GENERAL GRANT

AND

HIS CAMPAIGNS.

By JULIAN K. LARKE.

Illustrated with a Portrait on Steel,

AND VIEWS OF THE

SURRENDER OF FORT DONELSON AND VICKSBURG, AND
THE BATTLES AT PITTSBURG LANDING
AND CHATTANOOGA.

"No terms except unconditional and immediate surrender can be accepted. I propose to move immediately on your works."—Grant to Buckner.

NEW YORK:
J. C. DERBY & N. C. MILLER,
COMMISSION BOOKSELLERS AND PUBLISHERS.
1864.

C. A. ALVORD, STEREOTYPER AND PRINTER.

INTRODUCTION.

The best introduction to this volume that can be written, is to state that the subject of it is but forty-one years of age; has participated in two great wars; has captured during the present struggle five hundred guns, one hundred thousand prisoners, and a quarter of a million of small arms; has redeemed from rebel rule over fifty thousand square miles of territory; has reopened to the commerce of the world the mightiest highway on the globe; has stubbornly pursued his settled path in spite of all obstacles, and has never been beaten. All this has been realized not with any desire to gain glory for himself, but for the sole and patriotic purpose of securing the restoration of the Union. Modestly and quietly he moved along, almost unknown until the capture of Fort Donelson, and even now but few are fully acquainted with all that he has accomplished for the honor of his country. If a work should be written at all of any man, while living, no apology is needed for the present book. The author has had special opportunities of watching the career of General Grant during the whole war, and is thus enabled to give something of the history of one of the most successful military men of modern times.

J. K. L.

March, 1864.

LIST OF CONTENTS.

PAGE

CHAPTER XXXI.—OUTSIDE OPERATIONS.

CHAPTER XXXII.—THE ADVANCE TOWARDS JACKSON.—BATTLE OF RAYMOND.

CHAPTER XXIII.—THE CAPTURE AND OCCUPATION OF JACKSON.

CHAPTER XXXIV.—THE ADVANCE RENEWED.—CHAMPION'S HILL.

CHAPTER XXXV.—BATTLE OF BIG BLACK RIVER.

CHAPTER XXXVI.—APPROACHING VICKSBURG.—INVESTMENT.—FIRST ASSAULT.

CHAPTER XXXVII.—THE SECOND ASSAULT UPON VICKSBURG.

CHAPTER XXXVIII.—THE SIEGE OF VICKSBURG.

GENERAL GRANT AND HIS CAMPAIGNS.

CHAPTER I.

GRANT'S EARLY DAYS.

No military man of modern times has accomplished as much, with so little noise, as he of whom this narrative is written. From his earliest history down to the present time, his works and not his words have always spoken for him. Whenever he intended to do any thing of importance he would ask for, and listen to, the counsels of others, and, if good, adopt their plans, giving them the credit, if successful, and taking the blame upon himself if failure should ensue. He was never guilty of petty oppressions—such as many in office practise, to show they possess a power, which, in point of fact, they never know how to wield—nor did he ever find it necessary or politic to push himself into notoriety. And yet there is no one living who possesses more fame and celebrity.

Lieut-General Ulysses S. Grant,* of the United States

* The second initial of General Grant's name has thus been accounted for, on the authority of General William T. Sherman, who is a warm admirer of that officer. He is reported to have stated that General Grant's baptismal name was Hiram Ulysses, and he bore that appellation until he was appointed a cadet at West Point. General Hamer, who

regular army, the victorious commander of the principal portion of the Union forces in the West, and hero of Fort Donelson, Shiloh, Vicksburg, and Chattanooga, was born at Mount Pleasant, better known as Point Pleasant,* Clermont county, in the State of Ohio, on the 27th day of April, 1822. Point Pleasant is a post village of the county, and is situated on the Ohio River, about twenty-five miles above Cincinnati. Clermont county is in the southwestern part of the State of Ohio, and has an area of four hundred and sixty-two square miles, or 295,680 acres. The Ohio River forms the county boundary on the southwest, and the Little Miami River runs along its western lines. The land of the county is well drained by the east fork of the Little Miami River, into which the creeks mostly run. The surface of the country is of a rolling character, and is quite hilly in the vicinity of the Ohio River. The soil generally is of a rich nature, and the surface rock is formed of the

nominated him for the cadetship, by some means got his name mixed up with that of his brother. He was, therefore, appointed as "Ulysses Sydney Grant," and that name, once so recorded on the books of the Military Academy, could not be changed. He was baptized into the military school as U. S. Grant, and he has ever since been thus designated.

* This fact has been disputed by several of the newspapers of Scotland, Great Britain. One journal, the Montrose *Standard*, asserts that General Grant is a native of Kirriemuir, in that county; that his father had once been grieve on Kinordine, then farmer of Ballhall, and latterly a manufacturer in Kirriemuir. It further states that young Grant, having a military spirit, disdained the humble life of his father, and entered the British army as a private in the Life Guards. But finding the road to fame could not be travelled with ease on the horse of one belonging to the ranks, he deserted, and left for parts unknown, which, as the *Standard* asserts, has turned out to be America. The reader will see the fallacy of this assertion as he pursues the course of our narrative; it being only necessary to state in this note that no private is admitted into the ranks of the British Life Guards that is under six feet in height, or less than eighteen years of age.

blue limestone. A railroad now passes along its northern border, some distance from Grant's birthplace; but at the time when that general entered upon his career, the iron tramway was entirely unknown in that region of country.

During the year 1823, his parents, who were Scotch settlers, found it necessary to change their residence, and removed to Georgetown, a post village of Pleasant township, and capital of Brown county, Ohio. This village is situated in the midst of a rich farming district, and is located at about seven miles from the Ohio River. Here young Grant spent his early days, and obtained the rudiments of his education at the ordinary village school. While at school the embryo conqueror did not betray any remarkable talent for learning—that is, he was not considered a "brilliant lad." He was slow in acquiring knowledge; but such was his determination, that he would never give up his task until he had mastered it, and, when once impressed upon his mind, he seemed never to forget what he had learned. On one occasion he had a difficult piece of work placed before him by his teacher, and it seemed to puzzle poor Grant's brains more than any of his preceding studies.

"You can't master that task," remarked one of his school-fellows.

"Can't?" returned Grant, "what does that mean?"

"Well, it means that—that you can't, *there*."

Grant took up the old dictionary that was in constant use in the school, and searched through it; but could not find the word. It seemed to puzzle him, as to its definition, far more than his task had done. At last he determined to go to his teacher, to whom he made the following remarks:

"What is the meaning of can't? The word is not in the dictionary."

The teacher explained its origin, and how it came to be corrupted by abbreviation; and then, wishing to improve the opportunity to impress it on the young scholar's mind, he called all his school around him, and told his pupils the anecdote. He then wound up by saying: "If, in the struggles through life, any person should assert that 'you can't' do any thing that you had set your mind upon accomplishing, let your reply be, if the work be a good and lawful one, 'The word *can't* is not in the dictionary.'"

Grant conquered his studies, and never forgot the incident. In after years he often replied to those who would assert that he would fail in accomplishing his object, that "the word can't is not in the dictionary," and pertinaciously would he pursue that object until he had brought it down.

While Grant was at school, his companions used to tell a story about a horse trade that he was once engaged in. It appears that when he was about twelve years of age, his father sent him to purchase a horse of a farmer, named Ralston, who resided some short distance in the country. The elder Grant wanted the horse, but still desired to get it as cheaply as possible. Before starting, the old gentleman impressed upon young Grant's mind that fact in these words:

"Ulysses, when you see Mr. Ralston, tell him I have sent you to buy his horse, and offer him fifty dollars for it. If he will not take that, offer him fifty-five dollars, and rather than you should come away without the horse, you had better give him sixty dollars."

Off started the boy, and in due course of time arrived at Ralston's farm-house. He had carefully studied over in his mind his father's instructions, and of course intended to do as his parent had told him. Mr. Ralston, however, threw him off his balance, by putting the following direct, but natural question to him:

"How much did your father tell you to give for him?"

Young Ulysses had always had it impressed upon his mind by his mother, that the truth must be spoken at all times, and therefore he replied:

"Why, father told me to offer you fifty dollars at first; and if that would not do, to give you fifty-five dollars; and rather than come away without the horse I was to pay sixty dollars."

Of course, Ralston could not sell the horse for less than sixty dollars.

"I am sorry for that," returned Grant, "for, on looking at the horse, I have determined not to give more than fifty dollars for it, although father said I might give sixty. You may take fifty if you like, or you may keep the horse."

Ulysses rode the horse home.

Young Grant had been brought up to revere and esteem the character of Washington as the redeemer of his country, and so great an impression did the teachings of his friends have upon him, that, even as a boy, he would never allow that name or memory to be insulted in his presence.

It so happened that the brother of General Grant's father had settled in Canada, and was impressed with that strong British antipathy to the Government of the United States, so characteristic of the people of that province. Notwithstanding this fact, the Canadian Grant did not object to send his son John to the same school where young Ulysses was studying, so that he might be able to gain a better education than he could at that time obtain in Canada.

John had been brought up with the same feelings as his parents, and it was very natural for him occasionally to loosen his tongue in a disparaging manner upon American affairs, to the praise and glory of the "old country." While it was confined to remarks about Great Britain, young

Grant would listen, and argue all in good part; but, on one occasion the following conversation ensued, after one of their debates on the merits of the two styles of government, the love of country, and duty to rulers.

"Ulysses," said John, "you talk a great deal about Washington. He was nothing better than a rebel. He fought against his king."

"Now, look here, Jack," returned Grant, quickly, "you must stop that, or I will give you a thrashing. Mother says I must not fight, but must forgive my enemies. You may abuse me as much as you please; but if you abuse Washington, I'll off coat and let into you, if you were ten times my cousin, and then mother may afterwards whip me as much as she likes."

Jack was determined not to give way in his assertion, and Grant was as firm in his defence of his country's idol, until, at last, from words, they came to hard blows.

During the contest, Jack got the worst of it, but still Grant did not escape scot free—his face betraying evidences of the struggle—and when he reached his home his mother cried out:

"So, young man, you have been fighting, notwithstanding all I have said to you about it!"

Ulysses explained the whole of the circumstances of the case in a straightforward manner, without either addition or detraction. The good and worthy matron, with the determination that her son should respect her admonitions, began making preparations to give young Ulysses the promised castigation, when her husband interfered to prevent the boy being flogged:

"I tell thee what it is, wife," said the old gentleman, "the boy does not deserve to be punished. He has only stood up for his country, and he, that, as a boy, will stand up and fight in defence of the honor and integrity of the name of Washington, will rise, if God spares his life, to be a man and a Christian too." *

* Many years after this little *contre-temps* the cousins met in Canada, and suddenly Jack, then a fine-looking man, broke out with:

"I say, U. S., do you remember the trashing you gave me at school for calling Washington a rebel?"

"Yes," replied Grant, laughing, "and I will do it again under the same circumstances."

CHAPTER II.

AT WEST POINT.

THE ordinary education of common schools may fit out youth for the general routine duties of life; but higher institutions are necessary to complete the studies of those who intend to employ themselves in after-life in the pursuits of war, science, art, or literature. Young Grant, having betrayed evidences of his desire to become a soldier, obtained an admission into the United States Military Academy at West Point, through the influence of the late General Thomas L. Hamer, then a member of Congress, from his native State of Ohio. He entered the institution as a cadet, during the year 1839, at the age of seventeen years, and steadily progressed in his studies, especially in the science of mathematics. His progress was of the slow and sure kind, holding firmly on to all he acquired, but having nothing of that dashing brilliancy which is thought so much of by collegiates. He did not, like many, only study to pass the examiner, and then forget what he had learned. Even if his seat was below those of some others in his classes, at the end of each year it would be found that his education was of a far more solid and substantial nature than that of several of his class-mates who stood higher in grades.

When the young cadet entered the West Point Institution, he had to submit to a thorough physical and mental examination,to see whether he was fit to enter upon the life of a soldier, and was possessed of the proper mental talents, to make him competent to be trained as an officer. He passed the examination successfully and was admitted into the fourth class, where his studies consisted of mathematics, English grammar, including etymological and rhetorical exercises, composition, declamation, geography of the United States, French, and the use of small arms. In the camp, for the cadets have to live part of the summer months in tents as if on the field, he ranked as a private of the battalion, and had to submit to all the inconveniences that privates in camp have to suffer.

During the year 1840 he was advanced into the third class of the West Point Academy. Here he ranked as corporal in the cadet battalion, and his studies consisted of higher mathematics, French, drawing, and the duties of a cavalry soldier. In this last study he received practical instruction for sixteen weeks, so as to make him a good horseman. He progressed steadily, but not rapidly. He however did not fall back from any advance he had made, and if he only gained one seat at a time, he held on to that, with the intention of never again going below the cadet sitting next lower in his class.

Cadet Grant, during 1841, entered the second class of the U. S. Military School at West Point, obtaining with this change the rank of a sergeant of cadets. His studies now were somewhat more laborious; but still Grant persevered, and gradually mastered them. From September, 1841, to June, 1842, he was engaged in the study of natural and experimental philosophy, chemistry, and drawing, and in receiving practical instruction in horsemanship. During the summer months he was again encamped, and was well drilled, in both infantry and artillery tactics. He passed out of this class with credit.

During the year 1842, the young soldier passed into the first and concluding class of instruction of the Military

Academy. In this class he ranked as a commissioned officer of cadets, and was first put into the position where he could learn how to command a section, troop, or company. This is generally the trying position for the cadet; for, being invested with a little brief authority, he will either use it with credit or abuse it. Grant, while holding this position, set forth all the nobleness of his nature. He was no petty tyrant, nor was he a spy upon the actions of those who for the time were his subordinates. In the camp he commanded respect for his position; but out of camp he was still nothing more than a fellow-cadet. In this trait of his character, he was always liked by his classmates, and esteemed by those whose class degree was below him.

Cadet Grant had now more serious duties to perform, and studies to master. From September, 1842, to June, 1843, he was engaged in acquiring the knowledge of civil and military engineering, and from the 1st day of April to the 15th of May, 1843, he received practical instruction in this branch of the service. While encamped previous to September, 1842, he received some practical lessons in this science, and during the whole classical year he was engaged either in the study of ethics, constitutional law, international law, or military law, or in perfecting himself in horsemanship. He is now reputed one of the best riders in the service, not being easily thrown.

While in this class, he also endeavored to gain a knowledge of the science of mineralogy and geology, and of the Spanish language. He also received instruction in ordnance, gunnery, and cavalry tactics, which are esteemed among the higher branches of military acquirements. He passed through this class with credit, and graduated from the Military Academy on the 30th day of June, 1843, with thirty-eight other classmates, he standing No. 21, or about the middle of the class. He had now acquired a practical knowledge of the use of the rifled musket, the field-piece, mortar, siege, and sea-coast guns, small sword and bayonet, as well as of the construction of field-works, and the fabrication of all munitions and *matériel* of war.

The school companions of great men are very often mixed up with their after-life, and this statement is the more applicable to the West Point cadets who graduate in the same class. Such being the case, it may be a matter of interest to the reader to know who were General Grant's fellow-graduates, and what their relative positions were at the time of writing this narrative.

The cadet who graduated first in the class was William Benjamin Franklin, who entered the Topographical Engineer Corps; and having passed through a series of adventures under various commanders, was, at the beginning of 1864, the general commanding the Nineteenth Army Corps, in the Department of the Gulf, under General Banks.

The names of the next three graduates do not now appear in the Army List of the United States.

Wm. F. Raynolds graduated fifth in the class, entered the infantry service, and was appointed an aid on the staff of General Fremont, commanding the Mountain Department, with the rank of colonel, from the 31st day of March, 1862.

The next graduate was Isaac F. Quinby. He had entered the artillery service, and had been professor at West Point, but had retired to civil life. The Rebellion, however, brought him from his retirement, and he went to the field at the head of a regiment of New York volunteers. He afterwards became a brigadier-general in the Army of the Potomac.

Roswell S. Ripley, the author of "The War with Mexico," graduated seventh; but his name does not now appear in the official Army Register of the United States, as he had attached himself to the rebel cause.

The next graduate was John James Peck, who entered the artillery service, and was, on January 1, 1864, the commander of the district of and army in North Carolina, which then formed a portion of General Butler's Department.

John P. Johnstone, the daring artillery lieutenant who fell gallantly at Contreras, Mexico, was the next graduate.

General Joseph Jones Reynolds was the next in grade. This officer had gained great credit while in the army, as a professor of sciences; but had resigned some time, when the Rebellion broke out. He was, however, in 1861, again brought forward as a general of three months volunteers, under General McClellan, in Western Virginia; was afterwards commissioned by the President; and latterly became attached to the Army of the Cumberland. He served on the staff of the general commanding that army, with the rank of major-general, until General Grant assumed command of the military division embracing the Departments of Ohio, Tennessee, and Cumberland, when he was transferred to New Orleans.

The eleventh graduate was James Allen Hardie, who, during the War of the Rebellion became an assistant adjutant-general of the Army of the Potomac, with the rank of colonel.

Henry F. Clarke graduated twelfth, entered the artillery service, gained brevets in Mexico, and became chief commissary of the Army of the Potomac, during the War of the Rebellion, with the rank of colonel.

Lieutenant Booker, the next in grade, died while in service at San Antonio, Texas, on June 26, 1849.

The fourteenth graduate might have been a prominent officer of the U. S. army, had he not deserted the cause of his country, and attached himself to the rebels. He had not even the excuse of "going with his State," for he was a native of New Jersey, and was appointed to the army from that State. His name is Samuel G. French, major-general of the rebel army.

The next graduate was Lieutenant Theodore L. Chadbourne, who was killed in the battle of Resaca de la Palma, on May 9, 1846, after distinguishing himself for his bravery at the head of his command.

Christopher Colon Augur, one of the commanders of the Department of Washington, and major-general of volunteers, was the next in grade.

We now come to another renegade. Franklin Gardner, a native of New York, and an appointee from the State of Iowa, graduated seventeenth in General Grant's class. At the time of the Rebellion he deserted the cause of the United States and joined the rebels. He was disgracefully dropped from the rolls of the U. S. army, on May 7, 1861, became a major-general in the rebel service, and had to surrender his garrison at Port Hudson, July 9, 1863, through the reduction of Vicksburg by his junior graduate, U. S. Grant.

Lieutenant George Stevens, who was drowned in the passage of the Rio Grande, May 18, 1846, was the next graduate.

The nineteenth graduate was Edmund B. Holloway, of Kentucky, who obtained a brevet at Contreras, and was a captain of infantry in the U. S. regular army at the commencement of the Rebellion. Although his State remained in the Union, he threw up his commission on May 14, 1861, and joined the rebels.

The graduate that immediately preceded General Grant was Lieutenant Lewis Neill, who died on January 13, 1850, while in service at Fort Croghan, Texas.

Joseph H. Potter, of New Hampshire, graduated next after the hero of Vicksburg. During the War of the Re-

2

bellion he became a colonel of volunteers, retaining his rank as captain in the regular army.

Lieutenant Robert Hazlitt, who was killed in the storming of Monterey, September 21, 1846, and Lieutenant Edwin Howe, who died while in service at Fort Leavenworth, March 31, 1850, were the next two graduates.

Lafayette Boyer Wood, of Virginia, was the twenty-fifth graduate. He is no longer connected with the service, having resigned several years before the Rebellion.

The next graduate was Charles S. Hamilton, who for some time commanded, as major-general of volunteers, a district under General Grant, who at that time was chief of the Department of the Tennessee.

Captain Wm. K. Van Bokkelen, of New York, who was cashiered for rebel proclivities, on May 8, 1861, was the next graduate, and was followed by Alfred St. Amand Crozet, of New York, who had resigned the service several years before the breaking out of the civil war, and Lieutenant Charles E. James, who died at Sonoma, Cal., on June 8, 1849.

The thirtieth graduate was the gallant General Frederick Steele, who participated in the Vicksburg and Mississippi campaigns, as division and corps commander under General Grant, and afterwards commanded the Army of Arkansas.

The next graduate was Captain Henry R. Selden, of Vermont, and of the Fifth U. S. Infantry.

General Rufus Ingalls, quartermaster-general of the Army of the Potomac, graduated No. 32, and entered the mounted rifle regiment, but was found more valuable in the Quartermaster's Department, in which he held the rank of major from January 12, 1862, with a local rank of brigadier-general of volunteers from May 23, 1863.

Major Frederick T. Dent, of the Fourth U. S. Infantry,

and Major J. C. McFerran, of the Quartermaster's Department, were the next two graduates.

The thirty-fifth graduate was General Henry Moses Judah, who commanded a division of the Twenty-Third Army Corps during its operations after the rebel cavalry general, John H. Morgan, and in East Tennessee, during the fall of 1863.

The remaining four graduates were Norman Elting, who resigned the service October 29, 1846; Cave J. Couts, who was a member of the State Constitutional Convention of California during the year 1849; Charles G. Merchant, of New York; and George C. McClelland, of Pennsylvania, no one of whom is now connected with the United States Service.

It is very interesting to look over the above list to see how the twenty-first graduate has outstripped all his seniors in grade, showing plainly that true talent will ultimately make its way, no matter how modest the possessor may be, and notwithstanding all the opposition that may be placed in its way by others. It will be seen that General Grant now commands a larger force and a greater extent of country than all his thirty-eight classmates put together, and has risen higher in the military scale than any in his class, notwithstanding the fact that he did not seem to possess the same amount of apparent dashing ability.

His Scotch blood, however, gave him a pertinacity of character that enabled him to push forward against all difficulties, and this stubborn perseverance even in the midst of disappointments has characterized the whole of his life, both civil and military. When, however, he found he was on the right track he kept to it without turning aside for even a moment, and so ultimately became successful.

The following incident occurred while young Grant was serving his first year as a cadet of the Military Academy at West Point, and is a very good illustration of the bravery of his nature:

When admitted into the institution, he, as before mentioned, merely ranked as a private, and was so placed in one of the companies in the cadet battalion. As a novice, he became the subject of many a practical joke, as it is the usual custom in the Military Academy for the older scholars to torment the latest arrivals until still greener ones should make their appearance.

After enduring several of these jokes with great patience, and without a show of resentment, Grant, one day, determined he would put a stop to their fun, and have peace for himself. The next occasion when a joke was attempted upon him, was when the company was on a mock parade. Grant then stepped out of the ranks, threw off his jacket, and said:

"Now, Captain, drop your rank for a few minutes and stand up fair and square; and we'll soon see who is the best man."

The captain accepted the challenge, and before long was soundly whipped.

"It is now your turn, Lieutenant," said Grant, "to revenge the captain, if you can!"

At it they went, and the second officer shared the fate of his senior. Then, turning to his companions in the line, he inquired:

"Who is next? I want peace, and I am willing to fight all the company, one by one, to gain that peace. I have no ill-will against any one; but I must and will have peace in the future."

At this wholesale exhibition of pluck, his companions raised a shout that could have been heard for a very great distance, and then all parties came forward and shook Grant by the hand.

"You'll do," said the captain, who had been so soundly thrashed.

"We won't bother you any more," was the general remark of his companions.

"Grant's a plucky fellow, and will make his way," said another.

And in the midst of similar expressions the victorious young cadet put on his coat, took his place in the ranks, and was never again troubled with practical jokes. In honor of the occasion, his companions gave him the *nom de plume* of "Company Grant," by which he was known to the day of his entering the army, and even afterwards.

CHAPTER III.

ENTERS THE ARMY.—MEXICAN WAR.

WHEN a youth enters the West Point Military Academy he takes upon himself obligations to serve a certain time in the U. S. Regular Army, to finish the eight years—the term for which he is sworn into the service of the United States at the time he receives his cadet warrant.

Cadet Grant, therefore, when he graduated, at once entered the United States army as a brevet second-lieutenant of infantry. The date at which this brevet rank was awarded to him was that of the succeeding day to his graduation, viz., July 1, 1843.

At the time Grant entered the army, the United States were at peace with all the world, and very few vacancies then occurred in the rolls of army officers. He was, therefore, attached as a supernumerary lieutenant to the Fourth Regiment of Regular United States Infantry, then stationed on the frontier in Missouri and Missouri Territory, and engaged in keeping down the Indian tribes, that at that time were very annoying and dangerous to the early settlers of that region, which, twenty years ago, was almost a wilderness, except on the immediate banks of the great rivers.

While in this part of the West, Brevet Second-Lieutenant Grant assisted his military companions in superintending the opening up of the country, as well as in maintaining the peace and safety of those who had settled and were settling in that region.

The young officer had not been many months in the

West before he was ordered, with his regiment, into Texas, to join the army of General Taylor, who had been appointed to the command of the United States troops then concentrating in that republic. This army occupation was made during the year 1845. The Mexicans and Americans had for some time held an imaginary line of boundary within what is now known as the State of Texas. As all imaginary lines become more or less subjects of dispute, it was quite natural that two armies of distinct races, and with great personal animosities daily arising, should at last find, or imagine they had found, the other overstepping its proper limits, and, as a natural sequel, quarrels would take place, supposed wrongs would have to be revenged, and bloodshed would be the ultimate result. Such was certainly the origin of the actual hostilities which ripened into the American war with Mexico.

Corpus Christi, an important port on the Texan shore, was soon taken possession of by the Americans as a base of operations, and Grant was stationed at this place when he received his commission as full second lieutenant of infantry. This commission was dated from the 30th day of September, 1845, and was made out for a vacancy in the Seventh Regiment of U. S. Regular Infantry. He had, however, become so attached to the members of the Fourth Regiment, that a request was sent to Washington to allow him to be retained with that force, and in the following November a commission was handed to him, appointing him a full second lieutenant in the Fourth Regiment of U. S. Regular Infantry.

Some time before the declaration by Congress of a war with Mexico, the struggle commenced in Texas. The primary cause of the actual commencement of hostilities was a trifle; but the spark was no sooner applied than the conflagration began to make its rapid way, drawing the whole within its fearful grasp. Several petty struggles ensued, until at last General Taylor learned that an immense force of Mexicans were marching with the intention of crossing the Rio Grande into Texas, to drive the Americans from that region of territory. Promptly General Taylor moved; but, in the mean time, Fort Brown, on the Texas shore of the Rio Grande, was besieged. The gallant American garrison defended the position with great bravery; but, unless relief could have been sent them, it must have fallen. To relieve the besieged was General Taylor's duty; and, under his command, Lieutenant Grant marched to his first battle-ground.

On the 8th day of May, 1846, he participated in the battle of Palo Alto, and, although not mentioned in the official reports, he is spoken of by his companions to have acted with gallantry; several officers of his regiment obtaining brevets for their gallant and meritorious conduct. With his characteristic modesty, the young lieutenant kept himself in the back-ground, while his seniors gained the reward.

The battle of Resaca de la Palma was fought the next day, and here again Lieutenant Grant acted with praiseworthy gallantry. As before, his seniors in the regiment gained the brevets, while he quietly remained behind, perfectly satisfied that he had done his duty, and that time would ultimately bring to him his recompense.

Fort Brown was relieved, and the Mexicans felt the weight of its metal as they, in disorder, rushed across the Rio Grande in full retreat from the battle so bravely fought and won by General Taylor, on May 9, 1846.

The American army then advanced to and up the Rio Grande, and Texas was relieved from the jurisdiction of the Mexicans. Lieutenant Grant also participated in the subsequent brilliant operations of General Taylor along the banks of that historic stream, and advanced into the

Mexican territory, at a point over a hundred miles above the mouth of the river, in the Republic of New Leon.

On the 23d of September, 1846, Lieutenant Grant took part in the splendid operation of General Taylor against Monterey, which place the Mexicans had strongly fortified. In these works were posted a far superior force of Mexicans; but General Taylor was determined to drive them out of their intrenchments, and succeeded.

The American campaign in Mexico was now about to assume a different phase of character. War had been regularly declared, and a systemized plan of attack was made out. The advance by the northern route was to be made secondary to the grand movement by way of Vera Cruz; and the army and navy, as in the present war, were both to be brought into active use.

After General Scott had effected a landing above Vera Cruz, the forces on the Rio Grande were in part brought down that river to co-operate with him; and among the others was the Fourth Infantry. Lieutenant Grant, following the fortunes of his regiment, was, with it, transferred to the command under that general, and participated in the siege operations which finally caused the surrender of Vera Cruz, on the 29th day of March, 1847.

It now began to be perceived by his commanding officers, that Lieutenant Grant possessed some talents more than ordinary, and during the early part of April, when the army was preparing to advance into the interior of the Mexican country, Lieutenant Grant was appointed the quartermaster of his regiment, a post both honorable and of vital importance to an army in a strange country—the home of an enemy. With this position he participated in the whole of the remainder of the Mexican campaign, to the occupation, by the United States forces, of the capital.

It was while holding this staff appointment that Lieutenant Grant's brave disposition came more prominently before his commanding officers. His position in the army did not of necessity call upon him to enter into the actual strife; but, at the same time, his nature would not allow of his keeping out of it, when he found that his services were needed in the field. At the battle of Molino del Rey, on the 8th of September, 1847, he behaved with such distinguished gallantry and merit, that he was appointed on the field a first-lieutenant, to date from the day of that battle. Congress afterwards wished to confirm the appointment as a mere brevet, but Grant declined to accept it under such circumstances.

At the battle of Chapultepec, on the 13th day of September, 1847, Lieutenant Grant behaved with the most distinguished gallantry,* and also during the subsequent

* In the report of Captain Horace Brooks, Second Artillery, of the battle of Chapultepec, he says:

"I succeeded in reaching the fort with a few men. Here Lieutenant U. S. Grant, and a few more men of the Fourth Infantry found me, and, by a joint movement, after an obstinate resistance, a strong field-work was carried, and the enemy's right was completely turned."

The report of Major Francis Lee, commanding the Fourth Infantry, of the battle of Chapultepec, says:

"At the first barrier the enemy was in strong force, which rendered it necessary to advance with caution. This was done, and when the head of the battalion was within short musket range of the barrier, Lieutenant Grant, Fourth Infantry, and Captain Brooks, Second Artillery, with a few men of their respective regiments, by a handsome movement to the left, turned the right flank of the enemy, and the barrier was carried. * * * Second-Lieutenant Grant behaved with distinguished gallantry on the 13th and 14th." * * *

The report of Brevet Colonel John Garland, commanding the First Brigade, of the battle of Chapultepec, says:

"The rear of the enemy had made a stand behind a breastwork, from which they were driven by detachments of the Second Artillery, under battles, which only ceased with the final surrender of the city of Mexico.

Lieutenant Grant received the brevet of captain of the regular army, for gallant and meritorious conduct in the battle of Chapultepec, his rank to date from September 13, 1847, the day of that battle. The brevet was awarded to him in 1849; the nomination sent into Congress during the session of 1849–50, and confirmed during the executive session of 1850.

On the 16th day of September, 1847, the brave second lieutenant was commissioned a first-lieutenant in the Fourth Regiment of Regular Infantry, still holding his brevet rank of captain of three days prior date.

The following were the officers of the Fourth Regiment of United States Regular Infantry during the war with Mexico:

LIEUTENANT-COLONEL

John Garland, who participated in the whole of the Mexican war, and commanded a brigade, received a brevet colonelcy from Resaca de la Palma, and a brevet as brigadier-general from Churubusco. He was severely wounded in the capture of the city of Mexico; was made colonel of the Eighth Regular Infantry Regiment in May, 1849, and died in the city of New York, June 5, 1861.

Captain Brooks, and the Fourth Infantry, under Lieutenant Grant, supported by other regiments of the division, after a short but sharp conflict. * * I recognized the command as it came up, mounted a howitzer on the top of a convent, which, under the direction of Lieutenant Grant, quartermaster of the Fourth Infantry, and Lieutenant Lendrum, Third Artillery, annoyed the enemy considerably. * * * I must not omit to call attention to Lieutenant Grant, Fourth Infantry, who acquitted himself most nobly, upon several occasions, under my own observation."

In this particular mention of officers for gallantry and good conduct, besides the officers of his own staff, General Garland names but one other officer, besides Lieutenant Grant, out of his whole brigade.

General Worth's report, September 16th, also speaks highly of Lieutenant Grant.

Major

Francis Lee, who had entered upon the campaign as captain in the Seventh Reg't U. S. Regular Infantry, was brevetted lieutenant-colonel from Churubusco, and colonel from El Molino del Rey. He became colonel of the Second Regiment of Regular Infantry, October 18, 1855, and died at St. Louis, Missouri, January 19, 1859.

Captains.

George W. Allen (who had been brevetted major from Florida) was further brevetted lieutenant-colonel from Resaca de la Palma. He was next promoted to be a major of the Second Regiment Regular Infantry, and died at Vera Cruz, on March 15, 1848.

John Page was mortally wounded in the first battle, Palo Alto, and died on the 12th of July, 1846.

William M. Graham (who had been brevetted major from Florida) continued with the regiment until February, 1847; was promoted major of the Second Regiment of Regular Infantry, on February 16, 1847, and afterwards to lieutenant-colonel of the Eleventh U. S. Infantry, a regiment especially organized for the Mexican war. He was several times wounded during the campaign, and was finally killed at El Molino del Rey, on September 8, 1847.

Pitcairn Morrison was brevetted major from Resaca de la Palma, became major of the Eighth Regiment of U. S. Infantry, on September 26, 1847; lieutenant-colonel of the Seventh Regular Infantry, on June 9, 1853, and colonel of the Eighth Regular Infantry, June 6, 1861, with which rank he retired from the service during the fall of 1863.

George A. McCall, was brevetted major and lieutenant-colonel from Resaca de la Palma, and afterwards appointed to the Adjutant-General's Department as inspector-general. He resigned the service on April 29, 1853, and came in as a volunteer at the commencement of the Rebellion.

Gouverneur Morris was brevetted major from Resaca de la Palma, promoted to major of the Third Infantry, on January 31, 1850, and lieutenant-colonel of the First Infantry, May 31, 1857. He was retired from the service on September 9, 1861.

Robert C. Buchanan, was brevetted major from Resaca de la Palma, and lieutenant-colonel from El Molino del Rey. He served through the whole of the Mexican war with great credit, and was, in 1848, appointed acting inspector-general. He resumed his regimental position, and was promoted major of the regiment on February 3, 1855, and lieutenant-colonel on the 9th of September, 1861, which rank he held at the commencement of 1864, when he was employed as Superintendent of Volunteer Recruiting in the State of New Jersey.

Charles H. Larnard was brevetted major from Resaca de la Palma, and was drowned in Puget's Sound, near Fort Madison, Washington Territory, on the 27th of March, 1854.

Benjamin Alvord was brevetted captain from Resaca de la Palma, and major from the National Bridge. He became a paymaster, with the rank of major, from June 22, 1854, and during the Rebellion was appointed a brigadier-general of volunteers.

Henry L. Scott was appointed aide and acting adjutant-general to General Scott, gained the brevet of major from Churubusco, and lieutenant-colonel from Chapultepec. He became special aide to General Scott on March 7, 1855, and retired from the service on the 30th of October, 1861.

First Lieutenants.

Henry Prince, the adjutant of the regiment, was brevetted captain from Churubusco, and was severely wounded at, and brevetted major from, El Molino del Rey. He was appointed paymaster, May 23, 1855, and brigadier-general of volunteers during the War of the Rebellion.

Charles Hoskins, the former adjutant of the regiment, was killed at Monterey, September 21, 1846.

Richard H. Graham was mortally wounded at Monterey, September 21, 1846, and died on October 12, 1846.

John H. Gore was brevetted captain from Churubusco, and major from El Molino del Rey. He died, August 1, 1852, in the Bay of Panama, New Grenada.

Richard E. Cochran was killed in the second battle of the war, Resaca de la Palma, on May 9, 1846.

Theodore H. Porter was killed in a skirmish near the Rio Grande, on April 19, 1846.

Sidney Smith was wounded at El Molino del Rey, and was mortally wounded in the attack upon the city of Mexico, on September 14, 1847, and died on September 16, 1847.

Granville O. Haller served through the whole of the Mexican war; was brevetted captain from El Molino del Rey, and major from Chapultepec; became captain in January, 1848, and Major of the Seventh Infantry, September 25, 1861; and was summarily dismissed from the service during the summer of 1863.

Henry D. Wallen was wounded at Palo Alto, May 8, 1846, became adjutant from February, 1849, to May, 1850; captain from January 31,

1850, and Major of the Seventh Infantry from November 25, 1861. He held this position at the beginning of 1864.

Henderson Ridgeley was acting assistant adjutant-general to Brigadier-General Lane, and was killed at the Pass of Guadalaxara, on the 24th of November, 1847.

Jenks Beaman participated in the battles of Palo Alto and Resaca de la Palma; commanded his company in the battle of El Molino del Rey, and died at Tampico, on the 6th of May, 1848.

SECOND LIEUTENANTS.

Christopher R. Perry, after participating in part of the campaign, died at sea, on his return home, October 8, 1848.

Christopher C. Augur was aide to General Hopping, and, after the war in Mexico, remained in the U. S. Army. During the War of the Rebellion he became a major-general of volunteers.

ULYSSES S. GRANT.

Henry M. Judah was brevetted a first lieutenant from El Molino del Rey, and captain from Chapultepec. During the War of the Rebellion he commanded a division in General Grant's Military Division of the Mississippi.

James S. Woods was brevetted first lieutenant from Resaca de la Palma, and was killed at Monterey, September 21, 1846.

Alexander Hays was brevetted first lieutenant from Resaca de la Palma, and became acting assistant adjutant-general to Brigadier-General Lane. He resigned the service on April 12, 1848, and volunteered during the War of the Rebellion.

Abram B. Lincoln was wounded at, and brevetted first lieutenant from, El Molino del Rey, and died at Pilatka, Florida, April 15, 1852.

Thomas J. Montgomery commanded his company at the battles of Churubusco and El Molino del Rey; became first lieutenant during December, 1847, and captain, in March, 1854, and died at Fort Steilacoom, Washington Territory, November 22, 1854.

David A. Russell was brevetted first lieutenant from the National Bridge, and, remaining in the regular army after the war, became a brigadier-general of volunteers during the War of the Rebellion.

Alexander P. Rodgers was wounded, and afterwards killed, at Chapultepec, September 13, 1847.

Delancey Floyd Jones was brevetted first lieutenant from El Molino del Rey, but is no longer on the roll of army officers.

Maurice Maloney was brevetted first lieutenant from El Molino del

Rey, and captain from Chapultepec; was wounded at the San Cosme Gate, on September 13, 1847; became first lieutenant during May, 1848, captain in November, 1854, and Major of the First Infantry, September 16, 1862, which rank he held at the beginning of 1864.

Archibald B. Botts died on the first of January, 1847, at Camargo, Mexico.

Thomas R. McConnell was brevetted first lieutenant at El Molino del Rey, and captain from Chapultepec; became captain, in February, 1855, and resigned the service on March 11, 1856.

Edmund Russell was wounded at Churubusco; was brevetted first lieutenant from El Molino del Rey, and was killed by the Indians, near Red Bluff, California, on March 24, 1853.

Of the foregoing, the following only have occupied prominent positions during the War of the Rebellion:

Captain George Archibald McCall was appointed the commander of the division of troops known as the "Pennsylvania Reserve Corps," which consisted of three brigades and fifteen regiments, and fought with the Army of the Potomac, with the rank of brigadier-general of volunteers, from May 17, 1861. He resigned his connection with the United States service on March 31, 1863.

Captain Robert C. Buchanan was appointed Lieutenant-Colonel of the Fourth Infantry on September 9, 1861, and afterwards nominated for a volunteer brigadier-general's commission; but being too far advanced in years to endure the fatigues and laborious marches in the field during the civil war, he was principally kept in command of posts and garrisons within the Union lines.

Captain Benjamin Alvord became a brigadier-general of volunteers during the War of the Rebellion.

Lieutenant and Adjutant Henry Prince obtained a commission as brigadier-general of volunteers, dating from April 28, 1862, and participated in the campaigns in North Carolina and Virginia. At the beginning of 1864, he was in command of the Second Division of the Third Army Corps.

Lieutenant Christopher C. Augur distinguished himself during the Rebellion in the various capacities of brigade, division, and corps commander, and, on January 1, 1864, held the command of the Department of Washington, and of the Twenty-Second Army Corps, with head-quarters at the national capital. Rank, major-general of volunteers, from August 9, 1862.

Lieutenant Henry M. Judah was appointed a brigadier-general of volunteers on the 21st of March, 1862; distinguished himself in the pursuit of the rebel guerilla chief, General John H. Morgan, and in the Eastern Tennessee campaign of 1863. On January 1, 1864, he held the command of a division in the Twenty-Third Army Corps, which formed a part of General Grant's Military Division of the Mississippi.

Lieutenant Alexander Hays was appointed a brigadier-general of volunteers from September 29, 1862, he having previously held the command of a company of the Sixteenth Regiment of U. S. Regular Infantry. At the beginning of 1864, he was in command of a division in the Second Army Corps, then with the Army of the Potomac.

Lieutenant David A. Russell, having held the rank of Major of the Eighth Regiment of Regular Infantry, was appointed a brigadier-general of volunteers, on November 29, 1862, and distinguished himself during 1863, while in command of a brigade, and afterwards of a division of the Second Army Corps, then with the Army of the Potomac.

It will thus be seen that the young second lieutenant, of the Mexican war, has far outstripped all his regimental companions—many of whom then outranked him; and he has done so by his military merit alone.

CHAPTER IV.

SUBSEQUENT SERVICES AND RESIGNATION—CIVIL LIFE.

The struggles in Mexico having at last settled down into the mere brigandage which always follows large wars, the various volunteer troops of the United States Army were disbanded, and the regular regiments ordered back to the United States. Lieutenant Grant came home with his regiment—the Fourth Regular Infantry—and disembarked within the harbor of New York. The regiment was then distributed in companies and sections among the various northern frontier defences, along the borders of the States of Michigan and New York; and in one of these forts the young brevet captain commanded his company.

The emigration furor to California of 1850–51, carried to that El Dorado region an immense number of the vilest characters of all parts of the world; and the thirst for gold rendered all moral law and obligations, in that territory, subservient to violent might. To preserve even a show of law and order, and to restrain the Indians from murderous attacks upon the whites, the Government dispatched a force of troops to that part of the country, and among others the Fourth Regular Infantry was ordered to the Department of the Pacific. The battalion to which Lieutenant Grant was attached was sent up into Orĕgon, and, for some time, had its head-quarters at Fort Dallas, in that territory.

It was while the regiment was engaged in this duty that

Lieutenant Grant received his full promotion to captain of infantry, with a commission dating from August, 1853.

Captain Grant shortly after became attached to the Department of the West; but, anticipating more chances of progress in civil life than in the military, during the then prospective happy times of peace, he resigned his connection with the United States Army, on the 31st day of July, 1854.

Thus, for a time, the valuable services of the embryo hero were lost to the country, and his talents hid from the world. But like a cork, held by the finger at the bottom of a vessel of water, the release of which is no sooner effected by the removal of the pressure than it springs higher than ever above the surface, has Grant again sprung into notoriety.

After Captain Grant had severed his connection with the military service, he made his residence near the city of St. Louis, Missouri, and was there engaged in commercial pursuits until the year 1859.

The following is extracted from the letter of one who had taken some pains to trace the history of Grant's life while a resident in and near St. Louis:

"General Grant occupied a little farm to the southwest of St. Louis, whence he was in the habit of cutting the wood, drawing it to Carondelet, and selling it in the market there. Many of his wood purchasers are now calling to mind that they had a cord of wood delivered in person by the great General Grant. When he came into the wood market he was usually dressed in an old felt hat, with a blouse coat, and his pants tucked in the tops of his boots. In truth, he bore the appearance of a sturdy, honest woodman. This was his winter's work. In the summer he turned a collector of debts; but for this he was not qualified. He had a noble and truthful soul; so when he was told that the debtor had no money, he believed him, and would not trouble the debtor again. One of the leading merchants of St. Louis mentioned this circumstance to me. From all I can learn of his history here, he was honest, truthful, indefatigable—always at work at something; but he did not possess the knack of making money. He was honorable, for he always repaid borrowed money. His habits of life were hardy, inexpensive, and simple. About his being an inebriate, I find nothing to confirm it. On a cold day, when he had brought a load of wood to the Carondelet market, he would take something to keep himself warm. This, so far as I can trace, is the foundation of many reports of his inebriety."*

During 1859, Grant entered into partnership with his father, in the leather trade, and opened business in the city of Galena, Jo Daviess county, Illinois. This city is located on the Fevre River, about six miles above the point where it falls into the Mississippi, of which it is properly an arm. The city is built upon a bluff, with the streets rising one above the other, and communicating by means of flights of steps. Large portions of the States of Wisconsin, Iowa, and Minnesota are tributary to this town, and consequently it is a place of considerable trade.

The leather house of Grant & Son soon became a very prosperous concern, and, at the time of the outbreak of the rebellion, presented one of the best business prospects of any house in Galena. The younger Grant devoted himself to his business, and made it a study, so that, after a short time, the recommendation of a piece of leather by either of the firm of Grant & Son, was a sure guarantee of its good quality.

While alluding to the leather business of this firm, it will not be out of place to repeat an anecdote connected with General Grant, while at Vicksburg.

The Illinois politicians were everlastingly trying to inveigle General Grant into some debate, or the rendering of some definite idea or opinion in relation to the state of the various political parties of the country, and their pro-

* St. Louis correspondence of the Milwaukie *Wisconsin*, January, 1864.

fessed tenets. General Grant, however, was not to be drawn out. He had never attached himself to any other party than that of the true patriot, and all minor issues were, to that feeling, made entirely subservient, even if he knew or cared any thing at all about them.

While operating in the vicinity of Vicksburg, his professed political friends paid a visit to his head-quarters, and after a short time spent in compliments, they touched upon the never-ending subject of politics. One of the party was in the midst of a very flowery speech, using all his rhetorical powers to induce the general, if possible, to view matters in the same light as himself, when he was suddenly stopped by Grant.

"There is no use of talking politics to me. I know nothing about them; and, furthermore, I do not know of any person among my acquaintances who does. But," continued he, "there is one subject with which I am perfectly acquainted; talk of that, and I am your man."

"What is that, General?" asked the politicians, in great surprise.

"Tanning leather," was the reply.

The subject was immediately changed.

On another occasion, an infamous proposal was made by a person to General Grant, while he was staying at his head-quarters "in the field." The general, irritated, administered a severe kick to the proposer with the toe of his great cavalry boot; and, after the fellow had been driven from the tent, one of his staff remarked to a companion, that he did not think the general had hurt the rascal.

"Never fear," was the reply; "that boot never fails under such circumstances, for the leather came from Grant's store, in Galena."

CHAPTER V.

THE REBELLION—GRANT VOLUNTEERS, AND BECOMES A BRIGADIER-GENERAL.

THE attacks made by the rebels upon the arsenals and forts of the United States were enough to inflame the patriotic ardor of Grant, as well as that of all the loyal West Pointers who had retired into civil life; but when Fort Sumter was fired upon, he at once gave up his business, prosperous as it was, and tendered his services to the Governor of the State in which he resided, in answer to the call of the President for volunteers. Governor Yates, of Illinois, at first retained him near his person, as an aide upon his staff as commander-in-chief of the Illinois forces, and gave him the responsible position of mustering officer of Illinois volunteers.

It is owing a great deal to the enthusiastic labors of Grant, as mustering officer, that Illinois was enabled to turn out as many men as she did at the early stages of the war. Her quota was more than filled, and the men were speedily put into the field. But Grant could not sit down in the office of the mustering department while his services were more actively needed against the enemy in the field; and he therefore requested, that the Governor would give him some position in connection with one of the three years' regiments, then being raised. He therefore, about the middle of June, 1861, resigned his appointment as mustering officer, and accepted the colonelcy of the Twenty-first

Regiment of Illinois Volunteers, with a commission dating from June 15, 1861.

Colonel Grant at once left the capital of the State to join his regiment, then organizing at Mattoon, Illinois, and removed the men to the camp at Caseyville, where he personally superintended their drill and equipment.

As soon as the regiment was considered fit to enter upon active duties in the field, it was removed across the Mississippi River into Missouri, and formed part of the guard of the Hannibal and Hudson Railroad, a line running across the northern part of the State, from the Mississippi River to St. Joseph, on the border of Kansas, and one of the branches of the main lines which connected the East with the West.

On the 31st of July, 1861, Colonel Grant was placed in command of the troops at Mexico, on the North Missouri Railroad. Colonel Grant's force, at this time, formed a portion of Brigadier-General John Pope's command, which embraced the section of country north of the Missouri River, then known as the "District of North Missouri." It was, however, shortly after transferred to Pilot Knob, which was fortified and garrisoned. The regiment next marched to Ironton, Missouri; thence to Marble Creek, which it garrisoned. These movements occupied most of the time until about the 23d of August, 1861, when Colonel Grant was detached from his regimental command and appointed to the rank of brigadier-general of volunteers, with a commission dating from May 17, 1861.

The following table will show the relative position of General Grant, on May 17, 1861, with the others of the same rank, appointed on the same day, and how each of these generals was employed at the beginning of 1864:

Generals.	*January* 1, 1864.
Samuel P. Heintzelman,	Not in active field service.
Erasmus D. Keyes,	do. do.
Andrew Porter,	do. do.
Fitz John Porter,	Cashiered.
Wm. B. Franklin,	Commanding 19th Army Corps.
Wm. T. Sherman,	Commanding a Department under General Grant.
Charles P. Stone,	Chief of Staff to General Banks.
Don Carlos Buell,	Not in active field service.
Thomas W. Sherman,	Temporarily invalided.
James Oakes,	Not in service.
John Pope,	Commanding Department of the Northwest.
George A. McCall,	Resigned.
William R. Montgomery,	Not in active field service.
Philip Kearney,	Dead.
Joseph Hooker,	Commanding Grand Division under General Grant.
John W. Phelps,	Resigned.
ULYSSES S. GRANT,	———.
Joseph J. Reynolds,	Commanding troops at New Orleans.
Samuel R. Curtis,	Not in active field service.
Charles S. Hamilton,	do. do.
Darius N. Couch,	Commanding Department of the Susquehanna.
Rufus King,	Foreign Minister.
J. D. Cox,	Comm'ding Corps under Gen. Grant.
Stephen A. Hurlbut,	do. do.
Franz Sigel,	Not in active field service.
Robert C. Schenck,	In Congress.
B. M. Prentiss,	Resigned.
Frederick W. Lander,	Dead.
Benj. F. Kelly,	Commanding Department of Western Virginia.
John A. McClernand,	Not in active field service.
A. S. Williams,	Commanding a Division.
I. B. Richardson,	Dead.
William Sprague,	Declined.
James Cooper,	Dead.

By referring to the foregoing, it will be perceived that the name of Ulysses S. Grant stood No. 17—exactly half way down the list,—at the time he received his brigadier-general's commission. When this narrative was written, General Grant commanded as much territory and as many troops in the field as all the other thirty-three generals combined—a rapid rise in position scarcely equalled by any officer of modern times, Napoleon excepted.

CHAPTER VI.

POST AND DISTRICT COMMANDER.—BELMONT.

As soon as General Grant had been invested with the rank and authority sufficient to enable him to take the command of a post, he was placed in charge of the one at Cairo, and his forces were increased by the addition of another brigade, which had been organized for, and was under the command of, Brigadier-General John A. McClernand.

The post at Cairo included within its jurisdiction the Missouri shore of the Mississippi River, from Cape Girardeau to New Madrid, and the opposite Illinois shore, to the point of land on which Cairo stood. This post commanded the mouth of the Ohio River, and was the key to the Upper Mississippi and the Missouri Rivers. Its importance as a defensive military position, and also as a base of operations, at the early stages of the war, was without estimate; and even now as a permanent base of supplies, its value is great, and its loss would be severely felt by the Union army.

At this time, the State of Kentucky was in that incomprehensible condition designated as neutral; but as the line that separated Tennessee, which had seceded, from Kentucky, which had not, was a mere imaginary one; and as the rebel forces of the seceding States were stationed so closely on these borders, it is not to be wondered at that they often crossed the line into the neutral State, especially when it was to their advantage so to do.

General Grant no sooner found out that this course of policy was being adopted by the rebels, and that they had actually encroached upon the State of Kentucky, and were fortifying Columbus and Hickman, on the Mississippi River, and Bowling Green, on the Big Barren River, than he ordered the seizure of Paducah, a valuable post at the mouth of the Tennessee River. This village was occupied on September 6, 1861, and within nineteen days he also held possession of Smithland, at the mouth of the Cumberland River. By these movements he not only blockaded the rivers leading up into the Rebel States, against the running of supplies and contraband articles for the use of those who were up in arms against the government; but he also secured two fine bases for further operations, and cleared out the guerillas, who were trying to blockade the Ohio River, below those points. He also garrisoned each of these places with a force sufficient to hold them; but still retained his head-quarters at Cairo, which had then become the head-quarters of the sub-department or District of Southeast Missouri.

At the time when General Grant took possession of Paducah, he found secession flags flying in different parts of the city, in expectation of greeting the arrival of the rebel forces, which were reported to be nearly four thousand strong, and not many miles distant. The landing of the Union troops was a signal for a general uprising of the loyal citizens of the place, who, being properly supported, in effect, if not in fact, at once tore down from the houses of the rebel sympathizers the secession flags which they had raised.

General Grant immediately took possession of the telegraph office, railroad depot, hospitals, etc., and other points of importance, after which he issued the following proclamation to the citizens:

PADUCAH, KY., *September* 6, 1861.

To the citizens of Paducah:

I am come among you, not as an enemy, but as your fellow-citizen. Not to maltreat you nor annoy you, but to respect and enforce the rights of all loyal citizens. An enemy, in rebellion against our common government, has taken possession of, and planted its guns on the soil of Kentucky, and fired upon you. Columbus and Hickman are in his hands. He is moving upon your city. I am here to defend you against this enemy, to assist the authority and sovereignty of your government. *I have nothing to do with opinions*, and shall deal only with armed rebellion, and its aiders and abettors. You can pursue your usual avocations without fear. The strong arm of the government is here to protect its friends, and punish its enemies. Whenever it is manifest that you are able to defend yourselves, and maintain the authority of the government, and protect the rights of loyal citizens, I shall withdraw the forces under my command. U. S. GRANT, *Brig.-Gen. Commanding.*

The tone of the above proclamation speaks well for the temper of the soldier, who, although in the midst of enemies, and with the power in his hands, yet refused to use that power further than he, of actual necessity, was called upon to do by the exigencies of his position.

General Grant, when in camp at Cairo, presented little, in fact nothing, of the gewgaws and trappings which are generally attached to the attire of a general; and in this respect, he showed a marked contrast between himself and some of his sub-lieutenants, whose bright buttons and glittering shoulder-straps were perfectly resplendent. The general, instead, would move about the camp with his attire carelessly thrown on, and left to fall as it pleased. In fact, he seemed to care nothing at all about his personal appearance, and in the place of the usual military hat and gold cord, he wore an old battered black hat, generally designated as a "stove-pipe," an article that neither of his subordinates would have stooped to pick up, even if unobserved. In his mouth he carried a black-looking cigar, and he seemed to be perpetually smoking.

In connection with these facts, a detractor of General Grant was, on one occasion, speaking rather sarcastically of the stove-pipe General and his passion for cigars, when he was taken up by one of Grant's friends, who said: "Such a bright stove-pipe as Grant, should be excused for smoking."

Several reconnoissances were made down the Mississippi River and inland from the Ohio River, and occasionally skirmishes would also take place. At these contests prisoners would sometimes be taken on both sides, and the following correspondence was the result of these captures:

HEAD-QUARTERS, FIRST DIVISION,
WESTERN DEPARTMENT, *October*, 1861.

To the Commanding Officer at Cairo and Bird's Point:

I have in my camp a number of prisoners of the Federal army, and am informed there are prisoners belonging to the Missouri State troops in yours. I propose an exchange of these prisoners, and for that purpose send Captain Polk of the artillery, and Lieutenant Smith of the infantry, both of the Confederate States Army, with a flag of truce, to deliver to you this communication, and to know your pleasure in regard to my proposition.

The principles recognized in the exchange of prisoners effected on the 3d of September, between Brigadier-General Pillow, of the Confederate Army, and Colonel Wallace, of the U. S. Army, are those I propose as the basis of that now contemplated.

Respectfully, your obedient servant,
L. POLK, *Major-General Commanding.*

To which communication General Grant dispatched the following reply:

DISTRICT OF SOUTHEAST MISSOURI,
HEAD-QUARTERS, CAIRO, *October* 14, 1861.

GENERAL:—Yours of this date is just received. In regard to an exchange of prisoners, as proposed, I can, of my own accordance, make none. I recognize no "Southern Confederacy" myself, but will communicate with higher authorities for their views. Should I not be sustained, I will find means of communicating with you.

Respectfully, your obedient servant,

U. S. GRANT, *Brig.-Gen. Commanding.*

To Major-General POLK, *Columbus, Ky.*

On the 16th of October, 1861, General Grant ordered a portion of his forces under Colonel Plummer, then stationed at Cape Girardeau, Mo., to march towards Fredericktown, by way of Jackson and Dallas, and in conjunction with Colonel Carlin, who was moving in another direction, to check the advance of, and, if possible, defeat the rebel forces, then advancing northward under Brigadier-General Jeff Thompson. The movement was a success; and on the morning of October 21, 1861, the rebels were defeated, and the U. S. troops afterwards returned to their former posts.*

Having thus secured the information he required relative to the position of Jeff Thompson's forces, and also having learned that others were concentrating at the rebel camp at Belmont, Mo., General Grant at the head of two brigades, commanded respectively by General McClernand and himself, left Cairo on November 6, 1861, for that point. On the opposite Kentucky shore, the rebels had fortified a position at Columbus, which was to command the camp at Belmont, as well as to blockade the Mississippi River.

The two U. S. brigades landed at Belmont, at eight o'clock of the morning of November 7, were at once formed into line of battle, and immediately attacked the rebel works, where they found the enemy in force under General Cheatham. The rebel forces were driven to and through their camp, and their battery of twelve guns was

* See Appendix A.

captured. The camp was then burned, and the enemy's baggage and horses taken. Several prisoners also fell into the hands of the Union troops, and the attack was a complete triumph.

But at the very moment when victory was deemed certain, several large bodies of rebel troops from Columbus and Hickman crossed the Mississippi River, and re-enforced those at Belmont. This re-enforcement made the enemy numerically stronger than the forces under General Grant, and after another severe fight, the Union troops had to withdraw to their transports, their retreat being well covered by the ordnance of the gunboats.*

The following is from a private letter from General Grant to his father, written on the night of the 8th:

"Day before yesterday I left Cairo with about three thousand men in five steamers, convoyed by two gunboats, and proceeded down the river to within about twelve miles of Columbus. The next morning the boats were dropped down just out of range of the enemy's batteries, and the troops debarked. During this operation our gunboats exercised the rebels by throwing shells into their camps and batteries. When all ready, we proceeded about one mile toward Belmont, opposite Columbus,

---

* See Appendix B.

[NOTE.—Now that the clouds which mystified the view of this battle have cleared away, it is far from established that the Union troops were defeated on this occasion. General Polk's dispatch (Appendix B.) plainly shows the rebels to have suffered heavily, and to have lost part of their artillery. Nor should General Grant be blamed for the result of the expedition. He was ordered to make the attack, and, being only a District Commander, he had to obey his superior officer at the head of the Department, except as to the time and manner of fighting. That the attack was well planned and brilliantly executed there can be no manner of doubt, the troops displaying great bravery; and but for the heavy re-enforcements of the enemy, Belmont certainly would have been classed as one of the early victories for the Union arms. All this is established; and had the North nothing worse to contemplate than the affair at Belmont, the record of the war would be almost stainless.]

when I formed the troops into line, and ordered two companies from each regiment to deploy as skirmishers, and push on through the woods and discover the position of the enemy. They had gone but a little way when they were fired upon, and the ball may be said to have fairly opened.

"The whole command, with the exception of a small reserve, was then deployed in like manner and ordered forward. The order was obeyed with great alacrity, the men all showing great courage. I can say with great gratification that every colonel, without a single exception, set an example to their commands that inspired a confidence that will always insure victory when there is the slightest possibility of gaining one. I feel truly proud to command such men.

"From here we fought our way from tree to tree through the woods to Belmont, about two and a half miles, the enemy contesting every foot of ground. Here the enemy had strengthened their position by felling the trees for two or three hundred yards and sharpening their limbs, making a sort of abatis. Our men charged through, making the victory complete, giving us possession of their camp and garrison equipage, artillery, and every thing else.

"We got a great many prisoners. The majority, however, succeeded in getting aboard their steamers and pushing across the river. We burned every thing possible and started back, having accomplished all that we went for, and even more. Belmont is entirely covered by the batteries from Columbus, and is worth nothing as a military position—cannot be held without Columbus.

"The object of the expedition was to prevent the enemy from sending a force into Missouri to cut off troops I had sent there for a special purpose, and to prevent re-enforcing Price.

"Besides being well fortified at Columbus, their number far exceeded ours, and it would have been folly to have attacked them. We found the Confederates well armed and brave. On our return, stragglers, that had been left in our rear (now front), fired into us, and more recrossed the river and gave us battle for a full mile, and afterward at the boats when we were embarking.

"There was no hasty retreating or running away. Taking into account the object of the expedition, the victory was complete. It has given us confidence in the officers and men of this command, that will enable us to lead them in any future engagement without fear of the result. Gen. McClernand (who, by the way, acted with great coolness and courage throughout, and proved that he is a soldier as well as a statesman) and myself, each had our horses shot under us. Most of the field-officers met with the same loss, beside nearly one-third of them being themselves killed or wounded. As near as I can ascertain, our loss was about two hundred and fifty killed, wounded, and missing."

General McClernand, in his official report of this battle, after speaking of the hotness of the engagement, and narrow escapes of some of his officers, makes use of the following words:

"Here the projectiles from the enemy's heavy guns at Columbus, and their artillery at Belmont, crashed through the woods over and among us. * * * And here, too, many of our officers were killed or wounded; nor shall I omit to add, that this gallant conduct was stimulated by your (Grant's) presence, and inspired by your example. Here your horse was killed under you."

After the U. S. troops had returned to their base of operations at Cairo, General Grant issued the following order:

HEAD-QUARTERS, DISTRICT OF SOUTHEAST MISSOURI,
CAIRO, *November* 8, 1861.

The General commanding this military district, returns his thanks to the troops under his command at the battle of Belmont on yesterday.

It has been his fortune to have been in all the battles fought in Mexico by Generals Scott and Taylor, save Buena Vista, and he never saw one more hotly contested, or where troops behaved with more gallantry.

Such courage will insure victory wherever our flag may be borne and protected by such a class of men.

To the brave men who fell, the sympathy of the country is due, and will be manifested in a manner unmistakable.

U. S. GRANT, *Brig.-Gen. Commanding.*

But, while General Grant was engaged in congratulating those who had returned safe, he was not unmindful of the sufferers who had fallen wounded into the hands of the enemy. Knowing the incomplete state of the Medical and Surgical Departments of the rebel army opposed to him, he addressed the following dispatch to the rebel general under a flag of truce:

HEAD-QUARTERS, DISTRICT OF SOUTHEAST MISSOURI,
CAIRO, *November* 8, 1861.

General commanding forces, Columbus, Ky.

SIR:—In the skirmish of yesterday, in which both parties behaved with so much gallantry, many unfortunate men were left upon the field of battle, whom it was impossible to provide for. I now send, in the interest of humanity, to have these unfortunates collected and medical attendance secured them. Major Webster, Chief of Engineers, District Southeast Missouri, goes bearer of this, and will express to you my views upon the course that should be pursued under the circumstances, such as those of yesterday.

I am, very respectfully, your obedient servant,
U. S. GRANT, *Brig.-Gen. Commanding.*

To this communication, the commander of the rebel post returned the following answer:

HEAD-QUARTERS, FIRST DIVISION, WESTERN DEPARTMENT,
COLUMBUS, KY., *November* 8, 1861.

Brigadier-General U. S. GRANT, *U. S. A.:*

I have received your note in regard to your wounded and killed on the battle-field, after yesterday's engagement. The lateness of the hour at which my troops returned to the principal scene of action prevented my bestowing the care upon the wounded which I desired.

Such attentions as were practicable were shown them, and measures were taken at an early hour this morning to have them all brought into my hospitals. Provision was also made for taking care of your dead. The permission you desire under your flag of truce to aid in attention to your wounded, is granted with pleasure, under such restrictions as the exigencies of our service may require. In your note you say nothing of an exchange of prisoners, though you send me a private message as to your willingness to release certain wounded men, and some invalids taken from our list of sick in camps, and expect, in return, a corresponding number of your wounded prisoners. My own feelings would prompt me to waive again the unimportant affectation of declining to recognize these States as belligerents, in the interests of humanity; but my government requires all prisoners to be placed at the disposal of the Secretary of War. I have dispatched him to know if the case of the severely wounded held by me will form an exception.

I have the honor to be, your obedient servant,

L. POLK, *Major-General C. S. A.*

CHAPTER VII.

DISTRICT OF CAIRO.—GRAND RECONNOISSANCE.

AFTER General Halleck had assumed the command of the Department of the Missouri, he began to organize the same into proper military districts, so as to allow each district commander to have full control of the section of country embraced within his lines.

On the 20th of December, 1861, General Halleck, appreciating the military ability of General Grant, issued an order defining what should constitute the District of Cairo, and extending the command until it became one of the largest divisions in the country. He then appointed General Grant to be chief commander of the same. In accordance with that appointment, General Grant assumed the command of the new district on December 21, 1861, and announced the same in the following order:

HEAD-QUARTERS, DISTRICT OF CAIRO,
CAIRO, *December* 21, 1861.

[*General Order No.* 22.]

In pursuance of Special Order No. 78, from Head-Quarters, Department of the Missouri, the name of this Military District will be known as the "District of Cairo," and will include all the southern part of Illinois, that part of Kentucky west of the Cumberland River, and the southern counties of Missouri, south of Cape Girardeau.

The force at Shawneetown will be under the immediate command of Colonel T. H. Cavanaugh, Sixth Illinois Cavalry, who will consolidate the reports of his command weekly, and forward to these head-quarters.

All troops that are, or may be, stationed along the banks of the Ohio, on both sides of the river, east of Caledonia, and to the mouth of the Cumberland, will be included in the command, having head-quarters at Paducah, Ky.

Brigadier-General E. A. Paine is assigned to the command of the forces at Bird's Point, Missouri.

All supplies of ordnance, Quarter-Master and Commissary stores, will be obtained through the chiefs of each of these departments, at district head-quarters, where not otherwise provided for.

For the information of that portion of this command, newly attached, the following list of Staff Officers is published:

Captain John A. Rawlins, Assistant Adjutant-General.

Captain Clark B. Lagow, Aide-de-Camp.

Captain Wm. S. Hillyer, Aide-de-Camp.

Major John Riggin, Jr., Volunteer Aide-de-Camp.

Captain R. B. Hatch, Assistant Quarter-Master U. S. Volunteers, Chief Quarter-Master.

Captain W. W. Leland, A. C. S. U. S. Volunteers, Chief Commissary.

Captain W. F. Brinck, Ordnance Officer.

Surgeon James Simons, U. S. A., Medical Director.

Assistant Surgeon, J. P. Taggart, U. S. A., Medical Purveyor.

Major I. N. Cook, Pay-Master.

Colonel J. D. Webster, Chief of Staff, and Chief of Engineers.

By order, U. S. GRANT, *Brig.-Gen. Commanding.*

General Grant at once began organizing, under his personal supervision, the new troops added to his command, and as soon as deemed fit for such service, they were sent to the various posts belonging to the district, including Fort Jefferson and Paducah, in Kentucky. By this plan of operation General Grant had all his troops well in hand, and yet so distributed that it was a matter of great difficulty, if not an actual impossibility, for the enemy to learn his strength.

On the 10th of January, the forces under the immediate command of General McClernand, left Cairo in transports, and disembarked at Fort Jefferson. The transports were protected by two gunboats, which were next ordered to lie off the fort. The rebels, with three armed vessels, attacked these gunboats the next morning; but, after a brisk engagement, had to beat a retreat—the Union vessels chasing them until they took refuge under the guns of Columbus.

As picket shooting had existed to a fearful extent in the vicinity of Cairo, General Grant, on the 11th of January, issued an order, as follows:

HEAD-QUARTERS, CAIRO, *January* 11, 1862.

Brigadier-General PAINE, *Bird's Point:*

I understand that four of our pickets were shot this morning. If this is so, and appearances indicate that the assassins were citizens, not regularly organized in the rebel army, the whole country should be cleared out for six miles around, and word given that all citizens, making their appearance within those limits, are liable to be shot.

To execute this, patrols should be sent out in all directions, and bring into camp, at Bird's Point, all citizens, together with their subsistence, and require them to remain, under penalty of death and destruction of their property, until properly relieved.

Let no harm befall these people, if they quietly submit; but bring them in and place them in camp below the breastwork, and have them properly guarded.

The intention is not to make political prisoners of these people, but to cut off a dangerous class of spies.

This applies to all classes and conditions, age and sex. If, however, women and children prefer other protection than we can afford them, they may be allowed to retire beyond the limits indicated—not to return until authorized.

By order of U. S. GRANT, *Brig.-Gen. Commanding.*

As General Grant states in the above order, it was necessary to keep spies away from his vicinity, as he was then about to start on a perilous expedition. He had already divided his forces into three columns—under Generals Paine, McClernand, and C. F. Smith—General Grant commanding the whole expedition in person.

Before starting on this adventure, General Grant issued the following order to his troops:

HEAD-QUARTERS, DISTRICT OF CAIRO,
CAIRO, *January* 13, 1862.

[*General Order No.* 3.]

During the absence of the expedition, now starting upon soil occupied almost solely by the rebel army, and when it is a fair inference that every stranger met is an enemy, the following orders will be observed:

Troops, on marching, will be kept in the ranks; company officers being held strictly accountable for all stragglers from their companies. No firing will be allowed in camp or on the march, not strictly required in the performance of duty. While in camp, no privilege will be granted to officers or soldiers to leave their regimental grounds, and all violations of this order must be promptly and summarily punished.

Disgrace having been brought upon our brave fellows by the bad conduct of some of their members, showing on all occasions, when marching through territory occupied by sympathizers of the enemy, a total disregard of the rights of citizens, and being guilty of wanton destruction of private property, the general commanding *desires and intends to enforce a change in this respect.*

The interpreting of confiscation acts by troops themselves has a demoralizing effect—weakens them in exact proportions to the demoralization, and makes open and armed enemies of many who, from opposite treatment, would become friends, or, at most, non-combatants.

It is ordered, therefore, that the severest punishment be inflicted upon every soldier who is guilty of taking, or destroying, private property; and any commissioned officer, guilty of like conduct, or of countenancing it, shall be deprived of his sword and expelled from the camp, not to be permitted to return.

On the march, cavalry advance guards will be thrown out, also flank guards of cavalry or infantry, when practicable. A rear-guard of infantry will be required to see that no teams, baggage, or disabled soldiers are left behind. It will be the duty of company commanders to see that rolls of their company are called immediately upon going into camp each day, and every member accounted for.

By order, U. S. GRANT, *Brig.-Gen. Commanding.*

On the morning of Tuesday, January 14, 1862, General McClernand's column moved forward from Fort Jefferson, and the columns under Generals Paine and Smith, at Paducah, commenced similar movements. The three columns combined made a force of nineteen regiments of infantry, four regiments of volunteer cavalry, two companies of regular cavalry, and seven batteries of artillery.

At the time this expedition commenced its march, the Mississippi River was nearly filled with floating ice, thus making the transportation of troops a serious difficulty. Demonstrations were made by General McClernand's column, as if with the intention of attacking Columbus in the rear, by way of Blandville, Ky., while the real object was to concentrate with the troops marching from Paducah, Ky. The feint proved successful, and a great alarm was manifested by the rebel forces in Columbus.

As General McClernand's column advanced, it was at intervals joined by a regiment from the other columns, and, on the night of January 15th, his force encamped in line of battle ten miles to the rear of Columbus, threatening that post by two roads.

Here General Grant, who had been with the column from Paducah, came up with this part of the expedition, and personally superintended the disposition of the troops.

The first division was next morning marched to Milburn, apparently *en route* for Mayfield; but instead of following that path, the troops, after passing through Milburn, turned northward, so as to communicate with the force from Paducah; and, on the 17th, were within eight miles of Lovelaceville. They then turned westward, and, on the nights of the 18th and 19th, encamped about a mile from Blandville. On January 20th, the column returned to Fort Jefferson. During the interval between the 14th and 20th of January, the infantry of this column marched over seventy-five miles, and the cavalry about one hundred and forty miles, over icy and miry roads, and during a most inclement season. This march was a very heavy one for troops who had never before been in the field. The reconnoissance developed the fact, that the rebel army was not in large force west of the Paducah and Mayfield railroad, except, perhaps, in the rebel works at Columbus, and led to the discovery of valuable side-roads, not laid down in any map of that time. It also showed that Columbus was far from being as strong as was supposed, and that it could be attacked in the rear by several different roads, along which large forces of troops could be moved.

As soon as General Grant had communicated with General McClernand, at his encampment, on the night of the 15th, and had received his report, he at once discovered the mere shell of rebel defence which held that part of the State of Kentucky, and allowing General McClernand's column to keep up the appearance of an advance, he withdrew the other two columns to Cairo. He had, in fact, accomplished and ascertained all that he had desired when he first moved.

During the fall and winter of 1861, several gunboats had been ordered to be constructed on the Mississippi River, above Cairo, and by this time the majority of them were completed. In order to obtain sailors to man these gunboats, General Grant issued the following important order:

HEAD-QUARTERS, DISTRICT OF CAIRO,
CAIRO, *January* 20, 1862.

CIRCULAR.

Commanders of Regiments will report to these head-quarters, without delay, the number of river and seafaring men of their respective commands, who are willing to be transferred from the military to the gunboat service. Seeing the importance of fitting out our gunboats as speedily as possible, it is hoped there will be no delay or objections raised by company or regimental commanders in responding to this call. Men thus volunteering will be discharged at the end of one year, or at the end of the war, should it terminate sooner.

By order, U. S. GRANT, *Brig.-Gen. Commanding.*

A few days afterwards, General McClernand's forces were withdrawn from Kentucky, and again rendezvoused at Cairo, the commander being placed in temporary charge of the District during the necessary absence of General Grant.

CHAPTER VIII.

FORTS HENRY AND DONELSON.

A FEW days soon developed the whole object of the movement made by General Grant's forces in the western part of the State of Kentucky. It must also not be forgotten, that his troops still held the posts at Paducah and Smithland, at the mouth of the Tennessee and Cumberland Rivers.

By keeping up a false show of an advance upon the rear of Columbus, which had several times been attacked in the front by armed vessels, the rebels were led to believe that post to be in actual danger, and consequently concentrated all their available forces in that vicinity.

In the mean time, General Grant was preparing for an advance into the State of Kentucky, by an entirely different route, and, to have his forces well in hand, he issued the following order brigading the same:

HEAD-QUARTERS, DISTRICT OF CAIRO,
CAIRO, *February* 1, 1862.

[*General Order No.* 5.]

For temporary government, the forces of this military district will be divided and commanded as follows, to wit:

The First Brigade will consist of the Eighth, Eighteenth, Twenty-seventh, Twenty-ninth, Thirtieth, and Thirty-first Regiments of Illinois Volunteers, Schwartz's and Dresser's batteries, and Stewart's, Dollin's, O'Harnett's, and Carmichael's cavalry. Colonel R. J. Oglesby, senior colonel of the brigade, commanding.

The Second Brigade will consist of the Eleventh, Twentieth, Forty-fifth, and Forty-eighth Illinois Infantry, Fourth Illinois Cavalry, Taylor's and McAllister's Artillery. (The latter with four siege-guns.) Colonel W. H. L. Wallace commanding.

The First and Second Brigades will constitute the First Division of the

District of Cairo, and will be commanded by Brigadier-General John A. McClernand.

The Third Brigade will consist of the Eighth Wisconsin, Forty-ninth Illinois, Twenty-fifth Indiana, four companies of artillery, and such troops as are yet to arrive. Brigadier-General E. A. Paine commanding.

The Fourth Brigade will be composed of the Tenth, Sixteenth, Twenty-second, and Thirty-third Illinois, and the Tenth Iowa Infantry; Houtaling's battery of Light Artillery, four companies of the Seventh and two companies of the First Illinois Cavalry. Colonel Morgan commanding.

General E. A. Paine is assigned to the command of Cairo and Mound City, and Colonel Morgan to the command at Bird's Point.

By order of U. S. Grant, *Brig.-Gen. Commanding.*

John A. Rawlins, *A. A.-G.*

A subsequent order placed General E. A. Paine in command at Cairo.

This order having been publicly announced, if it even fell into the hands of the rebels—and there was but little doubt that such would be the case—would give them the idea that the above were all the troops that comprised the forces under General Grant; whereas the divisions then organizing under Generals C. F. Smith and Lewis Wallace, at the posts of Paducah and Smithland, are not mentioned at all.

General Grant, having secured his base, left Cairo on the night of February 2d, and, with Generals McClernand and Smith's Divisions, soon after began moving from Paducah upon Fort Henry, a defensive work erected near the border-line of the States of Kentucky and Tennessee, on the east side of the Tennessee River, so as to command the stream at that point. The gunboats had also advanced up that river from the Ohio, and at about half-past eleven o'clock, on the morning of February 6, 1862, opened fire upon the works. After about two hours and a quarter's engagement, the rebels, finding their retreat cut off by the Union troops in the rear, lowered their flag, and the work and garrison surrendered before the military forces were called into action. General Grant, however, arrived at the fort within an hour after it had capitulated, when Commodore Foote gave up the post and his prisoners into the hands of the military.*

General Grant, as a conqueror, possessed the virtue and true nobleness of character which plainly set forth the imprint of the hero. The captured General Tighlman thus speaks of him in his report to the rebel authorities:

FORT HENRY, *February* 9, 1862.

Colonel W. W. MACKALL, *A. A.-General, C. S. A., Bowling Green:*

SIR:—*Through the courtesy of* Brigadier-General U. S. GRANT, commanding Federal forces, I am *permitted to communicate* with you in relation to the result of the action between the fort under my command at this place, and the Federal gunboats, on yesterday.

At eleven o'clock and forty minutes, on yesterday morning, the enemy engaged the fort with seven gunboats, mounting fifty-four guns. I promptly returned their fire, with the eleven guns from Fort Henry bearing on the river. The action was maintained with great bravery by the force under my command until ten minutes before two P. M., at which time I had but four guns fit for service. At five minutes before two, finding it impossible to maintain the fort, and wishing to spare the lives of the gallant men under my command, and on consultation with my officers, I surrendered the fort. Our casualties are small. The effect of our shot was severely felt by the enemy, whose superior and overwhelming force alone gave them the advantage.

The surrender of Fort Henry involves that of Captain Taylor, Lieutenant Watts, Lieutenant Weller, and one other officer of artillery; Captains Hayden and Miller, of the engineers; Captains H. L. Jones and McLaughlin, Quartermaster's Department; A. A.-General McConnico and myself, with some fifty privates and twenty sick, together with all the munitions of war in and about the fort.

I communicate this result with deep regret, but feel that I performed my whole duty in the defence of my post.

* It will be seen by reference to General Grant's report and order (Appendix C.), that the disposition of the troops was perfectly satisfactory, and must have secured a victory, even if the gunboats had not accomplished that object.

I take occasion to bear testimony to the gallantry of the officers and men under my command. They maintained their position with consummate bravery, as long as there was any hope of success. *I also take great pleasure in acknowledging the courtesies and consideration shown by Brigadier-General U. S. Grant and Commodore Foote, and the officers under their command.*

I have the honor to remain, very respectfully,

Your obedient servant,

LLOYD TIGHLMAN, *Brig.-Gen. C. S. A.*

The reduction of Fort Henry was but a portion of the grand work that was to be accomplished; therefore, General Grant had no time to waste in sitting and contemplating the result of his movements, even if he had so wished. He at once ordered all available troops in his district to be sent to his command, and on the morning of the 11th of February, re-enforcements left Cairo, under orders to join him on the strip of Kentucky land which lies between the Cumberland and Tennessee Rivers.

Having properly disposed of these troops, in brigades and divisions, he placed the latter under the command of the following generals:

First Division, Acting Major-General J. A. McClernand.
Second Division, Acting Major-General C. F. Smith.
Third Division, Acting Major-General Lewis Wallace.

The last-mentioned division assembled at Smithland, and moved from that place towards the objective point.

On the evening of February 11th, General Grant issued the following important order:

HEAD-QUARTERS, DISTRICT OF CAIRO,
FORT HENRY, TENN., *Feb.* 11, 1862.

[*General Field Orders, No.* 12.]

The troops designated in General Field Orders No. 9 will move to-morrow, as speedily as possible, in the following order:

One brigade of the First Division will move by the Telegraph road directly upon Fort Donelson, halting for further orders at a distance of two miles from the fort. The other brigades of the First Division will move by the Dover Ridge road, and halt at the same distance from the fort, and throw out troops so as to form a continuous line between the two wings.

The two brigades of the Second Division, now at Fort Henry, will follow as rapidly as practicable, by the Dover road, and will be followed by the troops from Fort Heiman, as fast as they can be ferried across the river.

One brigade of the Second Division should be thrown into Dover *to cut off all retreat by the river*, if found practicable to do so.

The force of the enemy being so variously reported, it is impossible to give exact details of attack; but the necessary orders will be given on the field.

By order of Brig.-Gen. U. S. GRANT, *Commanding.*
JOHN A. RAWLINS *A. A.-G.*

In accordance with the above order, the troops moved from Fort Henry on the morning of February 12, and being well started, were soon followed by General Grant and staff. The troops moved rapidly, and by noon the advance of the First Division came upon the rebel outposts and drove in the pickets.

General Grant soon got his troops into line of battle, and, to prevent the enemy from holding the high ground, ordered the hills to be occupied by our forces. The movement was made in line of battle order, and gallantly executed—the men pushing forward with even front through brush, over brooks and fences, until the desired point had been reached—speaking volumes for their drill and discipline.

Reconnoitring forces were sent out and slight skirmishing ensued; but after the woods had been thoroughly scoured, it was soon ascertained that all the enemy's main forces were in General Grant's front.

The proper dispositions were made of the troops; the First Division forming the right of the extended line, the extreme right resting on Dover, while the Second Division occupied the left, its extreme extending to a creek on the north of the fort. In this order they passed the night, without any disturbance worthy of mention.

On the morning of the 13th of February, the gunboat Carondelet, under the direction of General Grant, approached the fort by the Cumberland River, and an engagement, which lasted two hours, ensued, when the boat was withdrawn. The object of this attack was to give time for the other gunboats and the troops belonging to the Third Division to arrive by way of the river.

The gunboats and troops having joined General Grant, preparations were made to attack the rebel works by a concerted action of both the military and naval forces.

At two o'clock on February 14th, the gunboats moved up the river and received the fire of the batteries. The water battery was silenced and the gunners driven from their position; but the plunging shots from the upper batteries having crippled the flag-ship, by shattering her wheel and pilot-house, and otherwise injuring the other vessels, Commodore Foote ordered a withdrawal from the action. And thus ended the contest on the 14th.

General Grant now determined to thoroughly invest the fort, and either reduce it by siege, or wait until the gunboats could be repaired. A change, for that purpose, was therefore made in the disposition of the troops. A sortie of the enemy the next morning, however, caused General Grant somewhat to alter his plans of operation.

On the morning of the 15th, a heavy body of rebel troops attacked the extreme right of General Grant's line. The suddenness of the attack, as well as the overpowering numbers of the enemy on that particular portion of the line, caused the Union troops to give way, after a very stubborn resistance, and the rebels captured two batteries of artillery. Re-enforcements were soon sent up by the general in command, and after a desperate struggle, in which both armies displayed great bravery and endurance, all the captured guns but three were retaken.

The rebels were then also re-enforced, and made a renewed and violent attack upon the wearied troops, who were again compelled to give way. On rushed the enemy, with frightful yells, flanking the Union forces, with every prospect of final success. Other Union regiments were then brought into action; but, by mistake, they took their friends for the enemy, and caused some serious loss in one of the wearied regiments, thus increasing the confusion. Another Union brigade was brought into action, with similar results; but the rebels had so concentrated their forces that the new arrivals also had to fall back.

On another part of the line, in obedience to General Grant's orders, the Union troops had driven back the enemy with great gallantry; but, in spite of this success, the day appeared to be lost; and, although to ordinary observers the prospect was dreary, General Grant seemed to perceive a most encouraging future.

The reports of the various commanders were handed in to him at his head-quarters, and on comparing them he said to one of his staff: "Good! we have them now exactly where we want them." General Grant then ordered General C. F. Smith to make a strong assault on the left of the line, and to carry the position, no matter at what sacrifice. He also directed certain movements on the right, with the intention of not only recovering the lost ground, but also to gain a solid position in front of the enemy's works.

General Smith carried out his orders with praiseworthy gallantry, and the position was gained, after a very desperate struggle. The column of attack moved forward without firing a gun, charged desperately upon the works, and drove the rebels out of them at the point of the bayonet.

THE SURRENDER OF FORT DONELSON.

It was a brave assault, and reflects honor on every man engaged in it.

The position was occupied, and the flag of the United States waved over the works; but the loss with which it was purchased was enormous. The success, however, which attended the assault, inspired the troops with both hope and courage, and all along the lines rang the wildest shouts of enthusiasm. The heights were all carried by storm; and when the day ended, notwithstanding the disasters that had attended the contest in the morning, the Union army held a better position than they had ever had before.

The soldiers again slept on their arms, with the intention of renewing the attack at daybreak; but the morning sun found a flag of truce waving over the enemy's works. The rebels wished to treat for a surrender.

The following correspondence then passed between the commanding generals of the contending armies:

GENERAL BUCKNER TO GENERAL GRANT.

HEAD-QUARTERS, FORT DONELSON,
February 16, 1862.

SIR:—In consideration of all the circumstances governing the present situation of affairs at this station, I propose to the commanding officer of the Federal forces the appointment of commissioners to agree upon terms of capitulation of the forces and fort under my command, and in that view suggest an armistice until twelve o'clock to-day.

I am, sir, very respectfully, your obedient servant,

S. B. BUCKNER, *Brig.-Gen. C. S. A.*

To Brigadier-General GRANT, *commanding the United States forces near Fort Donelson.*

To the bearer of this dispatch General Buckner gave the following orders:

HEAD-QUARTERS, FORT DONELSON,
February 16, 1862.

Major Cashy will take or send by an officer, to the nearest picket of the enemy, the accompanying communication to General Grant, and request information of the point where future communication may reach him; also inform him that my head-quarters will be, for the present, in Dover.

S. B. BUCKNER, *Brigadier-General.*

Have the white flag hoisted on Fort Donelson, not on the battery.

S. B. BUCKNER, *Brigadier-General.*

The communication reached General Grant in due course of time; but it did not take him long to make up his mind as to his reply. In a few minutes, the following document was placed in the hands of the bearer of General Buckner's message:

HEAD-QUARTERS, ARMY IN THE FIELD,
CAMP NEAR DONELSON, *Feb.* 16, 1862.

To General S. B. BUCKNER, *Confederate Army:*

Yours of this date, proposing an armistice and appointment of commissioners to settle terms of capitulation, is just received. *No terms other than an unconditional and immediate surrender can be accepted. propose to move immediately upon your works.*

I am, sir, very respectfully your obedient servant,

U. S. GRANT, *Brig.-Gen. U. S. A., Commanding.*

The reply was far from a pleasing one to the rebel commander; but, on looking around his position, he found he could not stand another assault, and his followers were anxious for a cessation of the strife. He therefore sent the following acceptation of General Grant's terms of capitulation:

HEAD-QUARTERS, DOVER, TENNESSEE,
February 16, 1862.

To Brigadier-General U. S. GRANT, *U. S. A.:*

SIR:—The distribution of the forces under my command, incident to an unexpected change of commanders, and the overwhelming force under your command, compel me, notwithstanding the brilliant success of the Confederate arms yesterday, to accept the ungenerous and unchivalrous terms which you propose.

I am, sir, your very obedient servant,

S. B. BUCKNER, *Brig.-Gen. C. S. A.*

And thus fell into the hands of General Grant and his army, the whole of the forces that garrisoned the works of Forts Henry and Donelson, with the exception of one small brigade of rebel troops, which escaped during the night with Generals Floyd and Pillow. The troops under the former general were stationed in the extreme rear of the works; and when it was ascertained that the day was certainly lost, the two generals, with this brigade, left General Buckner to please himself, as to whether he would run, fight, or surrender.*

The rebel loss in the surrender of Fort Henry, was the commander, General Tighlman, his staff, and about sixty men, the rest of the garrison having moved to support the troops at Fort Donelson. At Fort Donelson the rebels lost General Buckner, over thirteen thousand prisoners, three thousand horses, forty-eight field-pieces, seventeen heavy guns, twenty thousand stand of arms, and a large quantity of commissary stores. The rebels killed in the last engagement were 231, and wounded, 1,007, some of whom were prisoners. The Union loss was 446 killed, 1,735 wounded, and 150 prisoners. The Union troops having to fight in an open field, against the works of the rebels, accounts for the disparity of numbers in killed and wounded.

Two regiments of rebel Tennesseeans, who had been ordered to re-enforce the garrison at Fort Donelson, marched into that work on the day after the capitulation, being unaware of its capture. They went along with their colors flying and their bands playing, and were allowed to enter the camp without any warning as to the character and nationality of those who held it in possession. The whole force (1,475 men and officers) were at once captured.

The result of this campaign was far more valuable than

* See Appendix D.

would at the first sight appear. The rebel line, at this particular part of the country, may be said to have extended from Columbus to Bowling Green, Ky., a distance of one hundred and twenty miles, with the extreme points of each wing resting on those two places, which had been strongly fortified. The reduction of Forts Henry and Donelson, and the opening of the rivers at this point broke the centre or backbone of this whole line, and, as a natural sequence, the wings had to fall. In a few days after, both Bowling Green and Columbus were in the possession of the Union troops, the rebels having evacuated those defences.

When the victory was telegraphed to Washington,* the following words were added to the dispatch:

"The United States flag now waves over Tennessee. It shall never be removed."

* The following was the report of Gen. Cullum:

CAIRO, *February* 17, 1862.

To Major-General McCLELLAN:

The Union flag floats over Fort Donelson. The Carondelet, Capt. Walke, brings the glorious intelligence.

The fort surrendered at nine o'clock yesterday (Sunday) morning. Gen. Buckner and about fifteen thousand prisoners, and a large amount of matériel of war, are the trophies of the victory. Loss heavy on both sides.

Floyd, the thief, stole away during the night previous, with five thousand men, and is denounced by the rebels as a traitor. I am happy to inform you, that Flag-Officer Foote, though suffering with his foot, with the noble characteristic of our navy, notwithstanding his disability, will take up immediately two gun-boats, and with the eight mortar-boats, which he will overtake, will make an immediate attack on Clarksville, if the state of the weather will permit. We are now firing a national salute from Fort Cairo, General Grant's late post, in honor of the glorious achievement.

[Signed] GEO. W. CULLUM,
Brig.-Gen. Vols. and U. S. A. and Chief of Staff and Engineers.

For this victorious campaign General Grant was at once nominated for, and received the confirmation of the appointment of major-general of volunteers, to date from the day of the surrender of Fort Donelson, February 16, 1862.

The following is a very amusing incident connected with General Grant's victory on the rivers Tennessee and Cumberland:

Several rumors had appeared in the newspaper press, and had otherwise been publicly proclaimed, that General Grant was in the habit of getting intoxicated. This idea may have arisen from his slovenly mode of attiring himself, or from some other equally unreliable cause. The friends of the *Illinois* troops under General Grant's command, being anxious for their safety, selected a delegation to visit General Halleck, and have Grant removed.

"You see, General," said the spokesman, "we have a number of Illinois volunteers under General Grant, and it is not safe that their lives should be intrusted to the care of a man who so constantly indulges in intoxicating liquors. Who knows what blunders he may commit?"

"Well, gentlemen," said General Halleck, "I am satisfied with General Grant, and I have no doubt you also soon will be."

While the deputation were staying at the hotel, the news arrived of the capture of Fort Donelson and thirteen thousand prisoners. General Halleck posted the intelligence himself on the hotel bulletin, and as he did so he remarked, loud enough for all to hear:

"If General Grant is such a drunkard as he is reported to be, and can win such victories as these, I think it is my duty to issue an order that any man found sober in St. Louis to-night shall be punished with fine and imprisonment."

The people of St. Louis took the hint, and nearly all, that

night, entered into the spirit of jollification. The temperance delegation from Illinois were not behind their neighbors in celebrating the occasion, and with whiskey too.*

* It is scarcely necessary to contradict a charge of drunkenness made against so successful a general as Grant; but it may not be out of place to quote the following extract from a private letter from one of his staff officers to a friend in New York:

"I have seen it stated in the public prints that General Grant is a drunkard. I have seen him in every phase of his military life, and I can assert that the accusation is false. I have been in the same tent with him at all hours of the day and night, and I *never* knew him to be under the influence of liquor, or any thing even approaching to it. I do not know what his former life may have been, but I do know that now he is a temperate man."

CHAPTER IX.

DISTRICT OF WEST TENNESSEE.

THE operations of the early part of February, 1862, had brought General Grant and his army into the State of Tennessee, and to enable him to act with promptitude and success, it became necessary to increase his line of operations. Therefore, on the 14th day of February, General Halleck issued an order creating the new district of West Tennessee, to embrace all the country between the Tennessee and Mississippi Rivers, to the Mississippi State line, and Cairo, making the head-quarters temporarily at Fort Donelson, or wherever the general might be.

The first order issued by General Grant, after the assumption of the command of that district, was a congratulatory order to his troops on their late victory. The order was worded as follows:

HEAD-QUARTERS, DISTRICT OF WEST TENNESSEE,
FORT DONELSON, *February* 17, 1862.

[*General Order No.* 2.]

The general commanding takes great pleasure in congratulating the troops of this command for the triumph over rebellion, gained by their valor, on the thirteenth, fourteenth, and fifteenth instant.

For four successive nights, without shelter, during the most inclement weather known in this latitude, they faced an enemy in large force, in a position chosen by himself. Though strongly fortified by nature, all the additional safeguards suggested by science were added. Without a murmur this was borne, prepared at all times to receive an attack, and, with continuous skirmishing by day, resulting ultimately in forcing the enemy to surrender without conditions.

The victory achieved is not only great in the effect it will have in breaking down rebellion, but has secured the greatest number of prisoners of war ever taken in any battle on this continent.

Fort Donelson will hereafter be marked in capitals on the map of our United Country, and the men who fought the battle will live in the memory of a grateful people.

By order,

U. S. GRANT, *Brig.-Gen. Commanding.*

Although one of the principal objects of the campaign—the reopening of the Tennessee and Cumberland Rivers—had been accomplished, General Grant did not allow his forces to remain long idle. After Fort Donelson had been reduced, the gunboats, under Commodore Foote, were pushed up the Cumberland River, while, at the same time, a co-operating land force, consisting of a division of General Grant's army, marched along the western bank. On the 20th of February, the town of Clarksville was taken, without a fight; and at this depot were found supplies enough for subsisting General Grant's army for twenty days. The place was at once garrisoned and held, while the gunboats moved still further up the river, to open the way for the army of the Ohio to occupy Nashville.

The Union army had by this time advanced some distance into the territory of the rebels; and it became necessary, in order to protect the *morale* as well as the persons of those composing that army, that a most rigid discipline should be exacted, and a searching law imposed upon all, both friend and foe. General Grant, therefore, appended to his army orders of February 22d, the following:

HEAD-QUARTERS, DISTRICT OF WEST TENNESSEE,
FORT DONELSON, Tenn., *Feb.* 22, 1862.

[*General Orders, No.* 7.] [*Extract.*]

Tennessee, by her rebellion, having ignored all laws of the United States, no courts will be allowed to act under State authority; but all cases coming within the reach of the military arm, will be adjudicated by the authorities the government has established within the State.

Martial law is, therefore, declared to extend over West Tennessee. Whenever a sufficient number of citizens return to their allegiance to maintain law and order over the territory, the military restriction here indicated will be removed.

By order of Major-General U. S. GRANT.

J. A. RAWLINS, *A. A. G.*

In addition to the above, General Grant also caused the following order from the head of the department, to be read at dress parade:

HEAD-QUARTERS, DISTRICT OF WEST TENNESSEE,
February, 1862.

The following order from the commander of the department is published for the information of this command:

HEAD-QUARTERS, DEPARTMENT OF MISSOURI,
ST. LOUIS, *February* 23.

The major-general commanding this department desires to impress upon all officers the importance of preserving good order and discipline among these troops and the armies of the West, during their advance into Tennessee and the Southern States.

Let us show to our fellow-citizens of these States, that we come merely to crush out this rebellion, and to restore to them peace and the benefits of the Constitution and the Union, of which they have been deprived by selfish and unprincipled leaders. They have been told that we come to oppress and plunder. By our acts we will undeceive them. We will prove to them that we come to restore, not violate, the Constitution and the laws. In restoring to them the glorious flag of the Union, we will assure them that they shall enjoy, under its folds, the same protection of life and property as in former days.

Soldiers! Let no excesses on your part tarnish the glory of our arms! The orders heretofore issued from this department in regard to pillaging, marauding, and the destruction of private property, and the stealing and concealment of slaves, must be strictly enforced. It does not belong to the military to decide upon the relation of master and slave. Such questions must be settled by the civil courts. No fugitive slave will, therefore, be admitted within our lines or camps, except when especially ordered by the general commanding. *Women and children, merchants, farmers, and all persons not in arms, are to be regarded as non-combatants, and are not to be molested, either in their persons or property.* If, however, they assist and aid the enemy, they become belligerents, and will be treated as such. As they violate the laws of war, they will be made to suffer the penalties of such violation.

Military stores and public property of the enemy must be surrendered; and any attempt to conceal such property by fraudulent transfer or otherwise will be punished. But no private property will be touched, unless by order of the general commanding.

Whenever it becomes necessary, forced contributions for supplies and subsistence for our troops will be made. Such levies will be made as light as possible, and be so distributed as to produce no distress among the people. All property so taken must be receipted fully and accepted for as heretofore directed.

These orders will be read at the head of every regiment, and all officers are commanded strictly to enforce them.

By command of Major-General HALLECK.

W. H. MCLEAN, *Adjutant-General.*

By order of Major-General U. S. GRANT.

J. A. RAWLINS, *A. A. G.*

It will thus be seen, that, although strict martial law was to be exacted, and every effort made to crush the rebellion, still non-combatants were to be respected in their persons and property.

After Nashville had been occupied, the gunboats were taken down the Cumberland River for further operations; and, among others, a reconnoissance was made up the Tennessee River, as far as the northern State lines of Mississippi and Alabama. It was ascertained by the officers of the fleet, that along the banks of this river the Union feeling was strongly manifested, and that the gunboats were welcomed with enthusiasm. It was also discovered that no large rebel force was concentrated near the river itself, and that a base of operations might be established near the borders of the southern Tennessee State line. In consequence of this discovery, General Grant removed his headquarters to Fort Henry, on the Tennessee River, where he began fitting out his expedition for operations at a distance of about one hundred miles further up that stream.

About this time another very strong effort was made, by General Grant's detractors, to get him removed, and it was even reported that he had been deprived of his command. Subsequent events explained the origin of the rumor, in the fact that General C. F. Smith had been placed in command of the troops in the field, while General Grant was still kept at Fort Henry, organizing and fitting out the forces with which he was about to operate. The advance troops were sent by transports up the Tennessee River, to Savannah, Tennessee, and while *en route*, and even after disembarking, General Smith held the command until the arrival of General Grant at that place.*

On the 11th of March, 1862, General Grant, while at Fort Henry, was presented with a handsome sword, by the regimental commanding officers. The handle of the sword was made of ivory, mounted with gold, and the blade was of the finest tempered steel. Two scabbards were attached to the sword, the service one being of fine gilt, while the parade scabbard was of rich gilt, mounted at the band. The sword was enclosed in a fine rosewood case, and ac

* The Florence (Ala.) *Gazette*, of March 12, 1862, had the following very significant article:

"We learned yesterday that the Unionists had landed a very large force at Savannah, Tenn. We suppose they are making preparations to get possession of the Memphis and Charleston Railroad. *They must never be allowed to get this great thoroughfare in their possession, for then we would indeed be crippled.* The labor and untiring industry of too many faithful and energetic men have been expended on this road to bring it up to its present state of usefulness, to let it fall into the hands of the enemy to be used against us. It must be protected. We, as a people, are able to protect and save it. If unavoidable, let them have our river; but we hope it is the united sentiment of our people, *that we will have our railroad.*"

companied by a suitable sash and belt. The inscription on the sword was very simple, being merely:

"Presented to General U. S. Grant, by G. W. Graham, C. B. Lagow, C. C. Marsh, and John Cook, 1862."

While the Tennessee operations were thus being carried out, General Grant was not unmindful of the fact that he had the enemy's forces scattered about at posts nearer home. He, therefore, sent expeditions and reconnoitring parties in all directions; and on the 12th of March, 1862, one portion of his forces, consisting of artillery and cavalry, attacked the enemy's works which were located at a point about a mile and a half west of Paris, and commanding the various roads leading to that place. The rebels were driven out, with a loss of about one hundred killed, wounded, and prisoners, and the Union forces occupied the works.

As the tendency of the movements of the different armies of the West was towards the mouth of the Mississippi River and the Gulf, it became necessary that one chief should have the direction of the whole, so as to cause the combinations to take place at the proper time. Such being the case, a new department was created, to be known as the "Department of the Mississippi," which embraced all the country west of a line drawn north and south through Knoxville, as far as Kansas and the Indian Territory, and running north to the lakes. Of this large department General Grant commanded a very important district.

The enemy also began concentrating a large force in the Southwest, under General Albert Sydney Johnston, and of this force, General P. G. T. Beauregard commanded the troops which constituted the rebel army of the valley of the Mississippi. The head-quarters of this army were located at Corinth, Mississippi, with the intention of holding the line of the Memphis and Charleston Railroad; of preventing any advance of the Union forces below the line of the Tennessee River; and, also, for the purpose of having a force ready to move into Kentucky and across the Ohio River, if an opportunity should occur for so doing. The Mississippi River was also blockaded, by fortified positions, at Island No. 10, and other points above Memphis, and at Vicksburg, New Orleans, etc., below that city. It was, therefore, considered certain by the rebels, that Corinth could not be attacked by the way of the Mississippi, and they determined to mass their forces to resist the advance of Grant's army from the Tennessee River.

As the remainder of the troops under General Grant passed up the river, they encamped at Savannah and Pittsburg Landing, which positions were at a distance of about twenty miles from the rebel stronghold at Corinth.

On the 15th of March, 1862, the troops belonging to the Third Division of Grant's army advanced from Savannah, Tennessee, into McNairy County, and struck the line of the Jackson (Tenn.) and Corinth Railroad, at Purdy, where they burned the railroad bridge, and tore up the track for a long distance. This movement prevented a train, heavily laden with rebel troops, from passing over that line from Jackson, the cars arriving shortly after the bridge was destroyed. As the rebels held the road between Jackson and Grand Junction, thence to Corinth, the concentration of the rebel army was not prevented, but only delayed, by the destruction of this part of the line.

CHAPTER X.

PITTSBURG LANDING, OR SHILOH.

THE rebel forces which had concentrated at Corinth, about the 1st of April, 1862, were supposed to number, at least, forty-five thousand men, under General A. S. Johnston, commanding department; General P. G. T. Beauregard, commanding army at Corinth; and Generals Bragg, Hardee, Breckinridge, and Polk, in command of divisions. It was also expected, by General Johnston, that the forces under Generals Van Dorn and Price would have reached them within a few days, which re-enforcement would have swollen his numbers to at least seventy thousand.

General Grant's forces had, by this time, been nearly all brought together at Pittsburg Landing, Savannah, and other places within reach,—the cavalry pickets occupying the outposts of the army.

On the evening of April 2, 1862, the Union videttes of the Third Division, who had been stationed at Crump's Landing, were driven in, and a sharp skirmish ensued, during which several were wounded and a few taken prisoners.

The next day, April 3d, the rebel commanding general issued the following order:

SOLDIERS OF THE ARMY OF THE MISSISSIPPI:

I have put you in motion to offer battle to the invaders of your country, with the resolution and discipline and valor becoming men, fighting, as you are, for all worth living or dying for. You can but march to a decisive victory over agrarian mercenaries, sent to subjugate and despoil you of your liberties, property, and honor.

Remember the precious stake involved; remember the dependence of your mothers, your wives, your sisters, and your children, on the result. Remember the fair, broad, abounding lands, the happy homes, that will be desolated by your defeat. The eyes and hopes of eight million people rest upon you. You are expected to show yourselves worthy of your valor and courage, worthy of the women of the South, whose noble devotion in this war, has never been exceeded in any time. With such incentives to brave deeds, and with trust that God is with us, your general will lead you confidently to the combat, assured of success.

By order of General A. S. JOHNSTON, *Commanding.*

The rebel army of the Mississippi was then divided into three army corps, and was commanded as follows:

Commanding-General, General Albert Sydney Johnston.
Second in Command, General P. G. T. Beauregard.
First Army Corps, Lieutenant-General L. Polk.
Second Army Corps, Lieutenant-General Braxton Bragg.
Third Army Corps, Lieutenant-General W. J. Hardee.
Reserves, Major-General G. B. Crittenden.

Against this force, Major-General Grant had but a small army in comparison, consisting of five divisions. The organization of this army was as follows:

Commanding-General, Major-General U. S. Grant.
First Division, Major-General J. A. McClernand.
Second Division, Brigadier-General W. H. L. Wallace.
Third Division, Major-General Lewis Wallace.
Fourth Division, Brigadier-General S. A. Hurlburt.
Fifth Division, Brigadier-General W. T. Sherman.

On the evening of April 4th, the rebels made a reconnoissance with two regiments, and found the Union troops ready to receive them. A very slight skirmish ensued, after which the rebels retired, as they did not wish to bring on a general engagement, for the simple reason that the expected forces under Van Dorn and Price, had not arrived.

At the same time that the "Battle of Shiloh" or Pittsburg Landing, was opened by the main body of the rebels, a force of rebel cavalry made a dash upon the position held by the Third Division of Grant's army, at Adamsville, a village situated at about half way between Savannah and Purdy. This dash was made to prevent General Wallace from rendering any assistance to General Grant's forces at Pittsburg Landing.

Having thus glanced at the position of affairs previous to the opening of the battle of Shiloh, it will plainly be seen that the rebels held a great advantage over the Unionists, even without the assistance of Van Dorn and Price. Johnston and Beauregard had resolved to attack Grant before Buell should join him, for those rebel generals were perfectly aware that Buell was advancing from Nashville for that purpose. The rebel commanders had set apart April 5th, for the day of attack; but in consequence of the non-arrival of Price and Van Dorn's forces, they had resolved to wait one day longer. This gave General Buell further time to reach Grant; and, doubtless, saved the country from an irretrievable disaster, which must have been the result, had the re-enforcements not arrived, in spite of all General Grant could have done. A decisive defeat here would have been a crushing blow to the success of the Union, and would have been a sad reward to General Grant for the bravery manifested by him on the field.

At an early hour on Sunday morning, April 6, 1862, the Union pickets were driven in, and the rebel sharpshooters began picking off the officers. At about eight o'clock in the morning, heavy masses of rebel infantry were to be seen advancing on the front, and the Union troops were ready to receive them. There was no surprise; but a steady advance of men in overwhelming numbers, and with an apparent determination to attack with the greatest desperation. The Union troops fought well, and fell back foot by foot, until they reached the river. They were closely fol-

BATTLE OF SHILOH OR PITTSBURGH LANDING.

lowed in their retreat by the rebel forces, who seemed to gather more energy and desperation when they found the Union troops were falling back.

The following account from an eye-witness, being the first published of this terrific battle, will be found of great interest, inasmuch as it was the most complete, as well as the first, epitome of the contest, that found its way into print:

THE FIRST DAY'S STRUGGLE.

PITTSBURG, *via* Fort Henry,
April 9th, 3.20 A. M.

One of the greatest and bloodiest battles of modern days has just closed, resulting in the complete rout of the enemy, who attacked us at daybreak Sunday morning.

The battle lasted, without intermission, during the entire day, and was again renewed on Monday morning, and continued undecided until four o'clock in the afternoon, when the enemy commenced their retreat, and are still flying towards Corinth, pursued by a large force of our cavalry.

The slaughter on both sides is immense. We have lost in killed, wounded, and missing, from eighteen to twenty thousand; that of the enemy is estimated at from thirty-five to forty thousand.

It is impossible, in the present confused state of affairs, to ascertain any of the details; I, therefore, give you the best account possible from observation, having passed through the storm of action during the two days that it raged.

The fight was brought on by a body of three hundred of the Twenty-fifth Missouri Regiment, of General Prentiss's Division, attacking the advance guard of the rebels, which were supposed to be the pickets of the enemy in front of our camps.

The rebels immediately advanced on General Prentiss's Division on the left wing, pouring volley after volley of musketry, and riddling our camps with grape, canister, and shell. Our forces soon formed into line and returned their fire vigorously. By the time we were prepared to receive them, the rebels had turned their heaviest fire on the left centre, Sherman's Division, and drove our men back from their camps; then, bringing up a fresh force, opened fire on our left wing, under General McClernand. This fire was returned with terrible effect and determined spirit by both infantry and artillery, along the whole line, for a distance of over four miles.

General Hurlburt's division was thrown forward to support the centre, when a desperate conflict ensued. The rebels were driven back with terrible slaughter, but soon rallied and drove back our men in turn. *From about nine o'clock, the time your correspondent arrived on the field, until night closed on the bloody scene, there was no determination of the result of the struggle.* The rebels exhibited remarkably good generalship. At times engaging the left, with apparently their whole strength, they would suddenly open a terrible and destructive fire on the right or centre. Even our heaviest and most destructive fire upon the enemy did not appear to discourage their solid columns. The fire of Major Taylor's Chicago Artillery raked them down in scores, but the smoke would no sooner be dispersed than the breach would again be filled.

The most desperate fighting took place late in the afternoon. The rebels knew that, if they did not succeed in whipping us then, their chances for success would be extremely doubtful, as a portion of General Buell's forces had by this time arrived on the opposite side of the river, and another portion was coming up the river from Savannah. They became aware that we were being re-enforced, as they could see General Buell's troops from the river bank, a short distance above us on the left, to which point they had forced their way.

At five o'clock the rebels had forced our left wing back so as to occupy fully two-thirds of our camp, and were fighting their way forward with a desperate degree of confidence in their efforts to drive us into the river, and at the same time heavily engaged our right.

Up to this time we had received no re-enforcements, General Lewis Wallace failing to come to our support until the day was over. Being without other transports than those used for quartermaster's and commissary stores, which were too heavily laden to ferry any considerable number of General Buell's forces across the river, and the boats that were here having been sent to bring up the troops from Savannah, we could not even get those men to us who were so near, and anxiously waiting to take part in the struggle. *We were, therefore, contesting against fearful odds, our force not exceeding thirty-eight thousand men, while that of the enemy was upwards of sixty thousand.*

Our condition at this moment was extremely critical. Large numbers of men panic struck, others worn out by hard fighting, with the average percentage of skulkers, had straggled towards the river, and could not be rallied.

General Grant and staff, who had been recklessly riding along the lines during the entire day, amid the unceasing storm of bullets, grape, and shell, now rode from right to left, inciting the men to stand firm until our re-enforcements could cross the river.

Colonel Webster, Chief of Staff, immediately got into position the heaviest pieces of artillery, pointing on the enemy's right, while a large number of the batteries were planted along the entire line, from the river bank northwest to our extreme right, some two and a half miles distant. About an hour before dusk a general cannonading was opened upon the enemy, from along our whole line, with a perpetual crack of musketry. Such a roar of artillery was never heard on this continent. For a short time the rebels replied with vigor and effect, but their return shots grew less frequent and destructive, while ours grew more rapid and more terrible.

The gunboats Lexington and Tyler, which lay a short distance off, kept raining shell on the rebel hordes. This last effort was too much for the enemy, and ere dusk had set in the firing had nearly ceased, when, *night coming on, all the combatants rested from their awful work of blood and carnage.*

Our men rested on their arms in the position they had at the close of the night, until the forces under Major-General Lewis Wallace arrived and took position on the right, and General Buell's forces from the opposite side and Savannah, were being conveyed to the battle-ground. The entire right of General Nelson's division was ordered to form on the right, and the forces under General Crittenden were ordered to his support early in the morning.

THE SECOND DAY'S BATTLE.

General Buell, having himself arrived on Sunday evening, on the morning of Monday, April 7th, the ball was opened at daylight, simultaneously by General Nelson's division on the left, and Major-General Wallace's division on the right. General Nelson's force opened up a most galling fire on the rebels, and advanced rapidly as they fell back. The fire soon became general along the whole line, and began to tell with terrible effect on the enemy. Generals McClernand, Sherman, and Hurlburt's men, though terribly jaded from the previous day's fighting, still maintained their honors won at Donelson; but the resistance of the rebels at all points of the attack was terrible, and worthy of a better cause.

But they were not enough for our undaunted bravery, and the dreadful desolation produced by our artillery, which was sweeping them away like chaff before the wind. *But knowing that a defeat here would be the death-blow to their hopes, and that their all depended on this great struggle, their generals still urged them on in the face of destruction*, hoping by flanking us on the right to turn the tide of battle. Their success was again for a time cheering, as they began to gain ground on us, appearing to have been re-enforced; but our left, under General Nelson, was driving them, and with wonderful rapidity, and by eleven o'clock General Buell's forces had succeeded in flanking them, and capturing their batteries of artillery.

They, however, again rallied on the left, and recrossed, and the right forced themselves forward in another desperate effort. But re-enforcements from General Wood and General Thomas were coming in, regiment after regiment, which were sent to General Buell, who had again commenced to drive the enemy.

About three o'clock in the afternoon, General Grant rode to the left where the fresh regiments had been ordered, and, finding the rebels wavering, sent a portion of his body guard to the head of each of five regiments, *and then ordered a charge across the field, himself leading; and as he brandished his sword and waved them on to the crowning victory, the cannon-balls were falling like hail around him.*

The men followed with a shout that sounded above the roar and din of the artillery, and the rebels fled in dismay as from a destroying avalanche, and never made another stand.

General Buell followed the retreating rebels, driving them in splendid style, and by half-past five o'clock the whole rebel army was in full retreat to Corinth, with our cavalry in hot pursuit, with what further result is not known, not having returned up to this hour.

We have taken a large amount of their artillery and also a number of prisoners. We lost a number of our forces prisoners yesterday, among whom is General Prentiss. The number of our force taken has not yet been ascertained. It is reported at several hundred. General Prentiss was also reported as being wounded. Among the killed on the rebel side, was their General-in-Chief, Albert Sydney Johnston, who was struck by a cannon-ball on the afternoon of Sunday. Of this there is no doubt, and it is further reported that General Beauregard was wounded.

This afternoon, Generals Bragg, Breckinridge, and Jackson were commanding portions of the rebel forces.

THE SUMMING UP OF THE TWO DAYS.

There has never been a parallel to the gallantry and bearing of our officers, from the Commanding General to the lowest officer.

General Grant and staff were in the field, riding along the lines in the thickest of the enemy's fire during the entire two days of the battle, and all slept on the ground Sunday night, during a heavy rain. On several occasions General Grant got within range of the enemy's guns and was discovered and fired upon.

Lieutenant-Colonel McPherson had his horse shot from under him when along side of General Grant.

Captain Carson was between General Grant and your correspondent when a cannon-ball took off his head and killed and wounded several others.

General Sherman had two horses killed under him, and General McClernand shared like dangers; also General Hurlbut, each of whom received bullet holes through their clothes. *

The publication of the foregoing account so soon after the battle, created a great excitement among the citizens of New York, and during the day it was telegraphed to the national capital and to other parts of the Union. The proprietor of the newspaper in which it was published, telegraphed it immediately to the President and to both Houses of Congress, in which it was read aloud. In the Lower House, Mr. Colfax, on asking leave to read the dispatch, was greeted on all sides of the House with cries of "To the Clerk's desk." The previous noise and excitement subsided, and as the House listened to the brief and pregnant details of the bloody struggle which preceded the glorious victory over the concentrated strength of rebeldom, all hearts were stilled, and the very breathing almost suppressed, till the last word of the dispatch was read. The rejoicing was great at the victory, though somewhat saddened at the price of blood with which it had been purchased.

* From the *New York Herald*, Wednesday, April 9, 1862. See Appendix E.

The following extract from the official War Bulletin is complimentary to the commanding generals engaged.

"WAR DEPARTMENT, WASHINGTON,
"*April* 9, 1862.

[*Extract.*]

* * * * * *

"That the thanks of the Department are hereby given to Major-Generals Grant and Buell, and their forces, for the glorious repulse of Beauregard at Pittsburg, in Tennessee."

A salute of one hundred guns was fired at Washington, in honor of this and other victories which had recently taken place.

During this engagement, Major-General Grant was slightly wounded in the ankle, but not enough to prevent him from attending to his duties in the field.

It will be seen by the details of the struggle that on the first day, the success seemed to be entirely on the side of the rebels, and on that ground, General Beauregard, who succeeded General Johnston, telegraphed to the rebel government as follows:

CORINTH, *Tuesday*, *April* 8, 1862.

TO THE SECRETARY OF WAR, RICHMOND:

We have gained a great and glorious victory. Eight to ten thousand prisoners and thirty-six pieces of cannon. Buell re-enforced Grant, and *we retired to our intrenchments at Corinth*, which we can hold. Loss heavy on both sides.

BEAUREGARD.

From the following correspondence it does not appear that the rebels could have moved about at will, or had even the consolation of a victory:

HEAD-QUARTERS, DEPARTMENT OF MISSISSIPPI,
MONTEREY, *April* 8, 1862.

SIR:—At the close of the conflict yesterday, my forces being exhausted by the extraordinary length of the time during which they were engaged with yours on that and the preceding day, and it being apparent that you had received, and were still receiving, re-enforcements, I felt it my duty to withdraw my troops from the immediate scene of the conflict Under these circumstances, in accordance with the usages of war, I shall transmit this under a flag of truce, to ask permission to send a mounted party to the battle-field of Shiloh, for the purpose of giving decent interment to my dead. Certain gentlemen wishing to avail themselves of this opportunity to remove the remains of their sons and friends, I must request for them the privilege of accompanying the burial party; and in this connection, I deem it proper to say. I am asking what I have extended to your own countrymen under similar circumstances.

Respectfully, General, your obedient servant,

P. G. T. BEAUREGARD, *General Commanding.*

To Major-General U. S. GRANT, *Major-General Commanding United States Forces, Pittsburg Landing.*

HEAD-QUARTERS, ARMY IN FIELD,
PITTSBURG, *April* 9, 1862.

General P. G. T. BEAUREGARD, *Commanding Confederate Army on Mississippi, Monterey, Tenn.*

Your dispatch of yesterday is just received. Owing to the warmth of the weather I deemed it advisable to have all the dead of both parties buried immediately. Heavy details were made for this purpose, and it is now accomplished. There cannot, therefore, be any necessity of admitting within our lines the parties you desired to send on the ground asked. I shall always be glad to extend any courtesy consistent with duty, and especially so when dictated by humanity. I am, General, respectfully, your obedient servant,

U. S. GRANT, *Maj.-Gen. Commanding.*

On the morning of April 8th, General Sherman, the commander of the Fifth Division, at the head of a cavalry force and two brigades of infantry, made a reconnoissance along the Corinth road, where he found the abandoned camps of the rebels lining the roads with hospital flags for their protection. Shortly after he came upon the rebel cavalry, which, after a skirmish, was driven from the field. He then destroyed the rebel camp, including the ammunition intended for the rebels' guns.

General Sherman found the road to Corinth strewed

with abandoned wagons, ambulances, and limber-boxes,—evident sign of a hasty retreat. The enemy had succeeded in removing the guns; but had crippled his batteries by abandoning the limber-boxes of, at least, twenty pieces. The retreat of the enemy's infantry was evidently a disorderly one, and had not the cavalry been in great force, to protect the rear, might soon have been turned into a disastrous rout.

When the news of this battle reached St. Louis, General Halleck, the commander of the department, determined to take the field himself, and inquire into the real results of the "Battle of Shiloh."

On his arrival at Pittsburg Landing, he issued the following order to the troops:

HEAD-QUARTERS, DEPARTMENT OF THE MISSISSIPPI,
PITTSBURG, TENN., *April* 13, 1862.

I. The major-general commanding this department thanks Major-General Grant and Major-General Buell, and the officers and men of their respective commands, for the bravery and endurance with which they sustained the general attacks of the enemy on the 6th, and for the heroic manner in which, on the 7th instant, they defeated and routed the entire rebel army. The soldiers of the great West have added new laurels to those which they had already won on numerous battle-fields.

* * * * * * *

III. Major-Generals Grant and Buell will retain the immediate command of their respective armies in the field.

By command of Major-General HALLECK.

N. H. MCLEAN, *A. A. G.*

Cavalry skirmishes still continued, at intervals, to take place along the outposts of the Union army; but nothing important occurred until April 17, 1862, when the movement was made towards Corinth.

CHAPTER XI.

MOVEMENT AND SIEGE OF CORINTH.

On the morning of April 17, 1862, a heavy cavalry force under Brigadier-General Smith, Chief of Cavalry, was detailed to make a reconnoissance along the upper road from Pittsburg Landing to Corinth. The force arrived within two miles of Monterey without meeting any opposition. Several of the men dismounted to act as skirmishers, and steadily advanced until they discovered the exact position of a large force of the enemy, when they fell back upon the main body and returned.

On April 24th, another similar reconnoissance was made under the same commander, towards an elevation known as Pea Ridge, where a rebel camp was discovered and destroyed, and a few prisoners taken.

The operations along the Mississippi River, had also opened that highway some distance below Island No. 10, and on learning this, General Beauregard, who had assumed the sole chief command of the rebel troops, issued an address to the planters as follows:

"The casualties of war have opened the Mississippi to our enemies. The time has, therefore, come to test the earnestness of all classes, and I call upon all patriotic planters owning cotton in the possible reach of our enemies, to apply the torch to it without delay or hesitation."

It was thought that, by this mode of procedure, the Union troops would have less inducements to fight, as the profit of their victories would necessarily be greatly decreased. In this, however, the rebels had greatly deceived themselves.

On April 27th, Purdy, on the Jackson and Corinth Railroad, was abandoned by the rebels, and a cavalry skirmish took place near Monterey, a village situated at about ten miles from Corinth. Several prisoners were taken, and from them it was ascertained that Beauregard was concentrating all his available force at Corinth, which he had fortified, and where, he stated, he was determined to make a desperate resistance. On the 29th, a similar affair took place at Monterey, the rebels losing their camp and several prisoners.

A reconnoissance in force was made by the right wing of General Halleck's grand army, on April 30, 1862, to a point of the railroad four miles above Purdy, between Corinth and Jackson, Tennessee. The Union troops were met by a body of rebel cavalry, who fled to that town, closely pursued by the advancing forces. Purdy was taken possession of by the Unionists, who soon, by the destruction of bridges, etc., cut off all railroad communication along that route between Corinth and Northwestern Tennessee. On this day the siege of Corinth may be said to have commenced.

General Halleck, wishing to have a force of men under him that should be invincible in the event of a battle taking place, sent for all the unemployed troops in his large department, and ordered them to be concentrated at Pittsburg Landing, which was constituted a base of operations in the movement upon Corinth. This force he designated as the "Grand Army of the Tennessee," a special compliment to General Grant, the commander of the original Army of the Tennessee. The "Grand Army" was divided into three armies, as follows:

The Army of the Ohio (centre), under General Buell.
The Army of the Mississippi (left), under General Pope.
The Army of the Tennessee (right), under General Grant.

This grand army was composed of sixteen divisions, eight of which formed the Army of the Tennessee, and were placed under the immediate command of General Grant; four under General Pope, and four under General Buell. General Grant's command was, therefore, as large as the two other armies combined, and was divided into the "right" or active wing, under General Thomas, and the "reserve" under General McClernand.

About this time, an almost universal hue and cry was raised against General Grant, by the friends of those who had fallen at Donelson and Shiloh. The charges preferred against him were incapacity and inebriety, and the persons who made them had, doubtless, been stirred up by those who wished to kill the rising fame of the heroic commander. The feeling against him even found its way into the halls of Congress, and every effort was made to remove him from his command. The Hon. E. B. Washburne, representing, in Congress, the Galena District—the home of both General Grant and himself—promptly undertook his defence.* The Governors of the Western States went down in a body to General Halleck, at Pittsburg Landing, and tried to induce him to send General Grant away from that army. But General Halleck knew his worth too well to adopt such a course. He, instead, gave him, on May 1st, a far higher position, by placing him second in command to himself over the grand army, allowing him to retain the personal command of his own special forces on the right, and of the District of the Tennessee, in which the expected battle was to be fought.

* See Appendix F.

General Beauregard, being advised of the manner of procedure of the Union troops, and expecting a severe battle, called for all the re-enforcements he could obtain. On the 2d of May, 1862, a strong rebel force concentrated at Corinth, and to this united command, he issued a very spirited address.

Reconnoissances were continually being sent out by the Union commanders; and, on the 8th of May, the cavalry penetrated the rebel lines to within a mile and a half of Corinth. The rebels also made several dashes upon the Union lines, and even succeeded in causing the retirement of some of the forces on the left.

On the 11th of May, a consultation of the chief officers was held at General Halleck's head-quarters, and it was determined that a general advance should be made of the whole grand army. Shortly after this consultation, the movement of the troops commenced. Steadily and surely did they all push forward towards a common centre, which was understood to be Corinth, and the enthusiasm of the men was only kept within bounds by the knowledge that to secure victory, a terrific battle would have soon to be fought.

The rebels, however, were determined that the Union troops should not arrive at Corinth, or in its close vicinity, without a struggle. Therefore, on May 17, 1862, General Sherman's Fifth Division of General Grant's Army of the Tennessee, was brought into actual conflict with the rebel troops, at Russell's House, on the road to that city. The rebels were forced to give way, and fell back to their strongholds, while the Unionists continued to occupy this former rebel position, which they intrenched.

When the strength of Corinth was definitely ascertained, it was determined to reduce the fortified city by regular approaches. General Beauregard being, as an engineer officer, fully aware of the ultimate result of such a course of action, began to withdraw his garrison by the roads still open to him. This movement became the more necessary, as the U. S. naval forces were rapidly approaching Memphis from above, and New Orleans and other points of the Mississippi River below had already fallen into the hands of the Unionists. Should Memphis and Vicksburg be taken before his forces could escape from Corinth, it was more than likely that his whole command, which was becoming demoralized, would have surrendered, rather than endure the horrors of a siege.

To cover his retrograde movements, General Beauregard sent out a force to resist the advance of the Union troops, who were about to take possession of the ridge to the North of Phillip's Creek. On May 21st, the Second Division of General Grant's Army of the Tennessee, under General T. A. Davis, made the necessary movements to occupy the elevation; but found the rebels very strongly posted. By a feint of a retreat the garrison was brought out of their works, and, after a vigorous contest, was completely routed. The Union division then took possession of the heights, securing at the same time several prisoners, with their arms, camp equipage, etc. A reconnoissance was then made towards Corinth, to find out the position of the enemy, who still was able to show a bold front.

The parallels of the Union army began daily to get nearer and nearer to the city, and skirmishing was a constant occurrence along the whole line. A sharp fight between General Sherman's division and the rebels took place on May 27th; but as the latter, notwithstanding that they were in larger force than the Unionists, retreated, it is now plainly to be seen that the contest was merely for the purpose of delaying the advance of the Union army.

General Sherman, in his report of the engagement, says:

"The enemy was evidently surprised, and only killed two of our men, and wounded nine. After he had reached the ridge, he opened on us with a two-gun battery on the right and another from the front and left, doing my brigades but little harm, but killing three of General Veatch's men. With our artillery we soon silenced his, and by ten A. M. we were masters of the position. *Generals Grant and Thomas were present during the affair and witnessed the movement*, which was admirably executed, all the officers and men keeping their places like real soldiers."

The above extract plainly removes the impression which had been formed that General Grant had been relieved from actual command in the field for the result of the first day's engagement at Shiloh.

Three columns of Union troops advanced the next day, under the personal superintendence of General Grant, to within gunshot of the rebel works at Corinth, and made a reconnoissance in force. The rebels hotly contested the ground; but being closely pressed had to fall back, with considerable loss. The column on the left encountered the greatest opposition.

The following account of the advance is given by one who participated in the siege:

Though the task be a most difficult one, yet I will try to give your readers a faint idea of the scenes which an advance presents.

First, the enemy must be driven back. Regiments and artillery are placed in position, and generally the cavalry is in advance, but when the opposing forces are in close proximity the infantry does the work. The whole front is covered by a cloud of skirmishers, and then reserves formed, and then, in connection with the main line, they advance. For a moment, all is still as the grave to those in the background; as the line moves on, the eye is strained in vain to follow the skirmishers as they creep silently forward; then, from some point of the line, a single rifle rings through the forest, sharp and clear, and, as if in echo, another answers it. In a moment more the whole line resounds with the din of arms. Here the fire is slow and steady, there it rattles with fearful rapidity, and this mingled with the great roar of the reserves as the skirmishers chance at any point to be driven in; and if, by reason of superior force, these reserves fall back to the main force, then every nook and corner seems full of sound. The batteries open their terrible voices, and their shells sing horribly while winging their flight, and their dull explosion speaks plainly of death; their canister and grape go crashing through the trees, rifles ring, the muskets roar, and the din is terrific. Then the slackening of the fire denotes the withdrawing of the one party, and the more distant picket-firing, that the work was accomplished. The silence becomes almost painful after such a scene as this, and no one can conceive of the effect who has not experienced it; it cannot be described. The occasional firing of the pickets, which shows that the new lines are established, actually occasions a sense of relief. The movements of the mind under such circumstances are sudden and strong. It awaits with intense anxiety the opening of the contest, it rises with the din of battle, it sinks with the lull which follows it, and finds itself in fit condition to sympathize most deeply with the torn and bleeding ones that are fast being borne to the rear.

When the ground is clear, then the time for working parties has arrived, and as this is the description of a real scene, let me premise that the works were to reach through the centre of a large open farm of at least three hundred acres, surrounded by woods, one side of it being occupied by rebel pickets. These had been driven back as I have described.

The line of the works was selected, and at the word of command three thousand men, with axes, spades, and picks, stepped out into the open field from their cover in the woods; in almost as short a time as it takes to tell it, the fence-rails which surrounded and divided three hundred acres into convenient farm-lots were on the shoulders of the men, and on the way to the intended line of works. In a few moments more a long line of crib-work stretches over the slope of the hill, as if another anaconda fold had been twisted around the rebels. Then as for a time, the ditches deepen, the cribs fill up, the dirt is packed on the outer side, the bushes and all points of concealment are cleared from the front, and the centre divisions of our army had taken a long stride towards the rebel works. The siege-guns are brought up and placed in commanding positions. A log house furnishes the hewn and seasoned timber for the platforms, and the plantation of a Southern lord has been thus speedily transferred into one of Uncle Sam's strongholds, where the Stars and Stripes float proudly. Thus had the whole army (under the immediate charge of General Grant, the commander in the field) worked itself up into the very teeth of the rebel works, and rested there on Thursday night, the twenty-eighth, expecting a general engagement at any moment.

Soon after daylight, on Friday morning, the army was startled by rapid and long-continued explosions, similar to musketry, but much louder. The conviction flashed across my mind that the rebels were blowing up their loose ammunition and leaving. The dense smoke arising in the direction of Corinth strengthened this belief, and soon the whole army was advancing on a grand reconnoissance. The distance through the woods was short, and in a few minutes shouts arose from the rebel lines, which told that our army was in the enemy's trenches. Regiment after regiment pressed on, and passing through extensive camps just vacated, soon reached Corinth and found half of it in flames. Beauregard and Bragg had left the afternoon before and the rear-guard had passed out of the town before daylight, leaving enough stragglers to commit many acts of vandalism, at the expense of private property. They burned churches and other public buildings, private goods, stores and dwellings, and choked up half the wells in town. In the camps immediately around the town, there were few evidences of hasty retreat, but on the right flank where Price and Van Dorn were encamped, the destruction of baggage and stores was very great, showing precipitate flight. Portions of our army were immediately put in pursuit.

It seems that it was the slow and careful approach of General Halleck which caused the retreat. They would doubtless have remained had we attacked their positions without first securing our rear, but they could not stand a siege. Their position was a most commanding one and well protected.*

The works were first occupied by the Fifth Division of General Grant's Army of the Tennessee, under the command of Major-General William T. Sherman, which body of troops had, between the interval of leaving Shiloh and the occupation of Corinth, occupied and strongly intrenched seven distinct camps, in a manner to excite the admiration and high commendation of the commanding generals. This division had occupied the right flank of the grand army during the whole advance, and was consequently the more exposed by their position; having to detail a larger

* Corinth Correspondence of the *Cincinnati Gazette.*

guard and perform more work than their companion divisions.

Shortly before midnight, on May 29th, 1862, the remaining portion of the rebel army was withdrawn from the works, leaving their pickets unprotected. The evacuation of Corinth at the time, and the manner in which it was done, was a clear back down from the high and arrogant tone heretofore used by the rebels. They had chosen their own ground, which they had fortified, occupying a very large force for two months in the construction of their defences, and it was naturally supposed that the works were fully strong enough to secure the defeat of the assailants.

Corinth was, indeed, a stronghold, and its importance to whichever side should hold it cannot be over estimated. As an evidence of that fact, it was kept by the United States forces as a strong military post until the beginning of 1864, and a proper garrison there retained.

The following description of the occupation of Corinth, written on the spot, may not be uninteresting to our readers:

CORINTH, *May* 30, 1862.

The siege of Corinth, begun on April 30th, ended this morning. About half-past six, in the morning, orders to march were received, and at seven, the greater portion of the men were outside their breastworks, cautiously feeling their way through the dense underbrush which intervened between our fortifications and the defences of Corinth; but after proceeding three-eighths of a mile, they came to an open space, and the enemy's works, abandoned and desolate, burst upon their astonished gaze. The sight was entirely unexpected.

The opening was made by the rebels, who had felled the timber for about three hundred yards in front of their intrenchments, for the double purpose of obstructing our progress and giving them a fair view of our column when within rifle-range.

The view from the highest point of the rebel works, immediately in front of Davies's, now Rosecrans's division, of Grant's Army of the Tennessee, was truly grand. The circle of vision was at least five miles in extent, stretching from the extreme right to the extreme left, and the magnificent display of banners, the bristling of shining bayonets, and the steady step of the handsomely attired soldiers, presented a pageant which has seldom been witnessed on this continent.

Upon many of the regimental ensigns were printed 'Wilson's Creek,' 'Dug Springs, 'Donelson,' or 'Shiloh,' and one or two wave all these mottoes in the breeze. Those who passed through all these trying ordeals, unscathed, or who received honorable wounds in either, in future can look back upon a life devoted to their country's service, and feel that proud satisfaction which is denied to others not less patriotic, but less fortunate. In future pageants in honor of the nation's birthday, when the last relics of former struggles have become extinct, and when these shall be bowed down with age, they will be their country's honored guests, and receive that consideration due their noble deeds.

Notwithstanding the desire of the soldiers to possess themselves of relics of the retreating foe, perfect order was maintained in the lines. Your correspondent wandered around the large area lately occupied by the rebel troops, but found few trophies which were worth preserving. A broken sword and double-barreled shot-gun were picked up after an hour's search, but these were seized by the Provost-Marshal at the Landing, and confiscated.

The enemy, with the exception of the rear-guard, had left with the greatest deliberation. A few worthless tents, some heavy kettles, a large number of old barrels, tin cups, and articles of this description, were the only camp equipages not taken away.

There is nothing so desolate as a newly deserted camp. But yesterday, and all was life and animation; to-day the white tents have disappeared, the heavy footsteps have ceased to sound, and no evidence, save the desolated, hard-trodden ground, and a few tent-stakes, remain to tell the story.

Nothing surprised me more than the character of the rebel works. From the length of time Beauregard's army had been occupying the place, with a view to its defence, and from the importance the rebel general attached to it, in his dispatch which was intercepted by General Mitchel, I had been led to suppose that the fortifications were really formidable. But such was not the case. I admire the engineering which dictated the position of the intrenchments, and the lines they occupied, but that is all that deserves the slightest commendation.

But a single line of general fortifications had been constructed, and these were actually less formidable than those thrown up by our forces last night, after occupying a new position. There were, besides this general line, occasional rifle-pits, both outside and inside the works, but they could have been constructed by three relief details in six hours.

The only fortifications really worthy the name, were a few points where batteries were located, but these could not have resisted our Parrot and siege-guns half an hour. Yet the positions occupied by the breastworks were capable of being strengthened so as to render them almost invulnerable to a front attack, and no little difficulty would have been experienced in flanking the position, either on the right or left.

The works were on the brow of a ridge, considerably higher than any in the surrounding country, and at the foot of it was a ravine, correspondingly deep. The zigzag course of the line gave the defenders the command of all the feasible approaches, and hundreds could have been mowed down at every step made by an assailing army, even from the imperfect earth-banks which had been thrown up.

Had a fight occurred, it must have been decided by artillery, and in this respect we had the advantage, both in number and calibre of our guns; but had they improved the advantages they possessed, and fortified as men who really intended to make a stubborn defence, this superiority might have been overcome.

The conduct of the rebels is, indeed, beyond comprehension. Here is a place commanding several important railroads; a place, the seizure of which Beauregard confessed, in his celebrated dispatch to Davis, would open to us the valley of the Mississippi; a position capable of as stubborn a defence as Sebastopol, and yet scarcely an effort is made to fortify it, and its possessors fly at our approach. A stubborn resistance, even though followed by defeat, would command respect abroad; but a succession of evacuations, upon the slightest approach of danger, can insure only contempt.

The troops from every direction marched toward a common centre—Corinth; and as they neared each other and friends recognized friends, whom they had not seen for weeks or months, though separated but a few miles, greetings were exchanged, and as regiments met for the first time since leaving the bloody fields of Donelson and Shiloh, cheer after cheer resounded through the forests, and were echoed and re-echoed by the hills, as if the earth itself desired to prolong the sound.

As no rain had fallen for some time, the roads were exceedingly dusty, as was the whole camping-ground, which had been trampled solid by eighty thousand rebels. But all forgot obstacles and annoyances in the eagerness to see the town before which they had lain so long. A little after eight o'clock, a portion of the left and centre filed in, and were met by Mr. Harrington, the Mayor's clerk, who asked protection for private property, and for such of the citizens as had determined to remain. It is needless to add that his request was granted, and guards stationed at every door, as the object of our march is not to plunder, but to save.*

Corinth is built upon low lands and clay soil, so that in wet weather the place may very properly be denominated a swamp; but the soil is as easily affected by the drought as by rains. Just outside of the town are the ridges, which might be appropriately denominated hills, and upon which second, third, and fourth lines of defences could have been erected. The highest lands are in the direction of Farmington on the east, and College Hill on the south-west. The town is situated at the junction of the Mobile and Ohio and the Memphis and Charleston Railroads, both very important lines of communication, and indispensable to the enemy. The town is nearly all north of the Memphis and east of the Mobile road. Corinth was at one time a pleasant country village, of about 1,200 inhabitants, and the houses were built in the style only used in the South.

The rebel generals all had their head-quarters in houses during the siege, generally occupying the finest residences in the place. Beauregard's was on the east of the Purdy road, and at the outskirts of the village. The rebel chieftain was evidently surrounded by all the comforts and luxuries of life. Telegraph wires run in every direction from the building, but the wires were all cut, and the instruments taken away at the time the place was evacuated; so that when our army took possession of Corinth, they could only judge of, but could not use, these means of communication.

The Union forces engaged in the pursuit, which was con-

* Army correspondence.

ducted with great rapidity and skill, followed the rebels far down the Mobile and Ohio Railroad, through a difficult country much obstructed by the enemy. On the afternoon of the 30th of May the Union forces, which were sent out on the night of May 28th to cut off the rebel retreat, reached Boonesville, Miss., and there destroyed the track in many places both north and south of the town, blew up one culvert, burned the depot, locomotives and a train of twenty-six cars loaded with supplies, destroyed a quantity of arms, including artillery, clothing, and ammunition, besides taking a number of prisoners who belonged to the rear of the retreating forces. So desolated had the country become, that the pursuers had to live upon meat alone, such as they could find around them on their line of travel. Colonel Elliott, the commander of the cavalry, not having any wagons with him, could not collect food and forage: he, however, found a few sheep, which he devoted to the use of his followers; but the flesh was very poor and tough. The prisoners he captured were mostly infantry, and finding that he would have very great difficulty in looking after them, if he took them along with him, he merely disarmed them and sent them about their business.

Plans were laid by the rebels to cut off Colonel Elliott's command on its return; but the colonel judiciously chose another road, by which he escaped the snare, and arrived safely at Tuscumbia on June 1st, 1862. The route taken in the advance was by Iuka, Eastport, and Fulton, thence along the Tuscumbia and Jacinto road to Cartersville, thence to Padens and Boonesville, where the damage was principally inflicted on the rebels. The return was by the road to Tuscumbia.

On the 9th of June, 1862, General Halleck reported that the rebels had fallen back fifty miles from Corinth, by the nearest railroad route, and seventy miles by the wagon road, and that the estimated rebel loss, during the campaign near that place, was about forty thousand men. He also reported a state of demoralization existing in General Beauregard's army, and that the prisoners taken in many cases begged that they should not be exchanged, as they had purposely allowed themselves to be captured.

Holly Springs, Miss., on the railroad from Jackson, Tenn., to New Orleans, was taken possession of by General Sherman's forces of Grant's Army, on June 20th, 1862; and to prevent surprise by the rebels, several pieces of trestle-work on the Mississippi Central Railroad were destroyed. The rebels, before evacuating the place, had removed their machinery for the repairing and making of arms to Atlanta, in Georgia.

The campaign in this part of the country having virtually ended, General Halleck was, on July 11th, 1862, ordered to Washington, to assume the position of General-in-Chief, and, on the 17th, took leave of his army in a farewell address, congratulating the officers and soldiers belonging to it, on their endurance and bravery.

CHAPTER XII.

THE DEPARTMENT OF WEST TENNESSEE.—MEMPHIS.

THE removal of General Halleck from the command of so large a tract of country, naturally led to a reorganization of the forces in the West, and new departments were created out of the original Department of the Mississippi. General Buell's forces were separated, and formed into the Department of the Ohio, embracing the district of country north and east of the Tennessee River. Missouri was also formed into a distinct department.

All the country from the Mississippi River to the western shores of the Tennessee, Cairo, Forts Henry and Donelson, the western shore of the Mississippi River, and the northern part of the State of Mississippi, was formed into the "Department of West Tennessee." Of this department, General Grant was made the commander, with his head-quarters at Corinth.

Memphis, which had surrendered on June 6th, 1862, soon after the evacuation of Corinth, and had been occupied at once by the Union forces, now formed part of this department, and became, by this time, a very important post, both as a base of operations and of supplies. General Grant, while commanding the district, visited the post as soon as convenient, and placed it under the jurisdiction of a provost-marshal. Among other orders, he issued the following, as it was necessary to prevent the co-operation between the latent rebels in that city with those in arms outside our lines:

HEAD-QUARTERS, DISTRICT OF WEST TENNESSEE,
OFFICE PROVOST-MARSHAL GENERAL,
MEMPHIS, *June* 28, 1862.

[*Special Orders, No.* 4.]

* * * * * *

Passes issued for persons to pass out of the city will be understood to mean the person alone, and will not include goods, letters, or packages.

Where letters are found on persons passing out, without being marked PASSED by the Provost-Marshal, Post Commander, or General, Commanding, they will be seized and delivered to the Provost-Marshal and the offender arrested.

Powder, lead, percussion caps, and fire-arms of all descriptions, are positively prohibited from being carried out of the city by citizens. Citizens are also prohibited from carrying them within the city limits on pain of forfeiture of such weapons, and ten days' confinement, for the first offence, and expulsion south of our lines, to be treated as spies, if ever caught within them thereafter, for the second.

By command of Major-General U. S. GRANT.

WM. S. HILLYER, *Provost-Marshal General.*

Finding that the above appeared to have had no effect in stopping the illicit traffic, General Grant caused the following positive orders to be issued, which determination greatly aided him in restoring the city of Memphis to order and loyalty.

DISTRICT OF WEST TENNESSEE,
OFFICE OF THE PROVOST-MARSHAL GENERAL,
MEMPHIS, TENN., *July* 9, 1862.

[*Special Orders, No.* 13.]

* * * * * *

All passes heretofore issued to citizens, either by the Commanding General, the Provost-Marshal General, the Provost-Marshal of Memphis, or any other officer, which may have been issued without the party being required to take the Oath of Allegiance, or give the prescribed Parole of Honor, are hereby revoked.

No pass will be granted in any case hereafter, except upon the taking of the oath or parole.

The parole will be substituted for the oath only in special cases (at the discretion of the officer authorized to grant passes), where the party lives beyond the protection of our army.

By command of Major-General GRANT.

WM. S. HILLYER, *Provost-Marshal General.*

DISTRICT OF WEST TENNESSEE,
OFFICE PROVOST-MARSHAL GENERAL,
MEMPHIS, *July* 10, 1862.

[*Special Orders, No.* 14.]

The constant communication between the so-called Confederate army and their friends and sympathizers in the city of Memphis, despite the orders heretofore issued, and the efforts to enforce them, induced the issuing of the following order:

The families now residing in the city of Memphis of the following persons, are required to move south beyond the lines within five days from the date hereof:

First.—All persons holding commissions in the so-called Confederate army, or who have voluntarily enlisted in said army, or who accompany and are connected with the same.

Second.—All persons holding office under or in the employ of the so-called Confederate Government.

Third.—All persons holding State, county, or municipal offices, who claim allegiance to said so-called Confederate Government, and who have abandoned their families and gone South.

Safe conduct will be given to the parties hereby required to leave, upon application to the Provost-Marshal of Memphis.

By command of Major-General GRANT.

DISTRICT OF WEST TENNESSEE,
OFFICE OF THE PROVOST-MARSHAL GENERAL,
MEMPHIS, TENN., *July* 11, 1862.

[*Special Orders, No.* 15.].

* * * * * *

In order that innocent, peaceable, and well-disposed persons may not suffer for the bad conduct of the guilty parties coming within the purview of Special Order No. 14, dated July 10, 1862, they can be relieved from the operation of said order No. 14, by signing the following parole, and producing to the Provost-Marshal General, or the Provost-Marshal of Memphis, satisfactory guarantees that they will keep the pledge therein made:

PAROLE.

First. I have not, since the occupation of the city of Memphis by the Federal army, given any aid to the so-called Confederate army, nor given or sent any information of the movements, strength, or position of the Federal army to any one connected with said Confederate army.

Second. I will not, during the occupancy of Memphis by the Federal army and my residing therein, oppose or conspire against the civil or military authority of the United States, and that I will not give aid, comfort, information, or encouragement to the so-called Confederate army, nor to any person co-operating therewith.

All of which I state and pledge upon my sacred honor.

By command of Major-General GRANT.

WM. S. HILLYER, *Provost-Marshal General.*

And as a warning to the guerillas who were operating about Memphis, destroying cotton and plundering from friend and foe, the following order was also issued:

HEAD-QUARTERS, DIST. OF WEST TENNESSEE,
MEMPHIS, TENN., *July* 3, 1862.

[*General Order No.* 60.]

The system of guerilla warfare now being prosecuted by some troops organized under authority of the so-called Southern Confederacy, and others without such authority, being so pernicious to the welfare of the community where it is carried on, and it being within the power of the community to suppress this system, it is ordered that wherever loss is sustained by the Government, collections shall be made, by seizure of a sufficient amount of personal property, from persons in the immediate neighborhood sympathizing with the rebellion, to remunerate the Government for all loss and expense of the same.

Persons acting as guerillas without organization, and without uniform to distinguish them from private citizens, are not entitled to the treatment of prisoners of war when caught, and will not receive such treatment. By order of Major-General U. S. GRANT.

JOHN A. RAWLINS, *A. A.-G.*

The newspapers of Memphis had also continued to publish articles of a character likely to inflame the people against the United States authorities; and while such license of the press was allowed it would have been impossible to have restored order in that part of the district. The following documents have a very significant tone:

HEAD-QUARTERS DISTRICT OF WEST TENNESSEE,
OFFICE PROVOST-MARSHAL GENERAL,
MEMPHIS, TENN., *July* 1, 1862.

Messrs. WILLS, BINGHAM & Co., *Proprietors of the Memphis Avalanche.*

You will suspend the further publication of your paper. The spirit with which it is conducted is regarded as both incendiary and treasonable, and its issue cannot longer be tolerated.

This order will be strictly observed from the time of its reception.

By command of Maj.-Gen. U. S. GRANT.

WM. S. HILLYER, *Provost-Marshal General.*

MEMPHIS, *July* 1, 1862.

The Avalanche can continue by the withdrawal of the author of the obnoxious article under the caption of "Mischief Makers," and the editorial allusion to the same.

U. S. GRANT, *Major-General.*

TO OUR PATRONS.—For reasons apparent from the foregoing order, I withdraw from the editorial management of *The Avalanche.* Self-respect, and the spirit of true journalism, forbid any longer attempt to edit a paper. I approved and indorsed the articles in question. Prudence forbids my saying more, and duty less, to the public.

JEPTHA FOWLKES.

The ruinous system of guerilla warfare continuing, and it being found almost impossible to stop the contraband trade which was being carried on through Memphis, in aid of the rebellion, General Grant appointed General Sherman to the command of that city, with the full knowledge that his determination would soon check both operations. On the 21st of July, 1862, General Sherman assumed the command, and it was soon detected where the difficulty lay, as may be judged from the following order:

U. S. MILITARY TELEGRAPH, CORINTH, *July* 26, 1862.

To Brigadier-General J. T. QUIMBY, *Columbus, Ky.*

GENERAL:—Examine the baggage of all speculators coming South, and when they have specie turn them back. If medicine and other contraband articles, arrest them and confiscate the contraband articles. Jews should receive special attention.

(Signed) U. S. GRANT, *Major-General.*

He also ordered the most stringent measures to be adopted against all guerillas and their agents, and the following dispatch is an evidence of the manner with which his orders were carried out:

TRENTON, TENN., *July* 29, 1862.

GENERAL:—The man who guided the rebels to the bridge that was burned was hung to-day. He had taken the oath. The houses of four others who aided have been burned to the ground.

(Signed) G. M. DODGE, *Brigadier-General.*

On July 28th, General Grant ordered General Sherman to take possession of all unoccupied dwellings, manufactories, and stores, within the city of Memphis, to hire them out, and to collect the rents for the United States Government, in all cases where the owners were absent, engaged in arms against the United States. This plan was adopted to prevent the property being destroyed or abused, as well as to bring in a revenue from rebel sources to help pay the expenses of the war.

A portion of the rebel forces that had been engaged at Corinth were afterwards concentrated at Jackson, Miss., whence they were sent to Vicksburg, Baton Rouge, Port Hudson, and other places along the Mississippi River, for the purpose of again blockading that stream. On the 5th of August a battle was fought at Baton Rouge.*

The large number of negroes that had found refuge within the union lines, were about this time becoming a serious incubus upon the commanders of the army, and it was

* Although this battle occurred outside of the limits of General Grant's department, it is here alluded to—as it will be found in the course of the narrative, that these movements were more or less connected with his grand campaign of 1863.

decided that these men should be put at some useful employment. General Grant, therefore, to remedy the evil in his own special department, issued the following order, which contains certain regulations in relation to both the negro refugees and the carrying out of the Confiscation law, as passed by the Houses of Congress, and signed by the President:

HEAD-QUARTERS, DEPARTMENT OF WEST TENNESSEE,
CORINTH, MISS., *August* 11th, 1862.

[*General Orders*, *No.* 72.]

The recent Act of Congress prohibits the army from returning fugitives from labor to their claimants, and authorizes the employment of such persons in the service of the government. The following orders are therefore published for the guidance of the army in this matter.

1. All fugitives thus employed must be registered; the names of the fugitives and claimant given, and must be borne upon the morning report of the command in which they are kept, showing how they are employed.

2. Fugitives may be employed as laborers in the quartermaster's, subsistence, and engineer's department; and whenever by such employment a soldier may be saved to its ranks, they may be employed as teamsters and as company cooks, not exceeding four to a company, or as hospital attendants and nurses. Officers may employ them as private servants, in which latter case the fugitives will not be paid or rationed by the government. Negroes thus employed must be secured as authorized persons, and will be excluded from the camps.

3. Officers and soldiers are positively prohibited from enticing slaves to leave their masters. When it becomes necessary to employ this kind of labor, the commanding officer of the post or troops must send details, all under the charge of a suitable commissioned officer, to press into service the slaves of persons to the number required.

4. Citizens within reach of any military station, known to be disloyal and dangerous, may be ordered away or arrested, and their crops and stock taken for the benefit of the government or the use of the army.

5. All property taken from rebel owners must be duly reported and used for the benefit of the government, and be issued to the troops through the proper department, and, when practicable, the act of taking

should be accompanied by the written certificate of the officer so taking to the owner or agent of such property.

It is enjoined on all commanders to see that this order is executed strictly under their own direction. The demoralization of troops subsequent upon being left to execute laws in their own way without a proper head must be avoided.

By command of Major-General GRANT.

JOHN A. RAWLINS, *A. A.-G.*

It will be seen by the last clause of the above order that, although General Grant was perfectly willing to carry out the laws according to their letter and spirit, he was determined that wholesale plunder should not be allowed within the limits of his department.

Several had taken advantage of the advance of the armies to visit certain places in the Southern States within the Union lines. Among others were a number of individuals who had fled from their own States to avoid the enrolment ordered under the Conscription act. These men were generally of a disreputable character, and made their living by following the army, robbing the soldiers, or trading with the rebels. To meet the particular cases of these men, the following order was issued by General Grant from his departmental head-quarters.

HEAD-QUARTERS, DEPARTMENT OF WEST TENNESSEE,
CORINTH, MISS., *August* 16, 1862.

[*General Orders, No.* 74.]

1. All non-residents of this department, found within the same, who, if at home, would be subject to draft, will at once be enrolled under the supervision of the local commanders where they may be found, and, in case of a draft being made by their respective States, an equal proportion will be drawn from persons thus enrolled. Persons so drawn will at once be assigned to troops from the States to which they owe military service, and the executive thereof notified of such draft.

2. All violation of trade by army followers may be punished by

confiscation of stock in trade, and the assignment of offenders to do military duty as private soldiers.

By command of Major-General U. S. GRANT.

JOHN A. RAWLINS, *A. A.-G.*

As far as actual fighting was concerned, it may be safely stated that from June to September, 1862, General Grant's Department was particularly quiet. Skirmishes would occasionally take place between guerillas and the troops occupying small districts, as at Bolivar, on August 30th, and at Medon Station of the Mississippi Central Railroad, on August 31st. On all these occasions the rebel troops were generally worsted, so well had General Grant looked after the defences of these posts.

During the early part of September, 1862, the rebel forces in the Southwest began to make a general advance upon the Union positions. General Bragg issued an order on September 5, 1862, which he dated at Sparta, in the most southern part of Alabama, for the purpose of deceiving the Union troops as to his actual whereabouts, while, at the same time, he was at Chattanooga, Tenn., preparing to make a flank movement through East Tennessee and Kentucky, to the Ohio River. The deceitful order certainly misled the commander of the army of the Ohio; but did not impose upon General Grant, nor the officers under his command, as cavalry reconnoissances were continually being sent out to ascertain the whereabouts of the enemy.

The rebels soon discovered that General Grant was sending troops to re-enforce the army in Kentucky, and to prevent him from so doing, a portion of the rebel army in the State of Mississippi was detached, to operate against his lines. General Grant had, however, taken care of his own position while helping the others, and the results were the glorious victories of Iuka and Corinth.

CHAPTER XIII.

IUKA.—CORINTH AND THE HATCHIE.

The careful system of reconnoissance adopted in General Grant's army made the commander of the Department of West Tennessee and his subordinate general officers fully aware of the approach of the rebels upon their lines long before the actual attack took place. Even as early as September 10th, 1862, it was known that General Sterling Price, at the head of a far superior force of rebel troops, was marching upon the little camp at Jacinto, Tishamingo County, Miss. Orders were, of course, quickly given to break up this camp, and take the wagon trains to the defences at Corinth. The men who were ordered to remain behind were thereby compelled to sleep on their arms and in the open air for several nights.

On September 17th, a general advance was ordered by General Grant, and at four o'clock on the morning of September 18th the regiments from Corinth and Jacinto were pushing towards Iuka, where General Price had concentrated his forces. The march of the Union troops was made amidst a drenching rain, and along muddy roads, and they advanced upon the place by different routes, the force under General Rosecrans, known as the Army of the Mississippi, making the advance along the road from the south, while that under Generals Grant and Ord approached the town from the north, *via* Burnsville.

At daybreak, on the morning of September 19th, the march was renewed, and the advance of General Hamilton's Division encountered the rebel pickets at Barnett's Corners, on the road to Iuka. After a sharp skirmish, the pickets were driven six miles towards that town, losing slightly in killed and prisoners. The division again pushed forward until within two miles of Iuka, where they were received with a hot fire of musketry from the rebels who were posted on the ridge which commanded the country for several miles around. The engagement soon became general, on this part of the line, and lasted until dark, when the men threw themselves down on their arms, to take that rest so needed to enable them to renew the struggle on the morrow. The contest had been very sanguinary and fierce while it lasted, nearly one-third of the Union forces engaged being placed *hors de combat.*

During the night the rebel forces under Price evacuated the town, and in the morning General Rosecrans's troops entered Iuka from the south, and began pushing after the flying rebels. Shortly after, the forces under Generals Grant and Ord arrived by the northern route. As the intention of General Grant had been to cut off Price's retreat by that road, and as Price had chosen another towards the east, this part of the army was not engaged, although its position contributed towards forcing the enemy to evacuate the place.

The following extracts from a private letter of a rebel to a friend, under date of September 24th, 1862, contain matters of interest:

"We held peaceable possession of Iuka for one day, and on the next were alarmed by the booming of cannon, and were called out to spend the evening in battle array in the woods. On the evening of the 19th, when we supposed we were going back to camp, to rest awhile, the sharp crack of musketry on the right of our former lines told us that the enemy was much nearer than we imagined. In fact, they had almost penetrated the town itself. How on earth, with the woods full of our cavalry, they could have approached so near our lines, is a mystery. They had planted a battery sufficiently near to shell General Price's head-quarters, and were cracking away at the Third Brigade when the Fourth came up at double-quick, and then, for two hours and fifteen minutes, was kept up the most terrific fire of musketry that ever dinned my ears. There was one continuous roar of small arms, while grape and canister howled in fearful concert above our heads and through our ranks. General Little was shot dead early in the action. * * It was a terrible struggle, and we lost heavily. All night could be heard the groans of the wounded and dying, forming a sequel of horror and agony to the deadly struggle, over which night had kindly thrown its mantle. *Saddest of all, our dead were left unburied, and many of the wounded on the battle-field to be taken in charge by the enemy.*

"Finding that the enemy were being re-enforced from the north, and as our strength would not justify us in trying another battle, a retreat was ordered, and we left the town during the night. The enemy pressed our rear the next day, and were only kept off by grape and canister.

"It grieves me to state that acts of vandalism, disgraceful to any army, were, however, perpetrated along the line of retreat, and makes me blush to own such men as my countrymen. Corn-fields were laid waste, potato patches robbed, barn-yards and smoke-houses despoiled, hogs killed, and all kinds of outrages perpetrated in broad daylight and in full view of the officers. The advance and retreat were alike disgraceful, and I have no doubt that women and children along the route will cry for the bread which has been rudely taken from them by those who should have protected and defended them."*

The Army of the Mississippi bore the brunt of the fight, but the combinations caused the evacuation of the town. On the morning of the 20th of September, 1862, General Grant sent the following dispatch to the general-in-chief at Washington:

IUKA, MISS., *September* 20, 1862.

To Major-General H. W. HALLECK, *General-in-Chief:*

General Rosecrans, with Stanley's and Hamilton's Divisions and Misener's Cavalry, attacked Price south of this village about two hours before dark yesterday, and had a sharp fight until night closed in. General

* Private letter published in the Montgomery Advertiser, September, 1862.

Ord was to the north with an armed force of about 5,000 men, and had some skirmishing with the rebel pickets. This morning the fight was renewed by General Rosecrans, who was nearest to the town; but it was found that the enemy had been evacuating during the night, going south. Generals Hamilton and Stanley, with cavalry, are in full pursuit.

This will, no doubt, break up the enemy, and possibly force them to abandon much of their artillery. The loss on either side, in killed and wounded, is from 400 to 500. The enemy's loss in arms, tents, etc., will be large. We have about 250 prisoners.

I have reliable intelligence that it was Price's intention to move over east of the Tennessee. In this he has been thwarted. Among the enemy's loss are General Little killed, and General Whitefield wounded.

I cannot speak too highly of the energy and skill displayed by General Rosecrans in the attack, and of the endurance of the troops. General Ord's command showed untiring zeal; but the direction taken by the enemy prevented them from taking the active part they desired, Price's force was about 18,000.

U. S. GRANT, *Major-General.*

The examination of the field, after the first excitement of the battle was over, showed a still more favorable result for the Union forces, as may be judged by the following dispatch:

HEAD-QUARTERS, CORINTH, *September* 22, 1862.

Major-General HALLECK, *General-in-Chief:*

In my dispatch of the 20th our loss was over estimated, and the rebel loss under estimated. We found two hundred and sixty-one of them dead upon the field, while our loss in killed will be less than one hundred.

U. S. GRANT, *Major-General.*

General Grant, on the same day as he sent the above dispatch, issued the following order, complimenting his officers and men upon their bravery, not forgetting those who fell on that occasion:—

HEAD-QUARTERS, DEPARTMENT OF WEST TENNESSEE,
CORINTH, *September* 22, 1862.

[*General Field Orders, No.* 1.]

The General Commanding takes great pleasure in congratulating the two wings of the army, commanded respectively by Major-General Ord and Major-General Rosecrans, upon the energy, alacrity, and bravery displayed by them on the 19th and 20th inst., in their movement against the enemy at Iuka. Although the enemy was in numbers reputed far greater than their own, nothing was evinced by the troops but a burning desire to meet him, whatever his numbers, and however strong his position.

With such a disposition as was manifested by the troops on this occasion, their commanders need never fear defeat against any thing but overwhelming numbers.

While it was the fortune of the command of General Rosecrans, on the evening of the 19th inst., to engage the enemy in a most spirited fight for more than two hours, driving him with great loss from his position, and winning for themselves fresh laurels, the command of General Ord is entitled to equal credit for their efforts in trying to reach the enemy, and in diverting his attention.

And while congratulating the noble living, it is meet to offer our condolence to the friends of the heroic dead, who offered their lives a sacrifice in defence of constitutional liberty, and in their fall rendered memorable the field of Iuka.

By command of Major-General U. S. GRANT.

JOHN A. RAWLINS, *A. A.-G.*

General Bragg's forces were all this time pushing forward towards the Ohio River, and it became necessary, to enable General Grant to have full control over his department, that he should move his head-quarters to a more central position. He therefore chose Jackson, Tennessee, for that purpose; placing the commander of the Army of the Mississippi in local command at Corinth.

The rebel forces which had retreated from Iuka, were next concentrated near Ripley, Tippah County, Mississippi, and southwest of Corinth, at which point they were joined by those under Generals Van Dorn and Lovell. It appears that Price's forces, in retreating from Iuka, countermarched at a point several miles south of the Union position, crossed the Mobile and Ohio Railroad in the vicinity of Baldwyn, Tupello, etc., and were thus enabled to form a junction with the troops under the before mentioned Generals, and comprising all the available rebel forces in North Mississippi. The intention of the enemy was to retake Corinth at all hazards, or at least to break the Union line of communications, and force a retreat.

General Grant being duly advised of these facts, so arranged his forces that if the rebels were driven from Corinth—and he had not a doubt but that they would be—they should not be able to escape without a very severe punishment.

Cavalry scouts were sent out in all directions and demonstrated the fact that the rebels were on October 1st, 1862, moving from Ripley, *via* Buckersville, upon Corinth, while the main army was at Pocahontas. The question then was, where did they intend to strike the principal blow, as they were situated in such a position that they could attack with equal ease either of the posts at Bethel, Bolivar, Corinth, or Jackson. In fact, they held the centre of the base of the irregular triangle which had Jackson for its apex and Corinth for its right hand corner.

General Grant, however, was master of the situation, and to him it mattered little at what point the rebels struck, as he could move his forces to support the position attacked—so well had he arranged them within reasonable reach of each other. General Ord held the position at Bolivar, General Hurlbut was stationed nearer Pocahontas, General Rosecrans was at Corinth, and General Grant at Jackson. It will be seen that the rebels were hemmed in except on the south.

On the 4th of October, the enemy made a determined and vigorous attack upon the works at Corinth, and the most obstinate fighting ensued. General Grant was in constant telegraph communication with General Rosecrans, during the attack, and also with his other generals. He was enabled to move his forces knowingly so as to meet the movements made by the enemy.

The struggle at Corinth, was a fierce and sanguinary one, and bravely did the garrison defend the position during the morning of the 4th. By noon the battle was ended, and the enemy were in full retreat from the place. The rebels had even forced their way into the town, and severe fighting took place in the streets, but in the end they were driven out of Corinth, and their broken fragments chased into the woods.

The victory had, however, cost the Union army dearly, as may be judged from the following brief dispatch from General Grant to the general-in-chief:

GRANT'S HEAD-QUARTERS,
JACKSON, TENN., *October* 5,—8 A. M.

To Major-General H. W. HALECK, *General-in-Chief United States Army:*

Yesterday the rebels under Price, Van Dorn, and Lovell were repulsed from their attack on Corinth with great slaughter.

The enemy are in full retreat, leaving their dead and wounded on the field.

Rosecrans telegraphs that the loss is serious on our side, particularly in officers, but bears no comparison with that of the enemy.

General Hackleman fell while gallantly leading his brigade.

General Oglesby is dangerously wounded.

General McPherson, with his command, reached Corinth yesterday.

General Rosecrans pursued the retreating enemy this morning, and, should they attempt to move towards Bolivar, will follow to that place.

General Hurlbut is at the Hatchie River with five or six thousand men, and is no doubt with the pursuing columm.

From seven hundred to a thousand prisoners, besides the wounded, are left in our hands.

U. S. GRANT, *Major-General Commanding.*

As stated in the above dispatch, General Rosecrans chased the enemy, on the morning of the 5th of October, and pushed them towards the Hatchie River. General Hurlbut, who had moved forward to that position along the line of railroad from Grand Junction, had already on the previous day driven in the rebel videttes, but his advance had been somewhat disputed during the night. General Hurlbut was, on the morning of October 5th, joined by General Ord's forces from Bolivar. General Ord assumed command; but finding General Hurlbut had made excellent arrangements for the advance, he followed out the same plan. The road, narrow and winding, through swamp and jungle, and over precipitous ridges, across which at times the guns were with great labor dragged by hand, made the advance more than ordinarily dangerous in the face of the enemy, especially as the retreating forces from Corinth were likely soon to be joined with the others in the front. The rebels made use of every advantage the country gave them, using the swamps and jungles for their infantry, and the ridges for their artillery; but so valorous was the attack of the forces under Generals Ord and Hurlbut, that the enemy was driven for five miles to, and across the Hatchie, and up the heights beyond.

The following dispatch from General Grant, announces the victory on the Hatchie:

GRANT'S HEAD-QUARTERS,
JACKSON, TENN., *October* 5, 1862.

To Major-General H. W. HALLECK, *General-in-Chief United States Army:*

General Ord, who followed General Hurlbut, met the enemy to-day on the south side of the Hatchie, as I understand from a dispatch, and drove them across the stream, and got possession of the heights with our troops.

General Ord took two batteries and about two hundred prisoners.

A large portion of General Rosecrans's forces were at Chevalla.

At this distance every thing looks most favorable, and I cannot see how the enemy are to escape without losing every thing but their small arms.

I have strained every thing to take into the fight an adequate force, and to get them to the right place.

U. S. GRANT, *Major-General Commanding.*

The union of General McPherson's forces with those at Corinth, enabled General Rosecrans to continue vigorously the pursuit of that part of the enemy who had attacked his position at that place, and at about noon on the 6th of October General Grant was enabled to send the following dispatch, which sets forth the entire rout of the rebel forces on every side:

HEAD-QUARTERS OF GENERAL GRANT,
JACKSON, TENN., 12.20 P. M., *October* 6, 1862.

To Major-General HALLECK, *General-in-Chief:*

Generals Ord and Hurlbut came upon the enemy yesterday, and General Hurlbut having driven in small bodies of the rebels the day before, after seven hours hard fighting, drove the enemy five miles back across the Hatchie towards Corinth, capturing two batteries, about 300 prisoners, and many small arms.

I immediately apprised General Rosecrans of these facts, and directed him to urge on the good work. The following dispatch has just been received from him:

CHEVALLA, *October* 6, 1862.

To Major-General GRANT:

The enemy is totally routed, throwing every thing away. We are following sharply.

W. S. ROSECRANS, *Major-General.*

Under previous instructions, General Hurlbut is also following. General McPherson is in the lead of General Rosecrans's column. The rebel General Martin is said to be killed.

U. S. GRANT, *Major-General Commanding.*

The repulse of the rebels was really disastrous to them. The accounts published in the southern newspapers plainly manifest that their loss had been heavy, and that they failed in accomplishing the object of their movement—the capture of Corinth. But the same journals endeavored to console themselves and the people with the idea that General Grant had, at least, been prevented from sending re-enforcements to the aid of General Buell, who was then about to engage the rebel forces under General Bragg.

The following is the congratulatory order of General Grant to his troops relative to this campaign:

HEAD-QUARTERS, DEPARTMENT OF WEST TENN.,
JACKSON, TENN., *October* 7, 1862.

[*General Orders, No.* 88.]

It is with heartfelt gratitude the General Commanding congratulates the armies of the West for another great victory won by them on the 3d, 4th, and 5th instants, over the combined armies of Van Dorn, Price, and Lovell.

The enemy chose his own time and place of attack, and knowing the troops of the West as he does, and with great facilities for knowing their numbers, never would have made the attempt except with a superior force numerically. *But for the undaunted bravery of officers and soldiers, who have yet to learn defeat,* the efforts of the enemy must have proven successful.

Whilst one division of the army, under Major-General Rosecrans, was resisting and repelling the onslaught of the rebel hosts at Corinth, another, from Bolivar, under Major-General Hurlbut, was marching upon the enemy's rear, driving in their pickets and cavalry, and attracting the attention of a large force of infantry and artillery. On the following day, under Major-General Ord, these forces advanced with unsurpassed gallantry, driving the enemy back across the Hatchie, over ground where it is almost incredible that a superior force should be driven by an inferior, capturing two of the batteries (eight guns), many hundred small arms, and several hundred prisoners.

To those two divisions of the army all praise is due, and will be awarded by a grateful country.

Between them there should be, and I trust are, the warmest bonds of brotherhood. Each was risking life in the same cause, and, on this occasion, risking it also to save and assist the other. No troops could do more than these separate armies. Each did all possible for it to do in the places assigned it.

As in all great battles, so in this, it becomes our fate to mourn the loss of many brave and faithful officers and soldiers, who have given up their lives as a sacrifice for a great principle. The nation mourns for them.

By command of Major-General U. S. GRANT.

JOHN A. RAWLINS, *A. A.-G.*

President Lincoln, when he had received the intelligence from General Grant announcing the victories at Corinth and on the Hatchie, dispatched to him the following congratulations and inquiries:

WASHINGTON, D. C., *October* 8, 1862.

Major-General GRANT:

I congratulate you and all concerned in your recent battles and victories. How does it all sum up? I especially regret the death of General Hackleman, and am very anxious to know the condition of General Oglesby, who is an intimate personal friend.

A. LINCOLN.

The rebel forces of General Bragg were also by this time in full retreat from the Ohio river, and were being pursued by the Army of the Ohio.

Skirmishes with guerillas occurred occasionally within General Grant's lines; but otherwise this department was, by this time, once more reduced to quietness.

On the 16th of October, 1862, General Grant's Department was designated as the Department of the Tennessee, and was further extended so as to embrace the State of Mississippi as far as Vicksburg. General Rosecrans was shortly after relieved of his command under General Grant, and made commander of the Army of the Ohio in the place of General Buell. The combined troops under General Grant were now known as the Thirteenth Army Corps.

The victories of General Grant's forces were supposed in Washington to have had a beneficial effect upon the people of Tennessee; and to enable them to resume their own government under the auspices of the United States, the following document was sent to General Grant by the hands of the person therein named:

EXECUTIVE MANSION, WASHINGTON, *October* 21, 1862.

Major-General GRANT, Governor JOHNSON, *and all having Military, Naval, and Civil Authority under the United States within the State of Tennessee:*

The bearer of this, Thomas R. Smith, a citizen of Tennessee, goes to that State, seeking to have such of the people thereof as desire to avoid the unsatisfactory prospect before them, and to have peace again upon the old terms under the Constitution of the United States, to manifest such desire by elections of members to the Congress of the United

States particularly, and perhaps a Legislature, State Officers, and a United States Senator friendly to their object. I shall be glad for you and each of you to aid him, and all others acting for this object, as much as possible. In all available ways give the people a chance to express their wishes at these elections. Follow law, and forms of law, as far as convenient; but, at all events, get the expression of the largest number of the people possible. All see how much such action will connect with and affect the proclamation of September 22d. Of course, the men elected should be gentlemen of character, willing to swear support to the Constitution as of old, and known to be above reasonable suspicion of duplicity.

Yours, very respectfully,

A. LINCOLN.

To prevent the intention of the foregoing from being carried out, General Bragg marched his forces to within striking distance of the State Capital at Nashville.

CHAPTER XIV.

THE DEPARTMENT OF THE TENNESSEE.—DISCIPLINE.—TRADE.

General Grant assumed the command of his new department on the 25th day of October, 1862, and issued the following orders:

Head-Quarters, Department of the Tennessee,
Jackson, Tenn., *October* 25, 1862.

[*General Orders, No.* 1.]

I. In compliance with General Orders, No. 159, A. G. O., War Department, of date October 16th, 1862, the undersigned hereby assumes command of the Department of the Tennessee, which includes Cairo, Fort Henry and Fort Donelson, Northern Mississippi, and the portions of Kentucky and Tennessee west of the Tennessee river.

II. Head-quarters of the Department of the Tennessee will remain, until further orders, at Jackson, Tennessee.

III. All orders of the District of West Tennessee will continue in force in the Department.

U. S. Grant, *Major-General Commanding.*

Head-Quarters, Department of the Tennessee,
Jackson, Tenn., *October* 26, 1862.

[*General Orders, No.* 2.]

I. The geographical divisions designated in General Orders, No. 83, from Head-quarters District of West Tennessee, dated September 24th, 1862, will hereafter be known as districts. The First Division will constitute the "District of Memphis," Major-General W. T. Sherman commanding; the Second Division, the "District of Jackson," commanded by Major-General S. A. Hurlbut; the Third Division, the "District of Corinth," Brigadier-General C. S. Hamilton commanding; the Fourth Division, the "District of Columbus," commanded by Brigadier-General T. A. Davies.

II. The army heretofore known as the "Army of the Mississippi," being now divided and in different departments, will be continued as a separate army.

III. Until army corps are formed, there will be no distinction, known, except those of departments, districts, divisions, posts, brigades, regiments and companies.

By command of Major-General U. S. GRANT.

JOHN A. RAWLINS, *A. A.-G.*

As General Grant was now to have heavy work before him, it became necessary that he should also have his forces thoroughly well organized, and in this matter he determined to exercise his personal supervision. He began by rooting out, as far as possible, all guerilla bodies in his department, and in the affair at Clarkson his forces were very successful.

The following order shows that it was the intention during the approaching campaign to move light, and be spoke great activity with the command:

HEAD-QUARTERS, DEPARTMENT OF THE TENNESSEE,
JACKSON, TENN., *November* 1, 1862.

[*General Orders, No.* 3.]

I.—General Orders, No. 160, from the Adjutant-General's office, having been received at head-quarters, is published for the information of all concerned:

[*General Orders, No.* 160.]

The following regulations are established for army trains and baggage:

1. There will be allowed—

For head-quarters train of an army corps, four wagons; of a division or brigade, three; of a full infantry regiment, six; and of a light artillery battery or squadron of cavalry, three.

In no case will this allowance be exceeded, but always proportionably reduced, according to the officers and men actually present. All surplus wagons will be turned over to the Chief Quartermaster, to be organized under direction of the commanding Generals, into supply trains, or sent to the nearest depot.

The requisite supply trains, their size depending upon the state of the roads and character of the campaign, will be organized by the Chief

Quartermaster, with the approval of the commanding generals, subject to the control of the War Department.

2. The wagons allowed to a regiment, battery, or squadron, must carry nothing but forage for the teams, cooking utensils, and rations for the troops, hospital stores, and officers' baggage. One wagon to each regiment will transport exclusively hospital supplies, under direction of the regimental surgeon; the one for regimental head-quarters will carry the grain for the officers' horses, and the three allowed for each battery or squadron will be at least half loaded with the grain for their own teams.

Stores in bulk and ammunition will be carried in the regular or special supply trains.

3. In active campaign, troops must be prepared to bivouac on the march, the allowance of tents being limited, as follows:

For the head-quarters of an army corps, division, or brigade, one wall tent to the commanding General, and one to every two officers of his staff.

For the Colonel, Field and Staff of a full regiment, three wall tents; and for every other commissioned officer, one shelter tent each.

For every two non-commissioned officers, soldiers, officers' servants, and authorized camp followers, one shelter tent.

One hospital tent will be allowed for office purposes, at corps head-quarters, and one wall tent at those of a division or brigade. All tents beyond this allowance will be left in depot.

4. Officers' baggage will be limited to blankets, one small valise or carpet bag and a moderate mess-kit. The men will carry their own blankets and shelter tents, and reduce the contents of their knapsacks as much as possible.

The Depot Quartermaster will provide storage for a reasonable amount of officers' surplus baggage and the extra clothing and knapsacks of the men.

5. Hospital tents are for the sick and wounded, and except those allowed for army corps head-quarters, must not be diverted from their proper use.

6. Commanding officers will be held responsible for the strict enforcement of these regulations, especially the reduction of officers' baggage within their respective commands.

7. On all marches, Quartermasters, under the orders of their commanding officers, will accompany and conduct their trains in a way not to obstruct the movement of troops.

8. All Quartermasters and Commissaries will personally attend to the reception and issue of supplies for their commands, and will keep themselves informed of the condition of the depot, roads, and other communications.

9. All Quartermasters and Commissaries will report, by letter, on the first of every month, to the chiefs of their respective departments, at Washington, D. C., their station, and generally the duty on which they have been engaged during the preceding month.

By command of Major-General HALLECK.
(Signed) L. THOMAS, *Adjutant General.*

II. District Commanders will immediately cause an inspection of their command, with the view to a strict compliance of the above order, and see that all tents and transportation in excess of allowance are turned over to the Quartermaster; that all extra clothing and knapsacks of enlisted men are delivered for storage as provided; that the baggage of officers does not exceed the limitation prescribed; and that all hospital tents not in use for the sick and wounded are turned over to the Quartermaster at once.

III. Where there is a deficiency of clothing or tents, as allowed by regulations and said order, proper requisitions will be made on the Chief Quartermaster of the Department, Captain C. A. Reynolds, for same.

IV. The requirements of this order must be complied with without delay, and report of such compliance promptly made to these head-quarters.

By command of Major-General U. S. GRANT.
JOHN A. RAWLINS, *A. A.-G.*

About the latter end of October, 1862, a body of cavalry belonging to the army of General Grant, and under the command of Colonel [since Brigadier General] A. L. Lee, started on a reconnoissance below Ripley, Mississippi, which place was captured and held for twenty-four hours, as was also the town of Orizaba. Colonel Lee returned to Grand Junction on November 2d, with several prisoners.

On the evening of the 4th of November, General Grant removed his head-quarters to La Grange, west of Grand

Junction, occupying that place with a heavy body of troops, thereby out-generalling the rebels, who were concentrating their forces in the vicinity of Ripley, a long distance farther east.

Colonel Lee again made a successful reconnoissance with about fifteen hundred cavalry to Hudsonville, Mississippi. This was but the beginning of a grand reconnoissance, as follows:

On November 8th, General Grant ordered a strong force, consisting of two divisions of Infantry and Artillery and part of a cavalry division, upon a special reconnoissance. The cavalry was under the command of Colonel Lee, and the infantry under General McPherson. This force started from La Grange, the cavalry taking the lead. At Lamar, the infantry halted, while the cavalry pushed toward Hudsonville. On the road Colonel Lee encountered a body of rebel cavalry, which he engaged on the flank with one half of his force, while the other half proceeded to Hudsonville. After routing the cavalry, killing sixteen and capturing one hundred and thirty-four, with their horses and arms, Colonel Lee joined the remainder of his command at Hudsonville, and then returned to La Grange.

The following is General Grant's brief but complimentary dispatch to the General-in-Chief in relation to this movement:

LA GRANGE, *Nov.* 11, 1862, 10:30 P. M.

Major-General HALLECK, *General-in-Chief:*

One hundred and thirty-four prisoners were taken by Colonel Lee, of the Seventh Kansas Cavalry, and sixteen rebels killed. Our loss is two wounded. Colonel Lee is one of our best cavalry officers. I earnestly recommend him for promotion.

(Signed) U. S. GRANT.

The information gained by this reconnoissance was as follows:

General Lovell, who had been in command of the rebel forces north of Holly Springs, Mississippi, had fallen back through that place on November 2d; but while retreating, was met on November 5th by General Pemberton, who had come up from the State Capital—Jackson. General Lovell was ordered back to his old post, which he held, with two divisions, on the 8th of November. Price, with twelve thousand men, was seven miles below Holly Springs, on the Salem road; and twenty-two miles further south, at Abbeville, was a rebel conscript camp of about thirteen thousand men.

Some complaints having been made by the farmers in the vicinity, of the conduct of the rebel forces, while passing through their country, General Grant issued the following order, to prevent his troops from falling into the like disgraceful system of plunder:

HEAD-QUARTERS, DEPARTMENT OF THE TENNESSEE,
LAGRANGE, TENN., *November* 9, 1862.

[*Special Field Orders, No.* 2.]

Hereinafter stoppage will be made on muster and pay rolls *against divisions* for the full amount of depredations committed by any member or members of the division, *unless the act can be traced* either to the individuals committing them, or to the company, regiment, or brigade to which the offenders belong.

In all cases the punishment will be assessed to the smallest organization containing the guilty parties.

Confiscation acts were never intended to be executed by soldiers; and if they were, the general government should have full benefit of all property of which individuals are deprived. A stoppage of pay against offenders will effect this end, and it is to be hoped will correct this growing evil.

It is not only the duty of commissioned officers to correct this evil, but of all good men in the ranks to report every violation; and it is determined now that they shall have a pecuniary interest in doing so.

Assessments will also be made against commissioned officers, in the proportion of their pay proper.

Where offences of the nature contemplated in this order are traced to individuals, they will be summarily punished to the full extent formerly given to garrison court-martials, or be arrested and tried by a general court-martial, according to the enormity of the offence, and the severest penalties provided imposed and executed.

This order will be read on parade, before each regiment and detachment, for three successive evenings.

By order of Major-General U. S. GRANT.

By this means it was hoped that the evil would be remedied, or at least greatly ameliorated, and it was also by this strict discipline that General Grant was enabled to gather around him one of the finest working armies in the United States.

The change in the Department naturally led to a remodelling of the commander's staff, the officers of which were announced as follows:

HEAD-QUARTERS, THIRTEENTH ARMY CORPS,
DEPARTMENT OF THE TENNESSEE,
LAGRANGE, TENN., *November* 11, 1862.

[*General Orders, No.* 6.]

I. The following officers are announced as the staff and staff corps of this department, and will be recognized and obeyed accordingly;—

Brigadier-General J. D. Webster, Superintendent Military Railroads.

Lieutenant-Colonel John A. Rawlins, Assistant Adjutant-General and Chief of Staff.

Colonel T. Lyle Dickey, Chief of Cavalry.

Colonel William S. Hillyer, Aide-de-Camp and Provost-Marshal General

Colonel Clark B. Lagow, Aide-de-Camp and Acting Inspector-General.

Colonel George P. Ihrie, Aide-de-Camp and Acting Inspector-General.

Colonel John Riggin, Jr., Aide-de-Camp and Superintendent of Military Telegraphs.

Colonel George G. Pride, Chief Engineer of Military Railroads.

Lieutenant-Colonel W. L. Duff, Chief of Artillery.

Lieutenant-Colonel J. P. Hawkins, Chief of Subsistence Department

Lieutenant-Colonel C. A. Reynolds, Chief of Quartermaster's Department.

Surgeon Horace R. Wirtz, Chief of Medical Department.

Major William R. Rowley, Aide-de-Camp and Mustering Officer.

Captain T. S. Bowers, Aide-de-Camp.
Captain F. E. Prime, Chief of Engineers.
Lieutenant James H. Wilson, Chief of Topographical Engineers.
Lieutenant S. C. Lyford, Chief of Ordnance Department.

By command of Major-General U. S. GRANT.

JOHN A. RAWLINS, *A. A.-G.*

As it was found difficult to reduce the baggage and wagon trains of the army at a moment's notice, especially as the lighter material to be used in the place of the old fashioned tents had not been supplied to the troops, and as it was also necessary to make some provision for the cotton seized from the rebels, the following order was issued to remedy the evil as much as possible:

CHIEF QUARTERMASTER'S OFFICE,
LAGRANGE, TENN., *November* 13, 1862.

1. In compliance with General Orders, No. 160, from the War Department, and of General Orders, No. 3, from Head-Quarters, Department of the Tennessee, all officers of the Quartermaster's Department are required to reduce their means of transportation as much as possible until shelter tents are provided, when the transportation will be reduced in compliance with the above orders.

2. All surplus teams and wagons in charge of regimental quartermasters will be transferred to division quartermasters, who are hereby required to organize a supply train of from fifty to one hundred teams as the service of their division may require, and any teams in excess of the demands for division supply trains will be turned over to such officer as may be designated to take charge of the general supply train.

3. All division and brigade quartermasters are required to report immediately by letter their address and the division or brigade to which they belong, and the name of its commander to the Chief Quartermaster of the department; if an acting assistant quartermaster, they will report in addition the regiment to which they are attached.

4. Brigade quartermasters will not be required to have supply trains, as the division quartermaster will issue direct to regiments. Division, brigade, and regimental quartermasters are required to remain in camp with their respective commands. The only quartermasters allowed to take quarters or offices in towns which the army may occupy are the depot and post quartermasters; and no quarters will be occupied by any

officer whatsoever, unless duly assigned thereto by the post quarter master, under the direction of the Chief Quartermaster.

5. All cotton coming into the hands of quartermasters, seized south of Jackson, Tenn., will be sent to that point, and invoiced to Captain G. L. Fort, A. Q. M., or the post quartermaster, giving the name and residence of the parties from whom it was taken. And all cotton seized north of that place will be shipped to Captain Thomas O'Brien, A. Q. M., or the post quartermaster, at Columbus, Ky. The quartermasters above mentioned will hold such cotton until ordered to sell the same at public auction by the General Commanding or the Chief Quartermaster of the department.

6. All regimental and other quartermasters are required to show that they have sent the monthly papers and returns prescribed by regulations and existing orders to the Quartermaster-General and the proper Auditor of the Treasury at Washington, before they can receive funds for the payment of extra duty men. Extra duty rolls should have attached to the certificate, "and that I have forwarded a copy of the above roll to the Quartermaster-General at Washington." Estimates for funds should be approved by the Division General.

By command of Major-General U. S. GRANT.

CHARLES A. REYNOLDS, *Chief Quartermaster.*

The negro refugees at this time became a source of much anxiety, as well as an incubus on the army. Several of these men had played the parts of spies at the instigation of their rebel masters, by entering the Union lines under the pretence of being escaped slaves, and, after gaining what information they could, had made their way back to the rebel lines with the intelligence. To remedy this evil a special camp was organized for their accommodation and protection, and was placed under the charge of a responsible person. The following order located the camp and appointed the commander thereof:

HEAD-QUARTERS, 13TH ARMY CORPS,
DEPARTMENT OF THE TENNESSEE,
LAGRANGE, TENN., NOV. 14.

[*Special Field Orders, No.* 4.]

1. Chaplain J. Eaton, Jr., of the 27th Regiment Ohio Infantry Vol-

unteers, is hereby appointed to take charge of all fugitive slaves that are now, or may from time to time come within the military lines of the advancing army in this vicinity, not employed and registered in accordance with General Orders, No. 72, from Head-quarters District of West Tennessee, and will open a camp for them at Grand Junction, where they will be suitably cared for and organized into companies and set to work, picking, ginning, and baling all cotton now outstanding in fields.

2. Commanding officers of troops will send all fugitives that come within the lines, together with such teams, cooking utensils and other baggage as they may bring with them, to Chaplain J. Eaton, Jr., at Grand Junction.

3. One regiment of infantry from Brigadier-General McArthur's division will be temporarily detailed as guard in charge of such contrabands, and the Surgeons of said regiment will be charged with the care of the sick.

4. Commissaries of subsistence will issue on the requisitions of Chaplain J. Eaton, Jr., omitting the coffee rations, and substituting rye.

By order of Major-General U. S. GRANT.

JOHN A. RAWLINS, *A. A.-G.*

The Special Order No. 2, relative to plundering, began to have some effect in finding out who were the guilty parties engaged in such nefarious practices; and General Grant being fully determined to have his orders obeyed, not only in the spirit, but to the letter, assessed the guilty regiment for the whole amount of the injury inflicted, and punished the officers for neglect of duty.

The following order will explain his method of correcting the evil:—

HEAD-QUARTERS 13TH ARMY CORPS,
DEPARTMENT OF THE TENNESSEE,
LA GRANGE, TENN., Nov. 16, 1862.

[*Special Field Orders, No.* 6.]

The facts having been officially reported to the Major-General Commanding, that a portion of the Twentieth Regiment Illinois Infantry Volunteers did, on the night of the 7th of November inst., at Jackson, Tennessee, break into the store of G. W. Graham & Co., and take therefrom goods to the value of $841.40, the property of said Graham & Co., and did cut the tent of R. B. Kent and N. A. Bass, and take therefrom goods to the value of $345, the property of said Kent and Bass, and burn and destroy the tent and poles, also the property of said Kent and Bass, of the value of $56.26,—all of which damages amount to the sum of $1,242.66; and it further appearing from said report that Capt. C. L. Page, Co. D; Capt. J. M. North, Co. E; Capt. G. W. Kennard, Co. I; Lieutenants Harry King, Co. B; William Seas, Co. C; John Edmonston, Co. E; David Wadsworth, Co. F; J. Bailey, Co. F; Victor H. Stevens, Co. H; R. M. Evans, Co. I; Charles Taylor, Co. I, of said regiment, were absent from their commands at the time of the perpetration of these outrages, in violation of orders, and without proper cause, when they should have been present; and also that Captain Orton Frisbee, of Co. H, acting in the capacity of Major, and Captain John Tunison, of Co. G, the senior Captain, immediately after the commission of these depredations, did not exercise their authority to ferret out the men guilty of the offences, but that, on the contrary, Captain Tunison interposed to prevent search and discovery of the parties really guilty, and that Captain Frisbee, after the commission of the said depredations, being in command of the regiment, remained behind twenty-four hours after the regiment marched, and the names of the individual parties guilty not having been disclosed, it is therefore ordered—

1. That the said sum of $1,242.66 be assessed against said regiment and the officers hereinbefore named, excepting such enlisted men as were at the time sick in the hospital or absent with proper authority; that the same be charged against them on the proper muster and pay rolls, and the amount each is to pay noted opposite his name thereon,—the officers to be assessed *pro rata* with the men on the amount of their pay proper; and that the sum so collected be paid by the commanding officer of the regiment to the parties entitled to the same.

2. That Captain Orton Frisbee and Captain John Tunison of the Twentieth Regiment Illinois Infantry Volunteers, for wilful neglect of duty and violation of orders, are hereby mustered out of the service of the United States, to take effect this day.

By order of Major-General U. S. GRANT.

JOHN A. RAWLINS, *A. A.-G.*

The subject of trade in the insurrectionary States after they had again come within the Union lines, became a matter of much importance, and the Treasury Department had laid down certain rules for the guidance of those engaged in such traffic. These rules were, however, very deficient in many cases; and it also required certain stringent military regulations to be enforced to prevent the trade becoming a source of aid and comfort to the enemy. The following order was therefore issued, defining such trade within the lines of the Department of the Tennessee:

HEADQUARTERS 13TH ARMY CORPS,
DEPARTMENT OF THE TENNESSEE,
LAGRANGE, TENN., *November* 19, 1862.

[*General Orders, No.* 8.]

I. In addition to permits from the Treasury Department, all persons are required to have a permit from the local Provost-Marshal at the post before purchasing cotton or other Southern products in this Department, and shipping the same North.

II. *It will be regarded as evidence of disloyalty for persons to go beyond the lines of the army to purchase cotton or other products; and all contracts made for such articles in advance of the army, or for cotton in the field, are null and void, and all persons so offending will be expelled from the department.*

III. Freight agents on military railroads will report daily to the Post Provost-Marshal all cotton or other private property shipped by them; and when shipments are made by persons who have not the proper permits, notice will be given by telegraph, to the Provost-Marshal at Columbus, Ky., who will seize the goods for the benefit of the Government.

IV. The Federal army being now in the occupancy of West Tennessee to the Mississippi line, and it being no part of the policy of the Government to oppress, *or cause unnecessary suffering to those who are not in active rebellion*, hereafter, until otherwise directed, licenses will be granted by District Commanders to loyal persons, at all military stations within the department, to keep for sale, subject to the Treasury regulations, such articles as are of prime necessity for families, and sell the same to all citizens who have taken, or may voluntarily take the oath of allegiance, and who have permits from the Provost-Marshal, obtained under oath, that all goods to be purchased are for their own and for their family's use, and that no part thereof is for sale or for the use of any person other than those named in the permit. Permits so given will be good until countermanded; and all violations of trading permits will be punished by the forfeiture of the permit, fine and imprisonment, at the discretion of a military commission.

V. Particular attention is called to existing orders prohibiting the employment or use of Government teams for hauling private property. All cotton brought to stations or places for shipment in this department by Government teams will be seized by the Quartermaster's Department for the benefit of the Government, and persons claiming such property expelled from the Department. It is made the duty of all officers, and especially of local Provost-Marshals, to see that this order is rigidly enforced.

By command of Major-General U. S. GRANT.
JOHN A. RAWLINGS, *A. A.-G.*

But, despite the above orders, the Jewish camp followers were found to be continually engaged in an illegal traffic; whereupon General Grant expelled them all from his department. The following is his order of expulsion:

HEAD-QUARTERS, DEPARTMENT OF THE TENNESSEE,
OXFORD, MISS., *Dec.* 17, 1862.

[*General Orders, No.* 11.]

The Jews, as a class, violating every regulation of trade established by the Treasury Department, also department orders, are hereby expelled from the department within twenty-four hours from the receipt of this order by post commanders. They will see that all this class of people are furnished with passes and required to leave; and any one returning after such notification will be arrested and held in confinement until an opportunity occurs of sending them out as prisoners, unless furnished with permits from these head-quarters. No passes will be given these people to visit head-quarters for the purpose of making personal application for trade permits.*

By order of Major-General GRANT.

An anecdote is told of General Grant, relative to his refusal to engage in or authorize any movements for the reopening of trade with the rebellious States. On one occasion, especially, after his protests and orders suppressing such traffic, he was eagerly entreated by the agents of the Treasury Department to authorize some system of trade.

* This order was afterwards moderated and the Jews allowed to trade under certain regulations.

For a long time he refused, for the reason that he could not successfully conduct his military operations while such persons were moving around him; but at last he conceded, that a certain amount of trade in the recaptured districts of the South would be safe, proper, and even highly useful to the Union—provided it could be conducted through honest, unimpeachable Union hands. He was asked to name the persons to whom he would be willing to trust.

"I will do no such thing," was Grant's reply; "for if I did, it would appear in less than a week that I was a partner of every one of the persons trading under my authority."

CHAPTER XV.

ADVANCE INTO MISSISSIPPI.—A RETROSPECT.

The object of the advance of General Grant's army into the State of Mississippi was to reduce Vicksburg, and open the Mississippi River from its source to the Gulf. The river had been blockaded at different times, by the fortification of certain points, which had all been subdued by the gunboats, with the exception of Vicksburg; but in consequence of the natural, as well as artificial strength of that position, it could not be taken from the water-front. It became, therefore, necessary that the land forces should co-operate in the movement for the conquest of the rebels at this point.

It will be needful, for a clear understanding of the position of affairs when General Grant first undertook this responsible duty, to go back to the time when the great river of the West was first blockaded at Vicksburg by the rebels, and show how every previous effort had failed to reduce the stronghold which had been styled by the enemy, the "Gibraltar of the Mississippi."

On the 12th day of January, 1861, the Governor of the State of Mississippi first sent artillery to fortify Vicksburg, then supposed to be the strongest defensive position on the river, commanding as it did, from an important elevation, the channel for some miles, both above and below the city.

When it was found that the gunboat fleet had, with the

assistance of the army, reduced the strong position at Island No. 10, and had pushed down past the works constructed to blockade the river above Memphis, the rebels at once, under skilful engineers, began strengthening the fortifications at Vicksburg, until they were considered incapable of being stronger, and sufficient to resist the advance of any enemy either by land or from the water. Vicksburg, in fact, became a series of forts, inclosed and connected, as it were, within a larger fortress.

The operations of the army and the naval forces in the West up to May, 1862, had principally been for two grand objects—the reopening of the Mississippi River to the Gulf, and the suppression of the rebels in arms. The movements were therefore general in their character up to this date, and had not been directed to any one particular point, until the advance upon Corinth, under General Halleck.

About June, 1862, the reduction of Vicksburg and its neighboring batteries became a subject of more direct importance, and a special object to be accomplished; and on the 1st of that month, Commodore Farragut's fleet, which had taken New Orleans, and the other points of the Lower Mississippi, arrived off Grand Gulf, where it attacked a rebel battery of rifled guns. After a brief engagement the fleet passed up the river, without reducing the battery. It was the approach of this fleet from below and of the gunboat fleet from above, that warned General Beauregard that his army was in great danger, if he should remain too long at Corinth.

As before stated, Memphis was reduced on June 6th, and the next day, Farragut's fleet arrived off Vicksburg. On June 8th, a portion of the fleet returned to Grand Gulf, and for the time, silenced the rebel battery at that point. The gunboat fleet having cleared the river to Vicksburg from above, after reaching that place returned north, to operate on the rivers of Arkansas.

The movements of the Union army under General Grant, after the evacuation of Corinth, and the arrival of Farragut's fleet before Vicksburg, had such an effect upon the rebel inhabitants of the State of Mississippi, that they, on June 16th, 1862, removed their state archives from their capital—Jackson—to a more remote position. On the 27th of June, 1862, the fleet began bombarding Vicksburg, and with the aid of Porter's mortar fleet, kept shelling the rebel position at intervals, until the end of July, when the river was found to be so low, that the fleet had to retire to New Orleans, to prevent the larger vessels from becoming aground.

About twelve miles north of Vicksburg is the mouth of the Yazoo River, the waters of which stream are deep enough to float an ordinary river vessel, at almost any season of the year. Up this river, the rebels had established an improvised navy-yard; had there constructed a powerful iron-clad ram, which they had named the "Arkansas;" and, to prevent an enemy from passing up the Yazoo River to destroy this ship-building, the rebels had fortified Haines's Bluff, a strong elevation, a short distance above the point where the Yazoo falls into the Mississippi River. On July 15th, 1862, this ram came down the Yazoo, ran by the fleet, and laid up before the city of Vicksburg, adding thereby a floating battery to the works of that place. The gunboat "Essex" and the ram "Queen of the West," however, subsequently inflicted such injuries on this rebel vessel, that in a short time she was completely destroyed.

At this time, Vicksburg and its vicinity formed a portion of the Union Department of the Gulf, therefore, all military operations had to be made by troops having their base at New Orleans. While the United States vessels were engaged as just described, the troops, which consisted of one small division of infantry, under General Williams, were far from being idle.

An idea had been conceived that it was possible to isolate the city of Vicksburg, which was located on a bend of the Mississippi River, by turning the course of that stream, and thus force the city inland, some six miles.* As the only strategical value of Vicksburg to the rebels was its power in blockading the river, if the channel could be thus changed into another direction, the rebel works would be useless, and could be reduced without much bloodshed, even if they were not voluntarily abandoned. To effect this change in the channel of the river, it was deemed necessary to cut a canal across the neck of land between De Soto and Richmond, La., and nearly opposite Vicksburg. The troops were therefore employed on this work, while the fleet bombarded the city. If the channel had been thus changed, the piece of land cut off in this method would have been taken out of the State of Louisiana, and added to the State of Mississippi.

On the 22d of July, 1862, this canal was declared completed; but the waters of the river were too low to flow through it, at least it was then so supposed; but, afterwards, it was ascertained that the canal was located in the wrong spot, to cause any variation in the channel.

The waters of the river continuing to subside rapidly, it was deemed advisable to raise the siege; and the rebels took this opportunity to fill up the canal cut by the Union troops, and then to add their Vicksburg garrison to the force engaged against Corinth, during the early part of October. They, also, further fortified the hills around

* On many previous occasions, the course of the Mississippi River had been changed in one night, by merely running a plough across a neck of land, and thus making a previous peninsula into an island.

Vicksburg, on both the land and water sides, so as to render it, if possible, perfectly impregnable.

Such was the position of affairs, when General Grant commenced his advance into the State of Mississippi; and to prevent the naval vessels from N w Orleans from again ascending the river, to co-operate with him, the rebel forces, on November 25th, 1862, fortified Port Hudson, on the southwest corner of East Feliciana County, La., and a short distance above Baton Rouge.

CHAPTER XVI.

FIRST MOVEMENTS TOWARDS VICKSBURG.

General John A. Logan, one of the officers who had served under General Grant, from the first day he assumed command at Cairo, asserted, in the halls of the National Congress, that, if the Mississippi River could not otherwise be opened, "the men of the Northwest would hew their way to the Gulf," if the opportunity was only allowed them. The Government, finding this to be the temper of those hardy Western men, determined to foster that feeling, by not only enlarging General Grant's Department, but also by increasing his forces.

On the 28th of November, a force of infantry and cavalry, under Generals A. P. Hovey and Washburne, arrived at Delta, on the Mississippi River, near the mouth of the Yazoo Pass. They had started the previous day from Helena, on the Arkansas shore, at which point the Union troops about to join General Grant were being concentrated. General Washburne's cavalry made a reconnoissance to the mouth of the Coldwater River, where he captured a rebel camp, a number of horses, arms, and equipments, and routed the enemy. The reconnoissance was pushed along both the Coldwater and Tallahatchie Rivers, thence to Preston, after which an expedition was sent to Garner's Station, to destroy the railroad bridge and track. This expedition was completely successful, as were several others of a similar character. The cavalry then returned *via* Charleston, and formed a junction, near Mitchell's Cross-Roads, with General Hovey's forces. The reconnoissance was next pushed up to Panola, where an abandoned rebel camp was discovered, the occupants having fled during the previous night. The cavalry again moved in a southerly direction to Oakland, and along the road towards Coffeeville. After ascertaining the exact position of the rebel forces, and being engaged in a few skirmishes, this part of the expedition returned to the mouth of the Coldwater River. General Hovey's command also cut some portions of the railroad lines. This movement created quite a panic among the rebels of the Southwest.

Meanwhile, the main forces, under General Grant, moved steadily forward along the line of railroad leading from Grand Junction to Grenada. On November 28th, the advance left Davis's Mills for Holly Springs, Colonel Lee's cavalry pushing on ahead. All along the line of march were evidences of the recent cavalry operations of the Union forces. At ten o'clock of the morning of November 29th, the advance passed through Holly Springs, pushing on rapidly still further south, arriving near Waterford on the 30th. In this place was discovered several evidences of the illegal traffic that had been carried on through the rebel lines; one house, in St. Louis, having a branch clothing establishment for the supply of the rebels. This, and similar facts, led General Grant to issue his order, No. 11.

Cavalry reconnoissances were sent out under Colonel Lee, and discovered the enemy in force on the Tallahatchie. A skirmish took place on November 30th, near Abbeville, resulting in the retreat of the rebels to the defences at that place. On the 2d of December, Abbeville was evacuated, and occupied by the Union forces. A series of skirmishes occurred on December 3d, near Oxford, Miss., between the

Union cavalry advance and the rebels, and resulted in the retreat of the latter. The cavalry then pushed on after Van Dorn's retreating column, and, on December 4th, drove the rebels out of Water Valley, engaging them sharply near Coffeeville, on December 5th.

As the cavalry thus pushed on, they were followed by the main army under General Grant, whose generalship was plainly manifested in every movement he made. By sending General Hovey's forces, *via* Delta, toward the railroad lines, he created a panic in the very vicinity through which he was marching, thus making his advance almost a bloodless one. The gunboat fleet were also operating along the rivers, especially the Yazoo, in which torpedoes had been sunk by the rebels, to repel the advance. On December 11th, the gunboat Cairo was sunk by the explosion of one of these hidden weapons.

Skirmishes would occasionally take place at the posts left behind General Grant in his advance, but as he always took care that such places should be well guarded, these brief contests did not, at first, interfere with his movements. On December 12th, a skirmish took place at Corinth, but was handsomely repulsed by Colonel (since General) Sweeny.

General Grant's head-quarters had, by this time, been removed to Oxford, Mississippi; but, in consequence of the attack upon and disgraceful surrender of Holly Springs, on December 20th, with all its stores, etc., so necessary to the advance, General Grant's main forces had to fall back to that place, where he located his head-quarters, in order to recruit his supplies. Upon the investigation of the matter concerning this surrender, General Grant found that it was not warranted by any circumstances that attended it, and he expressed his displeasure in the following condemnatory order:—

HEAD-QUARTERS, 13TH ARMY CORPS,
DEPARTMENT OF THE TENNESSEE,
HOLLY SPRINGS, MISS., *December* 24, 1862.

[*Special Field Orders, No.* 23.] (*Extract.*)

It is with pain and mortification that the General Commanding reflects upon the disgraceful surrender of the place, with all the valuable stores it contained, on the 20th inst., and that without any resistance except by a few men, who form an honorable exception; and this, too, after warning had been giving of the enemy northward, the evening previous. With all the cotton, public stores, and substantial buildings about the dépôt, *it would have been perfectly practicable to have made, in a few hours, a defence sufficient to resist, with a small garrison, all the cavalry force brought against them* until the re-enforcements which the commanding officer was notified were marching to his relief could have reached him.

The conduct of officers and men in accepting paroles, under the circumstances, is highly reprehensible, and, to say the least, thoughtless. By the terms of the Dix-Hill cartel each party is bound to take care of their prisoners and to send them to Vicksburg, or a point on the James River, for exchange, or parole, unless some other point is mutually agreed upon by the generals commanding the opposing armies.

By a refusal to be paroled, the enemy, from his inability to take care of the prisoners, would have been compelled either to have refused them unconditionally, or to have abandoned further aggressive movements for the time being, which would have made their recapture, and the discomfiture of the enemy almost certain.

The prisoners paroled at this place will be collected in camp at once by the post commander, and held under close guard until their case can be reported to Washington for further instructions.

Commanders throughout the department are directed to arrest and hold as above all men of their commands and all stragglers who may have accepted their paroles upon like terms.

The General Commanding is satisfied that the majority of the troops who accepted a parole did so thoughtlessly and from want of knowledge of the cartel referred to, and that in future they will not be caught in the same way.

By order of Major-General U. S. GRANT.

JOHN A. RAWLINS, *A. A.-G.*

Other posts in General Grant's rear were attacked at about the same time as Holly Springs, but were bravely defended by their garrisons, and the rebel onslaughts repulsed. General Grant, therefore, caused a full investigation to be made, respecting the conduct of the troops at all the points that were assailed, and expressed his feelings concerning it, in the following order:—

HEAD-QUARTERS, DEPARTMENT OF THE TENNESSEE,
HOLLY SPRINGS, MISS., *January* 8, 1863.

[*General Orders, No.* 4.]

I. The Major-General Commanding the department takes just pride and satisfaction in congratulating *the small garrisons* of the posts of Coldwater, Davis's Mills, and Middleburg, for the heroic defence of their positions on the 20th, 21st, and 24th ultimo, *and their successful repulse of an enemy many times their number.*

The 90th Illinois, at Coldwater (its first engagement); the detachment of the veteran 25th Indiana, and two companies of the 5th Ohio Cavalry, at Davis's Mills; and the detachment of the gallant 12th Michigan at Middleburg, are deserving of the thanks of the army, which was in a measure dependent upon the road they so nobly defended for supplies, and they will receive the meed of praise ever awarded by a grateful public to those who bravely and successfully do their duty.

These regiments are entitled to inscribe upon their banners, respectively, Coldwater, Davis's Mills, and Middleburg, with the names of other battle-fields made victorious by their valor and discipline.

It is gratifying to know that at every point where our troops made a stand during the late raid of the enemy's cavalry, success followed, and the enemy was made to suffer a loss in killed and wounded greater than the entire garrisons of the places attacked. Especially was this the case of Davis's Mills and Middleburg. The only success gained by Van Dorn was at Holly Springs, where the whole garrison was left by their commander in ignorance of the approach of danger.

II. Colonel R. C. Murphy, of the 8th Regiment Wisconsin Infantry Volunteers, having, while in command of the post of Holly Springs, Mississippi, neglected and failed to exercise the usual and ordinary precautions to guard and protect the same; having, after repeated and timely warning of the approach of the enemy, failed to make any preparations for resistance or defence, or shown any disposition to do so; and having, with a force amply sufficient to have repulsed the enemy and protect the public stores intrusted to his care, disgracefully permitted him to capture the post and destroy the stores—and the movement of troops in the face of an enemy rendering it impracticable to convene a court-martial for his trial—is, therefore, *dismissed the service of the United States—to take effect from the* 20*th day of December*, 1862, *the date of his cowardly and disgraceful conduct.*

By order of Major-General U. S. GRANT.

JOHN A. RAWLINS, *A. A.-G.*

It will be seen, by the date of the above order, that it had not been issued in the heat of the moment, or without due consideration, but had been the result of a careful investigation of the merits and demerits of the case.

CHAPTER XVII.

COMMANDER OF FOUR ARMY CORPS.—SHERMAN'S EXPEDITION.

THE forces under General Grant having now been increased to such an extent as to authorize their division into Army Corps, the following order was issued, and gave directions for the arrangement of the forces by divisions into corps, and stated who were the commanders of the new organizations:

HEAD-QUARTERS, DEPARTMENT OF THE TENNESSEE,
HOLLY SPRINGS, MISS., *Dec.* 22, 1862.

[*General Orders, No.* 14.]

By directions of the General-in-Chief of the army, the troops in this department, including those of the Department of the Missouri operating on the Mississippi River, are hereby divided into four Army Corps, as follows:

1. The troops composing the 9th Division, Brigadier-General G. W. Morgan commanding; the 10th Division, Brigadier-General A. J. Smith commanding; and all other troops operating on the Mississippi River below Memphis, not included in the 15th Army Corps, will constitute the 13th Army Corps, under the command of Major-General John A. McClernand.

2. The 5th Division, Brigadier-General Morgan L. Smith commanding; the Division from Helena, Ark., commanded by Brigadier-General F. Steele; and the forces in the "District of Memphis," will constitute the 15th Army Corps, and be commanded by Major-General W. T. Sherman.

3. The 6th Division, Brigadier-General J. McArthur commanding; the 7th division, Brigadier-General I. F. Quinby commanding; the 8th Division, Brigadier General L. F. Ross commanding; the 2d Brigade of Cavalry, Colonel A. L. Lee commanding; and the troops in the "Dis-

trict of Columbus," commanded by Brigadier-General Davies, and those in the "District of Jackson," commanded by Brigadier-General Sullivan, will constitute the 16th Army Corps, and be commanded by Major-General S. A. Hurlbut.

4. The 1st Division, Brigadier-General J. W. Denver commanding; the 3d Division, Brigadier-General John A. Logan commanding; the 4th Division, Brigadier-General J. G. Lauman commanding; the 1st Brigade of Cavalry, Colonel B. H. Grierson commanding; and the forces in the "District of Corinth," commanded by Brigadier-General G. M. Dodge, will constitute the 17th Army Corps, and be commanded by Major-General J. B. McPherson.

District commanders will send consolidated returns of their forces to these head-quarters as well as to Army Corps head-quarters, and will, for the present, receive orders from Department head-quarters.

By order of Major-General U. S. GRANT.

JOHN A. RAWLINS, *A. A.-G.*

Another general order transposed the divisions of Generals McArthur and Quinby, of the 16th Army Corps, with those of Generals Lauman and Denver, of the 17th.

Two days before the issuance of the foregoing, General Sherman, who had been placed in command of an expedition down the Mississippi River to Vicksburg, and who had personally made certain reconnoissances in the vicinity of the Tallahatchie River, embarked his forces at Memphis, and they were ordered to rendezvous at Friar's Point, eighteen miles below Helena. The fleet consisted of one hundred and twenty-seven steamers, in addition to the gunboats. General Sherman's force was composed entirely of Western men, good fighters, hardy, daring, and used to a rough and adventurous life.

In order that the expedition might be composed entirely of fighting material, General Sherman issued the following, before embarking his forces:

HEAD-QUARTERS, RIGHT WING 13TH ARMY CORPS,
MEMPHIS, TENN., *Dec.* 18, 1862.

[*General Orders, No.* 8.]

1. The expedition now fitting out is purely of a military character, and the interests involved are of too important a nature to be mixed up with personal and private business. *No citizen, male or female, will be allowed to accompany it,* unless employed as part of a crew or as servants to the transports. Female chambermaids to the boats and nurses to the sick alone will be allowed, unless the wives of captains and pilots actually belonging to the boats. No laundress, officer's, or soldier's wife must pass below Helena.

2. No person whatever, citizen, officer, or sutler, will, on any consideration, buy or deal in cotton or other produce of the country. Should any cotton be brought on board of any transport going or returning, the brigade quartermaster, of which the boat forms a part, will take possession of it, and invoice it to Captain A. R. Eddy, Chief Quartermaster at Memphis.

3. Should any cotton or other produce, be brought back to Memphis by any chartered boat, Captain Eddy will take possession of the same, and sell it for the benefit of the United States. If accompanied by its actual producer, the planter or factor, the quartermaster will furnish him with a receipt for the same to be settled for, on proof of his loyalty at the close of the war.

4. Boats ascending the river may take cotton from the shore for bulkheads to protect their engines or crew, but on arrival at Memphis it will be turned over to the quartermaster with a statement of the time, place, and name of its owner. The trade in cotton must await a more peaceful state of affairs.

5. *Should any citizen accompany the expedition below Helena, in violation of these orders, any colonel of a regiment or captain of a battery will conscript him into the service of the United States for the unexpired term of his command. If he show a refractory spirit unfitting him for a soldier, the commanding officer present will turn him over to the captain of the boat as a deck hand, and compel him to work in that capacity without wages until the boat returns to Memphis.*

6. Any person whatever, whether in the service of the United States or transports, found making reports for publication, which might reach the enemy, giving them information, aid, and comfort, will be arrested and treated as spies. By order of Major-General SHERMAN.

J. H. HAMMOND, *Major and A. A.-G.*

The above order certainly gave speculators due warning of what they might expect, if they attempted to conceal themselves among the soldiers and were found out.

General Sherman, when he left Memphis, located his head-quarters on the "Forest Queen," and with his staff arrived at Friar's Point on December 21st. It will thus be seen that General Sherman was entirely unaware of the necessity which existed in General Grant retracing his steps from Oxford to Holly Springs; and as the plan had been for the latter to move upon Jackson by the railroad, thence to Vicksburg, while the former attacked the works, a proper combination was certainly needed to secure success.

Nor was it possible for General Grant to inform General Sherman of his retrograde movement; and it was only to be hoped that, having the moral support of supposing General Grant was successful, he would himself succeed.

As it was, the troops that had retreated before General Grant's advance, finding that they were released from the necessity of further resisting him—as it would have been a fatal madness for him to have pushed on to Jackson without supplies—were immediately transported to Vicksburg to resist the onslaught of General Sherman, of whose expedition the rebels had been duly apprised by their sympathizers in Memphis.

General Sherman, therefore, proceeded with his part of the expedition, and landed a small force under General Morgan L. Smith, at Milliken's Bend. These troops proceeded to Delhi and Dallas, on the Vicksburg and Texas Railroad, and destroyed the dépôts and a section of the track, so as to cut off the retreat of the rebels from Vicksburg.

It will be seen that General Grant's plan was a splendid one; and but for the surrender of Holly Springs, must have proved successful.

On the 27th of December, 1862, the main forces under General Sherman, having successfully disembarked at Johnston's Landing, near the mouth of the Yazoo River, the command next prepared for an assault upon the northern works that defended the city of Vicksburg.

CHAPTER XVIII.

SHERMAN'S ATTACK UPON VICKSBURG.—ARKANSAS POST.*

The forces under General Sherman consisted of four divisions, and were known as the "Right Wing of the Army of the Tennessee."

At about noon of December 26th, 1862, the fleet of transports arrived off Johnston's Landing, and under cover of the gunboats, the men were disembarked; the armed vessels having first silenced the battery which the rebels had planted. By early morning the whole force, infantry and artillery were landed—the advance having already moved some distance inland.

Vicksburg, from this point of landing, was peculiarly situated, being on a hill, with a line of hills surrounding it at a distance of several miles, and extending from Haines' Bluff, on the Yazoo River, to Warrenton, ten miles below the city, on the Mississippi River. The low country in the vicinity is swampy, filled with sloughs, bayous, and lagoons. To approach Vicksburg with a large force by this route, even in times of peace, would be a matter of great difficulty, and with an enemy in front, it was almost an impossibility.

* These two actions were not under the immediate supervision of General Grant; but as they occurred within his department, and were fought by his troops, they consequently form a portion of his military history. Under such circumstances, it is not necessary to fully describe each battle in detail, but briefly allude to them, so as to connect the links in the historic chain.

On Saturday morning, December 27th, 1862, the army was drawn up in line of battle, prepared to make the assault on the enemy's works. The general advance was then commenced from different points, and by dusk the enemy was driven at least a quarter of a mile from his former position.*

On the 28th, the men fought with great bravery and determination; but the non-arrival of the left wing had completely disarranged the plan of battle. The enemy had also by this time, been considerably re-enforced by the troops that had fled from before General Grant's advance; and the missiles from this concentrated body were thrown with great rapidity upon General Sherman's lines. The rebels, however, refused to come from behind their defences, which, on the morning of the 29th, extended for at least two miles up the bluffs—the newly arrived troops having been at once set to work, during the previous night, throwing up earthwork batteries in all directions, and at every assailable point. The position was naturally strong, but by the addition of art, it was made completely impregnable against so small a force as that commanded by General Sherman. The woods were also filled with sharpshooters, who picked off the officers with great rapidity.

During Monday, the 29th, several brilliant charges were made by the troops on the rebel works; but all was in vain, as the men were, on all occasions outnumbered by the enemy, and consequently could not hold the positions, even after they were taken. General Blair's brigade, headed

* General Sherman had so far successfully carried out his part of the programme; and it was by this time expected that General Grant would have been able to co-operate with him. The surrender of Holly Springs, as before described, had, however, prevented the latter from following out his portion of the plan; and thus, by the delinquency of one subordinate, the whole campaign was ruined.

by himself on foot, particularly distinguished itself, and suffered the greatest loss. As the men fell back upon their supports, the last man to leave the hill, was the brigade commander.

The following description of the charge is given by one who witnessed the whole action:

General Morgan, at eleven o'clock A. M., sent word to General Steele that he was about ready for the movement upon the hill, and wished the latter to support him with General Thayer's Brigade. General Steele accordingly ordered General Thayer to move his brigade forward, and be ready for the assault. The order was promptly complied with, and General Blair received from General Morgan the order to assault the hill. The artillery had been silent for some time; but Hoffman's Battery opened when the movement commenced. This was promptly replied to by the enemy, and taken up byGriffith's First Iowa Battery, and a vigorous shelling was the result. By the time General Blair's Brigade emerged from its cover of cypress forest, the shell were dropping fast among the men. A field battery had been in position in front of Hoffman's Battery; but it limbered up and moved away beyond the heavy batteries and the rifle-pits.

In front of the timber where Blair's Brigade had been lying was an abatis of young trees, cut off about three feet above the ground, and with the tops fallen promiscuously around. It took some minutes to pass this abatis, and by the time it was accomplished the enemy's fire had not been without effect. Beyond this abatis was a ditch fifteen or twenty feet deep, and with two or three feet of water in the bottom. The bottom of the ditch was a quicksand, in which the feet of the men commenced sinking, the instant they touched it. By the time this ditch was passed the line was thrown into considerable confusion, and it took several minutes to put it in order. All the horses of the officers were mired in this ditch. Every one dismounted and moved up the hill on foot.

Beyond this ditch was an abatis of heavy timber that had been felled several months before, and, from being completely seasoned, was more difficult of passage than that constructed of the greener and more flexible trees encountered at first. These obstacles were overcome under a tremendous fire from the enemy's batteries and the men in the rifle-pits. The line was recovered from the disorder into which it had been thrown by the passage of the abatis; and, with General Blair at their head, the regiments moved forward "upon the enemy's works." The first movement was over a sloping plateau, raked by direct and enfilading fires from heavy artillery, and swept by a perfect storm of bullets from the rifle-pits. Nothing daunted by the dozens of men that had already fallen, the brigade pressed on, and in a few moments had driven the enemy from the first range of rifle-pits at the base of the hill, and were in full possession.

Halting but a moment to take breath, the brigade renewed the charge, and speedily occupied the second line of rifle-pits, about two hundred yards distant from the first. General Blair was the first man of his brigade to enter. All this time the murderous fire from the enemy's guns continued. The batteries were still above this line of rifle-pits. The regiments were not strong enough to attempt their capture without a prompt and powerful support. For them it had truly been a march

> Into the jaws of death—
> Into the mouth of hell.

Almost simultaneously with the movement of General Blair on the left, Gen. Thayer received his command to go forward. He had previously given orders to all his regiments in column to follow each other whenever the first moved forward. He accordingly placed himself at the head of his advance regiment, the Fourth Iowa, and his order—"Forward, Second Brigade!"—rang out clear above the tumult. Colonel Williamson, commanding the Fourth Iowa, moved it off in splendid style. General Thayer supposed that all the other regiments of his brigade were following, in accordance with his instructions previously issued. He wound through the timber skirting the bayou, crossed at the same bridge where General Blair had passed but a few minutes before, made his way through the ditch and both lines of abatis, deflected the right and ascended the sloping plateau in the direction of the rifle-pits simultaneously with General Blair, and about two hundred yards to his right.

When General Thayer reached the rifle-pits, after hard fighting and a heavy loss, he found, to his horror, that only the Fourth Iowa had followed him, the wooded nature of the place having prevented his ascertaining it before. Sadly disheartened, with little hope of success, he still pressed forward and fought his way to the second line, at the same time that General Blair reached it on the left. Colonel Williamson's regiment was fast falling before the concentrated fire of the rebels, and with an anxious heart General Thayer looked around for aid.

The rebels were forming three full regiments of infantry to move down upon General Thayer, and were massing a proportionately formidable force against General Blair. The rebel infantry and artillery were constantly in full play, and two heavy guns were raking the rifle-pits in several places. With no hope of succor, General Thayer gave the order for a return down the hill and back to his original position. The Fourth Iowa, entering the fight five hundred strong, had lost a hundred and twenty men in less than thirty minutes. It fell back at a quick march, but with its ranks unbroken and without any thing of panic.

It appears that just at the time General Thayer's Brigade started up the hill, General Morgan sent for a portion of it to support him on the right. General Steele at once diverted the Second Regiment of Thayer's Brigade, which was passing at the time. The Second Regiment being thus diverted, the others followed, in accordance with the orders they had previously received from their commander. Notice of the movement was sent to General Thayer; but, in consequence of the death of the courier, the notification never reached him. This accounts for his being left with nothing save the Fourth Iowa Regiment. The occurrence was a sad one. The troops thus turned off were among the best that had yet been in action, and had they been permitted to charge the enemy they would have won for themselves a brilliant record.

When General Blair entered the second line of rifle-pits, his brigade continued to pursue the enemy up the hill. The Thirteenth Illinois Infantry was in advance, and fought with desperation to win its way to the top of the crest. Fifty yards or more above the second line of rifle-pits is a small clump of willows, hardly deserving the name of trees. They stand in a corn-field, and from the banks of the bayou below presented the appearance of a green hillock. To this copse many of the rebels fled when they were driven from the rifle-pits, and they were promptly pursued by General Blair's men. The Thirteenth met and engaged the rebels hand to hand, and in the encounter bayonets were repeatedly crossed. It gained the place, driving out the enemy; but as soon as our men occupied it the fire of a field-battery was turned upon them and the place became too hot to be held.

The road from Mrs. Lake's plantation to the top of the high ground and thence to Vicksburg, runs at an angle along the side of the hill, so as to obtain a slope easy of ascent. The lower side of this road was provided with a breastwork, so that a light battery could be taken anywhere along the road and fired over the embankment. From the nearest point of this embankment a battery opened on the Thirteenth Illinois, and was aided by a heavy battery on the hill. Several men were killed by the shell and grape that swept the copse.

The other regiments of the brigade came to the support of the Thirteenth, the Twenty-ninth Missouri, Colonel Cavender, being in the advance. Meantime the rebels formed a large force of infantry to bring against them, and when the Twenty-ninth reached the copse the rebels were already engaging the Union troops. The color-bearer of the Twelfth had been shot down, and some one picked up the standard and planted it in front of the copse. The force of the rebels was too great for our men to stand against them, and they slowly fell back, fighting step by step toward the rifle-pits, and taking their colors with them.

In this charge upon the hill the regiments lost severely. In General Blair's Brigade there were eighteen hundred and twenty-five men engaged in this assault, and of this number six hundred and forty-two were killed, wounded, and captured.*

Under a flag of truce the dead were buried and the wounded removed, after which General Sherman gave the order for his troops to re-embark.

The arrival of General McClernand at the scene of action next caused a change in the command, as he ranked General Sherman by over one month in the date of his commission; and an order was at once given by the former to withdraw from the Yazoo River, where the vessels were stationed, and return to the Mississippi River. General McClernand, on assuming the command, ordered the title of the army to be changed, and General Sherman announced the fact in the following order:

HEAD-QUARTERS, RIGHT WING ARMY OF TENNESSEE,
STEAMER FOREST QUEEN, MILLIKEN'S BEND, *January* 4, 1863.

[*General Orders, No.* 5.]

Pursuant to the terms of General Orders, No. 1, made this day by General McClernand, the title of our army ceases to exist, and constitutes in the future the Army of the Mississippi, composed of two "army corps," one to be commanded by General G. W. Morgan, and the other by myself. In relinquishing the command of the Army of the Tennessee, and restricting my authority to my own corps, I desire to express to all commanders, to soldiers and officers recently operating before Vicksburg, my hearty thanks for their zeal, alacrity, and courage manifested by them on all occasions. We failed in accomplishing one

* Correspondence of New York Herald, January, 1863.

purpose of our movement, the capture of Vicksburg; but we were part of a whole. *Ours was but part of a combined movement, in which others were to assist. We were on time; unforeseen contingencies must have delayed the others.* We have destroyed the Shreveport road, we have attacked the defences of Vicksburg, and pushed the attack as far as prudence would justify; and having found it too strong for our single column, we have drawn off in good order and good spirits, ready for any new move. *A new commander is now here to lead you.* He is chosen by the President of the United States, who is charged by the Constitution to maintain and defend it, and he has the undoubted right to select his own agents. *I know that all good officers and soldiers will give him the same hearty support and cheerful obedience they have hitherto given me.* There are honors enough in reserve for all, and work enough too. Let each do his appropriate part, and our nation must in the end emerge from this dire conflict purified and ennobled by the fires which now test its strength and purity. All officers of the general staff now attached to my person will hereafter report in person and by letter to Major General McClernand, commanding the Army of the Mississippi, on board the steamer Tigress, at our rendezvous at Gaines's Landing and at Montgomery Point.

By order of Major-General W. T. SHERMAN.
J. H. HAMMOND, *A. A.-G.*

For a short time this part of the army operated without being under the direct command of General Grant, and was, therefore, taken away from aiding in the grand object of the campaign—the reduction of Vicksburg. As such a diversion of General Grant's troops would necessarily lead to reduction of one-half of the force under his command, and perhaps a complete failure of the whole enterprise, for which he had so long labored, an application was made to the President to change the programme, which was done accordingly, and the two army corps—the 13th and 15th—again united to his forces, and ordered to report to him.

In the mean time the Army of the Mississippi, composed of those two corps, was taken up the Arkansas and White

Rivers to operate against Fort Hindman, a rebel work commanding the former stream.

The following dispatches will explain the result of the movement:

HEAD-QUARTERS, ARMY OF THE MISSISSIPPI,
POST OF ARKANSAS, *January* 11, 1863.

Major-General U. S. GRANT, *Commanding Department of the Tennessee:*

I have the honor to report that the forces under my command attacked the Post of Arkansas to-day, at one o'clock, having stormed the enemy's work. We took a large number of prisoners, variously estimated at from seven thousand to ten thousand, together with all his stores, animals, and munitions of war.

Rear-Admiral David D. Porter, commanding the Mississippi Squadron, effectively and brilliantly co-operated, accomplishing this complete success.

JOHN A. MCCLERNAND, *Major-General Commanding.*

UNITED STATES MISSISSIPPI SQUADRON,
ARKANSAS POST, *January* 11, 1863.

Hon. GIDEON WELLES, *Secretary of Navy:—*

SIR—The gunboats Louisville, De Kalb, Cincinnati, and Lexington, attacked the heavy fort at the Post, on the Arkansas, last night, and silenced the batteries, killing twenty of the enemy.

The gunboats attacked again this morning, and dismounted every gun, eleven in all.

Colonel Dunnington, late of the United States Navy, commandant of the fort, requested to surrender to the Navy. I received his sword.

The army co-operated on the land side. The forts were completely silenced, and the guns, eleven in number, were all dismounted in three hours.

The action was at close quarters on the part of the three iron-clads and the firing splendid.

The list of killed and wounded is small. The Louisville lost twelve, De Kalb seventeen, Cincinnati none, Lexington none, and Rattler two.

The vessels, although much cut up, were ready for action in half an hour after the battle.

The light draught Rattler, Lieutenant-Commander Wilson Smith, and the other light draughts, joined in the action when it became general, as did the Black Hawk, Lieutenant-Commander R. B. Breese, with her rifle-guns. Particulars will be given hereafter.

Very respectfully, your obedient servant,

DAVID D. PORTER, *Acting Rear-Admiral.*

CHAPTER XIX.

DISCIPLINE.—GUERILLAS.

During the investigation that followed the surrender of Holly Springs, it was discovered that political agencies had been brought to bear, to induce certain regiments to throw down their arms and refuse to fight, and even to surrender to the enemy. General Grant, in order to check an evil that would soon prove disastrous, if allowed to go unpunished, issued the following special order concerning one of the regiments so disaffected.

HEAD-QUARTERS THIRTEENTH ARMY CORPS,
DEPARTMENT OF THE TENNESSEE,
HOLLY SPRINGS, MISS., *December* 31, 1862.

[*Special Orders, No.* 58.]

It having been alleged that the 109th Regiment Illinois Infantry Volunteers has shown indications of disloyalty, and many members of the regiment having voluntarily hunted up citizens in the neighborhood of their camp to surrender and obtain parole from, is hereby placed in arrest.

The regiment will be disarmed by the commander of the brigade to which the regiment is temporarily attached, and the arms and ammunition of the regiment turned over to the Ordnance Officer, Lieutenant Carter, to be disposed of as may hereafter be ordered.

Officers and men will be confined within camp limits until other wise ordered.

The conduct of Company K, of said regiment, being in honorable contrast to the balance of the regiment, is exempt from the effect of the above order, and will be placed on duty with the brigade to which said regiment is attached.

By command of Major-General U. S. GRANT.

JOHN A. RAWLINS, *A. A.-G.*

The condition of this regiment was made the matter for a special court of inquiry, which was convened under an order from General Grant, bearing date January 2d, 1863. The case was carefully investigated, and exonerated the regiment as a body. The result of the investigation was publicly set forth by General Grant, in general orders, and read at the head of each regiment.

HEAD-QUARTERS, DEPARTMENT OF TENNESSEE,
YOUNG'S POINT, LA., *February* 1, 1863.

[*General Orders, No.* 12.]

The proceedings of the Court of Inquiry, convened at Holly Springs, Miss., by Special Orders, No. 2, of date of January 2d, 1863, from these head-quarters, and of which Lieutenant-Colonel Dewitt C. Loudon, of the 7th Ohio Volunteer Infantry, was president, to inquire into and investigate the allegations and charges of disloyalty against the 109th Illinois Infantry Volunteers, *exonerate said regiment, as a regiment, from all suspicion of disloyalty, satisfactorily vindicate its innocence, and place it where the commanding-general hoped to find it, among the pure and patriotic in their country's defence; that whatever cause for suspicion or charges of disloyalty there was arose from the conduct and declarations of the following named officers, who are hereby dismissed the service of the United States, with forfeiture of pay and allowances, to take effect from this date, for the offences of which they are severally shown to be guilty.*

Lieutenant-Colonel Elijah Willard, for disobedience of orders, and deserting his command in the face of an enemy, that he might be taken prisoner.

Captain John M. Richie, for disobedience of orders, encouraging his men to desert, and discouraging his men from fighting in the face of the enemy.

Captain Thomas Boswell, for encouraging his men to desert, that they might be captured and paroled, and advising them to apply for discharges for slight causes; also, for trying to impress upon the minds of the officers and men of his regiment that they were embraced in the surrender of Holly Springs by Colonel Murphy, on the 20th day of December, 1862, well knowing the same to be false.

Captain John McIntosh, for declaring in the hearing of his men, and in the presence of the enemy, that he would not fight if attacked, near Holly Springs, on the 20th December, 1862.

Captain Penninger, of Company G, for proposing a plan by which the regiment could be surrendered to the enemy, and attempting to induce others of the regiment to aid in carrying it into execution during the raid of the enemy's cavalry on Holly Springs, on the 20th day of December, 1862.

Second-Lieutenant John Stokes, for straggling from his command, and procuring for himself and a number of his men fraudulent paroles from a rebel citizen.

Second-Lieutenant Daniel Kimmel, for advising the colonel of his regiment, if attacked by the enemy, to surrender, and on feigned sickness procuring a surgeon's certificate, to go to the hospital, at Holly Springs, Miss., by reason of which he was captured and then paroled by the enemy during the raid on that place.

First-Lieutenant and Adjutant James Evans, for inciting dissatisfaction among the men of his regiment, and speaking in an improper manner of the war and President, in violation of the 5th Article of War.

Commissary-Sergeant Joshua Wisenheimer is reduced to the ranks for declaring that he would never fire a gun upon the enemy, and on hearing a camp rumor that Major-General Burnside was defeated with a loss of twenty thousand men, wished that it was so.

By order of Major-General U. S. GRANT.

JOHN A. RAWLINS, *A. A.-G.*

Cavalry operations were continually taking place in the vicinity of the Union posts, and on January 8th, 1863, a descent was made on a camp near Ripley, Tennessee, killing and wounding several rebel soldiers, and capturing forty-six, besides horses, arms, camp equipage, etc. The remainder of the force was dispersed. The commander at Memphis gave notice that, for all guerilla raids upon Union citizens and communications with the city, the resident secessionists should be punished in the forfeiture of their property and expulsion beyond the extreme limits of the Union army lines.

General Grant's immediate army, except the special posts held at Corinth and elsewhere, was also withdrawn from Northern Mississippi, after the diversion of the forces acting along the Mississippi River, and the head-quarters of the Department were located at Memphis. From this city General Grant announced the victory at Arkansas Post. After the withdrawal of the army, the rebel guerilla forces began to make raids upon all towns recently held by the Union troops, and any person or persons that had manifested to Grant's army any evidence of returning loyalty, were summarily punished, either in person or property.

On the 23d of January, the Army of Mississippi, having destroyed all offensive and defensive works at Arkansas Post, returned to Memphis and reported to General Grant.

General Grant was also determined that the President's Proclamation of Emancipation should be carried out in his department, and issued an order, relative to the negro regiments, of which document the following is an extract:—

MILLIKEN'S BEND, LA.

[*General Orders, No.* 25.]

I. Corps, Division, and Post Commanders will afford all facilities for the completion of the negro regiments now organizing in this Department. Commissaries will issue supplies, and Quartermasters will furnish stores on the same requisitions and returns as are required from other troops.

It is expected that all commanders will especially exert themselves in carrying out the policy of the administration, not only in organizing colored regiments, and rendering them efficient; but also in removing prejudice against them. * * * * *

By order of Major-General U. S. GRANT.

JOHN A. RAWLINS, *A. A.-G.*

CHAPTER XX.

CHANGE OF BASE.—WILLIAMS'S CANAL.

On the 29th of January, 1863, General Grant landed a portion of his army at Young's Point, Louisiana, and another portion at Milliken's Bend. He shortly followed these forces, and established his head-quarters at the former place, whence he could have good control of all the operations necessary to the reduction of the rebel stronghold. General Grant next thoroughly inspected the rebel works, and became convinced that it was impossible to take them from the water front. He then held a consultation with his generals as to the best plan to be adopted to turn the rebel position, and all agreed that the only method that promised success was to flank the works on the south side.

The most important object of consideration was the means to be adopted to transport his forces to the south side of the fortified city. But in this lay the great difficulty. The river was completely blockaded above by the works on the Walnut Hills and other elevations, and no advance could be made from New Orleans in consequence of the fortification of Port Hudson. General Grant, therefore, turned his attention to the reopening of the canal first cut by General Williams, opposite Vicksburg, across the Peninsula on the Louisiana side of the river. If this canal had been made successful, transports and gunboats could have been taken through it to the south side of the city, and the troops and supplies moved to a new base of operations.

The work, however, was of such a herculean nature, and was being continually interrupted by the heavy rains and the rapid rise of the river, that the number of men required to keep the water out of the camps and cuttings was much larger than those engaged on the canal, and more than could be conveniently detailed for the purpose.

It now became necessary that the utmost secrecy should be used concerning every thing that was being done or about to be done in General Grant's army, and the following order was issued to prevent any one from being admitted within the lines who did not properly belong to the army, and to prohibit those who were inside from going beyond the limits:

HEAD-QUARTERS, DEPARTMENT OF THE TENNESSEE,
YOUNG'S POINT, LA., *Feb.* 12, 1863.

[*Special Field Orders, No.* 2.]

I. The nature of the service the army is now called upon to perform, making it impracticable to transport or provide for persons unemployed by government, the enticing of negroes to leave their homes to come within the lines of the army is positively forbidden. They should be permitted to remain at their homes, in pursuance of the recommendation of the President, "in all cases where allowed to labor faithfully for reasonable wages." *Those at present within the lines will not be turned out; but in future, in the field, no persons, white or black, who are not duly authorized to pass the lines of sentinels, will be permitted to enter or leave camp.*

II. Whenever the services of negroes are required, details will be made by army corpsc ommanders for the purpose of collecting them, and they will be registered, provided for, and employed in accordance with law and existing orders.

III. The habit too prevalent of arresting citizens beyond the lines of the army, and bringing them into camp without charges, is prejudicial to the service, and must not be continued. When citizens are arrested hereafter without charges being preferred warranting the arrest, the citizen will be turned outside the lines, and the officer or soldier causing the arrest will be confined, and otherwise punished at the discretion of a court-martial.

IV. No flag of truce will hereafter be allowed to pass our outposts. Any message sent under it will be received by an officer and receipted for, and the flag directed to return immediately. All answers to such messages will be sent under our own flag of truce.

V. Attention of army corps commanders is particularly called to the 41st, 42d, 46th, and 50th Articles of War, which will be rigidly en forced.

By order of Major-General U. S. GRANT.

JOHN A. RAWLINS, *A. A.-G.*

The four Articles of War referred to in the foregoing order are as follows :—

ART. 41.—All non-commissioned officers and soldiers, who shall be found one mile from the camp, without leave in writing, from their commanding officer, shall suffer such punishment as shall be inflicted upon them by the sentence of a court-martial.

ART. 42.—No officer or soldier shall be out of his quarters, garrison, or camp, without leave from his superior officer, upon penalty of being punished according to the nature of his offence, by the sentence of a court-martial.

ART. 46.—Any sentinel who shall be found sleeping upon his post, or shall leave it before he shall be regularly relieved, shall suffer death, or such other punishment as shall be inflicted by the sentence of a court-martial.

ART. 50.—Any officer or soldier who shall, without urgent necessity, or without the leave of his superior officer, quit his guard, platoon, or division, shall be punished, according to the nature of his offence, by the sentence of a court-martial.

It will be seen at once that something of more than ordinary importance was being transacted, to require the issuance of such stringent orders as the foregoing.

The banks of the Mississippi River at this time were lined with guerilla parties, who would occasionally fire upon the supply boats and transports with light field-pieces, and when attacked would retreat into the jungles and cane-brakes. This partisan warfare proved to be a great annoyance, and sometimes destructive, but did not seriously interfere with General Grant in the prosecution of his work.

During the early part of February, a reconnoissance was made in the neighborhood of Lake Providence, and a skirmish took place at a point about five miles distant from the lake, resulting in the defeat of the rebels. Another skirmish took place at Old River, Louisiana, on the 10th of February, with a similar result. During the reconnoissance, Captain Prime, Chief of Engineers on General Grant's staff, ascertained certain facts that led him to believe that a water route could be made through the bayous which run from near Milliken's Bend, north of Vicksburg, and from New Carthage, south of that city, into the Tensas river.

Meanwhile, the work on the Williams Canal continued to be prosecuted with great vigor, and a large number of men were employed upon it. On the 8th of March the overflow of the river broke in the dam at the end of the canal, and flooded the whole of the low lands, before the cutting could be completed. As the season was too far advanced to renew experiments on this enterprise, it had to be abandoned.

CHAPTER XXI.

THE QUEEN OF THE WEST AND INDIANOLA.*

ACTING Rear-Admiral Porter's gunboat fleet ably co-operated with General Grant in his operations before Vicksburg, and, early in February, the ram Queen of the West, under command of Colonel Ellet, ran by the batteries at Vicksburg, and pushed down the Mississippi and up the Red Rivers on a reconnoisance. During the first trip Colonel Ellet captured three of the enemy's transports, and then returned to the lower end of the Williams Canal. On the 10th of February Colonel Ellet started on a second expedition in the same direction, and on the 12th arrived at the junction of the Red and Atchafalaya Rivers. The latter stream runs from the Red River to the Gulf through a curious swampy tract of country in Louisiana. The Queen, having left her tenders behind in a secure position, started down the Atchafalaya, and after passing along about six

* This chapter is written to point out one of the great difficulties under which General Grant labored. The Red River had been used by the rebels as a highway for the transportation of stores and supplies for the rebel garrisons at Vicksburg, Grand Gulf, Natchez, and Port Hudson, and until that source of supply was cut off, it would have been impossible to reduce the place by siege. To reach the mouth of the Red River it became necessary to run the batteries, and the experiment was first made by the Queen of the West, and next by the Indianola. These trials of the strength of the rebel batteries may also be looked upon as special reconnoissances for future use, as will be developed in the course of the narrative.

miles, succeeded in destroying an army wagon train, and a quantity of stores, ammunition, etc., belonging to the enemy.

On February 14th, Colonel Ellet captured a rebel steam transport on the Red River, at a point about fifteen miles above the mouth of the Black River. At the time of her capture this rebel vessel had on board two lieutenants and fourteen privates of the rebel army, and was laden with four thousand five hundred bushels of corn. The prisoners were put on shore, and the vessels sent under guard to a secure position.

Colonel Ellet then went about thirty miles further up the Red River, with the intention of capturing or destroying three other steamers which were lying under the protection of a rebel battery. The rebels opened upon the Queen with four pieces of artillery, and the pilot having purposely run the vessel aground, she was brought within easy range, and so crippled by the shots from the rebels that she had to be abandoned, Colonel Ellet and others escaping on bales of cotton, while the remainder of those on board were captured by the rebels.*

On the night of the 13th, the U. S. gunboat Indianola successfully ran by the batteries of Vicksburg, for the purpose of supporting the Queen of the West in her movements; but, after the former had passed Natchez, the captain was informed of the capture of the latter vessel by those who had escaped. The Indianola, under the guidance of Colonel Ellet, who had located his head-quarters on the captured vessel Era, then returned towards the Red River, with the intention of destroying the battery and retaking the Queen of the West.

* Including Mr. Finlay Anderson, a correspondent of the *New York Herald.*

On arriving at the mouth of the Red River, it was ascertained that the rebels had several armed vessels up that stream, and, under the circumstances, it was deemed advisable not to proceed farther, but to return at once to Vicksburg. While ascending the river, Colonel Ellet's vessel was fired upon several times.

The Indianola was then detailed to blockade the mouth of the Red River, barges of coal having been floated by the batteries, to keep her well supplied with fuel.

At about half-past nine P. M. on February 24th, four armed rebel vessels approached the Indianola under the cover of darkness. The captured Queen of the West, which the rebels had armed and manned, and another ram, made the first attack upon the Indianola, and in a short time the engagement became general at close quarters. The other two rebel vessels were merely cotton clad, and not being heavily armed, could do but little damage to the Union gunboat. The rebel rams plunged with their prows at the Indianola, with great violence, but it was not until the sixth blow was administered that any serious damage was inflicted.

The engagement lasted one hour and twenty-seven minutes, after which the Indianola became so damaged that the captain ran her ashore, and surrendered her to the rebels, first destroying all documents of value that had been on board. But, before the rebels could take possession of their prize, her stern had sunk under water, and her guns rendered useless, the lighter ones having been thrown overboard.

The Indianola was finally destroyed by the rebels about the beginning of March, 1863. The following extract from the Vicksburg *Whig*, of March 5th, 1863, explains the reason of her destruction:

DESTRUCTION OF THE INDIANOLA.

"We stated a day or two since that we would not enlighten our readers in regard to a matter which was puzzling them very much. We alluded to the loss of the gunboat Indianola, recently captured from the enemy. We were loath to acknowledge she had been destroyed, but such is the case. The Yankee barge sent down the river last week was reported to be an iron-clad gunboat. The authorities, thinking that this monster would retake the Indianola, immediately issued an order to blow her up. The order was sent down by a courier to the officer in charge of the vessel. A few hours afterwards another order was sent down countermanding the first, it being ascertained that the monstrous craft was only a coal boat; but before it reached the Indianola she had been blown to atoms—not even a gun was saved. Who is to blame for this folly—this precipitancy?"

About this time the commander at Memphis thought it necessary to suppress the circulation of an opposition newspaper, within the limits of the army lines; but General Grant, respecting the principle laid down with regard to the liberty of the press, at once rescinded the order, as soon as he had been made aware of the fact.

CHAPTER XXII.

THE LAKE PROVIDENCE CANAL.

THE success of a bayou canal in Missouri, near the vicinity of Island No. 10, induced the engineers on General Grant's staff to examine into the probable chances of success for a similar canal, from the bayous above Vicksburg to the bayous below the city. Captain F. E. Prime and Colonel G. G. Pride made a reconnoissance along a portion of the route, and reported the practicability of the plan. General Grant therefore determined to try the project, if for no other purpose than to engage the enemy's attention while he matured his own plans. Having more troops at Young's Point than could, at that moment, be there employed to advantage, and knowing that Lake Providence was connected by Bayou Baxter with Bayou Macon, a navigable stream, he set the men to work upon the canal between the Mississippi and the lake, so as to keep them from demoralizing idleness, and to divert the attention of the enemy.

To a person studying the map it would seem a very feasible project to connect the Mississippi River with the lake, especially when the level of the former lay somewhat higher than that of the latter. The lake is situated in Carroll County, La., about one mile west of the Mississippi River, which without doubt originally flowed through its bed, but had changed its course during one of the many freaks of Nature by which the channel of that great stream had been turned aside from its primary path. The length of the lake is about six miles, and it is fed by the Bayou Macon and the Bayou Tensas. One point of the lake, which is half-moon shaped, approaches nearer to the Mississippi River than the other, and at this point the canal was cut. It was supposed by the engineers that a highway could be made from the Mississippi, seventy-five miles above Vicksburg, through Lake Providence, thence by the bayous into the Tensas River, which falls into the Black River at Trinity, La. The Black River pursues its course and falls into the Red River, by three channels, at a point about thirty miles above the mouth of the latter, which opens into the Mississippi River at the northern limit of Point Coupee Parish, and at about fifty miles above the fortified position of Port Hudson. If this route had been made practicable, it would have opened a water communication between the positions above and below Vicksburg, and enabled General Grant to co-operate with General Banks, who was preparing to invest Port Hudson. Under cover of this engineering movement, General Grant began moving his forces below the line of the city of Vicksburg, and occupied certain points a short distance inland from the Louisiana shore of the Mississippi River.

The work of opening the Lake Providence route progressed rapidly, and one steamer and a number of barges were taken through the canal; but, about the middle of April, the Mississippi River began to fall with unusual rapidity, and the roads becoming passable between Milliken's Bend and New Carthage, the proposed water route was abandoned as unnecessary, and, with the low stage of water, mpracticable.

It appears from General Grant's report of the capitulation of Vicksburg, that he had but little faith in the success of the Lake Providence scheme; but was willing to allow the experiment to be tried, as it employed his men and covered his real movements from the enemy.

CHAPTER XXIII.

THE YAZOO PASS EXPEDITION.

During February, 1863, a plan was proposed to open a closed up route of water travel between the Mississippi River and the Coldwater and Tallahatchie Rivers, through the Yazoo Pass. This pass had for many years been unnavigable, stagnant, dreary, and wild, and had been almost forgotten. The primary object of this expedition was to enable a few troops with some light draft gunboats to reach the upper part of the Yazoo River, for the purpose of destroying the enemy's transports; but it was afterwards discovered that, when the snags and low timber had been cut away from that part of the water-course which had been so long closed, the navigation proved to be much better than was suspected. It was, therefore, deemed not impossible to use the route for a flank movement by water upon Haines's Bluff, which commanded the Yazoo River a short distance above the mouth. Had this plan been found practicable, a large body of troops would have been sent around by this route; but for want of proper vessels for transportation, the force detailed was insufficient to clear the way throughout.

On the 24th of February, 1863, the fleet entered the pass, after tearing down that part of the levee of the Mississippi River that closed up the entrance; and, by the 28th, after a series of dangers, slow travelling, etc., the vessels arrived in the Coldwater River. Some idea of the nature of the work to be accomplished in opening up this route may be gathered from the following extracts, from a description penned by one of the parties who took an active part in the expedition:

UNITED STATES GUNBOAT MARMORA,
COLDWATER RIVER, MISS., *Feb.* 28, 1863.

The Rubicon is passed. Three and a half days of most tedious, vexatious, bothersome, troublesome, and damaging steamboating has brought this expedition twenty miles on its way, and disclosed to its view the end of the now famous Yazoo Pass. A more execrable place was never known. Should one propose to run a steamboat to the moon he would be considered equally sane, by those who had seen the Yazoo Pass before this expedition forced its way through it, as the person who proposed this movement.

I would like to describe the Yazoo Pass. I would like to compare it to something that would be intelligible. But I know of nothing in heaven or on earth, or in the waters under the earth, that will compare with it. Had the immortal bard desired a subject from which to draw a picture of the way that leads to the realms of darkness and despair, he had only to picture the Yazoo Pass. Let me try, in the feeble language I can command, to describe it. Perhaps the reader has passed through the Dismal Swamp of Virginia; or, if not, he has read accounts of travellers who have enjoyed that privilege. Then he has heard of the famous jungles of India. He has seen or read of the unbroken silence of the boundless tall forests of the John Brown tract in Western New York. Conceive the ugliest features of these three varieties of territory, and he will be able, by combining them, to form a tolerably correct idea of the region through which the Yazoo Pass runs. Those who have watched the course of a snake as he trails his way along the ground, winding this way and that, hither and yonder, going in all directions at the same time, and yet maintaining something of a regular course in the average, will, by exaggerating the picture in their own minds, understand something of the tortuous course of the Yazoo Pass. I have passed through it from one end to the other, and I assert candidly that there is not throughout its entire length a piece two hundred feet long of perfectly straight river. The orders under which this expedition moved required that boats should keep three hundred yards apart; but there was no place to be found in the whole stream where they could see one-third of this distance ahead or behind them. Once, indeed, we did catch a glimpse of the Rattler, flagship. She was just abreast of us, and about one hundred yards away, going in an opposite direction to us. We fancied we were close on to her, and, as it was near night, concludea to tie up, so as to let her get away from us. The next morning we got under way at daylight, and just as the sun was at the meridian we passed the spot where we had seen our file leader eighteen hours before.

Much has been said and written of the efforts put forth by the rebels to obstruct this pass. Their labor was all thrown away. Nature had placed greater obstructions in the way than any an enemy could place there, no matter how powerful he might have been or how long he had been employed. Cypress and sycamore trees lined the banks in great profusion, intermixed with gigantic cotton-woods bearing the wildest entanglement of wild grape-vines. The stream itself is never to exceed a hundred feet in breadth, and frequently not more than fifty or seventy-five. Over this the timber forms a most perfect arch, frequently, as good fortune would have it, so high as to admit the easy passage of the tall smokestacks beneath it, but sometimes grazing their tops, and again angrily toppling over these intruders. But Providence evidently did not intend this pass for a military highway. Providence opposed the movement, not so much by this high arch enclosing the river and shutting it out from view, as by the long, jagged limbs it thrust out from the trees directly across the channel, and the numerous crooked and leaning trees that formed a most effective blockade.

It may be possible, from what I have written, to get an idea of the Yazoo Pass. A short account of the trip through it will be more profitable for this purpose. The total length of the pass from the Mississippi to the Coldwater River is twenty miles. From the Mississippi to the east side of Moon Lake, where the pass proper commences, is called eight miles, leaving the distance from Moon Lake to the Coldwater twelve miles. We left the lake on Wednesday morning, the 25th inst., and reached the Coldwater this afternoon just after dinner, making the trip in exactly three days and a half! To be sure, we did not travel nights, but we made, usually, about twelve hours time each day. This gives the rapid progress of one mile in three and a half hours. Does the progress made express any thing of the character of the route? If it does not, I hardly know what will. In the upper end of the pass the stream is confined, and runs along with great rapidity through its narrow channel, the rate being not less than five or six miles per hour. Lower down there are strips of bottom-land along the sides which are now overflown, giving greater width, and consequently less rapidity to the current. But in no place were we able even to drift with the current. That would inevitably have dashed us into the timber and have torn our boat to atoms. From the time we entered the pass until we emerged from it, we could only keep our wheels backing, and even this was not enough. A small boat was requisite on either side, by which lines were passed out and made fast to the trees, to check our headway or ease us around the sharp bends. The expedition has been facetiously called "the stern-wheel expedition," from the circumstance of there being none but stern-wheel boats (which are narrower than side-wheel steamers) engaged in it; but it might with equal propriety be called "the back-water expedition," or "the hold-back expedition," because of our advancing only by holding back.

But with all our care and labor, it has been impossible to save our boats from much damage. Frequently it was impossible to check the headway of a vessel in time to save its smokestacks, and away would go these tall iron cylinders, crashing through the hurricane deck, and making a complete wreck of the cabin and light upper works. Again a huge limb would come crashing and smashing along the side, tearing away stanchions and braces, and sometimes even the light bulkheads around the upper works. The flagship was thus visited, and Acting Commander Smith's cabin turned into a complete wreck. In fact, all the vessels looked as if they had been in a hard fought battle and had been badly worsted, only that none of them were damaged in machinery or hull. It has been a most exciting trip; but I believe or hear all have survived it save one poor old nigger—a contraband—belonging to this vessel. He was lying in his hammock, in the sick bay, being on the sick list, when a huge limb, broken off by the persistence of our smokestacks, came down endwise upon the deck, and, passing through, administered the death blow to poor Cuffee.

COLDWATER RIVER, *March* 3, 1863.

We are progressing towards our destination, though slowly. To-day we have made about six miles down stream, and are now catching our breath after this rapid locomotion, preparatory to an early start to-morrow morning. The Coldwater River is but a slight improvement on the Yazoo Pass. It is a trifle wider, it is true—so wide, in fact, that the branches seldom meet above it—but in other respects we have gained nothing, so far as ease of navigation is concerned. Rather we have lost as much as we have gained, since the increased width of the stream is quite counterbalanced by the sluggishness of the current. The course of the stream is nearly as tortuous as that of the pass, so that we cannot yet venture to steam ahead, and as floating and backing up continues to be the order, the progress made is provokingly slow.

Since my last date we have lain quiet at the mouth of the pass, waiting for all the boats to come up. This detained us until this morning, when we once more started forward.*

The rebels had, however, gained information of the Union movement through Yazoo Pass; but at first scouted the idea of its success, prophesying the destruction of every vessel connected with the expedition. When, however, they ascertained that the fleet had safely arrived in the Coldwater River, they, knowing that the other part of the stream was navigable, at once began diligently closing up the lower end of the Tallahatchie River, into which the Coldwater empties itself. This was accomplished by erecting a fort across the neck of land caused by a change of course of the stream after the Yalabusha had formed a junction with the Tallahatchie. These united waters were named the Yazoo River, which, after flowing through several hundred miles of country, empties itself into the Mississippi River a little above Vicksburg.

The advance of the expedition under General Ross proceeded without serious interruption through the Coldwater and Tallahatchie Rivers until it reached this newly erected fort, which was designated Fort Pemberton—it having been constructed by some of the forces that had been sent from Vicksburg for that purpose. At the point where the fort was erected, the distance from the Tallahatchie shores above the defences, to the Yazoo shores below that work, was but a few hundred yards by land, but was several miles by water. The fort, having been built across the neck, commanded both streams for a long distance. The rebels had well chosen their defensive position, as the land about the fort was low, and at the time of the

* Correspondence of the New York *Herald*, March 14th, 1863.

expedition was entirely overflowed. General Ross, therefore, in attacking this work, could not make use of his land forces to reduce it, and had to depend on the armed vessels under his command. After an engagement of several hours, these vessels had to withdraw without silencing the battery.

Finding that this obstruction prevented the water route from being used by the army, General Grant, on March 23d, sent orders for the withdrawal of the forces.

One advantage, however, arose from the movement. It caused a diversion of a portion of the rebel force at Vicksburg, and engaged the attention of the rebel authorities while General Grant was perfecting his own plans.

CHAPTER XXIV.

THE STEELE'S BAYOU EXPEDITION.

ADMIRAL PORTER, having made a naval reconnoissance up Steele's Bayou, and through Black Bayou to Duck Creek, returned to General Grant, and on March 14th, 1862, informed him that those water-courses were navigable for small gunboats and light draft transports. It was supposed that by following this route Deer Creek could be navigated to Rolling Fork, and thence by the Sunflower River into the Yazoo. Of the navigation of these two latter streams there was no doubt.

As the forces by way of the Coldwater and Tallahatchie Rivers had been prevented from proceeding further in consequence of the construction of Fort Pemberton, it was deemed necessary to ascertain whether this new route could be made practicable. General Grant, therefore, accompanied Admiral Porter on the morning of March 15th on another reconnoissance. The vessel in which the two commanding officers had temporarily taken up their head-quarters, proceeded along Steele's Bayou—several iron-clads taking the lead to prevent a surprise—until it reached the Black Bayou. General Grant then returned to Young's Point, for the purpose of sending up a pioneer corps to clear away the overhanging trees, which appeared to be the only important obstruction to the successful navigation of the route, at least so far as it had been explored.

Soon after General Grant had reached Young's Point, a

message was received from Admiral Porter, who had proceeded on the reconnoissance, requesting the co-operation of a good military force. General Grant promptly sent to him a division of the Fifteenth Army Corps, with General Sherman at its head. The number of steam transports suitable for such an expedition being limited, the major part of the military force was sent up the Mississippi River to Eagle Bend, a point where the river runs within a mile of Steele's Bayou.

The only cause of the failure of this expedition was the want of knowledge of the country to be passed through, and this ignorance led the expedition on until it encountered serious difficulties, which could not be removed without great delay. This gave the rebels time to place obstructions in the way of further progress, and the movement had to be abandoned when within a few hundred yards of a point, which, if attained, would have secured complete success.

The following is an interesting account of the expedition, from an eye witness:

U. S. TRANSPORT SILVER WAVE,
BLACK BAYOU, MISS., *March* 21.

On the 16th inst., late in the afternoon, General Grant ordered General Stuart to prepare the infantry of his division to move at daylight next morning. Leaving transportation, horses, tents, and every thing except ammunition, arms, and rations, the division embarked and proceeded up the Mississippi to Eagle Bend. A few days before the embarkation, Admiral Porter and General Grant had made a personal reconnoissance of a proposed route to the Yazoo above Haines's Bluff, and General Sherman was ordered by General Grant to take charge of the opening of the route. General Sherman, with the pioneer corps of Stuart's Division and the Eighth Missouri, left at once with the steamer Diligent. In the evening General Grant received dispatches from Admiral Porter, announcing that his gunboats were meeting with great success, and asking that the land force be sent at once. Grant immediately ordered General Stuart to proceed with his division. The distance by land from the Mississippi, along the Muddy Bayou, is about one mile. On account of the impossibility of taking any thing but small steamers, of which we had but five, through Steele's Bayou, the infantry was ordered to cross by this route to the bayou. On reaching Eagle Bend, a personal examination of the ground, made by Generals Stuart and Ewing, disclosed the fact that two long bridges were necessary to the movement of troops. The levee near the plantation of Senator Gwin had been carried away by a crevasse, and the water was rushing across his fields in a rapid torrent of considerable depth. The building of the bridges occupied a day and a half. Soon as it was completed, the division marched across to Steele's Bayou. General Stuart at once embarked so much of the First Brigade as could be transported upon the steamer Silver Wave, and started up through the wilderness of forest and water.

Between the Mississippi and the line of railway from Memphis to Jackson, the country north of the Yazoo, for some fifty miles, is traversed by three considerable streams, Steele's Bayou, Deer Creek, and the Sunflower, all of which are fed by innumerable creeks, bayous, and lakes, and empty into the Yazoo—Steele's seven miles from the Mississippi, near the scene of the battle of Chickasaw Bayou; Deer Creek below, and the Sunflower above Haines's Bluff. Their course, as is that of all streams through low and level ground, is very tortuous, very like the streams in the wild marshes. Transform the reeds of such marshes into the luxuriant growth of a Southern swamp, and a better idea could not be had of the wet wilderness in which we were. The eastern part of Issaguena county, on Deer Creek, has higher land, and some of the most valuable cotton plantations in the State. The soil is exceedingly prolific. We found in it immense numbers of slaves, and great quantities of cotton and grain. The Admiral called it one of the granaries of the Confederacy.

It was supposed to be so inaccessible, that the plantations were in the usual process of cultivation, the fields planted with corn, which was up, instead of cotton. They believed themselves beyond the reach of the devastations of war—had their gardens well stocked with vegetables, which were growing most temptingly, and, fancying that "the invader" could not penetrate, with gunboats and armies, the lagoons and forests which surrounded them, devoted their fancied security to the raising of crops to feed their brother rebels in the field. The appearance of the iron-clads was the first notice they had had of our approach. The overseer hastily fled, giving notice of the presence of the Yankees in the garden. A contraband told us, his master called the Deer Creek country the Confederate snuff-box, that the Yankees could not open.

Going up the Yazoo river seven miles, thence up Steele's Bayou twelve miles, the fleet came to Muddy Bayou, which runs across from the Mississippi into Steele's. At this point the troops came over on floating bridges and embarked. Hence they were transported up Steele's and Black Bayou about twenty miles to Hill's plantation, and marched thence twenty-one miles on a levee north along Deer Creek nearly to Rolling Fork. It was proposed at that point to embark the troops again on transports, and proceed on that creek a distance of seven miles, until we reached the Sunflower. Once upon the Sunflower, a stream of considerable width, we could reach the Yazoo, between Haines's Bluff and Yazoo City, and would be in a position to operate against the enemy at various points with great effect. So much for the object of the expedition and the route through which it was to pass.

General Grant and Admiral Porter, with the Musquito Rattler, and a tug, made a reconnoissance far enough to establish the fact that gunboats could pass from the Yazoo into Steele's Bayou. Admiral Porter immediately started with his gunboats up the Bayou. General Grant ordered General Sherman, with a division of his army corps, to form the land force. General Sherman started at once with a regiment, and the pioneer corps, to clear the bayou of obstructions—there was no delay. The reconnoissance was made on the 15th, General Grant's tug returning the morning of the 16th. Before night the advance of the land force and gunboats were at Muddy Bayou. Dispatches were received by General Grant that evening of the progress of the expedition, and General Stuart was ordered to follow with the rest of the division in the morning. Arriving at Eagle Bend on the 17th, a reconnoissance in small boats, made by General Suart and his brigade commanders, and another made twenty miles above, at Tullahola, by Colonel Giles A. Smith, demonstrated that the troops could not be marched across, a crevasse having swollen the Muddy Bayou to a rapid deep stream. The construction of two long floating bridges occupied the 18th and the forenoon of the 19th, and the division marched at once to Steele's Bayou. Arriving there, we found only one transport, the Silver Wave. Embarking two regiments, Stuart started up at once. During the three succeeding days, the boats which we had were used with all the dispatch possible, in transporting the troops to the rendezvous. At the mouth of Black Bayou they were transported from the steamers to a coal-barge, which was towed

9

by a tug up Black Bayou. In the mean time the gunboats had gone through Black Bayou into Deer Creek. The great might and strength of the iron-clads enabled them to ride over almost any ordinary growth of willow and cypress in the creek—the water was deep, and they moved slowly and surely along up Deer Creek some fifteen miles, without much labor, and without any obstruction from the enemy. On the 20th, the rebels commenced annoying them with sharp-shooters, and by felling trees in the creeks. The boats were obliged to lay by at night, and on the morning of the 21st, the Admiral found considerable obstructions in the river, and an enemy, some 600 strong, with a field battery of rifles, disputing his passage. This was near some old Indian mounds, and for the greater part of the day they were kept quite busy, making but a half mile progress.

Large bodies were kept a good distance from the fleet, but sharpshooters would come up behind trees and fire, taking deliberate aim at our men. The Admiral sent a dispatch back to General Sherman, stating the condition of affairs, and a force was at once sent to the relief of the gunboats, and to assist in getting them through. They made a forced march, skirmishing a part of the way, and reaching the gunboats before night of the 22d, a distance of twenty-one miles, over a terrible road. During the day the enemy had been largely re-enforced from the Yazoo, and now unmasked some 5,000 men—infantry, cavalry, and artillery. The boats were surrounded with rebels, who had cut down trees before and behind them, were moving up artillery, and making every exertion to cut off retreat and capture our boats. A patrol was at once established for a distance of seven miles along Deer Creek, behind the boats, with a chain of sentinels outside of them, to prevent the felling of trees. For a mile and a half to Rolling Fork, the creek was full of obstructions. Heavy batteries were on its bank, supported by a large force. To advance was impossible; to retreat seemed almost hopeless. The gunboats had their ports all closed, and preparations made to resist boarders. The mortar-boats were all ready for fire and explosion. The army lines were so close to each other that rebel officers wandered into our lines in the dark, and were captured. It was the second night without sleep aboard ship, and the infantry had marched twenty-one miles without rest. But the faithful force, with their energetic leader, kept successful watch and ward over the boats and their valuable artillery. At 7 o'clock that morning (the 22d), General Sherman received a dispatch from the Admiral, by the hands of a faithful contraband (who came along through the rebel lines in the night), stating his perilous condition. Leaving a dispatch for General Stuart, who was bringing up Ewing's Brigade, and orders for Stuart to follow him with the remainder of the division, General Sherman at once marched with the Second Brigade, and a part of the First Brigade. Our gunboats at that time were in a bend of the creek, the three regiments of the First Brigade had been brought in and placed in position near the boats. A rebel battery of fifteen guns was in front, at Rolling Fork. The creek was barely the width of a gunboat—the boats were so close up that only one bow gun apiece of four could be used, and then at an inconvenient angle—in fact, in only one position—and the broadsides of several were useless on account of the bank. Our immense superiority of metal was thus rendered almost useless for the purpose of engaging an enemy that was endeavoring to encircle the Admiral's boats. If his rear was gained, their superior numbers could board the first or the last boat, and, having captured her, use her guns with fearful effect on the others.

About mid-day the enemy commenced moving upon us, with the purpose of reaching the bank of the creek below the gunboats and below the infantry. General Sherman was some six miles distant. The rebels are believed to have advanced with about 4,000 men. It must be borne in mind that our troops were on a belt of land which forms the bank of the creek, of not great width, back of which the bottom land was under water and impassable. The rebels came down with the intention of turning his right and reaching the creek below. The gunboats and four mortars opened upon them, as soon as they discovered themselves in bodies. This firing embarrassed their movements and considerably retarded them. They debouched through the wood and became engaged with the skirmishers. The fight was beginning to be in earnest, but the rebels were gaining ground. The object was not a battle, but to pass by our forces. The first firing of the gunboats was heard by General Sherman near the Shelby plantation. He urged his troops forward, and after an hour's hard marching, the advance, deployed as skirmishers, came upon a body of the enemy who had passed by the force which had been engaged. Immediately engaging them, the enemy stood a while disconcerted by the unexpected attack, fought a short time, and gave way. Our forces pressed them, driving them back some two miles. The gunboats opened upon them thus hemmed in, and the day was ours. The rebels retreated, and the gunboats were saved for that day. Our loss was but one killed and none wounded. The loss of the rebels was heavy. One shell from a mortar killed twenty-six, as they were rallying as skirmishers. Another is stated to have killed and wounded forty persons. They suffered very much, but, as we did not attempt to occupy the field, it cannot be ascertained. It being obvious that further advance was impracticable, the boats at once commenced moving backward, and made several miles that evening.

The next effort of the rebels was to pass around our lines in the afternoon and night, and throw their whole force still further below us. General Stuart, with four regiments, marched on Hill's plantation the same morning, having run his transports in the night, and immediately advanced one regiment up Deer Creek, and another still further to the right. The rebels, who were making a circuit about General Sherman, thus found the whole line occupied, and abandoned the attempt to cut off the gunboats for that day. During the afternoon the troops and gunboats all arrived at Hill's plantation. Rebel scouts followed them within two miles of the division head-quarters. During the night the picket about one-half mile out was attacked by a squadron of cavalry, It immediately, upon the return of their fire, fell back. In the afternoon of the next day, another regiment was attacked by three regiments of infantry and a squadron of cavalry. Acting under instructions to draw them on, and to develop their whole force, a skirmish ensued, but they refused to follow. The enemy, the night before, landed a steamer and two flatboats, loaded with troops and artillery, about six miles above. We remained two days at Hill's plantation, waiting for the rebels to prepare; but they would not give or receive battle. We embarked on the transports and gunboats, and returned. The troops, gunboats, ammunition, and supplies, with a considerable quantity of cotton and fifty good mules, are all safe, and approaching Young's Point, as I write.

There were destroyed by our troops and by the rebels at least 2,000 bales of cotton, 50,000 bushels of corn, and the gins and houses of the plantations whose owners had obstructed our progress, and joined in the warfare. The resources of the country we found ample to subsist the army at Vicksburg for some length of time, and by the destruction of them we crippled the enemy so far.

There were features about this expedition novel and exciting.

Black Bayou, a narrow stream heretofore, only navigated by dugouts, was made of the width of our steamers, with great labor of felling trees and sawing stumps below the surface. Every foot of our way was cut and torn through a dense forest, never before traversed by steamers. I never witnessed a more exciting and picturesque scene than the transportation, on the last day, of the Third Brigade, by General Stuart. Crowded with men, the steamer, at the highest possible speed, pushed through overhanging trees and around short curves. Sometimes wedged fast between trees, then sailing along smoothly, a huge cypress would reach out an arm and sweep the whole length of the boats, tearing guards and chimneys from the decks. The last trip through the Black Bayou was in a night pitchy dark and rainy.

While the adventure was of uncertain success—when the result seemed almost accomplished, and when our gunboats were surrounded with an enemy confident of victory, and their extrication seemed almost an impossibility—officers and men worked with equal alacrity, whether in building bridges or making forced marches, both by day and in the night. The whole time was used in labor—constant and severe. It seems almost a miracle that the boats were saved. If Generals Sherman and Stuart, by their utmost exertions and labor, had forwarded their troops a single half day later, if the second forced march under General Sherman had been retarded a single hour, in all human probability the whole force would have been lost.*

All these expeditions proved to be excellent feints to distract the enemy's attention; but there is no doubt that if they had succeeded, one of them would have been adopted, and might not have produced so glorious a result as the final campaign and plans which General Grant had himself laid out. In fact, he states in his report, that the failure of these expeditions "may have been providential in driving him ultimately to a line of operations which has proven eminently successful."

The losses inflicted on the enemy in the destruction of supplies, and the withdrawal of certain portions of his garrison to meet the expeditionary movements were of inestimable value to General Grant in his final Vicksburg campaign.

* Correspondence of the Chicago *Tribune*, April, 1863.

CHAPTER XXV.

THE HEALTH OF THE ARMY.

It has often been stated by generals in the field, that they had far less dread of the enemy in their front than they had of their friends at home. A slight word of alarm, uttered by the latter in a careless moment, would soon be increased until it became a perfect panic. While General Grant was engaged in the before described expeditions, letters to friends were for a time prohibited, to prevent information reaching the enemy through a mail captured by guerillas; and this absence of regular communication between those in the army and their friends at home, led the latter to believe that the former were sick. An interchange of such news between the friends of various absentees, and the return of a few invalids, settled it as a matter of fact that the whole army was dying of disease.

An official inquiry was at once made by the Surgeon-in-chief, and General Grant, under date of March 6th, 1863, wrote to Surgeon-General Hammond, as follows:

No army ever went into the field better provided with medical stores and attendance than is furnished to the army before Vicksburg. There was a deficiency in volunteer surgeons, but that is now supplied. The hospital boats are supplied with their own surgeons, nurses, and every thing for the comfort of the sick. The purveyor's department not only has every thing furnished the sick, but more than it ever dreamed of was furnished to the army, and more than the great majority of men could have at home. Then, too, there is not that amount of sickness that persons would be led to believe, from the statements in the public prints. I question whether the health of the St. Louis force is better than that of this command. On my arrival here, the men who had to put up with straw for so long a time, and then with camping on low ground and in the most terrible weather ever experienced, there was for a time, of necessity, a great number of sick.

U. S. GRANT, *Major-General.*

The foregoing letter was informal; but shortly after General Grant sent, in answer to the official inquiry, the following document for registry in the departmental offices at Washington:

HEAD-QUARTERS, DEPARTMENT OF THE TENNESSEE,
BEFORE VICKSBURG, *March* 12, 1863.

Brigadier-General W. A. HAMMOND, *Surgeon-General, United States Army.*

SIR:—Surgeon J. R. Smith's letter of the 20th of February is just received, inquiring into the sanitary condition of this command, and asking for suggestions for its improvement. *I know a great deal has been said to impress the public generally, and officials particularly, with the idea, that this army was in a suffering condition, and mostly from neglect. This is most erroneous.* The health of this command will, I venture to say, compare favorably with that of any army in the field, and every preparation is made for the sick that could be desired.

I will refer Surgeon Smith's letter to my medical director for a fuller report of the condition of the medical department here.

I am, sir, very respectfully, your obedient servant,

U. S. GRANT, *Major-General.*

General Grant, desirous of having a good supply of sanitary stores, and to provide for the proper transportation and care of the same, issued the following order on the date specified.

HEAD-QUARTERS, DEPARTMENT OF THE TENNESSEE,
YOUNG'S POINT, LA., *March* 27, 1863.

[*Special Orders, No.* 86.]

I. The Quartermaster's Department will provide and furnish a suitable steamboat, to be called the "United States Sanitary Store Boat," and put the same in charge of the U. S. Sanitary Commission, to be used by it exclusively for the conveyance of goods calculated to prevent disease

—and supplement the government supply of stores for the relief of the sick and wounded.

II. No person will be permitted to travel on said boat, except sick officers of the Army and Navy (and they only on permits from their proper commanding officers), discharged soldiers, and employés of said Sanitary Commission, and no goods whatever for trading or commercial purposes will be carried on said boat, and no goods will be taken for individuals, or with any conditions which will prevent their being delivered to those most needing them in the Army or Navy.

III. The contents of all packages to be shipped on said U. S. Sanitary Store Boat, will be inspected before shipment by an agent of said Sanitary Commission, at the point of shipment, unless an invoice of their contents has been received, the correctness of which is assured by the signature of some person of known loyalty and integrity. A statement, showing what goods have been placed on board at each trip, will be sent to the Medical Director of the Department at these head-quarters.

IV. A weekly statement will also be made by said Sanitary Commission to the Department Medical Director, showing what sanitary supplies have been issued by said commission, and to whom issued.

V. All orders authorizing the *free* transportation of sanitary stores from Cairo south, on boats other than the one herein provided for, are hereby rescinded.

By order of Major-General U. S. GRANT.

JOHN A. RAWLINS, *A. A.-G.*

CHAPTER XXVI.

THE OVERLAND MOVEMENTS.—RUNNING THE BATTERIES.

It having been plainly manifested to General Grant that all the former operations would not reach the desired end, he at once determined to move his forces below Vicksburg on the Louisiana shore, so as to take the rebel works in the rear. On the 29th of March, 1863, the movement commenced; the Thirteenth Corps taking the lead, followed by the Seventeenth and Fifteenth, while to the Sixteenth Corps was left the charge of the communications and supplies.

Shortly before this, Admiral Farragut had run by the batteries at Port Hudson with his flag-ship, the Hartford, and her tender, the Albatross; and on March 17th was lying off Natchez, Miss. On March 21st the Hartford arrived off Vicksburg, and anchoring below the batteries, communicated with Admiral Porter and General Grant.

On the 25th of March, the U. S. rams Lancaster and Switzerland attempted to run by the batteries at Vicksburg, but were so crippled in the attempt that the former was sunk and the latter temporarily disabled. The rams had been made by altering river steamboats, and were far too light to withstand the shock of a heavy fire from such batteries as those at Vicksburg.

Two days after this event Admiral Farragut, with the Hartford, engaged the batteries at Warrenton, and succeeded in passing below them *en route* for the Red River.

On the 1st of April he engaged the batteries at Grand Gulf, and passed farther down the river with the Albatross and Switzerland in his company, arriving at the mouth of the Red River on the evening of April 2d.

In the mean time the army kept on the move, and on the 30th of March, Richmond, a village of Madison county, La., and on a direct line with Vicksburg, a few miles inland from the Mississippi River, was taken possession of by a portion of the Thirteenth Army Corps, who drove out the rebel cavalry after two hours sharp fighting. The Corps then pushed on towards New Carthage. The roads, although level, were in a very bad condition, and the march was necessarily slow and tedious. It was important that supplies and ammunition should travel with this corps, and consequently the movements were considerably delayed, as it became at times necessary to drag the wagons by hand.

When the corps was within two miles of New Carthage, it was found that, in consequence of the recent floods and the breaking of the levee of Bayou Vidal, that place was isolated, and located on an island. Boats were collected from the neighboring bayous, and barges were built; but by this method the progress of the army was too slow for the purpose intended. The corps was therefore marched to Perkins's plantation, twelve miles below New Carthage, and thirty-five miles from the point of starting. Over these thirty-five miles supplies and ordnance stores had to be transported; and as the roads were soft and spongy, owing to the floods, the labor of this movement is almost inconceivable. Provisions and ammunition had to be hauled in wagons, and until a sufficient quantity had reached the camp near the Mississippi River, below Vicksburg, it would have been impossible to have commenced a campaign, if a successful issue was to be desired.

While these army movements were in progress, Admiral Porter was not idle; but was engaged in making preparations for the running of transports and gunboats by the batteries at Vicksburg, so as to be able to co-operate with General Grant, and transport his troops from the Louisiana shore of the river to the Mississippi side. Until this was accomplished, the troops were no nearer reducing Vicksburg than they would have been at Young's Point or Milliken's Bend.

On the night of the 16th of April, Admiral Porter's fleet and three transports ran by the batteries at Vicksburg, and all but one succeeded in passing without being too much injured for service. These injuries were soon after repaired under the direction of Admiral Porter.

The success of this enterprise induced General Grant to send six more transports down the river, the fleet below being ready to receive them on their arrival. Volunteers were called for to man the transports, and a large number of men and officers tendered their services to take the vessels through on this dangerous trip. The enthusiasm of the volunteers for this expedition has scarcely ever been exceeded during the war. Five out of the six vessels arrived, on April 22d, safely below the batteries.

The transports injured in running this blockade were repaired by order of Admiral Porter, who was supplied with the material for such repairs as they required. The army supplied the requisite artisans and mechanics, and in a very short time five of the transports were in running order, and the remainder were in condition to be used as barges for the removal of troops. Twelve barges loaded with forage and rations were sent in tow of the six transports that passed the batteries on the 22d, and of these barges one-half got through in a condition to be used.

CHAPTER XXVII.

GRIERSON'S EXPEDITION.

BEFORE leaving the north side of Vicksburg, to take command of his army in person, General Grant determined to cut all the enemy's communications with that city, so as to secure his forces from an attack in the rear, should it become necessary to invest the place. He therefore detailed the First Cavalry Brigade, under Colonel B. H. Grierson, to this duty. On April 17th, 1863, this force left La Grange, Tenn., at about two o'clock in the morning, and after travelling a distance of thirty miles along the turnpike road, encamped within four miles of Ripley, Miss.

At eight o'clock the next morning the force was again on the march, and passing through Ripley moved southwardly toward New Albany. One battalion occupied the place, while the main body passed to the east, but all encamped about four miles south of New Albany.

Before leaving Ripley a part of the force, under Colonel Hatch, was detached to march on the left flank of the column, and taking a southeasterly direction, crossed the Tallahatchie about five miles northeast of New Albany.

It was impossible for a large force to move through the enemy's country without meeting some of the foe; and as a natural result, skirmishing took place all along the route, and several prisoners were taken. At one time the advance was engaged with the pickets of Chalmers's rebel brigade, but the latter was soon overpowered, and the main body of the rebels retreated.

The rebels attempted to fire the bridge at New Albany; but so rapid was Colonel Grierson's advance, that his forces were across the river before they could accomplish their purpose.

It now became necessary to mislead the enemy as to the actual destination of the main body; therefore, on April 19th, Colonel Grierson ordered a portion of his force to march back to New Albany, thence by Kingsbridge, where a rebel camp was said to be in existence. A second force he ordered east, and a third northwest, while the main body marched due south. It had been raining all the previous night; consequently this day's march was performed under great difficulties. The centre column then proceeded to Pontotoc, where a small rebel force was dispersed, and their camp equipage and a quantity of salt seized and destroyed. At eight o'clock that evening the command encamped six miles south of Pontotoc on the road to Houston.

On the 20th, a portion of the force was detached and sent back to La Grange with the prisoners and captured baggage. They were ordered to make as much noise in returning as possible, so as to give the rebels the idea that the expedition was over, while in fact the main body would still proceed south. This feint succeeded admirably.

The next day another force was detached, under Colonel Hatch, and ordered to destroy as much as possible of the Mobile and Ohio Railroad; to attack Columbus near the State line, between Mississippi and Alabama, and then to march back to La Grange. In this Colonel Hatch was successful, and the movement drew off General Chalmers's rebel forces from following Colonel Grierson, thus giving him three days fresh start.

The main body next moved to Starkville, where they captured and destroyed a rebel mail. After travelling four miles further, the command divided; one-half swimming the Dismal Swamp to destroy a tannery, which at the time contained a very large stock of boots and shoes, saddles, bridles, and several thousand dollars worth of leather; the other half proceeding on its course.

The command being again united, it pushed on towards Louisville, Miss. This part of the march was of the most dangerous character, as streams and blind marshes had to be crossed without any guide. Sometimes the horses would sink in the mud and be left to perish, and it is wonderful that some of the men did not share the same fate. Notwithstanding the horrible nature of this route, the men preserved their fortitude, and pushed on vigorously for Philadelphia, Miss., where another mail was destroyed. Private property, however, was in all cases respected.

On April 23d, the force pushed on to the Southern Railroad at Newton, moving by way of Decatur, and arrived at the former place about daylight on the 24th. Here two trains, bound to Vicksburg, *via* Jackson, were captured, and the whole thirty-eight cars, with the loads of quartermaster, commissary, and ordnance stores destroyed. The locomotives were also rendered useless. Several bridges and a quantity of trestlework were destroyed in this vicinity, after which, on the 25th, the raiding force moved towards Montrose, thence to Raleigh, Miss., where they encamped for the night.

At this time the rebels were close upon Colonel Grierson's heels, on ascertaining which, he moved over the Leaf River, destroying the bridge behind him, and then marched to Westville. Here two battalions were detached, and made a forced march to Hazlehurst station, on the Jackson and New Orleans Railroad, where they destroyed forty cars, four of which were loaded with shell and ammunition, and the remainder with quartermaster and commissary stores.

A detachment also made a raid upon Enterprise, on the Mobile and Ohio railroad, and thus diverting the enemy's attention from the movements of the main body.

When near Gallatin, the cavalry captured and spiked a thirty-two pound Parrot gun, which the rebels were hauling towards Vicksburg.

A detachment was next ordered to Bahala, on the Jackson and New Orleans Railroad, where they destroyed several miles of track and telegraph wire, a number of cars, water-tanks, and a considerable amount of government property.

On the morning of April 28th, the advance arrived at Brookhaven, where it surprised a body of rebels, taking about two hundred prisoners. Here a camp of instruction, about five hundred tents, and a large supply of small arms were destroyed.

Colonel Grierson, after making feints of moving towards Port Gibson and Natchez, marched, on April 30th, along the New Orleans and Jackson Railroad, destroying all the bridges between Brookhaven and Bogue Chito station. At the latter place, a number of loaded cars were found and destroyed. He next moved on to Summit, where he destroyed another train of cars.

The Union cavalry force then passed along the country road towards Clinton, and on their way met a body of rebel cavalry, which they engaged and routed. They again pushed on steadily towards the Mississippi River.

On Friday, May 1st, at about noon, the inhabitants of Baton Rouge were startled by the arrival of a courier, who announced thát a brigade of cavalry from General Grant's army had cut their way through the heart of the rebel country and were then only five miles outside of the city.

The information seemed too astounding for belief. At four o'clock, however, there was no longer doubt of the fact, for Colonel Grierson and his heroes were escorted into the city by a company of cavalry belonging to that post. At the picket lines they were welcomed by the commander and his staff, and the cheers of the garrison, as the adventurers entered Baton Rouge, could have been heard for miles.

The value of this expedition can scarcely be appreciated by merely reading the preceding account; but when it is considered that, in fifteen days this cavalry force marched over eight hundred miles, travelling through the very heart of the enemy's country, killed and wounded a number of the enemy, destroyed over four million dollars worth of property, cut off all communication with the rebel stronghold at Vicksburg, captured over a thousand prisoners, and twelve hundred horses, besides menacing the enemy at points where they deemed themselves secure, it will be at once seen that the expedition was one of the most important, as well as the most successful of the war, and is exceedingly creditable to all concerned.

About the same time cavalry raids were being made into Alabama and Georgia, under Colonel Streight, and to the rear of General Lee's army in Virginia, under General Stoneman, the various movements carrying consternation and terror into the midst of the enemy's dominions, and making it shake at its very centre.

The following table will show the work accomplished by Colonel Grierson during his expedition.

Locomotives destroyed, 2; cars destroyed, nearly 200; bridges burned, etc., 9; telegraph wires cut, 2; railroad tracks destroyed and broken, 3; rebel camps destroyed, 3; important rebel mails destroyed, 3; prisoners taken, over 1,000; tannery burned, 1; horses captured, over 1,200; miles travelled, over 800; value of property destroyed, over $4,000,000. Besides cutting off all railroad communication with the rebel strongholds on the Mississippi, as well as entirely destroying muskets, tents, stores, leather, boots, saddles, etc., of great value to the rebels in a military point of view.

Although the loss to the rebels was very great, the gain to General Grant was of corresponding value.

The following is General Grant's first announcement of the success of the expedition:

GRAND GULF, MISS., *May* 6.

Major-General HALLECK, *General-in-Chief:*

I learn that Colonel Grierson, with his cavalry, has been heard of, first, about ten days ago, in Northern Mississippi.

He moved thence and struck the railroad thirty miles east of Jackson, at a point called Newton's Station.

He then moved southward, towards Enterprise, demanded the surrender of the place, and gave one hour's grace, during which General Lormniey arrived.

He left at once and moved towards Hazelhurst, on the New Orleans and Jackson Railroad. At this point he tore up the track. Thence he pushed to Bahala, ten miles further south, on the same road, and thence eastward, on the Natchez road, where he had a fight with Wirt Adams's cavalry.

From this point he moved back to the New Orleans and Jackson Railroad, to Brookhaven, ten miles south of Bahala, and when last heard from he was three miles from Summit, ten miles south of Brookhaven, and was supposed to be making his way to Baton Rouge.

He had spread excitement throughout the State, destroying railroads, trestleworks, and bridges, burning locomotives and railway stock, taking prisoners, and destroying stores of all kinds.

U. S. GRANT, *Major-General.*

CHAPTER XXVIII.

OTHER PRELIMINARY MOVEMENTS.—ATTACK UPON GRAND GULF.

THE day after Colonel Grierson had started on his expedition, a party of Union troops, consisting of three regiments of infantry and one of cavalry, left Memphis, Tenn., on a reconnoissance into Mississippi. At Nanconnah they met a body of rebel cavalry, which, after a brisk fight, was repulsed with some loss. On the 19th another body of mounted rebels were met and driven over the Coldwater in confusion. The Union troops having been re-enforced at Hernando, Miss., again crossed the Coldwater and engaged the rebels at that point.

At about the same time General Banks's forces were making a demonstration in the neighborhood of Baton Rouge.

Owing to the limited number of transports below Vicksburg, it was deemed advisable by General Grant to extend his line of land travel to a little place in Louisiana, on the Mississippi River shore, locally known by the designation of Hard Times. As this place could only be reached by a very circuitous land route, the distance between the base of supplies at Milliken's Bend and the advance of the army was increased to seventy miles, with roads entirely unsuited for the operations of an army. But as the place was nearer to the point at which General Grant had intended to land his troops, on the Mississippi side of the river, he was determined that the roads should not prove an obstacle to thwart him in his plans. He therefore detailed a portion of his pioneer force to prepare the line of travel, and to keep it in order after it was constructed.

The Thirteenth Army Corps was embarked during the night of the 28th and early on the morning of the 29th of April, 1863, and the Seventeenth Corps being well on its way to take their place, General Grant ordered the transports to move over to the front of Grand Gulf. The plan had been for the navy to attack the rebel works, and for the military forces to land under cover of the guns, for the purpose of taking the place by storm. At eight o'clock in the morning Admiral Porter's fleet opened upon the works, which he engaged for five hours in the most brilliant manner. It, however, soon became evident that the enemy's batteries could not be silenced or taken from the water front, as the whole range of hills was lined with rifle-pits, supported by field artillery, that could be moved from one position to the other with the greatest ease. General Grant therefore determined to change his plan and effect a landing, if possible, at Rodney, some distance below Grand Gulf. But to effect this it became necessary again to run the rebel batteries. A consultation was therefore held between General Grant and Admiral Porter, and a plan soon agreed upon.

At dark Admiral Porter's fleet again engaged the batteries, and under cover of this contest the transports ran by the rebel works, receiving but two or three shots in the passage, and these not inflicting any material injury.

During the whole of the naval engagement at Grand Gulf, General Grant was on board a tug in the middle of the stream, a witness of the contest, and ready to move his forces to the assault as soon as the time appeared propitious.

CHAPTER XXIX.

THE LANDING AT BRUINSBURG, AND ADVANCE.

After the withdrawal of the fleet from before Grand Gulf, the troops were again landed at Hard Times, so that the transports might run easily by the rebel batteries without endangering more lives than was actually necessary. These disembarked troops were then marched overland, across the upper end of Coffee's Point and D'Schron's plantation, to the Louisiana shore of the Mississippi River below Grand Gulf.

A reconnoitring party was next sent out to discover the best point at which the troops could cross the river to the Mississippi shore. General McClernand says in his report of June 17th, 1863: "The reconnoissance made by my cavalry, in pursuance of Major-General Grant's order, indicated Bruinsburg to be the point. Hence, embarking on the morning of the thirtieth, my corps immediately proceeded to that place, and disembarked before noon."

The advance was now on the Vicksburg side of the river, and every thing was to be subservient to activity and rapid motion. The orders were that there should be no delay under any circumstances. Promptitude was especially necessary, as by that only could success be guaranteed.

At four o'clock in the afternoon, after having halted just long enough to distribute three days' rations, the advance of the Thirteenth Army Corps took up its line of march for the bluffs, three miles from the river. In this movement the corps commander states in his report that he acted "agreeably with General Grant's instructions." The bluffs were, therefore, reached and taken possession of some time before sunset.

The army had started in very light marching order, without trains or baggage, so that nothing should interfere with their rapid movements. Each man carried his allotted quantity of rations, and the bivouac and not the camp was to be the order of the night.*

The Thirteenth Army Corps, after reaching the Bluffs, pushed on toward Port Gibson, for the purpose of surprising any enemy that might be found in that neighborhood, and if possible to prevent him from destroying the bridges over Bayou Pierre, on the roads leading to Grand Gulf and to Jackson. To accomplish this object, the corps had to make forced marches, and to travel as far as possible along the road during that night.

The following account is given by one who participated in this movement of the rear column of the Thirteenth Army Corps:

Events have followed each other so rapidly within the last three days,

---

* The following is related of the very light manner in which General Grant commenced the campaign:—

A gentleman who participated in the Vicksburg campaign of General Grant, up to the time the enemy crossed the Big Black in the retreat towards Vicksburg, states that "in starting on the movement the General disencumbered himself of every thing, setting an example to his officers and men. He took neither a horse nor a servant, overcoat nor blanket, nor tent nor camp chest, nor even a clean shirt. *His only baggage consisted of a tooth-brush.* He always showed his teeth to the rebels. He shared all the hardships of the private soldier, sleeping in the front and in the open air, and eating hard tack and salt pork. He wore no sword, had on a low-crowned citizen's hat, and the only thing about him to mark him as a military man was his two stars on his undress military coat."

that it seems utterly impossible to keep pace with them as they have occurred.

When I wrote to you from Bruinsburg, it was long past midnight, and at the conclusion of my letter I was forced to throw myself upon the ground, under the friendly shelter of a thrifty cottonwood, to gain a little sleep for the labors of the coming day. Since eleven o'clock of the preceding (Thursday) night we had heard the occasional boom of cannon, followed by the sharp rattle of musketry, and I was not surprised, soon after I went into bivouac, to learn that an order was issued to march at daylight. At five reveille was beaten, and swallowing a cup of coffee and securing within haversack a cracker or two, just as the first rays of the tropical sun came glittering along the surface of the Mississippi, we left our bivouac, and taking the levee, moved in the direction of Port Gibson.

The steamers, which a few nights before had run the rebel batteries at Vicksburg and Grand Gulf were then used to carry troops from Bromly's plantation to Bruinsburg. Among others the Moderator and Horizon were thus used. The Moderator, on her return trip, met the Horizon coming down the river, having on board one hundred and fifty thousand rations and a full battery of artillery. Whether it was owing to the fog or the carelessness of the pilot has not been ascertained; but somehow the two vessels collided, and the Horizon, rations and battery, sank in deep water and disappeared from mortal vision. Every horse on board was drowned. Every gun lies fathoms deep in water, rations are ruined, and I regret to add that two or three soldiers found a watery grave. At this juncture the loss is almost irreparable.

But to describe our march from Bruinsburg:—The road to Port Gibson lies along the inner side of the levee for a couple of miles, until it branches to the right and strikes the bluffs or series of hills extending to Grand Gulf and Vicksburg. The route over these bluffs differs so materially from that over the dead levels of the preceding days, that we were continually finding something to wonder at and admire. The abrupt acclivities, the deep ravines, the waving corn, the beautiful flowers and magnificent magnolias, just now in full blossom, diffusing most delicious perfumes, and the long line of soldiers winding along the green trees, formed a truly beautiful picture. The harmony of this scene, normally so suggestive of peace, was sadly marred by the constantly recurring evidences that man was at variance with his fellow. As we approached a point six miles from Bruinsburg, we could hear the more rapid firing of cannon and the sharper rattle of musketry. When we arrived within four miles of Port Gibson we met a small force of stragglers, and received orders to move forward to the front.

The peculiar features of the region a little east of Bruinsburg are rigidly maintained at Thompson's Hills, except that, if possible, the hills are steeper, the ravines deeper, and ingress much more difficult. As we approached the plantation, whence the battle takes its name, we found at the bottom of a deep ravine a clear running stream of water—a rarity in this latitude. Ordinarily the streams are muddy and turbid, but here was one as clear as crystal. Beyond this stream the road over the hill rises abruptly until it reaches an open field, upon which the plantation mansion stands. Just beyond is a road to the left leading to Grand Gulf, and to the right a road leading south. We followed the latter, and reached a primitive church just in the edge of a grove of magnolias, with an open lawn in front. A half mile beyond, this road again forks, the left leading to Port Gibson and the right to Rodney. Taking this church as a centre, and striking a semicircle towards the east whose periphery shall be everywhere two miles from the common centre, and your line will strike a chain of hills and valleys, upon which and between which the battle, known as that of Thompson's Hills, was fought. Just beyond these hills is Port Gibson.*

* Army correspondence under date of May 3d.

CHAPTER XXX.

THE BATTLE OF THOMPSON'S HILLS, OR PORT GIBSON.—EVACUATION OF GRAND GULF.

The advance of the Thirteenth Army Corps approached the church, spoken of in the foregoing correspondence, at about one o'clock on the morning of the first of May, 1863. This church was distant from Bruinsburg about thirteen miles, and from Port Gibson about four miles. As the Fourteenth Division of Grant's army drew near the place, they were accosted by a light fire of rebel musketry, followed at a quick interval by a sharp attack with field artillery. The Union troops were at once formed into line of battle, and their batteries replied to the fire of the rebels. After a short but brisk engagement, the guns of the latter were silenced.

The Union troops then withdrew out of range, and patiently waited until daylight. At daybreak the fight was renewed by the ordering of the Ninth Division of Grant's army on to the road to the left. The First Brigade, while hastening forward to execute this order, encountered the enemy in force at about half-past five in the morning; and although the rebel position was strong, and the enemy apparently determined to keep it, he was forced to yield up possession after a hard struggle of over an hour's duration.

The Ninth Division, consisting only of two brigades, pressed forward; but the enemy had so obstructed the road by this route, that it was soon discovered a front attack would only result in disaster. A flank movement was then resolved upon, and by a spirited assault upon the right carried the rebel works, captured three pieces of cannon, and routed the enemy.

The following interesting account of the fight is given by an eye-witness:

General McClernand's army corps was marching in the direction of Port Gibson, and had reached the ravine and the running brook alluded to. It was his intention to encamp on the opposite hill, but the enemy had placed a three-gun battery there, and, as our advance reached the ravine, he began most persistently to shell us. His range was not good, and the guns did no damage. We withdrew out of range, and patiently waited until daylight. At daybreak the fight was renewed, first by the advance skirmishers, and afterwards by the main body. The battery placed upon the hill opposite was annoying us, and two regiments were ordered to take it. Across the running water and up the steep ascent advanced the brave soldiers, with bayonets firmly set, nor faltered a single step until the enemy were driven from the position and their guns fell into our hands.

From here the enemy retired to the right, following the road which led past the church, near which they had stationed another battery. Here the battle raged fearfully, and several of our men were wounded and killed. After the rebels had left this point I was able to find, where the fight raged the fiercest, the dead bodies of twenty men within a circuit of half as many rods. Driven from this position by the impetuous attack of the federal soldiers, the rebel general sought a convenient circlet of hills, and established his battle line. His centre rested on the Port Gibson road, with his right and left on the right and left of that thoroughfare. The attack was first made with artillery upon his centre, then skirmishers advanced, and the engagement became general in that locality. After heavy firing, the enemy gave way, and massed his forces on his left with the evident intention of flanking our right. This intention was discovered in season to avoid it by a proper disposition ol our reserves, when the enemy wheeled over to his right and massed his forces, making a most formidable demonstration. The attack against this wing was resisted with great determination and with partial success in the earlier part of the day, and the enemy gained several important positions, from which, for some hours, we tried in vain to dislodge him. On our extreme left and their right there was an elevation, protected in front by an impenetrable canebrake, and defended from flank approach by ravines, where the attacking party would be forced to undergo an enfilading fire. The enemy had mounted his guns upon the hill, and posted his skirmishers in the thicket before it. Several hours' most strenuous efforts were made to dislodge them, but our boys were unable to penetrate the dense thicket. The deadly missiles came singing through the air with fearful accuracy, and many a brave soldier was laid low. General Osterhaus and a portion of the Ninth Division were opposite. At length re-enforcements were called for, and the First Brigade of the Third Division, belonging to the Seventeenth Army Corps, came rushing along the road towards Grand Gulf. They were quickly formed in battle array, and with a shout, which must have struck terror in the hearts of the enemy, the boys fixed bayonets and boldly charged the position. Down upon their hands and knees, they worked their way through the young cane, and mercilessly slaughtered all who did not yield. One hundred and fifty men were taken prisoners in this glorious charge, and scores of rebels were killed and wounded. They gained the other side of the thicket, and picked off the men and horses serving the rebel battery. The Union batteries finished the good work, and the position and guns fell into our hands.

Beaten at every point, losing one hundred and fifty killed, three hundred wounded, and more than five hundred prisoners, the enemy sullenly and rapidly retreated to Port Gibson, harassed in his flight by volleys of musketry and the most strenuous efforts of our artillery.

Without difficulty they reached Port Gibson, blowing up, when near the village, a caisson filled with shot, shell, and powder.

Night was wrapping her sable mantle over hill and valley, and the silver moon shone out clear and bright, casting a flood of beautiful light over friend and foe, when the order was given to cease pursuit. We rested on the battle-field, wearied and exhausted, and soon deep silence reigned supreme where Mars so recently held high carnival.*

The commander of the corps, in his official report of this engagement, states that during the heat of the battle, "Major-General Grant came up from Bruinsburg, and soon after he had the pleasure of meeting him on the field."

* *New York Herald* correspondence, May 3d.

It also appears from the official reports, that the second position taken by the enemy was much stronger than the first, being located in a creek bottom, covered with trees and underbrush, the approach to which was over open fields, and ragged and exposed hill-slopes.

At break of day on the morning of Saturday, May 2d, the Thirteenth Army Corps triumphantly entered Port Gibson, through which place, and across the south branch of the Bayou Pierre, the enemy had hastily fled the night before, burning the bridge across that stream in his rear. This bridge was even burning when the advance entered Port Gibson, and it was necessary to remain a few hours in that village, until a floating bridge could be constructed.

While this bridge was being built, the rebels appeared on the opposite side of the Bayou Pierre, both above and below the town, and a desultory fire ensued between the belligerents, without any material damage to either side. In the afternoon the bridge was completed, and the advance crossed over.

Three miles beyond Port Gibson, on the Raymond road, the Union Army came across two large piles of bacon belonging to the rebel army, and at least of fifty thousand pounds weight. The army next came upon the upper causeway across the Bayou Pierre, which being a substantial iron suspension bridge, the rebels had not time to completely destroy, although they left behind them evidences of their attempts at its destruction.

This bridge repaired, the Union army passed over it, and came to the cross-roads near the site of an old town which once rejoiced in the name of Willow Springs. As the army was proceeding leisurely along the road, a battery opened upon them with shell at short range, causing a few casualties. The advance was next drawn up in line of battle, and moved slowly forward until the rebel position was attained. The enemy, however, then soon retired with unusual haste.

The advance of the Union army then pushed on to the bank of the Big Black River, where it arrived shortly before dark, and was received with a sharp fire of musketry. Lines of skirmishers were quickly formed, and the rebel troops driven across the river. Their rearguard attempted to destroy the pontoon bridge; but in this design they were frustrated by the rapid movements of the sharpshooters of the Union army. After exchanging a few shell and shot, all was quiet for a time.

This part of the army was seven miles beyond Grand Gulf, and within eighteen miles of Vicksburg. While passing through a deep ravine to reach the above position, the Union troops met a strong line of rebel skirmishers, and, after an engagement of about two hours, the latter retired, closely followed by the Unionists. Several prisoners were taken, from whom it was ascertained that Grand Gulf had been evacuated and the rebel magazine blown up. This was owing to two causes; first, the flanking of the position by General Grant, and secondly, the severe bombardment it received at the hands of Admiral Porter.

Finding that Grand Gulf had been evacuated, and that the advance of the Union forces was already fifteen miles on the road they would have to take to reach either Vicksburg, Jackson, or any point of the railroad between those cities, General Grant determined not to stop the troops in their victorious course, for the purpose of furnishing himself with an escort due to his rank, but took with him some fifteen men, and proceeded in person to the evacuated position, where he made the necessary arrangements for changing his base of supplies from Bruinsburg to Grand Gulf.

From this point General Grant telegraphed to the Government the complete success of the first part of his movement. It will be seen that the document was worded in the most modest manner, considering the value of the work accomplished, and was as follows:

GRAND GULF, MISS., *May* 3, 1863.

Major-General HALLECK, *General-in-Chief:*

We landed at Bruinsburg April 30th, moved immediately on Port Gibson, met the enemy, 11,000 strong, four miles south of Port Gibson, at two o'clock A. M., on the 1st inst., and engaged him all day, entirely routing him, with the loss of many killed, and about 500 prisoners, besides the wounded. Our loss is about 100 killed and 500 wounded.

The enemy retreated towards Vicksburg, destroying the bridges over the two forks of the Bayou Pierre. These were rebuilt, and the pursuit has continued until the present time.

Besides the heavy artillery at the place, four field-pieces were captured, and some stores, and the enemy were driven to destroy many more.

The country is the most broken and difficult to operate in I ever saw.

Our victory has been most complete, and the enemy is thoroughly demoralized. Very respectfully,

U. S. GRANT, *Major-General Commanding.*

Governor Yates, of Illinois, who was on a visit to the army at the time of the movement, and had necessarily to participate therein, telegraphed at the same time to the officials at his State Capital, as follows:

GRAND GULF, MISS., *May* 3, 1863.

We gained a glorious victory at Port Gibson, on the 1st instant.

The enemy are in full retreat. Our forces are in close pursuit. The Illinois troops, as usual, behaved with the greatest gallantry. The loss on our side is 150 killed and 500 wounded.

We have taken 1,000 prisoners. The loss of the enemy in killed and wounded was much greater than ours. RICHARD YATES.

On the same night that Grand Gulf had been taken possession of, several barges, loaded with stores, were sent down past the Vicksburg batteries. The firing was very heavy upon some of them, and a shell bursting in the midst of a quantity of cotton and hay, destroyed the vessels, and compelled those on board to surrender. The following is the rebel official dispatch of the occurrence:

VICKSBURG, *May* 4, 1863.

To General S. COOPER:

Last night two large barges, heavily laden with hospital and commissary stores, with a small tug between them, attempted to pass here. They were burned to the water's edge, and twenty-four prisoners taken from them, among whom are one correspondent of the New York *World*, two of the New York *Tribune*, and one of the Cincinnati *Times*.*

J. C. PEMBERTON, *Lieut.-Gen. Commanding.*

The day after the occupation of Grand Gulf, Governor Yates sent the following report of the operations of the few preceding days:

GRAND GULF, MISS., *May* 4, 1863.

Our arms are gloriously triumphant. *We have succeeded in winning a victory which, in its results, must be the most important of the war.* The battle of May 1st lasted from eight o'clock in the morning until night, during all which time the enemy was driven back on the right, left, and centre. All day yesterday our army was in pursuit of the rebels, they giving us battle at almost every defensible point, and fighting with desperate valor. Last night a large force of the enemy was driven across Black River, and General McClernand was driving another large force in the direction of Willow Springs. About two o'clock yesterday I left General Logan, with his division, in pursuit of the enemy, to join General Grant at Grand Gulf, which the enemy had evacuated in the morning, first blowing up their magazines, spiking their cannon, destroying tents, etc. *On my way to Grand Gulf I saw guns scattered all along the road, which the enemy had left in their retreat.* The rebels were scattered through the woods in every direction. *This army of the rebels was considered, as I now learn, invincible; but it quailed before the irresistible assaults of Northwestern valor.*

I consider Vicksburg as ours in a short time, and the Mississippi River as destined to be open from its source to its mouth.

I have been side by side with our boys in battle, and can bear witness to the unfaltering courage and prowess of our brave Illinoisans.

RICHARD YATES, *Governor.*

---

* Some of the unfortunate correspondents were in Libby Prison at the commencement of 1864.

CHAPTER XXXI.

OUTSIDE OPERATIONS.

General Grant, in order to deceive the rebel authorities at Richmond, Chattanooga, and elsewhere, as to the precise direction from which he intended to strike at Vicksburg, and also to prevent heavy re-enforcements from being sent to Grand Gulf from that place, ordered some very excellent feints to be made in all directions.

Among others, General Grant ordered Colonel Corwyn, with his Cavalry Brigade, to go down the Mobile and Ohio Railroad, on the east of his line of operations, and threaten an attack upon all the rebel posts along that road. On the 6th of May a fight took place between the Union cavalry and the rebel forces under General Ruggles, at Tupello, a railroad station in Itawamba county, Mississippi, and, after a half-hour's conflict, the rebels retreated in disorder, leaving behind them their arms, equipments, and ninety of their men prisoners.

On the north General Grant ordered a still more valuable feint. In moving from Milliken's Bend, the Fifteenth Army Corps had been set apart to bring up the rear, and, consequently, under that order, it was to be the last to start upon the southern march. General Sherman, commanding the Fifteenth Corps, had made every preparation to move by April 26th, 1863, on which day he received a letter from General Grant, who was then near New Carthage, ordering him to delay his march, *in consequence of* *the state of the roads*, until the system of canals, then in process of construction, could be completed.*

On the 28th of April, General Sherman received a letter in cipher, fixing the time when General Grant proposed to attack Grand Gulf, and stating that a simultaneous feint on the enemy's batteries near Haines Bluff, on the Yazoo River, would be most desirable, provided it could be done without the ill effect on the army and the country of an appearance of a repulse. Knowing full well that the army could distinguish a feint from a real attack, by succeeding events, General Sherman made the necessary orders, embarked the Second Division on ten steam transports, and sailed for the Yazoo River.

At about ten o'clock on the morning of April 29th, General Sherman with this force proceeded to the mouth of the Yazoo River, where he found several vessels of the fleet, ready to co-operate with the feigned movement. This fact alone proves how well General Grant and Admiral Porter had agreed upon the plan of operations, and how they worked in harmony together; neither one being jealous of the other's fame, but both being ready to do battle in their country's service, and for the common cause.

The united forces then proceeded at once up the Yazoo River, in proper order, and lay for the night of April 29th at the mouth of the Chickasaw Bayou. The next morning, at an early hour, the fleet proceeded up within easy range of the enemy's batteries. The gunboats at once made an attack upon the works, and for four hours a very pretty demonstration was kept up. The vessels were then called out of range, and toward evening General Sherman disembarked his troops, *in full view of the enemy*, making

* If this document had fallen into the hands of the enemy, no idea could have been obtained of the true motive of the delay.

preparations as if to assault the works. As soon as the landing was effected the gunboats reopened their fire upon the rebel defences.

The perceptible activity of the enemy, in moving the guns, artillery, and infantry, gave evidence that they expected a real attack; and keeping up a show of this intent until dark, General Sherman succeeded in accomplishing the full object of his *ruse*. At night the troops re-embarked; but during the whole of the next day similar movements were made, accompanied by reconnoissances of all the country on both sides of the Yazoo River. While thus engaged, General Sherman received instructions from General Grant to hasten and rejoin him at Grand Gulf.

The two divisions of General Sherman's Corps, that had remained at Milliken's Bend, were at once ordered to march, and to join General Grant by way of Richmond, Louisiana, while General Sherman, at the head of the Second Division, kept up his feint on the Yazoo River until night. General Sherman then quietly dropped back to his camp at Young's Point, when the whole corps, with the exception of one division left behind as a garrison, marched to Hard Times, four miles above Grand Gulf, on the Louisiana shore, where it arrived on the morning of May 6th, after travelling sixty-three miles on foot. During the night of the 6th, and the morning of the 7th, the forces were ferried over the river, and on the 8th commenced their march into the interior.

It appears also that a junction was to have been formed between the forces under General Grant and those under General Banks, but, in consequence of the position of the troops under the latter general, this movement was found to require a much greater delay and loss of time than General Grant could, under the circumstances, have afforded, as will be seen from the following extract from his official report:

About this time (May 4th), I received a letter from General Banks, giving his position west of the Mississippi River, and stating that he could return to Baton Rouge by the 10th of May; that by the reduction of Port Hudson he could join me with twelve thousand men.

I learned about the same time, that troops were expected at Jackson from the southern cities, with General Beauregard in command. To delay until the 10th of May, and for the reduction of Port Hudson after that, the accession of twelve thousand men would not leave me relatively so strong as to move promptly with what I had. Information received, from day to day, of the movements of the enemy, also impelled me to the course I pursued.

CHAPTER XXXII.

THE ADVANCE TOWARDS JACKSON.—BATTLE OF RAYMOND.

The army had, as before stated, advanced in light marching order, up to the occupation of Grand Gulf, after which it became necessary that trains should follow, as the three days rations set apart for each man at starting, had by this time been consumed. This naturally led to a short delay; but no longer time was occupied than was actually necessary. General Grant personally superintended the landing and distribution of the supplies, with the full determination that his campaign should not fail through any dereliction of duty on the part of his quartermasters or commissaries. In this he manifested one of the traits of a good soldier; as it is not merely essential to put an army into the field to secure victory, but it is also superlatively necessary, to insure the same result, that the army shall be properly fed, clothed, and sheltered, from the commencement to the close of the campaign. It is this forethought and care for the soldiers, that has secured for General Grant the love and veneration of every man under his command.

Having secured a sufficient amount of supplies to last him for a certain time, and having made arrangements for others to follow, General Grant removed his head-quarters, on the morning of May 7th, to Hawkinson's Ferry, on the Black River, leaving General Sherman's forces to garrison Grand Gulf for the few hours it was necessary to hold it, during the landing of the remainder of the supplies.

While lying at Hawkinson's Ferry, waiting for the wagons, supplies, and Sherman's Corps to come up, demonstrations were made to induce the enemy to believe, that the routes to Vicksburg by that ferry and the one by Hall's Ferry, which was a short distance higher up the river, were very desirable to General Grant. To impress this idea still further upon the minds of the rebel generals, reconnoitring parties were sent out along the roads, on the west side of the Big Black River, to within six miles of Warrenton. The artifice was completely successful.

In the mean time, all Mississippi was called to arms to resist the advance of General Grant. The following proclamation of the Governor of the State, will show the anxious feeling that existed in the hearts of the State authorities:

EXECUTIVE OFFICE,
JACKSON, MISS., May 5, 1863.

To the People of Mississippi:

Recent events, familiar to you all, impel me, as your Chief Magistrate, to appeal to your patriotism *for united effort in expelling our enemies from the soil of Mississippi. It can and must be done.* Let no man capable of bearing arms withhold from his State his services in repelling the invasion. Duty, interest, our common safety, demand every sacrifice necessary for the protection of our homes, our honor, liberty itself.

The exalted position won in her name upon every battle-field where Mississippi's sons have unfurled her proud banner, and hurled defiance in the face of overwhelming numbers, forbids that her honor, the chivalry of her people, the glory of her daring deeds on foreign fields, should be tarnished and her streaming battle flag dragged to the dust by barbarian hordes on her own soil.

Awake, then—arouse, Mississippians, young and old, from your fertile plains, your beautiful towns and cities, your once quiet and happy but now desecrated homes, come and join your brothers in arms, your sons and neighbors, who are now baring their bosoms to the storm of battle, at your very doors, and in defence of all you hold dear.

Meet in every county with your arms; organize companies of not less than twenty (under the late act of Congress), forward your muster rolls to this office, and you will be received into the service with all the protection and rights belonging to other soldiers in the field.

Ammunition will be furnished you, and every aid in my power extended to you for your security and efficiency

Fathers, brothers, Mississippians—while your sons and kindred are bravely fighting your battles on other fields, and shedding new lustre on your name, the burning disgrace of successful invasion of their homes, of insult and injury to their wives, mothers, and sisters, of rapine and ruin, with God's help and by your assistance, shall never be written while a Mississippian lives to feel in his proud heart the scorching degradation.

Every moment's inaction and delay but strengthens your enemy and weakens your brothers in arms. Let every man, then, make it his business, laying all else aside, to assist in organizing as many companies as can be raised in each county, and report immediately to this office for orders. By this course you will enable our arms in a short time to repel the invader, secure the safety of your homes, and shed imperishable honor on your cause. You will not be without assistance. *Let no man forego the proud distinction of being one of his country's defenders, or hereafter wear the disgraceful badge of the dastardly traitor who refused to defend his home and his country.*

JOHN J. PETTUS, *Governor of Mississippi.*

General Grant's plans had been too carefully studied and followed out, to be thwarted by any suddenly improvised forces that the Governor could then raise.

On the morning of the 7th of May, a general advance was ordered by General Grant. The Thirteenth Army Corps was directed to move along the ridge road from Wilton Springs; the Seventeenth Army Corps was to keep the road nearest the Black River to Rocky Springs; and the Fifteenth Army Corps was to divide in two parts and follow. All the ferries were closely guarded until the troops were well advanced, to prevent surprise on the flanks, and also to mislead the enemy as to the intention of the movement.

Before the troops were started on this march, the following congratulatory order was read at the head of every regiment:

HEAD-QUARTERS, ARMY OF THE TENNESSEE, IN THE FIELD,
HAWKINSON'S FERRY, *May 7th.*

Soldiers of the Army of Tennessee:

Once more I thank you for adding another victory to the long list of those previously won by your valor and endurance. *The triumph gained over the enemy near Port Gibson, on the 1st, was one of the most important of the war.* The capture of five cannon and more than one thousand prisoners, the possession of Grand Gulf, and a firm foothold on the highlands between the Big Black and Bayou Pierre, from whence we threaten the whole line of the enemy, are among the fruits of this brilliant achievement.

The march from Milliken's Bend to the point opposite Grand Gulf was made in stormy weather, over the worst of roads. Bridges and ferries had to be constructed. Moving by night as well as by day, with labor incessant, and extraordinary privations endured by men and officers, such as have been rarely paralleled in any campaign, not a murmur of complaint has been uttered. A few days continuance of the same zeal and constancy will secure to this army crowning victories over the rebellion.

More difficulties and privations are before us; let us endure them manfully. Other battles are to be fought; let us fight them bravely. *A grateful country will rejoice at our success, and history will record it with immortal honor.* U. S. GRANT, *Major-General Commanding.*

It appears from General Grant's official report of the Vicksburg Campaign, that it had been his intention, while at Hawkinson's Ferry, to have moved the Thirteenth and Fifteenth Army Corps in such a manner as to hug the Black River as closely as possible, in order that they might be able to strike the Jackson and Vicksburg Railroad at some point between Edwards's Station and Bolton. The Seventeenth Army Corps was to move by way of Utica to Raymond, thence to Jackson, at which place, and in its vicinity, it was intended that the railroad, telegraph, public stores, etc., should be destroyed, after which the corps was to move west and rejoin the main army.

The following is an account of the primary movements of the army, by one who took part in its operations from its organization to the capitulation of Vicksburg:

On Thursday, the 7th of May, General McPherson, commanding the Seventeenth Army Corps, moved his troops to Rocky Springs, and his camp was occupied next day by General Sherman, with the Fifteenth Army Corps. On Saturday, the 9th, General McPherson again moved to the eastward, to the village of Utica, crossing the road occupied by the Thirteenth Army Corps under General McClernand, and leaving the latter on his left. On Sunday morning, the 10th, General McClernand marched to Five Mile Creek, and encamped on the south bank at noon, on account of broken bridges, which were repaired the same day. On Monday morning, the 11th, General Sherman's Corps came up, passed, General McClernand's, and encamped that night at the village of Auburn, about ten miles south of Edwards's Station, which is on a portion of the railroad from Vicksburg to Jackson. As soon as it passed, General McClernand's corps followed a few miles, and then took a road going obliquely to the left, leading to Hall's Ferry, on the Big Black River. Thus on Monday evening, May 11th, General McClernand was at Hall's Ferry; General Sherman was at Auburn, six or eight miles to the northeast, and General McPherson was about eight miles still further to the northeast, a few miles north of Utica. The whole formed an immense line of battle; Sherman's Corps being in the centre, with those of McPherson and McClernand forming the right and left wings. It will be observed, also, that a change of front had been effected. From Grand Gulf the army marched eastward; but, by these last movements, it had swung on the left as a pivot, and fronted nearly northward.

Up to this the enemy had not appeared on our line of march. On Tuesday morning, May 12th, General McClernand's advance drove in the enemy's pickets near Hall's Ferry, and brisk skirmishing ensued for an hour or two, with little loss to either side. By noon the rebels had disappeared from his front, and seven wounded and none killed was the total Union loss. General Sherman put Steele's Division in motion early in the morning, and came upon the enemy at the crossing of Fourteen Mile creek, four miles from Auburn. The cavalry advance was fired into from the thick woods that skirt the stream, and was unable, owing to the nature of the ground, to make a charge or clear the rebels from their position. A battery was taken to the front, supported by the two infantry regiments, and threw a few shell into the bushy undergrowth skirting the stream which gave them cover. Skirmishers was thrown out and advanced to the creek, driving the enemy slowly. A brigade was thrown to the right and left flanks, when the rebel forces, mainly cavalry, withdrew towards Raymond. The bridge was burned during the skirmish; but a crossing was constructed in two hours, and trains were passing before noon.*

General Grant was not behind his troops; but as they advanced, he continually changed his head-quarters and his line of communications, keeping with the centre of the army for the purpose of better directing the movements of his three columns.

When he had advanced far enough into the field to be sure of his position, he sent the following telegraphic message to the government at Washington:

IN THE FIELD, *May* 11, 1863.

To Major-General HALLECK, *General-in-Chief:*

My force will be this evening as far advanced along Fourteen Mile Creek, the left near Black River, and extending in a line nearly east and west, as they can get without bringing on a general engagement.

I shall communicate with Grand Gulf no more, except it becomes necessary to send a train with a heavy escort.

You may not hear from me again for several days.

U. S. GRANT, *Major-General.*

The foregoing dispatch plainly sets forth that General Grant in his plans had intended to cut an opening through the enemy's lines, and communicate with the General-in-chief by a more northern route. When the dispatch was sent from General Grant, he plainly foresaw the success of this plan, and as he personally superintended all the movements of his army, and had not to depend upon any other outside co-operation than that of the fleet, he doubtless felt sure he could not fail through any lack of proper combination at the right time. He also, by breaking up this line of communication by way of Grand Gulf, prevented the enemy from cutting off his supplies, and he

* Army correspondence of the *New York Herald.*

had taken the precaution to have with him all that was needed until he was ready to open up the new line by the Yazoo.

The Fifteenth Army Corps moved forward on the Edwards Station road, and crossed the Fourteen Mile Creek at Dillon's plantation. The Thirteenth Army Corps crossed the same Creek, some short distance further west, making a demonstration along the road towards Bald win's Ferry, as if to advance upon Vicksburg or Warrenton by that route.

While crossing the Fourteen Mile Creek, both corps had to skirmish considerably with the enemy in order to gain possession of the right of way; but under the persistent attacks of the determined Union troops, the rebels had to give way, and the Union army moved towards the railroad in splendid order.

In the meantime the Seventeenth Army Corps was steadily advancing upon Raymond, but met with no small opposition from the rebels, who were stationed in two brigades under Generals Gregg and Walker, at a point of the road about two miles southwest of that village. General Logan's Division came upon the rebel troops, estimated at about ten thousand, posted on Fondren's Creek, at ten o'clock on Tuesday morning, May 12th, and brisk skirmishing began at once, followed by a general engagement. The enemy (as in front of General Sherman) was almost wholly concealed at first by the woods bordering the stream, behind which their forces were posted. Their artillery was on an eminence that commanded the approach, and the Union troops had to cross an open field, exposed to a terrible fire. The First and Second Brigades were in the thickest of the contest, and suffered most. After three hours' hard fighting, the enemy withdrew sullenly in two columns, the principal one taking the road to Jackson.

General Grant, in his report of this action, states that the fighting was very hard; that the enemy were driven, with heavy loss in killed, wounded, and prisoners; and that many of the rebels threw down their arms and deserted their cause.

When General Grant discovered that the enemy had retreated from Raymond to Jackson, he, on the night of May 12th, diverted the Thirteenth and Fifteenth Army Corps from their intended route, and ordered them both to move towards Raymond, at which place he established his head-quarters on the evening of May 13th.

The next day General Grant sent the following dispatch by way of Memphis:

RAYMOND, MISS., *May* 14, 1863.

Major-General HALLECK, *General-in-Chief:*

McPherson took this place on the 12th inst., after a brisk fight of more than two hours.

Our loss was fifty-one killed, and one hundred and eighty wounded. The enemy's loss was seventy-five killed (buried by us) and one hundred and eighty-six prisoners captured, besides the wounded.

McPherson is now at Clinton. General Sherman is on the direct Jackson road, and General McClernand is bringing up the rear.

I will attack the State capital to-day.

U. S. GRANT, *Major-General.*

The commander at Memphis, before receiving the above dispatch from General Grant, sent the following to Wash ington:

MEMPHIS, TENN., *May* 17, 1863.

Major-General HALLECK, *General-in-Chief:*

Papers of the 14th from Vicksburg and Jackson report that Grant defeated Gregg's Brigade at Raymond, on Tuesday, the 12th. The rebel loss is admitted in the papers at seven hundred.

The next day Gregg was re-enforced by General W. H. T. Walker, of Georgia, when he was attacked at Mississippi Spring, and driven toward Jackson on Thursday.

General Joseph Johnston arrived at Jackson on the 13th, and went out toward Vicksburg with three brigades.

The force which General Grant fought, viz., Gregg's Brigade, was from Port Hudson, while Walker's was from Jordan.

Every horse fit for service in Mississippi is claimed by the rebel government to mount their troops.

Grant has struck the railroad.

S. A. HURLBUT, *Major-General.*

CHAPTER XXXIII.

THE CAPTURE AND OCCUPATION OF JACKSON.

THE Seventeenth Army Corps had moved up to Clinton, on the Jackson and Vicksburg Railroad, during the previous day, May 13th, so as to be able to make the movement along that railroad to Jackson, simultaneously with that of the Fifteenth Army Corps by way of the Raymond and Jackson turnpike road.

Clinton was no sooner taken possession of, than parties were sent out to destroy the track and telegraph, and while engaged on this duty, several important dispatches from General Pemberton to General Gregg, both of the rebel forces, were captured and taken to General Grant's head-quarters.

As the Seventeenth Army Corps advanced along the railroad, a parallel line of march was kept up by the Fifteenth Army Corps, along the turnpike road by way of Mississippi Springs, while the Thirteenth Army Corps occupied Raymond.

On May 14th, the Fifteenth and Seventeenth Corps moved with their whole force then present on the field, upon Jackson—the march being made amidst a heavy storm of rain, which fell in torrents from midnight of the 13th until noon of the 14th. The roads were therefore in the most horrible condition, at first slippery, next ankle deep in mud. "Notwithstanding this," says General Grant, in his report, "the troops marched in excellent order, without straggling, and in the best of spirits, nearly fourteen miles, and engaged the enemy at about twelve o'clock, noon, near Jackson."

As the two corps marched toward Jackson, the Thirteenth Corps garrisoned the places they had vacated, one division occupying Clinton, another holding Mississippi Springs, while a third took possession of Raymond. General Blair's division of the Fifteenth Corps guarded the wagon train at New Auburn, and the road to Utica was held by an advancing brigade of the Seventeenth Corps that had not, since the movement commenced, been joined to the main column. These forces were kept back as a corps of reserve, if necessary, and ready to move in either direction towards Jackson or Vicksburg.

When General Joseph E. Johnston, who commanded the rebel forces at Jackson, discovered that Grant's troops were marching upon him, he determined to meet them on the outside of the city, and delay this advance as long as possible, to give him an opportunity to remove a portion if not the whole of the property of the rebel government, then at Jackson. As his forces were small in numbers, he ordered a feigned resistance to be made with artillery, supported by a small force of infantry, against the advance of the Fifteenth Army Corps by the turnpike road, while, with the bulk of his army, he marched out on the Clinton road and engaged the Seventeenth Corps about two and a half miles from the city.

The determined advance of the skirmishers of the Fifteenth Corps soon drove in the resistance in their front, and the rebels took refuge in their rifle-pits, which had been thrown up just outside the city of Jackson. General Sherman, the commander of the Fifteenth Corps, soon discovered the weakness of the enemy by means of a reconnoissance to his right, and this flank movement caused an evacuation of the rebel position on this part of their line.

Meanwhile, General McPherson, at the head of two divisions of the Seventeenth Corps, engaged the main bulk of the rebel forces from Jackson without any support, or requiring any further aid. After a very spirited contest of over two hours' duration, he defeated the rebel forces, and the dispirited and beaten troops retreated northward, along the Canton road, leaving the city in the hands of the conquerors. A pursuit was immediately ordered; but the rebels had escaped; their retreat having been made in the greatest haste.

The following is General Grant's modest dispatch concerning this brilliant operation:

JACKSON, MISS., *May* 15, 1863.

Major-General H. W. HALLECK, *General-in-Chief, Washington:*

This place fell into our hands yesterday, after a fight of about three hours.

Joe Johnston was in command.

The enemy retreated north, evidently with the design of joining the Vicksburg forces.

U. S. GRANT, *Major-General.*

General Grant entered the town of Jackson on the afternoon of the 14th, and held a consultation with the commanders of the two corps which had taken possession of the city. To prevent any unjustifiable plunder or marauding, the troops were encamped on the outskirts of the city during the night. General Grant ordered the rifle-pits to be occupied at once, and on the following day to destroy effectually the railroad tracks in and about Jackson, and all the property belonging to the enemy.

Accordingly, on the morning of May 15th, one division was set to work to destroy the railroad and property to the south and east of the city, including the Pearl River bridge, while another division was engaged on the road to the north and west. This work of destruction was so well performed, that the utility of Jackson as a railroad or military centre, or as a dépôt of stores or military supplies, was completely destroyed for the time being. The roads were laid waste for at least four miles to the east of Jackson, three miles south, three miles north, and nearly ten miles west. Cavalry raids were also sent along the road running towards Meridian, and cut the railroad at Brandon and elsewhere.

In the city itself, the arsenal building, government foundery, a gun carriage establishment, including the carriages for two complete batteries of artillery, military carpenter's shop, stables and paint shops were at once destroyed. Some convicts who had broken loose succeeded in setting fire to the penitentiary during the time the military were thus engaged. A valuable cotton factory was also demolished. General Sherman, in speaking of the destruction of this establishment, says: "This factory was the property of the Messrs. Greene, who made strong appeals, based on the fact that it gave employment to very many females and poor families; and that, although it had woven cloth for the enemy, its principal use was in weaving cloth for the people. But I decided that machinery of that kind could so easily be converted into hostile uses, that the United States could better afford to compensate the Messrs. Greene for their property, and for the poor families thus thrown out of employment, than to spare the property. I therefore assured all such families that if want should force them, they might come to the river, where we would feed them until they could find employment or seek refuge in some more peaceful land."

The following letter from an army correspondent contains incidents of interest concerning the march to and occupation of the city of Jackson:—

The Union army have undisturbed possession of Jackson, the capital of Mississippi, and the head-quarters of the Rebel Department of Mississippi and Eastern Louisiana. The Federal flag floats gracefully from the dome of the State House, Yankee soldiers are patroling the streets, prisoners are gathering at the guardhouse, the sick in the hospitals are being paroled, negroes are grinning from the sidewalks, citizens look silently and sullenly at us from behind screens and closed window-blinds, and all the details of military government are in full operation.

We encamped at Raymond on Tuesday night, and early Wednesday morning started for Clinton, a small town on the Vicksburg and Jackson Railroad. It was considered indispensably necessary for the success of our movement upon Vicksburg, that we should have possession of the railroad and the city of Jackson. We reached Clinton at nightfall, and went into camp.

During the night, a regiment, under the command of Captain Tresilian, of General Logan's staff, moved out on the railroad east and west of Clinton, and destroyed it, tearing up the rails and burning every bridge and the timbers across every cattle guard for four miles each side of the village. The telegraph office and the post office were seized and rifled of their precious contents. From this source most valuable information of the enemy's future movements was obtained. In the express packages left by the train of cars which steamed out of town just as our advance came in sight, several orders from General Johnston were discovered, and a package of Confederate scrip.

At Clinton a hundred prisoners were found, occupants of rebel hospitals. These were paroled, and taken in charge by the citizens.

At daylight Thursday morning, the army was on the road to Jackson, moving in line of battle. A strong advance guard was thrown out, and a heavy line of skirmishers on the right and left flank, and thus we moved in the direction of the city,

All was quiet for the first five or six miles, until we reached a hill overlooking a broad open field, through the centre of which, and over the crest of the hill beyond which the road to Jackson passes. On the left of this hill the enemy had posted his artillery, and along the crest his line of battle. From the foot of the acclivity, and not a mile removed, we could see the long line of rebel infantry awaiting in silence our onset. Slowly and cautiously we moved up the hill until we came within range, when all at once, upon the heights to the right, we discovered a puff of white smoke and heard the report of booming cannon, followed by the shrill scream of an exploding shell. One of our batteries was moved to the left of a cotton gin in the open field, midway between the enemy's line of battle and the foot of the hill, and played upon the rebel battery with telling effect. The duel was kept up with great spirit on both sides for nearly an hour, when all at once it ceased by the withdrawal of the enemy's guns. Two brigades were thrown out to the right and left of this battery, supported by another brigade at proper distance. A strong line of skirmishers had been pushed forward and posted in a ravine just in front, which protected them from rebel fire. After a little delay, they were again advanced out of cover, and for several minutes a desultory fire was kept up between both lines of skirmishers, in which, owing to the topographical nature of the ground, the enemy had the advantage.

At last General Crocker, who was on the field and had personally inspected the position, saw that, unless the enemy could be driven from his occupation of the crest of the hill, he would be forced to retire. He therefore ordered a charge along the line. With colors flying, and with a step as measured and unbroken as if on dress parade, the movement was executed. Slowly they advanced, crossed the narrow ravine, and, with fixed bayonets, rose the crest of the hill in easy range of the rebel line. Here they received a tremendous volley, which caused painful gaps in their ranks. They held their fire until they were within a distance of thirty paces, when they delivered the returning volley with fearful effect, and, without waiting to reload their muskets, with a terrific yell they rushed upon the staggered foe.

Over the fences, through the brushwood, into the enclosure, they worked their way, and slaughtered right and left without mercy. The enemy, astonished at their impetuosity, wavered and fell back, rallied again, and finally broke in wild confusion. The brave Union soldiers gained the crest of the hill, and the rebels fled in utter terror. Our boys reloaded their muskets and sent the terrible missiles after the fleeing rebels, adding haste to their terrified flight. They cast muskets and blankets to the ground, unslung their knapsacks, and ran like greyhounds, nor stopped to look back until they reached the intrenchments just within the city.

Meantime General Sherman, who had left Raymond the day before, and taken the road to the right just beyond the town, came up with the left wing of the enemy's forces and engaged them with artillery. They made a feeble resistance, and they, too, broke and ran.

After a delay of half an hour, to enable our wearied soldiers to take breath, our column moved forward again.

We reached the fort, and found a magnificent battery of six pieces, which the enemy had left behind him, and a hundred new tents, awaiting appropriation.

The hospital flag was flying from the Deaf and Dumb Institute, and this was crowded with sick and wounded soldiers, who, of course, fell into our hands as prisoners of war. Opposite and all around this building were tents enough to encamp an entire division, and just in front of it, hauled out by the roadside, were two small breech-loading two-pounder rifles, which had been used to pick off officers.

Further down the street we found a pile of burning caissons, and on the opposite side of the street, directly in front of the Confederate House, the stores, filled with commissary and quartermaster's supplies, were briskly consuming.

Directly in front of us the State House loomed up in ample proportions. Two officers, taking possession of the flag of one of the regiments, galloped rapidly forward, and hoisted it from the flag-staff surmounting its broad dome. The beautiful flag was seen in the distance by the advancing column, and with cheers and congratulations it was greeted.

We had captured Jackson, the hotbed of the rebellion. Guards were established, a provost-marshal appointed, and the city placed under martial law. The citizens, particularly those who sustained official relations to the State and rebel governments, had left the city the evening before; but there were many soldiers left behind, and a large number in hospital, who fell into our hands.

The State Treasurer and Governor Pettus* were gone, taking the funds and State papers with them. A large amount of government and military property fell into our hands; but private property was altogether unmolested. The offices of the Memphis *Appeal* and Jackson *Mississippian* were removed the preceding night—the former to Brandon and the latter to Mobile.

We now have quiet and undisturbed possession of Jackson.

One portion of the rebel force has moved out on the Canton road, and the other on the road south of the city, whence they will both doubtless make a detour around Jackson, outside of our lines, and unite at Edwards's Station, on the Vicksburg and Jackson Railroad, where the citizens say they will give us battle.†

---

* See Proclamation in Chapter XXXII., pages 228, 229.

† *New York Herald* correspondence, under date of Jackson, Miss., May 14th, 1863.

CHAPTER XXXIV.

THE ADVANCE RENEWED.—CHAMPION'S HILL.

General Grant, after he had taken possession of the State capital of Mississippi on May 14th, obtained some very important information relative to the plans of the rebel army, and among other things ascertained that General Johnston had ordered General Pemberton peremptorily to move out of Vicksburg and attack the United States forces in the rear. As soon as General Grant was satisfied of the correctness of this information, he at once ordered the Thirteenth Army Corps and General Blair's Division of the Fifteenth Army Corps to face their troops toward Bolton, with a view of marching upon Edwards's Station. These troops being admirably located for such a move, marched along different roads converging near Bolton, and the movement resulted in a complete success. The Seventeenth Army Corps was ordered to retrace its steps to Clinton, and commenced its march early on the morning of the 15th of May. The balance of the Fifteenth Army Corps was left at Jackson to destroy every thing that might have been or was capable of being used in a hostile manner by the enemy.

At half past nine o'clock on the morning of the 15th of May, a division of the Thirteenth Army Corps occupied Bolton, capturing a number of prisoners, and driving away the rebel pickets from the post.

On the afternoon of the same day, General Grant removed his head-quarters to Clinton,* where he arrived at about a quarter to five o'clock P. M.

The Seventeenth Army Corps having passed through Clinton to the support of the right of the Thirteenth Corps, General Grant ordered General McClernand to move his command early the next morning upon Edwards's station, marching so as to feel the enemy; but not to bring on a general engagement unless he felt sure of defeating the force before him. In accordance with this order, cavalry reconnoissances were sent out toward the picket lines of the enemy; three good roads were discovered leading from the Bolton and Raymond road to Edwards's station; and on the night of the fifteenth of May, the necessary orders were given for the advance of the corps on the morrow.

The following account of the battle of Champion's Hill is given by a participant:

The programme of the advance was arranged by General Grant and General McClernand as follows:—Extreme left, General Smith, supported by General Blair: on the right of General Smith, General Osterhaus, supported by General Carr: General Hovey in the centre, with General McPherson's Corps on the extreme right, with General Crocker, as reserve. In this order the advance was made. General McClernand's Corps, with the exception of General Hovey's Division, reaching the position by way of the several roads leading from Raymond to Edwards's Station.

On the evening of the 15th, General McClernand heard that the enemy were advancing from Edwards's Station, and quickly placed his troops in order of battle to repel the anticipated attack. Extensive reconnoissances revealed the fact, however, that he was merely feeling his position and force, and that no attack need be expected that day.

The enemy's first demonstration was upon our extreme left, which

* It will be plainly seen that during the successive changes in the position of the army, General Grant was always in the immediate vicinity of his fighting troops, directing their movements.

they attempted to turn. This attempt was most gallantly repulsed by General Smith, commanding the left wing. At seven o'clock the skirmishers were actively engaged; and as the enemy sought the cover of the forest our artillery fire was opened, which continued without intermission for two hours. At this time General Ransom's Brigade marched on the field, and took up a position as reserve behind General Carr.

Now the battle raged fearfully along the entire line, the evident intention of the enemy being to mass his forces upon Hovey on the centre. There the fight was most earnest; but General McPherson brought his forces into the field, and after four hours hard fighting the tide of battle was turned and the enemy forced to retire.

Disappointed in his movements upon our right, the rebels turned their attention to the left of Hovey's division, where Colonel Slack commanded a brigade of Indianians. Massing his forces here, the enemy hurled them against the opposing columns with irresistible impetuosity, and forced them to fall back: not, however, until at least one quarter of the troops comprising the brigade were either killed or wounded. Taking a new position, and receiving fresh re-enforcements, our soldiers again attempted to stem the tide, this time with eminent success. The enemy was beaten back, and compelled to seek the cover of the forest in his rear. Following up their advantage, without waiting to reform, the soldiers of the Western army fixed their bayonets and charged into the woods after them. The rebels were seized with an uncontrollable panic, and thought only of escape. In this terrible charge men were slaughtered without mercy. The ground was literally covered with the dead and dying. The enemy scattered in every direction, and rushed through the fields to reach the column now moving to the west along the Vicksburg road. At three o'clock in the afternoon, the battle was over and the victory won.

Of the part taken in this battle by McPherson's Corps, it is only necessary to say that it rendered the most efficient and satisfactory assistance. To it belongs the credit of winning the fight on the extreme right.

The battle ended, the left wing was speedily advanced upon the Vicksburg road, driving the enemy rapidly before them, and picking up as they advanced numbers of prisoners and guns.

On the left of the road we could see large squads of rebel soldiers and commands cut off from the main column, and whom we engaged at intervals with artillery.

Thus we pursued the enemy until nearly dark, when we entered the little village, known by the name of Edwards's Station, just as the enemy was leaving it.

When within rifle range of the station, we discovered, on the left, a large building in flames, and on the right a smaller one from which, just then, issued a series of magnificent explosions. The former contained commissary stores, and the latter shell and ammunition—five car-loads—brought down from Vicksburg on the morning of the day of the battle. In their hasty exit from Edwards's Station the rebels could not take this ammunition with them, but consigned it to the flames rather than it should fall into our hands. We bivouac in line of battle to-night, and to-morrow move upon the bridge across Big Black River.*

The following extracts from General McClernand's official report will also prove interesting, inasmuch as it sets forth the part taken by General Grant in this brilliant affair:

The different divisions were started at different hours, in consequence of the different distances they had to march, which was designed to secure a parallel advance of the different columns. Believing that General Hovey's Division needed support, I sent a dispatch to General Grant, requesting that General McPherson's Corps should also move forward. Assurances altogether satisfactory were given by the General, and I felt confident of our superiority.

After alluding to the demonstrations made in the early part of the contest, General McClernand continues:—

Early notifying Major-General Grant and Major-General McPherson what had transpired on the left, I requested the latter to co-operate with my forces on the right, and directed General Hovey to advance promptly but carefully, and received a dispatch from General Hovey informing me that he had found the enemy strongly posted in front; that General McPherson's Corps was behind him; that his right flank would probably encounter severe resistance; and inquiring whether he should bring on the impending battle. My command was now about four miles from Edwards's Station, and immediately informing Major-General Grant, *whom I understood to be on the field*, of the position of affairs, I inquired whether I should bring on a general engagement. A dispatch from the General,

* Army correspondence of the *New York Herald*, May 30, 1863.

dated at thirty-five minutes past noon, came, directing me to throw forward skirmishers as soon as my forces were on hand, to feel and attack the enemy in force, if opportunity occurred, *and informing me that he was with Hovey and McPherson, and would see that they fully co-operated.* Meanwhile, a line of skirmishers had encountered Generals Osterhaus and Smith's Divisions, closing up the narrow space between them. * * These measures had been taken in *compliance with General Grant's orders, based on information of which he had advised me, that the enemy was in greatest strength in front of my centre and left, and might turn my left flank and gain my rear.* * * * Instantly upon the receipt of *General Grant's order to attack*, I hastened to do so.

Then follows an account of that part of the battle in which the Thirteenth Army Corps participated, the details of which will be found in the army correspondence immediately preceding the foregoing extracts, and in General Grant's report.*

The following is General Johnston's dispatch announcing the defeat of the rebel forces:

CAMP BETWEEN LIVINGSTON AND BROWNSVILLE, MISS.,
May 18, 1863.

To General S. COOPER:

Lieutenant-General Pemberton was attacked by the enemy on the morning of the 16th inst., near Edwards's Dépôt, and, after nine hours fighting, was compelled to fall back behind the Big Black.

J. E. JOHNSTON, *General-Commanding.*

The dispatch also shows the position of the forces that retreated from Jackson, and how, by General Grant's rapid movements, they had been cut off from forming a junction with Pemberton.

---

* Appendix G.

CHAPTER XXXV.

BATTLE OF BIG BLACK RIVER.

Before leaving Clifton, General Grant notified General Sherman of the approaching engagement at Edwards's Station, and ordered him to advance upon Bolton as quickly as possible. The dispatch was received on the morning of May 16th, and with his usual promptitude one of his divisions marched at ten o'clock in the forenoon, and he followed with the other at noon.

The whole corps marched during that day from Jackson to Bolton, nearly twenty miles, and the next morning, May 17th, by order of General Grant, resumed the march by a road lying north of Baker's Creek to Bridgeport on the Big Black River, where it arrived at noon. At this point General Blair's Divison, also by order of General Grant, rejoined the command.

The success at Champion's Hill was the cause of this change of route, and as the enemy had fallen back over the Big Black River towards Vicksburg, it was necessary that means of crossing should be supplied to the pursuing troops. When General Sherman arrived at Bridgeport, he found that General Grant had looked after this vital point, for in his official report he says: "There I found General Blair's Division *and the pontoon train.*" The pontoon bridge was laid, and two divisions crossed the river that night, the third following the next morning.

The defeated rebels fell back from Edwards's Station to

the Black River, which they crossed by means of the railroad bridge. At daylight on May 17th, the pursuit was renewed with General McClernand's Thirteenth Army Corps in the advance. The enemy was found strongly posted on both sides of the Black River. At this point of the stream the bluffs extend to the water's edge on the west or Vicksburg bank, while on the east side is an open, cultivated bottom of nearly one mile in width, surrounded by a bayou of stagnant water from two to three feet in depth, and from ten to twenty feet in width, running from the river above the railroad to the river below. The enemy, by constructing a line of rifle-pits along the inside edge of this bayou, had formed it into a natural ditch before a fortified work. The spot was well chosen for defence, and gave to the enemy every advantage.

The position had, however, to be carried before Vicksburg could be reached; and notwithstanding the level ground over which a portion of the troops had to pass without cover, and the great obstacle of the bayou in front of the enemy's works, the charge was gallantly and successfully made, and in a few minutes the entire garrison with seventeen pieces of artillery were the trophies of this brilliant and daring movement.

When the rebels on the west bank of the river discovered that the position on the level below was sure to be taken, they destroyed the railroad bridge by fire with the intent of preventing General Grant's army from crossing the Big Black River: but in this operation they merely cut off every chance of escape for the garrison on the eastern bank, and the men were therefore all taken prisoners with their arms and equipments.

An eye-witness of the struggle at the Black River bridge gives the following account of the battle:

The battle of Big Black bridge was fought on Sunday, May 17th, the day after the battle of Cham)on's Hill. In this spirited engagement only the Thirteenth Army Corps was engaged. It is superfluous to add that the troops comprising this corps fought as they always do, excellently well.* In the morning, after a night's bivouac on the hill overlooking the village of Edwards's Station, the column with McClernand at its head moved towards Black River bridge. The citizens who were questioned on the subject, said the position was strongly fortified at the crossing, and we naturally thought the enemy would make stubborn resistance there. We were not surprised, therefore, to learn that our advance guard was fired upon by the rebel pickets as the column moved towards the river.

The country between Edwards's Station and the bridge loses that hilly and broken character which distinguishes the region further east, and spreads out into a broad and fertile plain, over which we moved rapidly. There were no commanding hills whence they could pour a deadly fire into our ranks; but there were numerous patches of forest, under the cover and from the edge of which they could easily enfilade the open fields by the roadside. There was such a one a mile east of the intrenchments where the main picket-guard was stationed. Here determined resistance was first made.

General Carr's division had the extreme advance of the column, and opened and ended the engagement. Hastily deploying a heavy line of skirmishers to the right of the road, backed up by the two brigades of Carr's Division in line of battle behind it, with General Osterhaus's Division on the left of the road similarly disposed, General McClernand gave the order to advance. Soon in the depths of the thick forest the skirmishers of both armies were hotly engaged, while batteries of artillery planted on the right and left of the road poured shot and shell into the fort most furiously. The guns in the intrenchments replied with vigor and spirit. Almost the first shot dropped in the caisson belonging to a Wisconsin battery, and exploded its contents, slightly wounding General Osterhaus, and Captain Foster, of the battery, and very seriously injuring two gunners. General Osterhaus being thus disabled, the command of his division was temporarily given to Brigadier-General A. L. Lee.

After skirmishing had continued for an hour, during which the enemy gave way and sought the cover of his intrenchments, the order was given to the several brigade commanders, on the right, to advance and charge

* It will be remembered that this corps was mostly composed of troops who had participated in the contests of Fort Donelson, Shiloh, and Corinth, under General Grant.

the enemy's works. The order was received with cheers; and when the word "Forward" was spoken, steadily and splendidly the brave boys moved up to the assault. The enemy crouched down behind the breastworks. A portion of them, stationed in a curtain of the fort, whence they were able to get a cross-fire upon the column, reserved their volley until we were within easy musket range of the intrenchments, when they swept the advancing line with their terrible fire. The brave boys lost in that fearful volley one hundred and fifty men; yet they faltered not nor turned their steps backward. They waded the bayou, delivering their fire as they reached the other bank, and rushed upon the enemy with fixed bayonets. So quickly was all this accomplished, that the enemy had not time to reload their guns, and were forced to surrender.

The battle was ended, and the fort, with three thousand prisoners, seventeen pieces of artillery—some of them captured from ourselves, and bearing appropriate inscriptions—several thousand stand of arms, and a large supply of corn and commissary stores, fell into our hands.

The enemy had, earlier in the day, out of the hulls of three steamboats, constructed a bridge, over which he had passed the main body of his army. As the charge was made, and it became evident that we should capture the position, they burned this bridge, and also the railroad bridge across the river just above.

In the afternoon several attempts were made to cross the river, but the sharpshooters lined the bluffs beyond and entirely prevented it. Later, the main body of sharpshooters were dispersed by our artillery. It was not, however, safe to stand upon the bank, or cross the open field east of the bridge, until after dark, when the enemy withdrew altogether.*

---

* *New York Herald* correspondence, under date of May 17th, 1863.

CHAPTER XXXVI.

APPROACHING VICKSBURG.—INVESTMENT.—FIRST ASSAULT.

General Sherman, with the Fifteenth Corps, during the time the battle of Black River was being fought, had as before stated, reached Bridgeport. By the morning of May 18th, he had crossed his command to the west side of the Black River, and was ready for the onward march. It appears, by General Grant's report, that "the only pontoon train with the expedition was with him;" and as the rebels had destroyed the railroad bridge, it became necessary, in order to get the Thirteenth and Seventeenth Corps across the river, to build floating bridges, which were constructed during the night of May 17th, and early morning of the next day.

At eight o'clock, on the morning of May 18th, the two army corps were ready to make the crossing. The Fifteenth Corps was now ordered in the advance, and commenced moving along the Bridgeport and Vicksburg road at a very early hour.

As the corps arrived within three and a half miles of Vicksburg, the men turned to the right, to get possession of the Walnut Hills, and to open a communication with the fleet in the Yazoo River. This manœuvre was successfully accomplished by the evening of May 18th.

The Seventeenth Corps followed the Jackson road until it connected with the same road previously taken by the Fifteenth. The former then took up the line of march to the rear of the latter, and at about nightfall arrived at the point of the road where General Sherman had turned off towards the Yazoo River.

The Thirteenth Corps had moved by the Jackson and Vicksburg road to Mount Albans, whence it turned to the left, for the purpose of striking the Baldwin's Ferry road.

"By this disposition," says General Grant, "the three army corps covered all the ground their strength would admit of, and by the morning of the 19th of May the investment of Vicksburg was made as complete as could be by the forces under my command."

As the army advanced, it was continually met by the rebel skirmishers, who fell back steadily to their works before the city. "Relying," says General Grant, "upon the demoralization of the enemy, in consequence of repeated defeats outside of Vicksburg, I ordered a general assault at two P. M., on this day."

At the appointed signal, the line of the Fifteenth Army Corps advanced, and made a vigorous assault; but the other two corps succeeded only in securing advanced positions, where they were covered from the enemy's fire.

The ground to the right and left of the road by which the Fifteenth Corps advanced, was cut up in deep chasms, filled with standing and fallen timber, and was so impracticable that the line was slow and irregular in reaching the trenches. The object was, however, finally attained, and the colors of the Thirteenth U. S. Infantry planted on the exterior slope of the works. But this was not accomplished without serious loss. General Sherman reports that the "commander of the regiment was mortally wounded, and five other officers were wounded more or less severely. Seventy-seven, out of two hundred and fifty men, are reported killed or wounded." Two other regiments reached the position about the same time, held their ground, and fired upon any head that presented itself above the parapet;

but it was found impossible to enter the works. The fight was continued till night; but the men were still outside the defences, and the assaulting column was then withdrawn to a more sheltered position, for the purpose of bivouac.

The following account of the advance and assault, is given by one who accompanied the main army:

The army crossed the river early on Monday morning, over the bridge constructed during the night. General Osterhaus's Division first crossed, followed by General A. J. Smith's, which in turn was followed by McPherson's Army Corps. Sherman had continued north of the railroad from Jackson, striking Big Black River a little west of Bridgeport. Here he crossed on his pontoon bridge, and moved upon the Vicksburg and Haines Bluff and Spring Dale roads. McPherson moved out on the main Vicksburg and Jackson road, while McClernand took possession of the Baldwin's Ferry road.

On the summit of the high bank across the river the column moved through the camp whence the night before the enemy made his hasty exit. On the plateau nearest the river, before the hill is reached, numerous tents were left standing, just as the occupants had hastily left them. They could not be destroyed under the heavy fire of our skirmishers posted on the hither bank of the river. When the hill was reached, we found abundant evidence of the demoralization of the enemy. Several piles of gun-barrels, with stocks but half consumed, were lying by the roadside. Tents, wagons, and gun-carriages were in ashes, corn was burning, and officers' baggage and soldiers' clothing were scattered all over the camp. The column moved to Bovina, where no evidence of the enemy was seen, save a rebel hospital filled with sick and wounded. *Here General Grant was joined by General Dwight from Banks's army.*

At Mount Albans, General McClernand turned off on the Baldwin's Ferry road, while McPherson kept along the railroad upon the main Vicksburg road. The approaches to Vicksburg were now all occupied, with the exception of that by way of Warrenton, which was afterwards occupied by McArthur. When General Sherman crossed the river at Bridgeport, he met the advance of the enemy, which immediately turned back, and, it is rumored, reached Vicksburg by way of Warrenton the next day. *That gap is now closed, and if we capture Vicksburg we shall capture the entire force.*

The night of the 18th, the command encamped in the open fields outside the outer works, and within easy artillery range of them—General McClernand, with the Thirteenth Army Corps on the left, General McPherson's Seventeenth Corps in the centre, and General Sherman's Fifteenth Corps on the right.

At daylight on the 19th, General Grant proceeded to move upon the enemy's works—*a series of redoubts arranged with great skill, and extending from the rear of Haines Bluff around to the Warrenton road, a distance of from eight to ten miles.*

The ground by which they are approached is singularly broken—a vast plateau upon which a multitude of little hills seem to have been sown broadcast, and of course *the rebel redoubts were so disposed as to sweep every neighboring crest and enfilade every approach.*

The corps of General Sherman moved up on the Haines' Bluff road, by a sort of poetic justice taking possession of the ground by the rear which he had once vainly attempted to gain from the front. McPherson advanced on the Jackson road, and covered the ground from the left of Sherman to the railroad, while McClernand's Corps occupied the front from the railroad to the extreme left.

The action began by a slow fire from our artillery along the whole line, our guns having a pretty long range, and eliciting but feeble response from the enemy.

About noon, Osterhaus's Division advanced on the left to within about six hundred yards of the enemy's works, to find themselves confronted by fifteen redoubts, with their rifle-pits, which opened fire upon us whenever we appeared on a crest or through a hollow.

The guns of the rebels appeared to be of small calibre, throwing principally grape and canister. Our skirmishers were thrown further up; but little firing was done on either side.

At two o'clock the order came for a general advance upon the rebel works, over ground which, on the left, at least, *was almost impassable under the most peaceful circumstances.* The order seemed a hard one; yet nothing is too hard for true soldiers to try.

General A. L. Lee, who commanded the First Brigade of Osterhaus's Division, and was in the advance, determined to carry out his orders if their execution was possible. Addressing a few words of cheer to his men, he placed himself in front of the centre of his brigade, led them forward in line of battle, and was the first man to gain the crest of the hill which he was attempting. He then found that it was only the first of several ridges which were to be crossed, the ravines between which were swept by the guns of the enemy's redoubt. Still he tried to press on, and his brigade of brave fellows to follow him, the air, in the mean time, thick with bullets and shells; but a ball from the rifle of a sharpshooter struck him on the face, and he fell. His brigade withdrew a few feet only, behind the crest of the hill on which they had just raised, and held their position; one of the regiments getting so favorable a point, that they were able to remain within about two hundred yards of one of the redoubts, and to prevent the gunners from firing a single shot.

I am glad to say that General Lee, though severely, was by no means dangerously wounded. His brigade sustained a much smaller loss than a distant observer could have believed possible.

The same degree of success, or want of success, attended the movement along the whole line. Our forces moved very close to the works, and then remained waiting and watching for the nearer approach of our artillery. At nightfall our troops retired a short distance and went into camp. During the night heavy siege-guns were planted by us for future use, our light artillery moved nearer, and a slight earthwork was thrown up to protect them.

To-day (Wednesday, May 20th), the heavy guns on our left opened long before daylight. As heretofore, the enemy have failed to reply. Our skirmishers are pushed forward within a hundred and fifty yards of the whole line of the redoubts, and keep so sharp a lookout that the enemy finds it impossible to work his guns.

On the centre two heavy siege-guns are in position less than half a mile from a strong fort just in front of them, so near that the Minié bullets were whistling merrily past the ears of the workmen. To-morrow they will open on the fort.

On the right, Sherman still holds his line of skirmishers well up to the rebel forts on his front, and the artillerists are trying to level the rebel works, so far without success. During our operations to-day thirty or forty men were wounded.*

General Sherman, in making his movement of May 18th, towards the Yazoo River, as before stated, acted under General Grant's instructions, for the purpose of opening communication with the fleet in those waters, and securing a base of supplies north of the city of Vicksburg. It is therefore necessary to show how Admiral Porter had co-

* Army correspondence to the *New York Herald*, under date of May 20th.

operated with General Grant's movements. The following report will, without comment, clearly explain his proceedings in the front of Vicksburg while General Grant was acting in the rear:

FLAGSHIP BLACK HAWK, HAINES BLUFF,
YAZOO RIVER, *May* 20, 1863.

Hon. GIDEON WELLES, *Secretary of the Navy:*

On the morning of the 15th, I came over to the Yazoo, to be ready *to co-operate with General Grant.* Leaving two of the iron-clads at Red River, one at Grand Gulf, one at Carthage, three at Warrenton, and two in the Yazoo, left me a small force. Still I disposed of them to the best advantage.

On the 18th, at meridian, firing was heard in the rear of Vicksburg, *which assured me that General Grant was approaching the city.* The cannonading was kept up furiously for some time, when, by the aid of glasses, I discerned a company of our artillery advancing, taking position, and driving the rebels before them. I immediately saw that General Sherman's Division had come on to the left of Snyder's Bluff, and that *the rebels at that place had been cut off from joining the forces in the city.* I dispatched the De Kalb, Lieutenant-Commander Walker; Choctaw, Lieutenant-Commander Ramsay; Romeo, Petrel, and Forest Rose, all under command of Lieutenant-Commander Breese, up the Yazoo, to open communication in that way with Generals Grant and Sherman.

This I succeeded in doing, and *in three hours received letters from Generals Grant,* Sherman, and Steele, informing me of this vast success, and asking me to send up provisions, which was at once done.

In the mean time, Lieutenant-Commander Walker, in the De Kalb, pushed on to Haines Bluff, which the enemy had commenced evacuating the day before, and a party remained behind in the hopes of destroying or taking away a large amount of ammunition on hand.

When they saw the gunboats, they ran out and left every thing in good order—guns, forts, tents, and equipage of all kinds, which fell into our hands.

As soon as the capture of Haines Bluff and fourteen forts was reported to me, I shoved up the gunboats from below Vicksburg to fire at the hill batteries, which fire was kept up for two or three hours, At midnight they moved up to the town and opened on it for about an hour, and continued at intervals during the night to annoy the garrison.

On the 19th I placed six mortars in position, with orders to fire night and day as rapidly as they could.

The works at Haines Bluff are very formidable. There are fourteen of the heaviest kind of mounted eight and ten inch and seven and a half inch rifled guns, with ammunition enough to last a long siege. As the gun-carriages might again fall into the hands of the enemy, I had them burned, blew up the magazine, and destroyed the works generally. I also burned up the encampments, which were permanently and remarkably well constructed, looking as if the rebels intended to stay for some time.

These works and encampments covered many acres of ground, and the fortifications and the rifle-pits proper of Haines Bluff extend about a mile and a quarter. Such a network of defences I never saw.

The rebels were a year constructing them, and all were rendered useless in an hour. As soon as I got through with the destruction of the magazines and other works, I started Lieutenant-Commander Walker up the Yazoo River, with sufficient force to destroy all the enemy's property in that direction, with orders to return with all dispatch, and only to proceed as far as Yazoo City, where the rebels have a navy-yard and store-houses.

In the mean time, General Grant has closely invested Vicksburg, and has possession of the best commanding points. In a very short time a general assault will take place, when I hope to announce that Vicksburg has fallen, after *a series of the most brilliant successes that ever attended an army.*

There has never been a case, during the war, where the rebels have been so successfully beaten at all points; and the patience and endurance shown by our army and navy, for so many months, are about being rewarded.

It is a mere question of a few hours, and then, with the exception of Port Hudson, which will follow Vicksburg, the Mississippi will be open its entire length.

D. D. PORTER,
Rear-Admiral commanding the Mississippi Squadron.

It will thus be seen that the most perfect harmony of plan had been agreed upon between General Grant and Admiral Porter, and that the latter rendered the former all the assistance in his power, towards accomplishing the grand object—the reduction of Vicksburg.

The following official dispatches from General Pemberton, the commander at Vicksburg, were sent to Jackson, Mississippi, and from thence telegraphed to the rebel President Davis:

VICKSBURG, *May* 20, 1863.

The enemy assaulted our intrenchments yesterday on our centre and left. They were repulsed with heavy loss. Our loss is small. The enemy's force is at least 60,000.

VICKSBURG, *May* 21, 1863.

The enemy kept up a heavy artillery fire yesterday. Two of our guns were dismounted in the centre. Our works, however, were uninjured. Their sharpshooters picked off officers and men all day. Our works were repaired, and our guns replaced last night. Our men are encouraged by a report that General Johnston is near with a large army, and are in good spirits.

We have had a brisk artillery and musketry firing to-day, also heavy mortar firing from gunboats.

During the past two days transports with troops have gone up the river. Their destination is unknown.

CHAPTER XXXVII.

THE SECOND ASSAULT UPON VICKSBURG.

AFTER the withdrawal of the forces from before Vicksburg on the night of the 19th of May, the army, for two days, was kept in a state of comparative inactivity, although lively skirmishing occurred all along the line. General Grant was, however, far from being idle, inasmuch as he was fully engaged in perfecting communications with the dépôts of supplies north of the invested city. The greater part of the troops had been marching and fighting battles for twenty days, on an average of about five days' rations, drawn from the commissary department. Although the men had not suffered from short rations up to this time, still they had begun to feel the want of bread to accompany the other food with which they had been supplied, and to remedy this deficiency was for the time General Grant's first and greatest object.

By the 21st of May, General Grant had completed his arrangements for the drawing of every description of supply, and having secured this desirable aim, he was determined to make another effort to take the city of Vicksburg by storm.

General Grant was induced to again make the assault upon the rebel defences of Vicksburg from several causes, some of which he sets forth in his official report. "There were many reasons," said he, "to determine me to adopt this course. I believed an assault, from the position gained by this time, could be made successfully. It was known that Johnston was at Canton with the force taken by him from Jackson, re-enforced by other troops from the East, and that more were daily reaching him. With the force I had, a short time must have enabled him to attack me in the rear, and, possibly, succeed in raising the siege. Possession of Vicksburg at that time would have enabled me to have turned upon Johnston, and driven him from the State, and possess myself of all the railroads and practical military highways, thus effectually securing to ourselves all territory west of the Tombigbee, and this before the season was too far advanced for campaigning in this latitude. I would have saved the Government sending large re-enforcements, much needed elsewhere; and, finally, the troops themselves were impatient to possess Vicksburg, and would not have worked in the trenches with the same zeal, believing it unnecessary, that they did after their failure to carry the enemy's works."

General Grant, therefore, gave orders on the 21st of May for a general assault upon the rebel defences, to be made at ten o'clock of the next morning, by the whole line; and that there should be no mistake or difference in the time of movement, and as a great deal would sometimes depend upon minutes, all the corps commanders set their chronometers by the one in the possession of General Grant.

The following is the copy of the order issued for the movement to the corps commanders:

HEAD-QUARTERS IN THE FIELD, *May* 21, 1863.

GENERAL:—A simultaneous attack will be made to-morrow at ten o'clock A. M., by all the army corps of this army.

During this day army corps commanders will have examined all practical routes over which troops can possibly pass. They will get in position all the artillery possible, and gain all the ground they can with their infantry and skirmishers.

At an early hour in the morning a vigorous attack will be commenced by artillery and skirmishers. The infantry, with the exception of reserves and skirmishers, will be placed in column of platoons, or by a flank, if the ground over which they may have to pass will not admit of a greater front, ready to move forward at the hour designated. *Promptly at the hour designated all will start, at quick time, with bayonet fixed, and march immediately upon the enemy, without firing a gun until the outer works are carried.* Skirmishers will advance as soon as possible after heads of columns pass them, and scale the walls of such works as may confront them.

By order of U. S. GRANT, *Major-General Commanding.*

In order the better to secure success, General Grant's order was, on the evening of May 21st, communicated to the division and brigade commanders, and, as far as practicable, every thing was done calculated to insure the grand object of the movement.

Five minutes before ten o'clock, on the morning of May 22d, the bugles rang along the line to prepare for the charge, and, at ten o'clock precisely, the three army corps commenced their movement in the following order: General McClernand, with the Thirteenth Army Corps on the left, General McPherson, with the Seventeenth in the centre, and General Sherman, with the Fifteenth on the right. General Grant himself took up a commanding position near the front of the Seventeenth Corps, by which he was enabled to see all the advancing columns from that corps, and part of each of those on the right and left.

The preliminary work had been performed by the artillery, and the outer works were breached in several places. Under cover of this fire, the infantry advanced to the charge all along the line. Brigade after brigade rushed forward, and slope and ditch were carried at the point of the bayonet. The Stars and Stripes were planted on several portions of the outer slopes of the enemy's bastions, and they were maintained in that position until night. The assault was a splendid one, and was gallantly performed by all the troops on every part of the line; but the position of the enemy was far too strong to be thus taken. Vicksburg had always been naturally strong, but art had greatly improved it by the cutting of ditches, felling of trees, construction of works, and, what is of far more importance, the proper location of batteries to guard every avenue of approach. General Sherman reported that the artillery fire from the rebel works, on one part of his line, was so steady and severe, that it was impossible for the infantry to pass that point; and even when an attempt was made to take the death-dealing works, it was found to be so well covered by other works, that the assaulting party recoiled under the effects of a staggering fire.

Notwithstanding this fearful artillery reply to the assault, several evidences of individual bravery were manifested by the soldiers.* The walls were scaled, but with no successful effect. Although assaulted at every point and at all of them at the same time, the enemy was enabled to show as much force as his work could cover. "The assault failed," says General Grant, in his report, "but without weakening the confidence of the troops in their ability to ultimately succeed." They knew well that the failure did not arise from lack of courage in themselves, or skill in their commander, but they also discovered that works of the character which defended Vicksburg could not be carried by storm.

The position taken up by General Grant enabled him to have a view of the whole field of action, and he states emphatically that "the assault of this day proved the quality of the soldiers of the Army of the Tennessee. Without either success, and with a heavy loss, there was no mur-

* See General Grant's Report, Appendix G.

muring nor complaining, no falling back, nor other evidence of demoralization." This fact alone proves the value of the discipline by which General Grant had reared his army, and the love the men bore their commanders.

The following sketch of the assault, by a participant, is of interest:

NEAR VICKSBURG, *May* 22, 1863.

It was rumored yesterday that this morning General Grant would order a charge simultaneously along the entire line of works. Late in the evening, the commanders of the different divisions and brigades received their orders, and prepared to execute them. The order contemplated a fierce cannonade from daylight until ten o'clock, but, for some reason, it was not opened until after eight.

During the night, however, the gunboats and mortars lying in front of Vicksburg kept up a continual fire, and dropped their fiery messengers right and left without distinction.

During this bombardment several buildings were set on fire by the exploding shells, and lighted up the darkness, revealing strange shapes and wonderful outlines standing out in relief against the dark sky, which added wonderful interest to the bombardment as witnessed by the distant observer. It is impossible to estimate the damage occasioned by thus dropping into Vicksburg those heavy eleven and thirteen inch shells. Imagination falls far short of its reality.

Before we approached the city, General Pemberton ordered all the women and children for miles around Vicksburg to come within the intrenchments, assuring them that in that way they would escape all danger. The consequence is, that there are a large number of non-combatants in Vicksburg, exposed to all the dangers of siege and bombardment.

At eight o'clock this morning the cannonading began, and continued, with scarcely a moment's intermission, along the entire line until ten o'clock. From every hill-top in front of the enemy's works cannon were placed, and the fiery tempest raged fearfully. Guns were dismounted, embrasures torn up, parapets destroyed, and caissons exploded. It was a fearful demonstration. The enemy were powerless to reply; for our line of skirmishers were pushed up close to the enemy's works, and unerringly picked off the gunners whenever they attempted to work the guns.

For two long hours did this cannonade continue, when a general charge was made. Winding through the valleys, clambering over the hills everywhere, subjected to a murderous enfilading and cross-fire, the advance pressed up close to the rebel works—to find that a deep ditch, protected by sharp stakes along the outer edge, lay between them and the intrenchments. They planted their flag directly before the fort, and crouched down behind the embankment, out of range of the rebel fire, as calmly as possible, to await developments. The soldiers within the forts could not rise above the parapet to fire at them, for if they did, a hundred bullets came whizzing through the air, and the adventurers died.

The rebels, however, adopted another plan. Taking a shell, they cut the fuse close off, lighted it and, rolled it over the outer slope of the embankment.

Subsequently, with picks and shovels, a way was dug into one fort, and through the breach the boys walked bravely in. The first fort on the left of the railroad was stormed by a portion of General Carr's Division, and gallantly taken. The colonel that led the charge was wounded.

On the centre the fire was persistent and terrible. Many brave officers were killed and many more wounded. Col. Dollins, of the Eighty-first Illinois, fell dead while leading his men to the charge.

Later in the afternoon General Ransom's Brigade charged the works opposite his position, with heavy loss.

Steele and Tuttle, on the right, were also heavily engaged, and the former is reported to have lost nearly a thousand men.*

The following account, also, gives interesting details of the action, as seen from General Grant's head-quarters:

For several days the disposition of the troops designed for the reduction of Vicksburg had been going on with unceasing energy. The peculiar formation of the country in this vicinity made it a matter of no small importance to thoroughly comprehend the ground before using it for military ends, because there were some localities which possessed striking advantages over others, yet they did not appear upon first sight. Accordingly, the day after the arrival of the army here, *General Grant*

---

* Army correspondence of the Chicago *Tribune*, under date, of May 22d, 1863.

spent most of his time in riding over the ground and studying out the positions. This being finished, on the following day the troops were moved to the positions which they were to occupy and hold, in corps, the Fifteenth (General Sherman) on the right, the Seventeenth (General McPherson) in the centre, and the Thirteenth (General McClernand) on the left.

General Sherman the day before had detached part of his command, with orders to march against a strong position in the enemy's possession at Chickasaw Bluffs. The movement was made, and resulted most eminently in our favor—that is, without the loss of a man. The enemy at this point, hearing of the presence of our army in the rear of Vicksburg, and its proximity to their own position, concluded that the better part of valor would be the evacuation of their works, which action was had immediately and without delay. The possession of this point is of great importance to this army in its present movements. It gives us a ready and short line of communication between our base of supplies at Young's Point and the army in the field, the distance being but fifteen miles by water and ten by land, making twenty-five miles; and by this time the arrangements are so far matured that *in a day from Young's Point supplies of all sorts can reach the army.*

Having every facility at his command, the troops in possession of every necessary to their comfort and efficiency, the men in the best of spirits after a victorious campaign from Grand Gulf to Big Black, and the positions we now hold in the rear of Vicksburg, General Grant planned the assault upon the enemy's works which came off to-day. The arrangement was to make a simultaneous move on all points, basing success upon the consideration that the insufficient garrison of the place would not be able to contest equally our assault at all points, and, as a consequence, the weaker places could be taken while the stronger were making their defence. This conclusion was very natural, and there seemed hardly a doubt that at this moment our troops would be at least in possession of several of the enemy's outer works, the occupation of which would insure us a decided advantage in position.

But from causes, perhaps beyond the control of the generals in the field, this enemy found us unsuccessful, and some of our lines were less advanced than in the morning. However, *due to the high state of discipline of the army,* instead of being disheartened at our repulse and severe loss, the men are even more determined than they were at first: they think of nothing but the capture of Vicksburg—a fact, under such circumstances, surely to be realized.

General Grant's "field order," issued last night, ordered that all the reserve troops should be formed in line at an early hour this morning, and that those commands selected for the storming of the fortifications should be drawn up in "column" by division, so as to be ready to move at precisely ten o'clock this morning, which was the hour designated for the assault to commence. The artillery opened a vigorous fire some time before the designated hour of the assault. The firing was excellent, almost every shot striking the crest of the parapet, and nearly all the shells exploding immediately over the inner side of the breastworks. Of course it is not possible to judge of the enemy's loss, but he certainly must have suffered severely during our heavy fire. Two large explosions occurred within the works, during the engagement, which were thought to be caissons. A large building was also destroyed by our shells.

At a given hour the troops were in motion, moving along the ravines, in which to assume the required formation and make the attack. The charges were most admirably executed. With perfect composure the men moved up the hill, though not under fire, yet under the influence of a dreadful anticipation of a deadly volley at close quarters. When within forty yards of the works, of a sudden the parapet was alive with armed men, and in an instant more the flash of thousands of muskets hurled death and destruction most appalling into the ranks of our advancing columns. Five hundred men lay dead or bleeding on one part of the field at the first fire. Bravely, against all odds, this command fought until its depleted ranks could no longer stand, when sullenly it withdrew under cover of a hill near by. In addition to the heavy musketry fire which repelled the assault, artillery played with dreadful havoc upon the fading ranks, which, after every effort to win the goal, were obliged to give way, not to numbers, but impregnability of position.

Upon the whole, as regards the designs of our movement, we were frustrated, but nothing more. Our troops, with but few exceptions, hold their own. The loss of this day's engagement has been exceedingly heavy, according to first accounts, which are not the most reliable, and it is to be hoped the authenticated returns will greatly lessen the casualties.

The failure of our endeavors to take the city by assault will be succeeded by an effort to reduce the place by means of the spade. The argument in favor of this course is economy of life, for even a successful attack upon the city would be attended with an extravagant loss of men.

The strength of Vicksburg towards the land is equally as strong as on the river-side. The country is broken to a degree, affording excellent defensive positions, and an attacking party must necessarily be exposed to a fire which could not be withstood by any troops. In addition to this, the ravines intervening the ridges and knolls, which the enemy has fortified, are covered with a tangled growth of cane, wild grape, etc., making it impossible to move the troops in well-dressed lines. The attempt of to-day has exhibited the impossibility of taking the city by storm; but a few weeks of the spade will show that Vicksburg can be taken.*

The following official report from Admiral Porter will explain the part taken by the fleet during this assault:

MISSISSIPPI SQUADRON, FLAGSHIP BLACK HAWK,
May 23, 1863.

SIR:—On the morning of the 21st, *I received a communication from General Grant, informing me that he intended to attack the whole of the rebel works at ten* A. M. *the next day, and asking me to shell the batteries from half-past nine until half-past ten, and annoy the garrison.* I kept six mortars playing rapidly on the works and town all night, and sent the Benton, Mound City, and Carondelet up to shell the water batteries and other places where troops might be resting during the night. At seven o'clock in the morning the Mound City proceeded across the river, and made an attack on the hill batteries opposite the canal. At eight o'clock I found her in company with the Benton, Tuscumbia, and Carondelet. All these vessels opened on the hill batteries and finally silenced them, though the main work on the battery containing the heavy rifled gun was done by the Mound City, Lieutenant-Commanding Byron Wilson. I then pushed the Benton, Mound City, and Carondelet up to the water batteries, leaving the Tuscumbia, which is still out of repair, to keep the hill batteries from firing on our vessels after they had passed by. The three gunboats passed up slowly, owing to the strong current, the Mound City leading, the Benton following, and the Carondelet astern. The water batteries opened furiously, supported by a hill battery on the starboard beam of the vessels. The vessels advanced to within four hundred and forty yards (by our marks). and returned the fire for two hours without cessation, the enemy's fire being very accurate and incessant.

Finding that the hill batteries behind us were silenced, I ordered up the Tuscumbia to within eight hundred yards of the batteries; but the

* Army correspondence of the *New York Herald*, dated May 22d, 1863.

turret was soon made untenable, not standing the enemy's shot, and I made her drop down. I had been engaged with the forts an hour longer than General Grant asked. The vessels had all received severe shots under water which we could not stop while in motion, and not knowing what might have delayed the movement of the army, I ordered the vessels to drop out of fire, which they did in a cool, handsome manner.

This was the hottest fire the gunboats have ever been under; but, owing to the water batteries being more on a level with them than usual, the gunboats threw in their shell so fast that the aim of the enemy was not very good. The enemy hit our vessels a number of times, but, fighting bow on, that did but little damage.

Not a man was killed, and only a few wounded. I had only enough ammunition for a few moments longer, and set all hands to work to fill up from our dépôt below.

After dropping back I found that the enemy had taken possession again of one of the lower hill batteries and was endeavoring to mount his guns, and had mounted a twelve-pounder field-piece to fire at General McArthur's troops, which had landed a short time before at Warrenton. I sent the Mound City and Carondelet to drive him off, which they did in a few moments.

I beg leave to inclose a letter from General McArthur, explaining why he did not (to use his own expression) take advantage of the results gained by the gunboats. *I have since learned through General Grant that the army did assault at the right time vigorously. In the noise and smoke we could not see or hear it. The gunboats were, therefore, still fighting when the assault had proved unsuccessful.*

The army had terrible work before them, and are fighting as well as soldiers ever fought before. But the works are stronger than any of us dreamed of. General Grant and his soldiers are confident that the brave and energetic generals in the army will soon overcome all obstacles and carry the works.

DAVID D. PORTER,

Acting Rear-Admiral, commanding Mississippi Squadron.

Hon. GIDEON WELLES, *Secretary of the Navy.*

Shortly after this assault some dissensions arose in the army relative to the merits of the troops, and in consequence of a congratulatory order issued by General McClernand on May 30th, the quarrel would have ended in a complete disruption of the whole force, had it not been for the prompt action of General Grant. It will be remembered that General McClernand had served with General Grant from the time he first took command at Cairo to the assault of Vicksburg; and that naturally there existed a friendship between them, that would have been provocative of great jealousy among the other commanders if General Grant had overlooked the matter in question, especially under the circumstances.* The objectionable order commenced as follows:

COMRADES:—As your commander, I am proud to congratulate you upon your constancy, valor and success. History affords no more brilliant example of soldierly qualities. Your victories have followed in such rapid succession, that their echoes have not yet reached the country. They will challenge its grateful and enthusiastic applause. Yourselves striking out a new path, your comrades of the Tennessee followed, and a way was thus opened for them to redeem previous disappointments.

After summing up the achievements of the corps, and speaking in high terms of his own men, General McClernand concludes in the following language:

On the 22d, in pursuance of the order of the Commander of the Department, you assaulted the enemy's defences in front at 10 o'clock A. M., and within thirty minutes had made a lodgment and placed your colors upon two of his bastions. This partial success called into exercise the highest heroism, and was only gained by a bloody and protracted struggle. Yet it was gained, and was the first and largest success gained anywhere along the whole line of our army.

For nearly eight hours, under a scorching sun and destructive fire, you firmly held your footing, and only withdrew when the enemy had largely massed their forces, and concentrated their attack upon you.

How and why the general assault failed, it would be needless now to explain. The Thirteenth Army Corps, acknowledging the good intentions of all, would scorn indulgence in weak regrets and idle criminations. According justice to all, it would only defend itself. If, while the enemy

* See General Grant's Report, Appendix G.

was massing to crush it, assistance was asked for by a division at other points, or by re-enforcements, it only asked what, in one case, Major-General Grant had specifically and peremptorily ordered, namely, simultaneous and persistent attack all along our line, until the enemy's outer works should be carried; and what, in the other, by massing a strong force in time upon a weakened point, would have probably insured success.

This order gave very great offence; in fact, it became the source of serious trouble in all the other parts of the army, the men openly expressing their disapprobation of it. This led to a correspondence between the commander of the Thirteenth Army Corps and the General commanding the army, and the following letter was sent from the former to the latter.

HEAD-QUARTERS THIRTEENTH ARMY CORPS,
BATTLE-FIELD NEAR VICKSBURG, *June* 4, 1863.

GENERAL:—What appears to be a systematic effort to destroy my usefulness and reputation as a commander, makes it proper that I should address you this note.

It is reported, among other things, as I understand, that I attacked the enemy's works on the 22d ult. without authority; again, that I attacked too late; again, that I am responsible for your failure and losses; again, that I am arrested and being sent North; again, that my command is turned over to another officer; and again, that you have personally assumed command of it. These reports are finding their way from the landings up the river.

I hardly need say to you that all these reports are false; that I obeyed orders in attacking; that my attack was more prompt, and in a large measure more successful, than any other; that the ultimate failure of the general attack, and losses attending the failure, were, under the circumstances, unavoidable consequences of obstacles found to be insurmountable, and in spite of a determined effort on my part to carry and hold the works in obedience to your express and peremptory order. I may add that I am not yet under arrest, or being sent away, or superseded in my command.

All these things being known to you, and these false reports being brought to your notice, it remains for you to determine whether truth, justice, and generosity do not call on you for such a declaration as will be conclusive in the matter. Your obedient servant,

JOHN A. MCCLERNAND, *Major-General Commanding.*

Major-General U. S. GRANT, *Commanding Department Tennessee.*

To this General Grant replied as follows:

HEAD-QUARTERS, DEPARTMENT OF THE TENNESSEE,
NEAR VICKSBURG, *June* 7 1863.

Major-General J. A. MCCLERNAND, *Commanding* 13*th Army Corps:*

GENERAL:—Inclosed I send you what purports to be your congratulatory address to the Thirteenth Army Corps.

I would respectfully ask if it is a true copy. If it is not a correct copy, furnish me one by bearer, as required both by regulations and existing orders of the Department.

Very respectfully,

U. S. GRANT, *Major-General.*

It appears that General McClernand was absent at the time General Grant's dispatch reached his head-quarters, and did not return until the 15th of June. As soon as he came back, and had read General Grant's communication, he at once telegraphed the following reply thereto:

HEAD-QUARTERS THIRTEENTH ARMY CORPS,
NEAR VICKSBURG, *June* 15, 1863.

Major-General GRANT:

I have just returned. The newspaper slip is a correct copy of my congratulatory order, No 72. *I am prepared to maintain its statements.*

I regret that my adjutant did not send you a copy promptly, as he ought, and I thought he had.

JOHN A. MCCLERNAND, *Major-General Commanding.*

This, of course, settled the matter as to the authenticity of the document in question; and as the order implied a direct censure of the commanding general, and an indirect breach of the sixth Article of War, General Grant therefore being equal to the urgent necessity of the case, with the desire to save his army even at the cost of his friend, immediately issued a special order, of which the following is an extract:

HEAD-QUARTERS, DEPARTMENT OF THE TENNESSEE,
NEAR VICKSBURG, MISS., *June* 15, 1863.

[*Special Orders, No.* 164.]—*Extract.*

Major-General John A. McClernand is hereby relieved from the command of the Thirteenth Army Corps. He will proceed to any point he may select in the State of Illinois, and report by letter to head-quarters of the army for orders.

Major-General E. O. C. Ord is hereby appointed to the command of the Thirteenth Army Corps, subject to the approval of the President, and will immediately assume charge of the same.

By order of Major-General U. S. GRANT.

JOHN A. RAWLINS, *A. A.-G.*

On receipt of this order, after turning over his command to General Ord, General McClernand sent the following to General Grant:

BATTLE-FIELD NEAR VICKSBURG, MISS.,
June 20, 1863.

Major-General U. S. GRANT, *Commanding Department Tennessee:*

Your note relieving me, and appointing Major-General Ord to the command of the Thirteenth Army Corps, is received.

Having been appointed by the President to the command of that corps, under a definite act of Congress, I might justly challenge your authority in the premises, but forbear to do so at present.

I am quite willing that any statement of fact in my congratulatory order to the Thirteenth Army Corps, to which you think just exception may be taken, should be made the subject of investigation, not doubting the result.

Your obedient servant,

JOHN A. MCCLERNAND.

That no ill feeling existed between the commanders is evident from the concluding paragraph of General McClernand's report of the part taken by himself and his corps in the Vicksburg campaign. The report is dated two days after he was removed from command, and closes with the following words:

"Sympathizing with the general commanding the noble army of the Tennessee, in the loss of so many brave men, killed and wounded, *I cannot but congratulate him in my thankfulness to Providence upon the many and signal successes which have crowned his arms in a just cause.*"

It had been reported in the rebel army that General Pemberton had "sold" the battle-fields of Champion's Hill and Big Black River Bridge. After the repulse of the Union assault upon the works at Vicksburg, General Pemberton made the following brief but pithy speech to his command:

> You have heard that I was incompetent and a traitor, and that it was my intention to sell Vicksburg. Follow me, and you will see the cost at which I will sell Vicksburg. *When the last pound of beef, bacon, and flour; the last grain of corn; the last cow, and hog, and horse, and dog shall have been consumed, and the last man shall have perished in the trenches, then, and only then, will I sell Vicksburg.*

The above will show with what determination the rebels intended to resist the advance of General Grant and the reduction of their fortified city.

In the mean time Colonel Corwyn's Brigade of Union cavalry was making very successful raids into Alabama, etc., destroying lines of communication, factories, mills, workshops, ammunition, ordnance stores, dépôts of supplies, and other valuable property belonging to the rebel government, or its military authorities. Private property, however, was almost universally respected, with the exception of such supplies as were needful for his command, and for which proper receipts were given.

CHAPTER XXXVIII.

THE SIEGE OF VICKSBURG.

After the failure of the assault of May 22d, upon the works of Vicksburg, General Grant determined to resort to the slow, but certain method of a regular siege. The troops having been now made fully aware of the necessity of taking the works by regular approaches, performed their part with alacrity, diligence and cheerfulness.

The advance of each corps was pushed up as close as possible to the rebel works, which were nearly invested by the troops already under General Grant's command. But still there were points at which portions of the rebel garrison would slip out, and supplies be taken into their works. The communication between General Johnston, who was at Canton, Miss., and General Pemberton at Vicksburg, was but partially interrupted, and while this leak existed, it was impossible to reduce the place by siege. General Herron's command was therefore withdrawn from northwestern Arkansas, and added to the force at the extreme left of the Union lines. This secured the complete investment of the fortified city.

The position of the army at the end of May was as follows:

General Grant was well up to the rebel fortifications, and was daily enlarging and strengthening his own. The extreme left, occupied by General Herron, was so situated topographically as to require less formidable opposing works than at any other point; but even there the works were on a scale sufficiently important to successfully oppose any demonstration the rebels might make in that direction.

The Thirteenth Army Corps had the perfect range of the forts opposite their position, and kept down the rebel sharpshooters, and prevented the successful working of rebel artillery.

The Seventeenth Corps planted a heavy battery of siege guns within a hundred yards of the opposing fort, and expected to do excellent service in battering down the earthworks. Advantage had been taken of the topographical peculiarities of the ground, and a covered pathway had been constructed, through which the canonniers could pass to and fro without danger from the sharpshooters.

The Fifteenth Corps, on the extreme right, was equally busy. General Tuttle, of this corps, had constructed a fort, the guns of which enfiladed one of the enemy's most important, and, to us, destructive positions. This, of course, rendered it practically useless, and, had it not been for the line of rifle-pits on the Vicksburg side, which commanded the interior, it might have been stormed and carried any time.

General Blair held Haines Bluff, and the country between the Yazoo and the Big Black River.

About this time, the Union commanding general discovered an intention on the part of the rebel forces under General Johnston to advance and attack General Grant's army in the rear. The manner in which General Grant obtained his information is thus related by one of the officers of his army:

General Pemberton was anxious to indicate to General Johnston his exact situation, and sent a trusty fellow, named Douglas—son of a prominent citizen of Illinois, who several years since migrated to Texas, and there joined the rebel service—through his lines, with instructions to make his way by night past the Union pickets, and, seizing the first horse he met, to ride to General Johnston at Jackson. On the night of May 27th, at dark, he started, and, holding a pass from Pemberton, was allowed to leave the inclosure in the rear of Vicksburg. Young Douglas had, unknown to his superiors, for a long time meditated escape, and he could not neglect this golden opportunity. Instead of trying to avoid our pickets, therefore, he marched boldly up to them, and surrendered himself a prisoner. General Lauman conversed with him long enough to discover that there was meat in that shell, and sent him to General Grant. To him he delivered the message he was instructed to deliver to Johnston. It was in effect as follows:—"I have 15,000 men in Vicksburg, and rations for thirty days—one meal a day. Come to my aid with an army of 30,000 men. Attack Grant in his rear. If you cannot do this within ten days you had better retreat. Ammunition is almost exhausted, particularly percussion caps." This is the substance of the message, although not its exact terms. Douglas volunteered also other valuable information, which leaves no doubt of the ultimate capture of the rebel army.

General Pemberton saw plainly that the siege might be a long one, and as his supplies had been cut off, he, for the sake of economizing rations, ordered every horse and mule, except those used by field and staff officers, to be turned outside his lines. Of those thus turned out, General Grant secured several thousand. When General Grant first opened a concentrated fire upon Vicksburg from his lines of circumvallation, the rebel herd of beef cattle was exposed and a large number killed. The rebels soon removed these animals to a place of greater safety.

In order to prevent Johnston's forces from getting to the rear of General Grant's army, General Osterhaus, with his division, was sent to the Big Black River to guard the crossings, and to resist any attempt of the enemy to force a passage. A reconnoissance was also sent out under General Blair to ascertain the position of Johnston's army, and reported no enemy within striking distance.

The following is a brief account of what was accomplished by the expedition under General Blair:

Information reaching the ears of the commanding general, that Johnston, in possession of a considerable force, was moving towards the Big Black River with an intention of making a demonstration on our army now in the rear of Vicksburg, induced the movement of a sufficient body of troops in that direction, to meet the approaching enemy, if found, as reported, and engage him before he could effect a crossing, or at every hazard to repel any attempt he might make to secure a foothold on this side. Accordingly, an expedition was sent out under General F. P. Blair, Jr., composed of men selected from each corps of the army, with their artillery and a command of cavalry. On the 27th of May, the party started on their mission, and marching hastily towards Mechanicsburg, the cavalry in advance, when near that place, fell in with about one thousand men, partly of the Twentieth Mississippi mounted infantry, commanded by Colonel Wirt Adams, and the rest, composed of detachments, all under command of General Adams. A brisk skirmish ensued, resulting in forcing back our cavalry. The infantry was soon formed and thrown forward, and after a brief engagement the enemy left the field in haste.

This affair being over, the troops pushed forward, scouring the country in all directions, seizing stock, bacon, and every other thing useful to the enemy. The advance marched within twenty miles of Yazoo City, without meeting any force, then struck across the country and returned to take their part in the investment of Vicksburg.

The facts collected concerning the enemy were, that Johnston had at his call twenty thousand men at Canton, and a similar number at Jackson. This force was composed of very old and young men, all conscripted for the occasion, and were without arms. His serviceable force did not number more than fifteen thousand, though by the inhabitants it is estimated much higher.

The expedition returned, confident that no fears should be entertained of serious difficulty from the direction of the Big Black, at any rate for some time. His last experience had so intimidated the rebel general that there was little danger of great boldness on his part, and so long as he remained on the other side of the river, General Grant was informed that he need have no concern about him. Our cavalry was always in movement in that direction, and kept close watch on all his plans.

The captures made during the expedition amounted to five hundred head of cattle, five hundred horses and mules, one hundred bales of cotton, and ten thousand pounds of bacon. All bridges were either burned or demolished, and all forage destroyed. In a word, the country was divested of every thing useful to the enemy.*

In the mean time, General Grant set the sappers and miners at work upon the most eligible sites. Mines were dug, powder planted, and every thing made ready to blow up the advanced works, at the shortest notice. The rebel works, in the front and rear, were also bombarded, at intervals, night and day, first by the fleet, then by the approaching parallels of General Grant, and so alternately, during the whole month of the siege. And as the shells would burst in the works, it would inspire the men to renew their task with greater vigor.

About the middle of June, the Ninth Army Corps, under General Parke, and a part of the Sixteenth Army Corps, under General Washburne, was added to General Grant's command, and by him stationed in the vicinity of the Big Black River, to resist any movement of Johnston, and, if necessary, to attack and drive him back.

It had also been reported that General Johnston was again approaching the Big Black River, with a very large improvised force. About this time a courier was captured, who had managed to get out of Vicksburg during the night, and had passed the picket lines under cover of the darkness. He had upon him a number of letters from the rebel soldiers, to their wives. The men wrote in a sad tone; but stated that they were resigned, and put their trust in the Lord. They, however, still lived in hopes of Joe Johnston coming to their relief. An expedition was then formed to resist the advance of General Johnston's forces, and General Sherman was placed in command. General Grant, in his letter to General Sherman, accompanying the order for the movement, spoke of these letters.

* Correspondence of the *New York Herald.*

"They seem," said he, "to put a great deal of faith in the Lord, and Joe Johnston, but *you* must whip Johnston at least fifteen miles from here."

The following order, to General Parke, shows the same decided determination with regard to Johnston's forces:

June 22, 1863.

General Parke:—Sherman goes out from here with five brigades, and Osterhaus's Division subject to his orders besides. In addition to this, another division, 5,000 strong, is notified to be in readiness to move on notice. In addition to this, I can spare still another division, 6,000 strong, if they should be required. We want to whip Johnston at least fifteen miles off, if possible. U. S. Grant, *Major-General.*

The result of the movement was, that General Johnston, finding General Grant's position to be as strong in the rear as it was in the front, and that Vicksburg was certainly doomed, gave up all hope of diverting the attacking general from his settled purpose, and retreated towards Jackson.

CHAPTER XXXIX.

THE EXPLOSION OF THE MINES.

THE sappers and miners pushed on their work with a steady perseverance, until, on June 25th, 1863, the mines were ready to be sprung. All the time the excavations had been in progress a most rigid guard had been kept upon the entrances, and even the field and line officers of General Grant's army were not allowed to inspect the saps and mines. The utmost possible secrecy was observed concerning them, and though some knew the intention to blow up the enemy's works, yet how or where it was to be done was a matter known to but few. The guards at the head of the saps leading to the entrance of the mine, were instructed to allow no one to pass under the rank of a general, with an exception in the case of engineers and workmen immediately in charge.

The following is a brief description of the mining operations that were performed under General Grant's directions:

In order to reach the main sap running to the mine, it was necessary to traverse a distance of three hundred yards, in front of the enemy's main work. To do this a series of trenches were dug, taking directions at no time exposed to an enfilading fire from the enemy, yet, at every yard, approaching nearer and nearer, with perfect safety to the sappers. In these works a number of sharpshooters were posted to keep the enemy from looking over and discovering or interfering with the labors of the mining party. In different locations along the works, batteries were thrown up and guns mounted, which had excellent battering positions.

A number of other heavy batteries were also in working order, but in locations that did not possess the advantages of those already mentioned.

From the head of the trench to the mouth of the mine ran a ditch about six feet wide and six feet deep, the earth of which was thrown upon the surface towards the enemy. This afforded double security and protection against the enemy's projectiles. The length of this trench was about thirty-five yards.

On approaching the mine, the visitor, on looking round, found himself in plain view and within five yards of the enemy's strongest work, the parapet of which was about twenty feet from the bottom of the ditch. This work was evidently of sod, almost perpendicular on its outer face, intended to mount four guns, and was supposed to be the keep of the rebel position. A few steps in advance, and the visitor was before the mine, which here had the appearance of a square shaft dug into the earth, with a gradual declivity as you penetrate. The entrance was made in the scarp of the enemy's fort, and presented an opening four feet square, well framed with timber to keep up the loose earth which the projectiles of the attacking party had broken from the face of the work. In order to protect the entrance a number of gabions and boxes had been piled up before the mouth, and afforded ample security from hand grenades and shell thrown over by the rebel troops inside.

The main gallery, from the mouth to the point of divergence of the other galleries, measured thirty-five feet. Here three smaller galleries set out, one ten feet deep, obliquely to the left; another eight feet, diverging to the right, and a third, eight feet in length, being a continuation of the main gallery. The chambers for the reception of the powder were let into the bottom of the shaft, and were about two feet in depth.

Having completed one gallery, the powder was brought up and packed into the chambers in almost equal quantities, the entire quantity used being twenty-two hundred pounds, one thousand of which were placed at the end of the main gallery, the remainder being distributed in the extremities of the smaller galleries. From each of the chambers a fuse was run out to the mouth of the shaft, where the match was to be applied at the designated time.

The working party engaged on the mines was formed of a detail from various regiments under General Grant, a call being made to forward to head-quarters all practical miners in the regiments. Accordingly in a few hours fifty picked men, chiefly Welsh, Scotch, English, and Irish, of experience in the old country, were immediately organized into a corps, under the direct command of a miner of reputation. This party reported to the chief of the corps of engineers, and the work at once commenced, the entire time occupied for the excavation being forty hours.

Another sap was also, on the last day, run off to the left, at an angle to the main one leading to the mine. This sap ran parallel to the enemy's breastwork and just outside of where ran the exterior end of the ditch, which had been partly filled. The object of this new sap was to afford a secure place for the Union sharpshooters, and enable them to hold their ground on the right by keeping down a flank fire. The length of the sap was about fifty yards.

It may be supposed by some that the running of mines is the mere operation of the pick and shovel, without interference on the part of the enemy by means of the same instruments, as well as by his riflemen picking off the men as they approach, or by throwing hand grenades and shell over the parapet amongst the men. This idea is quite different from the reality. A few facts connected with the proceedings may enable the reader to form some notion of this dangerous operation. The work is generally performed after dark; and on the night preceding the explosion of June 25th, 1863, the working party returned to the mine, already a depth of thirty-five feet, which was the entire number of feet of the main gallery. The men had but fairly commenced when they heard, as they supposed, near by, the picking and shovelling of another party, which they knew to be the enemy, endeavoring to intercept the Union mine. The men of the attacking side at once desisted from their labors, and applied their ears to the walls of the gallery in order to detect the direction of approach, if possible, of the enemy's countermine. Soon, however, the enemy himself ceased his labors. The Unionists once more resumed operations, and worked until midnight, the enemy working at the same time, and seemingly approaching the outside shaft. "At this juncture," says a correspondent, "an unexpected panic overcame the workers, and they hurried out of the mine with considerable dispatch. The cause of this excitement is said to have been a suspicion that the enemy was about to blow up his own mine, in view of counteracting our own. Accordingly nothing was done until morning, when the party, reassured, renewed their work."

The following interesting account of the firing and explosion of the mine is given by an army correspondent who witnessed the whole affair:

At three o'clock this afternoon a messenger arrived from the mine, bringing information that every thing was in readiness to apply the match. The troops in the outer works were all withdrawn, with the exception of a small body of sharpshooters, who were retained to keep up a demonstration until the fuse was ignited, when they, also, were to retire hastily to a respectful distance under cover of one of the parallels.

As part of the grand programme, Leggett's Brigade was ordered under arms, and marched into the trenches as near the front as safety would permit. Here they rested, awaiting the preconcerted signal, when they were to rush upon the work immediately on the heels of the forlorn hope, which dangerous duty was set apart for a detachment of one hundred men from the Forty-fifth Illinois Infantry, and another hundred from the Twenty-third Indiana. These bodies were thrown out in the extreme advance, with instructions for the Forty-fifth Illinois to assault on the right on Fort Hill, the moment the explosion had taken place, and the Twenty-third Indiana was to rush out the sap running to the left and attack the curtain of the fort extending towards the town. Here they were to keep down, by means of musketry, the enemy's riflemen; for without this accomplished, we would have suffered an enfilading fire on the attackers upon the main fort.

As a support to the brigade of Leggett, General Stephenson's command was ordered to hold itself in readiness to move at a moment's notice. As an additional force, and kind of reserve to the support, the Seventeenth Iowa and Fifty-sixth Illinois, of General John E. Smith's Division, and the Seventeenth Wisconsin, of Ransom's Brigade, McArthur's Division, were brought to the centre and held to the rear to await the development of the struggle. These troops carried nothing with them but their muskets and cartridge boxes; many of them were in their shirt sleeves, evidently anticipating warm work, if engaged.

As might be supposed, the explosion was designated as the signal for a general simultaneous co-operation all along the lines from right to left. In making an attack of this character, it was expected that the attention of the enemy would be distracted, and the force within be distributed along the entire line, instead of being concentrated upon the one fort in front of this corps, which would result in inevitable, perhaps irreparable defeat. All these contingencies were wisely considered, and the subsequent results exemplified how necessary was the co-operation of the other commands.

Every thing was finished. The vitalizing spark had quickened the hitherto passive agent, and the now harmless flashes went hurrying to the centre. The troops had been withdrawn. The forlorn hope stood out in plain view, boldly awaiting the uncertainties of the precarious office. A chilling sensation ran through the frame as an observer looked down upon this devoted band about to hurl itself into the breach—perchance into the jaws of death. Thousands of men in arms flashed on every hill. Every one was speechless. Even men of tried valor—veterans insensible to the shouts of contending battalions, or nerved to the shrieks of comrades suffering under the torture of painful agonies—stood motionless as they directed their eyes upon the spot where soon the terror of a buried agency would discover itself in wild concussions and contortions, carrying annihilation to all within the scope of its tremendous power. It was the seeming torpor which precedes the antagonism of powerful bodies. Five minutes had elapsed. It seemed like an existence. Five minutes more, and yet no signs of the expected exhibition An indescribable sensation of impatience, blended with a still active anticipation, ran through the assembled spectators. A small pall of smoke now discovered itself; every one thought the crisis had come, and almost saw the terrific scene which the mind had depicted. But not yet. Every eye now centered upon the smoke, momentarily growing greater and greater. Thus another five minutes wore away, and curiosity was not satisfied. Another few minutes, then the explosion; and upon the horizon could be seen an enormous column of earth, dust, timbers, and projectiles lifted into the air at an altitude of at least eighty feet. One entire face of the fort was disembodied and scattered in particles all over the surrounding surface. The right and left faces were also much damaged; but fortunately enough of them remained to afford an excellent protection on our flanks.

No sooner had the explosion taken place than the two detachments acting as the forlorn hope ran into the fort and sap, as already mentioned. A brisk musketry fire at once commenced between the two parties, with about equal effect upon either side. No sooner had these detachments become well engaged than the rest of Leggett's Brigade joined them and entered into the struggle. The regiments relieving each other at intervals, the contest now grew severe; both sides, determined upon holding their own, were doing their best. Volley after volley was fired, though with less carnage than would be supposed. The Forty-fifth Illinois charged immediately up to the crest of the parapet, and here suffered its heaviest, losing many officers in the assault.

After a severe contest of half an hour, with varying results, the flag of the Forty-fifth appeared upon the summit of the work. The position was gained. Cheer after cheer broke through the confusion and uproar of the contest, assuring the troops everywhere along the line that the Forty-fifth was still itself. The colonel was now left alone in command of the regiment, and he was himself badly bruised by a flying splinter. The regiment had also suffered severely in the line, and the troops were worn out by excessive heat and hard fighting.

Relief was necessary. Accordingly another Illinois regiment was ordered up and the Forty-fifth drawn off—this was six o'clock P. M. After this the action was kept up briskly but steadily for several hours, until dusk, when the firing lulled and the men took a respite. While the Forty-fifth was so hotly engaged in the fort, the Twenty-third Indiana followed its first detachment into the sap, from which place they were to hold the rebels at bay during the contest for the fort. The rebels fought desperately as well at this point as the other; but the character of the engagement was different, the troops firing at each other over breastworks of earth. This regiment displayed great gallantry and did excellent service in its way. In consequence of the limited space in which to fight, not more than one regiment could act in either place at the same time; accordingly regiments were relieved by regiments as rapidly as the necessities of the occasion demanded.

During the hottest of the action General Leggett was in the fort in the midst of his troops, sharing their dangers and partaking of their glory. While here, a shell from one of the enemy's guns exploded in a timber lying on the parapet, distributing splinters in all directions, one of which struck the General on the breast, knocking him over. Though somewhat bruised and stunned, he soon recovered himself, and taking a chair, sat in one of the trenches near the fort, where he could be seen by his men.

The explosion of the mine was the signal for the opening of the artillery of the entire line. The left division of General McPherson's Seventeenth or centre Corps opened first, and discharges were repeated along the left through General Ord's Thirteenth Corps, and Herron's extreme "left division," until the sound struck the ear like the mutterings of distant thunder. General Sherman, on the right, also opened his artillery about the same time and occupied the enemy's attention along his front. Every shell struck the parapet, and, bounding over, exploded in the midst of the enemy's forces beyond. The scene at this time was one of the utmost sublimity. The roar of artillery, rattle of small arms, the cheers of the men, flashes of light, wreathes of pale blue smoke over different parts of the field, the bursting of shell, the fierce whistle of solid shot, the deep boom of the mortars, the broadsides of the ships of war, and added to all this, the vigorous replies of the enemy, set up a din which beggars all description. The peculiar configuration of the field afforded an opportunity to witness almost every battery and every rifle-pit within seeing distance, and it is due to all the troops to say that every one did his duty.

After the possession of the fort was no longer in doubt, the pioneer corps mounted the work with their shovels and set to throwing up earth vigorously in order to secure space for artillery. A most fortunate peculiarity in the explosion was the manner in which the earth was thrown out. The appearance of the place was that of a funnel, with heavy sides running up to the very crest of the parapet, affording admirable protection not only for our troops and pioneers, but turned out a ready made fortification in the rough, which, with a slight application of the shovel and pick, was ready to receive the guns to be used at this point.

Miraculous as it may seem, amid all the fiery ordeal of this afternoon's engagement, one hundred killed and two hundred wounded is a large estimate of casualties on our side.

From a lookout on the summit of an eminence near the rebel works, the movements of the enemy could be plainly watched. An individual in the tower, just prior to the explosion of the mine, saw two rebel regiments marching out to the fort. Of a sudden—perhaps upon seeing the smoke of the fuse—the troops turned about and ran towards the town in perfect panic. They were not seen again during the fight; but other regiments were brought up to supply their place.*

Another correspondent gives the following brief sketch of the explosion:

This morning the work was completed, an immense quantity of gunpowder was stored in the cavity prepared to receive it, and the fuse train was laid. At noon the different regiments of the Seventeenth Corps, selected to make the assault upon the breach when it should have been effected, were marshalled in long lines upon the near slopes of the hills immediately confronting the doomed rebel fortifications, where, disposed for the attack, they impatiently awaited the *dénouement.* The rebels seemed to discover that some movement was on foot, for from the moment our troops came into position until the explosion took place their sharpshooters kept up an incessant fire from the whole line of their works.

At length all was in readiness; the fuse train was fired, and it went

* Mr. De B. Randolph Keim's dispatch of June 25th, to the *New York Herald.*

fizzing and popping through the zigzag line of trenches, until for a moment it vanished. Its disappearance was quickly succeeded by the explosion, and the mine was sprung. So terrible a spectacle is seldom witnessed. Dust, dirt, smoke, gabions, stockades, timber, gun-carriages, logs—in fact, every thing connected with the fort—rose hundreds of feet into the air, as if vomited forth from a volcano. Some who were close spectators even say that they saw the bodies of the poor wretches who a moment before had lined the ramparts of the work.*

As soon as the explosion had taken place, the greatest activity was manifested along the whole line, under the soul-inspiring orders of General Grant. The following is a specimen of the emphatic style with which that general calls for vigilance on the part of his troops:

June 25, 1863.

GENERAL ORD:—McPherson occupies the crater made by the explosion. He will have guns in battery there by morning. He has been hard at work running rifle-pits right, and thinks he will hold all gained. *Keep Smith's Division sleeping under arms to-night ready for an emergency.* Their services may be required particularly about daylight. *There should be the greatest vigilance along the whole line.*

U. S. GRANT, *Major-General.*

In the mean time, the gunboat fleet off Warrenton commenced a bombardment of the enemy's forts. This was kept up without intermission until midnight, when it was slackened to desultory shots. The fuses of the shells as they ascended in the air were easily distinguishable, and looked in their course like shooting meteors. When they would strike the shell would explode with a terrific report. Some of the shells exploded in the air, and the flashes which they emitted looked like an immense piece of pyrotechny.

* Mr. James C. Fitzpatrick's dispatch of June 25th.

CHAPTER XL.

THE SURRENDER OF VICKSBURG.

After the explosion of the mine, and the occupation of that part of the rebel works, General Grant resumed the operation of constructing parallels, for the purpose of approaching near enough to the rebel fortifications to take them by a sudden dash. As the U. S. troops advanced, the rebels retired, constructing inner lines of defences as the outer ones were taken. On the 28th of June the Union lines were thirteen hundred yards nearer the city than the original works. As these lines were advanced on all sides at the same time, the rebel area of operations became more and more circumscribed.

During this bombardment every effort was made to reduce the rebel works without unnecessarily damaging the city. On this subject a correspondent writes as follows:

Be it understood, that at no time has *General Grant sought the destruction of the city. He wishes to spare it for the city itself, and because it contains women and children.* As long as the rebel army confines its operations outside its limits the city will remain intact. If it had been necessary to destroy the city, our guns now in range could have accomplished the work.

The capture of Vicksburg is a foregone conclusion. We get the evidence of the fact from the rebels themselves. A few days ago a rebel mail was captured coming out from Vicksburg, in which were letters from prominent men in the rebel army, who state that they cannot hold out much longer, and informing their friends that they expect to spend their summer in northern prisons. Better evidence of the condition of things in the rebel army cannot be desired.

So far as the siege of this place goes, I presume the people at home, in their easy chairs, think it ought to have been finished long since. To such let me say, could they be present here, and make a tour of the country in this vicinity, and see the configuration of the country, its broken topography, its high and abrupt hills, deep gullies, gorges and dilapidated roads, they would then realize the difficulties of the work. Then there is a large army to feed, great *matériel* to be brought into position, all of which demands large transportation, and the united efforts of thousands of men.

General Grant acts independently of opinions of the public. He fully realizes the responsibility of his position, and in the duty before him, he is determined to accomplish his work with as great an economy of human life as possible. He feels now that the prize is within his grasp, and a little patience will achieve all, which, if rashly sought, might cost the lives of the brave army with whom he has gained so many victories.*

General Sherman's expedition returned from the special duty assigned it without meeting anywhere near the doomed city the rebel army under General Joseph E. Johnston. The commander, however, obtained sufficient intelligence of the rebel movements to decide General Grant as to his plan of operations immediately after the reduction of Vicksburg.

The bombardment and approaches steadily progressed, and it was whispered about among the troops that on the following anniversary of the day of Independence a grand assault was to be made, for the purpose of taking the place by storm. The rebels, doubtless, were apprised of this fact, or at least suspected it, for, on the morning of the previous day, July 3d, 1863, a flag of truce left the rebel lines, with a sealed communication for General Grant, borne by General Bowen and Colonel Montgomery. The bearers of the document having been taken to the nearest general head-quarters, a courier was at once dispatched with all possible haste to the chief commanding office.

* Mr. Charles H. Farrell's dispatch to the *New York Herald.*

On opening the document General Grant found the following communication addressed to himself:

HEAD-QUARTERS, VICKSBURG, *July* 3, 1863.

Major-General GRANT, *commanding United States forces:*

GENERAL:—I have the honor to propose to you an armistice for — hours, with a view to arranging terms for the capitulation of Vicksburg. To this end, if agreeable to you, I will appoint three commissioners, to meet a like number to be named by yourself, at such place and hour as you may find convenient. I make this proposition to save the further effusion of blood, which must otherwise be shed to a frightful extent, feeling myself fully able to maintain my position for a yet indefinite period. This communication will be handed you, under a flag of truce, by Major-General James Bowen.

Very respectfully, your obedient servant,

J. C. PEMBERTON.

To this General Grant replied as follows:

HEAD-QUARTERS, DEPARTMENT OF TENNESSEE,
IN THE FIELD, NEAR VICKSBURG, *July* 3, 1863.

Lieutenant-General J. C. PEMBERTON, *commanding Confederate forces, &c.:*

GENERAL:—Your note of this date, just received, proposes an armistice of several hours, for the purpose of arranging terms of capitulation through commissioners to be appointed, &c. The effusion of blood you propose stopping by this course, can be ended at any time you may choose, *by an unconditional surrender of the city and garrison.* Men who have shown so much endurance and courage as those now in Vicksburg, will always challenge the respect of an adversary, and I can assure you will be treated with all the respect due them as prisoners of war. I do not favor the proposition of appointing commissioners to arrange terms of capitulation, *because I have no other terms than those indicated above.*

I am, General, very respectfully, your obedient servant,

U. S. GRANT, *Major-General.*

General Bowen expressed a wish to converse with the chief General on this important matter; but the latter at once declined. General Bowen then requested that General Grant would meet General Pemberton on neutral ground, as more could be arranged at one personal interview than by an exchange of numerous dispatches. General Grant very readily replied he would willingly do so in person, offering to meet General Pemberton the same afternoon at three o'clock, and consult with him on the terms he would grant the garrison. This reply was placed in the hands of the rebel messengers, who, blindfolded, were conducted back to the place of entrance to the Union lines, and were there set at liberty, to return to General Pemberton with the answer.

Nothing more was now done until afternoon. The artillery re-opened, and the siege went on as before. By noon, however, the general promulgated his orders, requiring a temporary cessation of hostilities.

The following interesting account of the interview between Generals Grant and Pemberton, is given by one who had followed the army during the whole campaign:

At three o'clock precisely, one gun, the prearranged signal, was fired, and immediately replied to by the enemy. General Pemberton then made his appearance on the works in McPherson's front, under a white flag, considerably on the left of what is known as Fort Hill. General Grant rode through our trenches until he came to an outlet, leading to a small green space, which had not been trod by either army. Here he dismounted, and advanced to meet General Pemberton, with whom he shook hands, and greeted familiarly.

It was beneath the outspreading branches of a gigantic oak that the conference of the generals took place. Here presented the only space which had not been used for some purpose or other by the contending armies. The ground was covered with a fresh, luxuriant verdure; here and there a shrub or clump of bushes could be seen standing out from the green growth on the surface, while several oaks filled up the scene, and gave it character. Some of the trees in their tops exhibited the effects of flying projectiles, by the loss of limbs or torn foliage, and in their trunks the indentations of smaller missiles plainly marked the occurrences to which they had been silent witnesses.

The party made up to take part in the conference was composed as follows:

United States Officers.

Major-General U. S. Grant.

Major-General James B. McPherson.

Brigadier-General A. J. Smith.

Rebel Officers.

Lieutenant-General John C. Pemberton.

Major-General Bowen.

Colonel Montgomery, A. A.-G. to General Pemberton.

When Generals Grant and Pemberton met they shook hands, Colonel Montgomery introducing the party. A short silence ensued, at the expiration of which General Pemberton remarked:

"General Grant, I meet you in order to arrange terms for the capitulation of the city of Vicksburg and its garrison. What terms do you demand?"

"*Unconditional surrender*," replied General Grant.

"Unconditional surrender?" said Pemberton. "Never, so long as I have a man left me! I will fight rather."

"*Then, sir, you can continue the defence*," coolly said General Grant. "*My army has never been in a better condition for the prosecution of the siege.*"

During the passing of these few preliminaries, General Pemberton was greatly agitated, quaking from head to foot, while General Grant experienced all his natural self-possession, and evinced not the least sign of embarrassment.

After a short conversation standing, by a kind of mutual tendency the two generals wandered off from the rest of the party and seated themselves on the grass, in a cluster of bushes, where alone they talked over the important events then pending. General Grant could be seen, even at that distance, talking coolly, occasionally giving a few puffs at his favorite companion—his black cigar. General McPherson, General A. J. Smith, General Bowen, and Colonel Montgomery, imitating the example of the commanding generals, seated themselves at some distance off, while the respective staffs of the generals formed another and larger group in the rear.

After a lengthy conversation the generals separated. General Pemberton did not come to any conclusion on the matter, but stated his intention to submit the matter to a council of general officers of his command; and, in the event of their assent, the surrender of the city should be made in the morning. Until morning was given him to consider, to determine upon the matter, and send in his final reply. The generals now rode to their respective quarters.*

General Grant next conferred at his head-quarters with his corps and division commanders, and sent the following letter to General Pemberton, by the hands of General Logan and Lieutenant-Colonel Wilson:

HEAD-QUARTERS, DEPARTMENT OF TENNESSEE,
NEAR VICKSBURG, *July* 3, 1863.

Lieutenant-General J. C. PEMBERTON, *commanding Confederate forces*, *Vicksburg, Miss:*

GENERAL: In conformity with the agreement of this afternoon, I will submit the following proposition for the surrender of the city of Vicksburg, public stores, &c. On your accepting the terms proposed, I will march in one division, as a guard, and take possession at eight o'clock to-morrow morning. As soon as paroles can be made out and signed by the officers and men, you will be allowed to march out of our lines, the officers taking with them their regimental clothing, and staff, field, and cavalry officers one horse each. The rank and file will be allowed all their clothing, but no other property.

If these conditions are accepted, any amount of rations you may deem necessary can be taken from the stores you now have, and also the necessary cooking utensils for preparing them; thirty wagons also, counting two two-horse or mule teams as one. You will be allowed to transport such articles as cannot be carried along. The same conditions will be allowed to all sick and wounded officers and privates, as fast as they become able to travel. The paroles for these latter must be signed, however, whilst officers are present, authorized to sign the roll of prisoners.

I am, General, very respectfully,
Your obedient servant,
U. S. GRANT, *Major-General.*

The same correspondent, whose description of the interview between the generals has already been given, writes under date of July 4th, as follows:

From the time of the breaking up of the conference of generals, till

* Mr. Keim's dispatch to the *New York Herald.*

this morning, when the surrender became an irrevocable fact, the impatience and restlessness of the entire army was greater than can possibly be imagined. The troops ceased their customary vigilance and wandered from camp to camp in a state of listless reaction. There was no firing from the trenches or batteries, for orders had been promulgated that all operations of a hostile character should cease until resumed by authority from head-quarters. *This was the first instance of a cessation of firing since our arrival.* The existence of the two armies was not perceptible except in the presence of the troops. Everywhere silence and relaxation reigned. It was a change from the most exacting duty on the one hand, to the most extreme idleness on the other. The only appearance of duty by either army was on the part of a few sentinels, national and rebel, posted at various points along our lines and the rebel works, to keep back the curious of our own men, as well as to stay the desire of the enemy to penetrate within our lines and see the perfect network of approaches by means of which we have advanced unharmed up to the very ditches of their forts.

The remainder of yesterday was passed by many of the soldiers of both armies in chats upon various matters connected with the campaign. Knots of a half dozen of our men, and a like number of rebels, could be seen here and there reclining upon the exterior slope of the enemy's works, engaged in enthusiastic conversation, not unfrequently relieving its monotony by physical application upon each other, to enforce the veracity of their assertions, when doubted by the opposite party. Thus did they wile away the hours of the evening until tattoo, when the soldiers of each side, excepting those on sentinel duty, disappeared.

During the night no startling occurrences happened, all being quiet.

The morning of this thrice glorious Fourth dawned with a cloudless sky, and, even ere the sun had risen, the camps were alive with an anticipating and impatient set, whose loquacity poured itself forth, in a confusion of languages which might be heard ringing in the clear air at a distance several times the usual compass of the human voice. Nor were the speculations of the men less various than their language. One had his reasons for knowing that the rebels were using the present moments of respite to strengthen themselves, or to consolidate their force on some unexpected point of attack, or perhaps to effect some other designs equally as nefarious, of which we were not aware. Some said the enemy had no intention of surrendering, but, fearing a first class Fourth of July bombardment, they hit upon the present plan of eluding such a direful visitation and its necessary results. In this way reasoned many. Another set thought, if it really were the intention of the enemy to surrender, it was time they were coming to a conclusion. They "could not see why they did not do so at once," they "thought the rebels were playing a sharp game," and so forth; every man giving himself a vast amount of unnecessary trouble and concern.

Thus time moved along heavily, each moment passing like a duration of almost weeks, until the eventful time had arrived, and it was known to a certainty that Vicksburg had indeed surrendered.

Having a few hours leisure this morning, prior to the arrival of the dispatch from General Pemberton, stating he was ready to surrender, I took occasion to visit General Grant, and found everybody about his head-quarters in a state of the liveliest satisfaction. It was evident the glorious events of the day were duly appreciated.

The General I found in conversation more animated than I have ever known him. He is evidently contented with the manner in which he has acquitted himself of the responsible task which has for more than five months engrossed his mind and his army. The consummation is one of which he may well be proud. From Bruinsburg to Vicksburg, nineteen days, presents one of the most active records of marches, actions, and victories of the war. All the combined operations of our armies, for a similar length of time, cannot equal it. *It is unparalleled, the only campaign of the war which has involved celerity of movement, attack, victory, pursuit, and the annihilation of the enemy.* But of this I have occasion to speak in another place, and will therefore drop it for the present.

Among other things, the General signified his intention to enter into an immediate pursuit of the rebel Johnston. He was ready as soon as he received Pemberton's final reply to order the troops under Sherman (then resting this side of the Big Black) across the river, while the contingent forces held at Haines and Snyder's bluffs were to follow, overtake and effect a junction with the other troops. This would create a force equal to all the possibilities of the campaign, and irretrievably wrest Southern Mississippi, with the towns of Jackson, Canton, and Meridian, from the possession of the enemy. Such action would restore a large territory to the government, and weaken the enemy correspondingly by subtracting so much from his already limited resources.

From General Grant I returned to the head-quarters of the Seventeenth (McPherson's) Corps, and found the same prevailing good humor that I remarked everywhere else.*

---

* Mr. Keim's dispatch to the *New York Herald.*

The officers who received General Grant's letter stated that it would be impossible to answer it by night, and it was not till a little before the peep of day that the proposed reply was furnished. Early in the morning, however, a messenger arrived at the Union lines with the following letter from General Pemberton:

HEAD-QUARTERS, VICKSBURG, *July* 3, 1863.

Major-General GRANT, *commanding United States forces:*

GENERAL:—I have the honor to acknowledge the receipt of your communication of this date proposing terms for the surrender of this garrison and post. In the main your terms are accepted; but in justice both to the honor and spirit of my troops, manifested in the defence of Vicksburg, I have the honor to submit the following amendments, which, if acceded to by you, will perfect the agreement between us. At ten o'clock to-morrow I propose to evacuate the works in and around Vicksburg, and to surrender the city and garrison under my command by *marching out with my colors and arms and stacking them in front of my present limits,* after which you will take possession; officers to retain their side arms and personal property, and the rights and property of citizens to be respected.

I am, General, yours, very respectfully,

J. C. PEMBERTON, *Lieutenant-General.*

This was a proposal for the besieged to march out with the honors of war, only allowed to garrisons after a very obstinate and brave defence. It is entirely optional on the part of the victor to allow such a privilege, and many commanders have entirely refused it.

General Grant, however, with his accustomed magnanimity to the conquered, acquiesced in the request as follows:

HEAD-QUARTERS, DEPARTMENT OF TENNESSEE,
BEFORE VICKSBURG, *July* 4, 1863.

Lieutenant-General PEMBERTON, *commanding forces in Vicksburg:*

GENERAL:—I have the honor to acknowledge your communication of the 3d of July. The amendments proposed by you cannot be acceded to in full. It will be necessary to furnish every officer and man with a

SURRENDER OF VICKSBURG.

parole signed by himself, which, with the completion of the rolls of prisoners, will necessarily take some time. Again, I can make no stipulation with regard to the treatment of citizens and their private property. *While I do not propose to cause any of them any undue annoyance or loss, I cannot consent to leave myself under restraint by stipulations.* The property which officers can be allowed to take with them will be as stated in the proposition of last evening—that is, *that officers will be allowed their private baggage and side arms, and mounted officers one horse each. If you mean by your proposition for each brigade to march to the front of the lines now occupied by it, and stack their arms at ten o'clock* A. M., *and then return to the inside and remain as prisoners until properly paroled, I will make no objection to it.* Should no modifications be made of your acceptance of my terms by nine o'clock A. M., I shall regard them as having been rejected, and act accordingly. Should these terms be accepted, white flags will be displayed along your lines to prevent such of my troops as may not have been notified from firing on your men.

I am, General, very respectfully,

Your obedient servant,

U. S. GRANT, *Major-General U. S. A.*

After a very short consultation with his general officers, the commandant of Vicksburg sent the following reply:

HEAD-QUARTERS, VICKSBURG, *July* 4, 1863

Major-General U. S. GRANT, *commanding United States forces, etc.:*

GENERAL:—I have the honor to acknowledge the receipt of your communication of this date, and, in reply, to say that the terms proposed by you are accepted.

Very respectfully, your obedient servant,

J. C. PEMBERTON, *Lieutenant-General.*

At ten o'clock on the morning of July 4th, the above final dispatch was received from General Pemberton, and he stated that he was ready to capitulate. General Grant at once telegraphed to General McPherson's head-quarters with instructions that the Seventeenth Corps be ordered under arms immediately, to be in readiness to move instantly into the city upon the receipt of orders to that effect.

Shortly after the hour above mentioned, the rebel works

were surmounted by a large number of white flags along the entire lines, extending from right to left. This was the signal of surrender. Soon the enemy marched out by regiment, on McPherson's front, and stacked their arms and returned within, where they were paroled in a body, prior to the individual parole of each man.

The privilege allowed by General Grant to the enemy of stacking their arms outside of their fortifications somewhat crowded matters, as the Union works were so close that the enemy was pressed for room in order to avoid trespassing beyond the small strip of unoccupied territory lying between the works of the two armies. However, after considerable difficulty, the arms, excepting those of several regiments, were deposited according to the provisions of the surrender, without encroachment upon our approaches.

In attendance upon the capitulation of the rebels there were a number of line officers and privates of the Union army as lookers on. No one had been delegated by General Grant to superintend the matter, *out of courtesy to the enemy*, whose noble defence had won them the highest esteem of both officers and men. The surrender, therefore, appeared, as it were, a volition, and not of compulsion; and was hardly known until some time after, owing to the quietness with which it was conducted. General Grant had wisely taken this matter into consideration, and prevented the lips of the incautious and uncalculating from uttering remarks of no good to the Union cause, and not in the least calculated to keep alive that harmony of feeling which turned out to be one of the most noticeable features of the occasion. As it was, as the General had desired, the enemy was allowed to conduct the matter according to his own liking, so it was done within the limitations of the previously stipulated terms of capitulation.

Several regiments not having room to stack arms with the rest of the command, deposited them at the Court House.

Three hours elapsed before the last of the rebel regiments had surrendered their arms. During this time General John A. Logan was engaged in getting his troops in readiness for subsequent movements.

CHAPTER XLI.

OCCUPATION OF VICKSBURG.—THE LOSSES.

THE Fourth of July, 1863, was one of the most important in the history of the United States, and of its armies. On this day the glad tidings of victory in Pennsylvania was sounded throughout the land, and on this day the victorious "Army of Tennessee" took possession of the boasted stronghold of the rebels—"the Gibraltar of the Mississippi"—Vicksburg.

The entrance into the city of Vicksburg is thus described by a participant:

It was about one o'clock P. M., before matters had assumed such a stage of completion as would admit of the entrance of the city by our troops. A slight further detention was also occasioned awaiting the pioneer corps, thrown out in advance, to open a passage through the breastworks and across the ditches and rifle-pits of the enemy. After this was finished, no further obstructions presented themselves, and the column moved forward. The order of march was by a seniority of brigade commanders, with an exception in the case of the Forty-fifth Illinois Infantry, Colonel J. A. Maltby, *which was specially ordered to lead the column, in consequence of heroic conduct during the siege and operations in the campaign against Vicksburg.*

The order of formation, in the march into the city, was as follows:

Major-General U. S. Grant and staff.

Major-General J. B. McPherson and staff.

Major-General J. A. Logan and staff.

Brigadier-General M. D. Leggett, First Brigade, Third Division, led by the Forty-fifth Illinois Infantry.

Brigadier-General Z. E. G. Ransom, First Brigade, Seventh Division, temporarily assigned to Logan.

Brigadier-General John Stevenson, Second Brigade, Third Division; and with each brigade its batteries, baggage train, &c.

The division of General John E. Smith, though part of the Seventeenth Army Corps which was designated by General Grant to occupy the city, was held outside of the works as a kind of outer line of guards to prevent the escape of prisoners.

After passing through several inner lines of the rifle-pits and breastworks, the column of occupation penetrated the suburbs of the city, and marched through its principal streets to the Court House. As might be expected, from the long schooling the city had received under the influence of the secession conspirators, no demonstrations of satisfaction at our arrival were made along the line of march; but on the contrary, houses were closed, the citizens within doors, and the city was wrapped in gloom. It seems as if the population anticipated their next step would be into the grave.

Upon arriving at the Court House, the troops were drawn up in line facing the building. This done, the ceremony of possession was completed by the display of the flags of the Forty-fifth Illinois Infantry, and of the head-quarters of the Seventeenth Corps, from the dome of the Court House.

Upon the appearance of the flags the troops cheered vociferously, making the city ring to its very suburbs with shouts of the votaries of liberty. It was an occasion which few ever have the opportunity of witnessing, and one which will secure a life-long remembrance in the minds of all present.

In consideration of the active part taken by the Seventeenth Corps in the campaign which consummated in the capture of Vicksburg, that command was designated by General Grant to take possession of the city. General Logan's Division occupied within the works, while General John E. Smith held the Union works without. General McArthur continued with General Sherman's army in its operations against Johnston.

In view of General Grant's plans, Major-General McPherson was appointed to the command of the new district about to be formed, and having Vicksburg for its centre.

Major-General Logan commanded the city and its environs.

The Provost-Marshal's department was placed in charge of Lieutenant-Colonel James Wilson, Provost-Marshal of the corps—Provost-Guard, Forty-fifth Illinois Infantry.

A number of subordinate officers had to be created to carry out the laborious and endless details which naturally occur in the administration of a city in population as large as the present. However, as initiatory measures, the above answered every purpose, and the workings of the plans were harmonious and effective. There were no disgraceful scenes of rapine, violence or insult to note, nor had any thing occurred to compromise as a mass the soldiers of the government. There were a few instances of battering down store doors, to examine the contents of the establishments, *but this was soon stopped* upon the inauguration of the provost-guard. One rather unaccountable fact was the trouble the guard experienced in keeping down the rebel soldiery. The people feared the thieving proclivities of their own men even more than ours. It was not long, however, before the efficient guard patroling the city had picked up all vagrant individuals, compelled them to disgorge, and then quietly consigned them to the peaceable retirement of the guard-house, to await their trial before his worship, the Provost-Marshal. The aforesaid establishment is already quite populous with miscreant secesh, and a slight sprinkling of our own unfortunates. While they are amongst us they must expect to be obliged to conduct themselves like soldiers, and obey the newly inaugurated authority now ruling and insuring order and security to the inhabitants and property within the city. The quiet which now prevails everywhere is astonishing, *and reflects great credit upon the abilities and judgment of those at the head of affairs.*

After the surrender of the city was officially known to the transportation officers in charge of steamboats at Chickasaw Bayou, there was a general, mixed and laughable stampede of boats out of the Yazoo and down the Mississippi for the levee of Vicksburg. The John H. Groesbeck, being the office boat of the Chief of Transportation, appropriated the advance of the Yazoo River batch.

The transports, however, were not the first to arrive before the city, for the Neptune of the Mississippi was on the alert, and impatiently awaited the course of events under full steam. No sooner was the flag thrown to the breeze from the Court House than the Admiral's glass caught sight of its beautiful folds, and in due time his vessel steamed down to the city, followed by all the gunboats in the neighborhood, and took possession of a few feet of river front. All this was duly done, after the authority of the army of the United States was secured beyond doubt.

In less than four hours after the city had capitulated, the levees were lined with steamers as far as the eye could reach. At least seventy-five had arrived up to that time, and more were coming in hourly. All the boats from below, as well as those from above, were there to swell the number. The city had the appearance of a great inland commercial metropolis. The levees were almost instantaneously covered with a busy, moving crowd of humanity, pushing hither and thither, as if they were old residents, and the city had not experienced the *interregnum* of intercourse with the outer world, which had been her fate for nearly two years. Many of the boats had already commenced to discharge their cargoes, which, of course, occasioned a lively activity on shore, while teams and men were busily engaged in hauling the different stores to their respective destinations.

It may be said that Vicksburg is once more a living city. Reclaimed from her late oppressors, she is free to share with her sister cities the numerous opportunities which have been restored to them by the reinstated authority of our great, and glorious, and ever to be perpetuated republic.*

The value of the reduction of Vicksburg was not only great in a moral, political, and strategical point of view; but it possessed still further importance by inflicting a severe loss upon the rebels, in both men and material.

The following is a rough estimate of the number of officers, soldiers, and ordnance, which fell into the hands of the United States authorities with the city of Vicksburg:

One Lieutenant-General, John C. Pemberton, late commandant of the army for the defence of Vicksburg.

Nineteen Major and Brigadier-Generals, as follows:—Major-General Bowen, Major-General Martin L. Smith and Major-General Forney; Brigadier-Generals Barton, Cochran, Lee, Vaughn, Reynolds, Baldwin, Harris, Taylor, Cummings, Stevenson of Georgia, Hebart, Wall of Texas, commanding Texan Legion; Moore, Schoep, Buford, and Cockerell.

Over four thousand field, line, and staff officers.

About twenty-three thousand effective men, non-commissioned officers and privates, and over six thousand men in hospital.

* Mr. Keim's dispatch to the *New York Herald*.

Ninety siege-guns.

One hundred and twenty-eight field-pieces.

Thirty-five thousand (approximately) muskets and rifles, principally Enfield, and in excellent order.

Powder and shell for ordnance of different calibre in abundance.

A large quantity of miscellaneous matter, such as wagons, a few animals, armorers' tools, machinery, &c.

Among the military establishments taken possession of were the arsenal, well supplied with unused rifles, and the foundry, with all conveniences for casting shot, shell, and cannon, and capable of doing a great deal of other work of a similar character, such as casting.

The troops taken prisoners were mainly composed of Mississippians, called "The State troops," Georgians, Alabamians, Louisianians, Missourians, and regulars.

The following is a table compiled from various sources, and showing, at a glance, the estimated losses of the rebels, in men, from the commencement of the campaign, on April 30th, to the final surrender of the city:

Prisoners.	
Lieutenant-General	1
Major and Brigadier-Generals	19
Field, staff, and line officers	4,600
Non-commissioned officers and privates	30,000
Total, without regard to rank	34,620
Killed, Wounded, and Stragglers.	
Killed in battles and skirmishes	1,000
Wounded in battles and skirmishes	4,000
Captured in hospitals in Vicksburg and elsewhere	6,000
Stragglers, including men cut off and unable to rejoin their commands	800
Total	11,800

Recapitulation.

Total prisoners	34,620
Killed, wounded, and in hospital	11,000
Stragglers, &c.	800
Making a loss to the enemy, in sixty-five days, of	46,420

The following table also shows the losses of material sustained by the enemy during the same length of time:

Field Artillery.	*Pieces.*
Captured in battle	83
At Vicksburg	128
Total	211
Siege Artillery.	
At Vicksburg	90
Captured Small-Arms.	
In battle	10,000
At Vicksburg	35,000
Total	45,000

Recapitulation.

Artillery captured	301
Muskets and rifles	45,000

Besides this, a number of field-pieces and siege-guns were destroyed at Jackson, Haines and Snyder's Bluffs, which are not included in the above estimate.*

General Grant, in his official report, sums up the Union losses, during the series of battles of the Vicksburg campaign, as follows:

	Killed.	*Wounded.*	*Missing.*	*Total.*
Port Gibson,	130	718	5	853
Fourteen-Mile Creek (skirmish)	4	24	—	28
Raymond,	69	341	32	442
Jackson,	40	240	6	286
Champion's Hill,	426	1,842	189	2,457
Big Black Railroad Bridge,	29	242	2	273
Vicksburg,	245	3,688	303	4,236
Grand Total,	943	7,095†	537	8,575

* *New York Herald* estimates. See also Appendix G.

† Nearly one-half of the wounded returned to duty within a month.

General Recapitulation.

Rebel losses in killed, wounded, stragglers, and prisoners,					46,420
Union losses,	do.	do.	do.	do.	8,575
Balance in favor of Grant,					37,845

In addition, therefore, to the immense quantity of stores secured with the reduction of Vicksburg, a balance of nearly thirty-eight thousand men had to be placed to the credit of Grant's services during this campaign.

The following extract, from General Grant's report, will show how the army subsisted during the first twenty days of the Vicksburg campaign:

In the march from Bruinsburg to Vicksburg, covering a period of twenty days, before supplies could be obtained from government stores, only five days' rations were issued, and three days of those were taken in haversacks at the start, and were soon exhausted. All other subsistence was obtained from the country through which we passed. The march was commenced without wagons, except such as could be picked up through the country. The country was abundantly supplied with corn, bacon, beef, and mutton. The troops enjoyed excellent health, and no army ever appeared in better spirits, or felt more confident of success.

General Halleck, in his Annual Report of the War, thus speaks of the administration and success of the Department of the Tennessee:

At the date of my last Annual Report, Major-General Grant occupied West Tennessee and the northern boundary of Mississippi. The object of the campaign of this army was the opening of the Mississippi River, in conjunction with the army of General Banks.

General Grant was instructed to drive the enemy in the interior as far south as possible, and destroy their railroad communications; then to fall back to Memphis and embark his available forces on transports, and with the assistance of the fleet of Admiral Porter, reduce Vicksburg. The first part of this plan was most successfully executed, but the right wing of the army sent against Vicksburg, under Major-General Sherman, found that place much stronger than was expected.

Two attacks were made, on the 28th and 29th of December; but failing in their object, our troops were withdrawn, and while waiting for re-enforcements from General Grant, moved up the Arkansas River to Arkansas Post, which place was, with the assistance of the gunboats, captured on the 11th of January. Our loss at Vicksburg was 191 killed, 982 wounded, and 756 missing; at Arkansas Post, 129 killed, 831 wounded, and 17 missing. We captured at the latter place 5,000 prisoners, 17 pieces of cannon, 3,000 small-arms, 46,000 rounds of ammunition, and 563 animals.

General Grant now assumed the immediate command of the army on the Mississippi, which was largely re-enforced. Being satisfied by the result of General Sherman's operations that the north line of the enemy's works was too strong to be carried without a very heavy loss, he directed his attention to opening the canal, which had been commenced the year before by General Williams, across the peninsula on the west bank of the river.

This canal had been improperly located—its upper terminus being in an eddy, and the lower terminus being exposed to the enemy's guns; nevertheless, it was thought that it could be completed sooner than a new one could be constructed. While working parties, under Captain Prince, chief engineer of that army, were diligently employed upon this canal, General Grant directed his attention to several other projects for turning the enemy's position. These are fully described in his official report.* The canal proving impracticable, and his other plans being unsuccessful, he determined to move his army by land down the west bank of the river, some seventy miles, while transports for crossing should run past the enemy's batteries at Vicksburg.

The danger of running the batteries being very great, and the roads on the west side in horrible condition, this was a difficult and hazardous expedient; but it seemed to be the only possible solution of the problem. The execution of the plan, however, was greatly facilitated by Admiral Farragut, who had run two of his vessels past the enemy's batteries at Port Hudson and Grand Gulf, and cleared the river of the enemy's boats below Vicksburg; and finally, through the *the indomitable energy of the commanding-general* and the admirable dispositions of Admiral Porter for running the enemy's batteries, the operation was completely successful.

The army crossed the river at Bruinsburg, April 30th, turned Grand Gulf, and engaged the enemy near Port Gibson on the 1st, and at Fourteen-Mile Creek on the 3d of May. The enemy was defeated in both

---

* See Appendix G.

engagements, with heavy loss. General Grant now moved his forces by rapid marches to the north, in order to separate the garrison of Vicksburg from the covering army of Johnston. This movement was followed by the battles of "Raymond," May 12th; of "Jackson," May 14th; of "Champion's Hill," May 16th, and of "Big Black River Bridge," May 17th—in all of which our troops were victorious. General Grant now proceeded to invest Vicksburg.

In order to facilitate General Grant's operations by destroying the enemy's lines of communication, and prevent the early concentration of any re-enforcements, Colonel (now Brigadier-General) Grierson was sent with a cavalry force from La Grange on the 17th of April to traverse the interior of the State of Mississippi. This expedition was most successfully conducted. It destroyed many of the enemy's railroad bridges, dépôts, and much rolling stock, and reached Baton Rouge, Lousiana, in safety on the 2d of May. On returning to Vicksburg, General Grant found his forces insufficient to entirely invest the enemy's works. There was, therefore, danger that the two bodies of the enemy under Pemberton and Johnston might yet effect a junction, as it was known that the latter was being largely re-enforced from Bragg's army in Middle and East Tennessee. Under these circumstances General Grant determined to attempt to carry the place by assault.

Two unsuccessful attacks were made May 19th and 22d; but as re-enforcements reached him a few days after, sufficiently large to enable him to completely invest the rebel defences, he resorted to the slower but more certain operations of a regular siege. By the 3d of July his saps were so far advanced as to render his success certain, and on that day General Pemberton proposed an armistice and capitulation, which were finally accepted, and Vicksburg surrendered on the 4th of July. In the language of General Grant's official report, the results of this short campaign were:

"The defeat of the enemy in five battles outside of Vicksburg, the occupation of Jackson, the capital of the State of Mississippi, and the capture of Vicksburg and its garrison and munitions of war; a loss to the enemy of 37,000 prisoners, among whom were fifteen general officers; at least 10,000 killed and wounded; and among the killed, Generals Tracy, Tilghman, and Green, and hundreds, and perhaps thousands of stragglers, who can never be collected and organized. Arms and munitions of war for an army of sixty thousand have fallen into our hands, besides a large amount of other public property, consisting of railroad, locomotives, cars, steamboats, cotton, etc.; and much was destroyed to prevent our capturing it."

When we consider the character of the country in which this army oper-

ated, the formidable obstacles to be overcome, the number of forces and the strength of the enemy's works, we cannot fail to admire the courage and endurance of the troops, and the skill and daring of their commander. No more brilliant exploit can be found in military history. It has been alleged, and the allegation has been widely circulated by the press, that General Grant, in the conduct of his campaign, positively disobeyed the instructions of his superiors. *It is hardly necessary to remark that General Grant never disobeyed an order or instruction, but always carried out to the best of his ability every wish or suggestion made to him by the government.* Moreover he has never complained that the government did not furnish him all the means and assistance in its power, to facilitate the execution of any plan he saw fit to adopt.

While the main army of Tennessee was operating against Vicksburg, the enemy's force, on the west side of the river, made unsuccessful attacks on Milliken's Bend and Lake Providence on the 6th and 10th of June. Our loss in the former was 101 killed, and 285 wounded, and 266 missing. The loss in the latter was not reported. It is represented that the colored troops in these desperate engagements fought with great bravery; and that the rebels treated this class of prisoners of war, as well as their officers, with great barbarity. It has not been possible, however, to ascertain the correctness of these representations in regard to the treatment of these prisoners.

After the capture of Vicksburg, General Grant reported, that his troops were so much fatigued and worn out with forced marches and the labors of the siege as to absolutely require several weeks of repose before undertaking another campaign. *Nevertheless, as the exigencies of the service seemed to require it, he sent out those who were least fatigued on several important expeditions, while the others remained at Vicksburg to put that place in a better defensive condition for a small garrison.*

When the news of this glorious victory officially reached the President, he wrote an autograph letter to General Grant, of which document the following is a copy:

EXECUTIVE MANSION, WASHINGTON, *July* 13, 1863.

To Major-General GRANT:

MY DEAR GENERAL:—I do not remember that you and I ever met personally. I write this now as a greatful acknowledgment for *the almost inestimable service you have done the country.* I wish to say a word further. When you first reached the vicinity of Vicksburg, I thought you should do what you finally did—march the troops across the neck, run the batteries with the transports, and thus go below; and I never had any faith, except a general hope that you knew better than I, that the Yazoo Pass expedition and the like could succeed. When you got below and took Port Gibson, Grand Gulf, and vicinity, I thought you should go down the river and join General Banks; and when you turned northward east of the Big Black, I feared it was a mistake. I now wish to make a personal acknowledgment *that you were right and I was wrong.** Yours, very truly,

A. LINCOLN.

Several gentlemen were near the President at the time he received the news of Grant's success, some of whom had been complaining of the rumors of his habit of using intoxicating drinks to excess.

"So I understand Grant drinks whiskey to excess?" interrogatively remarked the President.

"Yes," was the reply.

"What whiskey does he drink?" inquired Mr. Lincoln.

"What whiskey?" doubtfully queried his hearers.

"Yes. Is it Bourbon or Monongahela?"

"Why do you ask, Mr. President?"

"Because, if it makes him win victories like this at Vicksburg, I will send a demijohn of the same kind to every general in the army."

His visitors saw the point, although at their own cost.

It is stated that General Grant entered Vicksburg on July 4th, 1863, with a cigar in his mouth. In alluding to

* It is currently stated that when Adjutant-General Thomas visited the Department of the Tennessee, early in April, 1863, he carried in his pocket an order from the President to displace and remove General Grant from his command, if the facts proved to be as they were reported at the national capital. Perhaps President Lincoln's note refers indirectly to that order. It is needless to add that General Thomas, on his arrival at Milliken's Bend, found matters far different than were represented at Washington, and he, therefore, thought it more judicious not to remove the order from his pocket, nor General Grant from his command.

this fact, a newspaper of strong Southern proclivities remarked as follows:

We pardon General Grant's smoking a cigar as he entered the smouldering ruins of the town of Vicksburg. A little stage effect is admissible in great captains, considering that Napoleon at Milan wore the little cocked hat and sword of Marengo, and that snuff was the inevitable concomitant of victory in the great Frederick. *General Grant is a noble fellow, and by the terms of capitulation he accorded to the heroic garrison, showed himself as generous as Napoleon was to Wurmser at the surrender of Mantua. His deed will read well in history, and he has secured to himself a name which posterity will pronounce with veneration and gratitude.* There is no general in this country or in Europe that has done harder work than General Grant, and none that has better graced his victories by the exercise of humanity and virtue. What we learn of the terms of capitulation is sufficient to prove *General Grant to be a generous soldier and a man.* A truly brave man respects bravery in others, and when the sword is sheathed considers himself free to follow the dictates of humanity. General Grant is not a general that marks his progress by proclamations to frighten unarmed men, women, and children; he fulminates no arbitrary edicts against the press; he does not make war on newspapers and their correspondents; he flatters no one to get himself puffed; but *he is terrible in arms and magnanimous after the battle.* Go on, brave General Grant; pursue the course you have marked out for yourself, and Clio, the pensive muse, as she records your deeds. will rejoice at her manly theme.

Among the results of the fall of Vicksburg is one that must not be overlooked—Port Hudson. As soon as the garrison had surrendered, General Grant notified General Banks of the fact, and that officer at once imparted the glorious intelligence to his command. Like lightning the welcome news flew along the line, and the Union pickets joyously informed the rebel sentinels that their boasted stronghold had fallen. It did not take long for the tidings to reach the rebel head-quarters, and the same day the commandant at Port Hudson sent the following dispatch to General Banks:

HEAD-QUARTERS, PORT HUDSON, LA., *July* 7, 1863.

GENERAL:—Having received information from your troops that *Vicksburg has been surrendered*, I make this communication to ask you to give me the official assurance whether this is true or not, *and if true I ask for a cessation of hostilities*, with a view to the consideration of terms for surrendering this position.

I am, General, very respectfully, your obedient servant,

FRANK GARDNER,

Major-General commanding Confederate States forces.

To Major-General BANKS, *commanding U. S. forces near Port Hudson.*

General Banks, early the next morning, replied as follows:

HEAD-QUARTERS, DEPARTMENT OF THE GULF,
BEFORE PORT HUDSON, *July* 8, 1863.

GENERAL:—In reply to your communication, dated the 7th instant, by flag of truce received a few moments since, I have the honor to inform you that I received yesterday morning, July 7th, at forty-five minutes past ten o'clock, by the gunboat General Price, an official dispatch from Major-General Ulysses S. Grant, United States Army, whereof the following is a true extract:—

HEAD-QUARTERS, DEPARTMENT OF THE TENNESSEE,
NEAR VICKSBURG, *July* 4, 1863.

Major-General N. P. BANKS, *commanding Department of the Gulf:*

GENERAL:—The garrison of Vicksburg surrendered this morning. The number of prisoners, as given by the officers, is twenty-seven thousand; field artillery, one hundred and twenty-eight pieces; and a large number of siege-guns, probably not less than eighty.

Your obedient servant, U. S. GRANT, *Major-General.*

I regret to say that, under present circumstances, I cannot, consistently with my duty, consent to a cessation of hostilities for the purpose you indicate.

Very respectfully, your obedient servant,

N. P. BANKS, *Major-General Commanding.*

To Major-General FRANK GARDNER, *Commanding Confederate States forces, Port Hudson.*

It appears that the unwelcome news was all that was wanting to decide the fate of Port Hudson. In fact, after Vicksburg had capitulated, Port Hudson was untenable.

The rebel commandant, therefore, immediately dispatched the following communication to General Banks:

PORT HUDSON, *July* 8, 1863.

GENERAL:—I have the honor to acknowledge the receipt of your communication of this date, giving a copy of an official communication from Major-General U. S. Grant, United States Army, *announcing the surrender of the garrison of Vicksburg.*

Having defended this position as long as I deem my duty requires, I am willing to surrender to you, and will appoint a commission of three officers to meet a similiar commission appointed by yourself, *at nine o'clock this morning,* for the purpose of agreeing upon, and drawing up the terms of surrender, and for that purpose I ask a cessation of hostilities. Will you please designate a point outside of my breastworks where the meeting shall be held for this purpose?

I am, very respectfully, your obedient servant,

FRANK GARDNER, *commanding Confederate States forces.*

To Major-General BANKS, *commanding United States forces.*

General Banks replied at once in the following language:

HEAD-QUARTERS, UNITED STATES FORCES,
BEFORE PORT HUDSON, *July* 8, 1863.

GENERAL:—I have the honor to acknowledge the receipt of your communication of this date, stating that you are willing to surrender the garrison under your command to the forces under my command, and that you will appoint a commission of three officers to meet a similar commission appointed by me, at nine o'clock this morning, for the purpose of agreeing upon and drawing up the terms of surrender.

In reply I have the honor to state, that I have designated Brigadier-General Charles P. Stone, Colonel Henry W. Birge, and Lieutenant-Colonel Richard B. Irwin, as the officers to meet the commission appointed by you.

They will meet your officers, at the hour designated, at a point where the flag of truce was received this morning. I will direct that active hostilities shall entirely cease on my part, until further notice, for the purpose stated.

Very respectfully, your obedient servant,

N. P. BANKS, *Major-General Commanding.*

To Major-General FRANK GARDNER, *commanding Confederate States forces, Port Hudson.*

The following announces the result of the surrender:

HEAD-QUARTERS, DEPARTMENT OF THE GULF,
NINETEENTH ARMY CORPS, PORT HUDSON, *July* 10, 1863.

To General H. W. HALLECK:

SIR:—I have the honor to inform you that, with this post, there fell into our hands over five thousand five hundred prisoners, including one Major-General and one Brigadier-General; twenty pieces of heavy artillery, five complete batteries, numbering thirty-one pieces of field artillery; a good supply of projectiles for light and heavy guns, 44,800 pounds of cannon-powder, five thousand stand of arms, and one hundred and fifty thousand rounds of small-arm ammunition, besides a small amount of stores of various kinds. We captured, also, two steamers, one of which is very valuable. They will be of great service at this time.

I am, General, very respectfully, your obedient servant,

N. P. BANKS, *Major-General Commanding.**

---

* General Banks, by his operations around Port Hudson during May and June, 1863, rendered valuable assistance to General Grant in the prosecution of the siege of Vicksburg.

CHAPTER XLII.

THE PURSUIT OF JOHNSTON.—SECOND CAPTURE OF THE CITY OF JACKSON.

General Grant having learned, as before stated, that General Joseph E. Johnston intended to attack him in the rear, if he could find an opportunity, or, at least, so harass him as to cause him, if possible, to raise the siege of Vicksburg, sent a force, under General W. T. Sherman, to resist his advance. General Johnston did not attack; therefore General Grant determined to attack him the moment Vicksburg fell, and of this fact General Sherman was notified.

It had been planned that the grand assault on Vicksburg should have taken place on July 6th, and General Grant therefore ordered General Sherman in the mean time to have up supplies of all descriptions, so that he might be able to move at a moment's notice, should the assault prove a success, of which fact the General appeared to have no doubt. General Sherman at once made his preparations, and (adds Grant in his report) "when the place surrendered on the 4th, two days earlier than I had fixed for the attack, General Sherman was found ready, and moved at once with a force increased by the addition of the remainder of both the Thirteenth and Fifteenth Army Corps, and is at present (July 6th) investing Jackson, where Johnston has made a stand."

The rebel general, on finding the Union troops had been sent in pursuit of his forces, fell back within the defences of the Mississippi State capital, where he issued the following proclamation to his troops:

HEAD-QUARTERS, ON THE FIELD, *July* 9, 1863.

FELLOW-SOLDIERS:—An insolent foe, *flushed with hope by his recent success at Vicksburg, confronts you,* threatening the people, whose homes and liberty you are here to protect, with plunder and conquest. Their guns may even now be heard as they advance.

The enemy it is at once the duty and the mission of you, brave men, to chastise and expel from the soil of Mississippi. The commanding general confidently relies on you to sustain his pledge, which he makes in advance, and he will be with you in the good work, even unto the end.

The vice of "straggling" he begs you to shun, and to frown on. If needs be, it will be checked by even the most summary remedies.

The telegraph has already announced a glorious victory over the foe, won by your noble comrades of the Virginia army on Federal soil; may he not, with redoubled hopes, count on you, while defending your firesides and household gods, to emulate the proud example of your brothers in the East?

The country expects in this, the great crisis of its destiny, that every man will do his duty.

JOSEPH E. JOHNSTON, *General Commanding.*

The army under General Sherman had advanced steadily, and was now gradually encircling the city. On the 12th of July he had invested the city from Pearl River, on the north of Jackson, to the same stream south of the place. The Pearl River runs directly through the city. By this means, General Sherman succeeded in cutting off many hundred cars from the Confederacy. While investing the city, General Sherman on the 11th of July sent a company of cavalry on a foraging expedition, and during the trip the command ascertained that the extensive library, forerly belonging to the rebel President, was secreted in a house near by. The cavalry at once proceeded to the house, and there found thousands of volumes of books, and *several bushels of private and political papers*, belonging to Davis, written by persons North and South, who had been engaged in the plot of inciting the rebellion. Some of these papers were carried into camp, and served as novel literature for the officers and men.

In addition to these, several valuable gold-headed walking-canes were found, one of them presented to Davis by Franklin Pierce. On another one was the inscription, "From a Soldier to a Soldier's Friend."

In many of the letters the subject of secession was warmly discussed. Some of these letters date back as far as 1852. Many of the more prominent writers accepted the separation of the North and South as a foregone conclusion, but only disagreed how and when it should be done. Davis is alluded to as the political Moses in this measure, and the allusions to him would seem as if he were looked upon in the light of a demi-god.

On the morning of July 12th, General Sherman sent a battalion of cavalry on an expedition about fifteen miles east of Jackson, for the purpose of destroying the railroad bridges, culverts, rolling stock, or any thing else of value to the rebel government or its military authorities.

During the greater part of the preceding night the investing forces made arrangements for a cannonade of the enemy's works. A premature movement of a portion of the line nearly caused a failure of the expedition, but a prompt action on the part of the commanding general remedied the evil.

On the 13th of July the rebels made a sortie from their works and advanced a brigade of infantry and several batteries of artillery against the right of the line, with the intention of breaking it. The advance was very sudden and was made under the cover of a heavy fog; but the sortie was met with a determined resistance. In a short time after the enemy had opened the attack, the whole of the right wing was in line of battle, ready for an emergency.

On the night of June 16th, General Joseph E. Johnston with a portion of his army evacuated Jackson and retreated in great haste towards the east. Had he not made good his retreat on that night, the whole garrison would have been the next day in great danger of capture by a complete investment of the city.

The following accounts from army correspondents give interesting details of the advance to, and second occupation of the city of Jackson:

While the surrender of Vicksburg was in progress, General Grant arranged his plans for the capture of this town, and intrusted the affair to General Sherman. Accordingly, on the morning of the 5th of July, the Ninth Army Corps, which was then encamped on the Yazoo River, in the vicinity of Haines Bluff, took up the line of march, forming the left wing of the advancing column. The other corps had marched on the right of the Ninth. After a few days of skirmishing, which resulted in the falling back of the rebels to their line of defensive works around the town, the siege regularly commenced, but was of even much briefer duration than the most sanguine expected. Our forces surrounded the city on the north, west, and south sides. As early as the morning of the 16th, suspicion was aroused that the rebels were or intended evacuating, and in order to ascertain the truth a charge of the whole line was ordered at eleven A. M. The signal was two cannon-shots. The troops of the whole force selected to make a feint of an assault were drawn up in line, and as the guns boomed the second shot, away they dashed at the rebel works. *They were received, however, with a steady and heavy fire, which gave no doubt of the presence of an enemy in force*, and the test having been successful, they were withdrawn, after suffering but slight loss. In the evening a reconnoissance was made to within a short distance of the rebel fortifications; and the tramp of a column of troops in motion, intermingled with the commands of the officers, and a confused bustle of noises, was distinctly heard, indicating that the evacuation had commenced.

Daylight on the morning of the 17th left little doubt that such was in fact the case. One brigade was ordered forward as skirmishers, with another in support. Approaching the rebel works, they found them tenantless, and the brigade, reforming in column, dashed into the town on the double quick. No enemy presented himself, but on the outskirts stragglers to the number of 157 were captured. The troops soon pushed to the centre of the town, and raised the Stars and Stripes on the State-House.

The town at this time was almost enveloped in smoke from the burning buildings. The troops all around the line soon observed so evident an indication of a retreat, and in a short time detachments of the Thirteenth and Fifteenth Corps sallied in from the south and west sides. A check, however, was suddenly given to this movement, when it was discovered that the rebels in leaving had planted torpedoes in the roads, which exploded when trodden upon. Fortunately, the injury inflicted by these cowardly instruments was not very extensive. The first killed was a citizen who was flying from the burning town. Another exploded under a group of soldiers, killing or wounding about six of them, and a third blew up a wagon while passing over it.

The evacuation by the rebels, as far as can be ascertained from the reports of citizens and prisoners, commenced soon after sundown and continued until two o'clock of the morning of the 17th, when only a rear guard was left to apply the torch to the buildings selected for destruction.

Of course the retreat was over the Pearl River, in the direction of Meridian, on the line of the Jackson Railroad. The burned district embraces the business portion of the town, though a number of private residences were also fired. The burned buildings lie principally on State, or Main and Capitol streets. In addition to these and their contents, the rebels destroyed a large quantity of cotton, the bales of which they rolled into the streets and ignited.

The tracks of the railroad are reported torn up for many miles beyond the river. In the town they are comparatively uninjured. A number of cars, which are in pretty good condition, also escaped destruction.

In addition to the one hundred and fifty-seven prisoners captured by General Ferrero's Brigade, many others were subsequently taken, swelling the number to nearly four hundred.

The defences of the town, on a close inspection, do not prove so formidable as they were conjectured to be. The roads leading out into the country are each fortified with large and strong works, constructed in many cases with cotton-bales, supplied with heavy guns, and connected with each other by a line of breastworks, rifle-pits, and intrenchments

The heavy artillery had not been removed, and with a large quantity of shot, shell, and powder, has fallen into our hands a prize.*

The annexed account is given by a participant with the right wing of the army:

The evacuation of Jackson was commenced by the rebels at dusk on the evening of the 16th of July, 1863. In the afternoon of that day the Ninth Army Corps (left wing), Major-General Parke, received orders from General Sherman to condense their lines by approaching four hundred yards nearer the rebel works from the line they then occupied. The movement was commenced, and our skirmishers, who were a short distance from the attacking column, were soon engaging the rebel pickets. The rebels on that flank at once comprehended our movement, and sent out a strong body of troops to repel our advance. In a few minutes the musketry fire increased, and in twenty minutes there was a terrific roar of musketry and artillery. The movement of General Parke received some support from the Fifteenth Corps (centre), Major-General Steele, which kept up a diagonal fire on the enemy. The engaging parties were soon enveloped in smoke, and for a time it was a problem which side was gaining ground. After three-fourths of an hour the matter was clearly decided, our troops having attained the objective point, and the rebels were driven back defeated, leaving hundreds of their dead and wounded on the field. After this there was a total cessation of firing on both sides. At dusk one of the rebel regimental bands took a position in one of the salients of their works and regaled our troops by playing the "Bonnie Blue Flag," "My Maryland," "Dixie's Land," and all the other plagiarized airs which they have adopted as national tunes. During the night of the 16th inst., tranquillity reigned throughout the camps. Early on the morning of the 17th inst., our advance pickets of the Thirteenth Corps discovered that the rebel pickets had been withdrawn during the night; and, on looking towards the rebel works, every thing indicated that "fighting Joe Johnston" and his army had left for more congenial parts. The news was communicated to Major-General Ord, commanding the right wing, and in turn was sent to General Sherman, commanding the expedition. Measures were subsequently adopted to take immediate possession of the city

General Blair established his head-quarters at the Governor's house,

---

* Mr. Jas. C. Fitzpatrick's dispatch to the *New York Herald.*

from which place he promulgated orders, and afforded the few remaining inhabitants of the city all the protection within his power. In this he was successful after his orders got into operation, and by one o'clock in the day order reigned supreme.

It would beggar description to attempt to portray the appearance of Jackson after the rebels retreated. Destruction was visible on all hands. Our own army, on its first visit to Jackson, destroyed much valuable property; and, to complete the catalogue, the rebels burned up fifty or sixty buildings on the street fronting the capitol, on the ground of military necessity, to accomplish the destruction of large quantities of army stores which they were not able to transport in their retreat. The day was sultry, scarcely a current of fresh air being felt, and the smoke from the ruins of the fires coursed along through the principal streets, making a trip through the city decidedly uncomfortable.

For nearly two months the rebels had worked night and day to fortify Jackson. Fortifications and rifle-pits arose as if by magic, and these works extended over a front of two miles. Every advantage was taken of the topography of the ground, and every convergent road to the city was covered by artillery. In front of these works and for one-fourth of a mile from their front a strong and impassable abatis was formed by felling trees, placed in such a manner as to render the approach to the works by an opposing army a matter of impossibility. An attempt to charge these works by our troops would have been certain defeat, if not annihilation, to our gallant army. Again, these obstructions afforded a cover to the real nature of the rebel works, and so complete was this concealment as to make them appear as ordinary field works. The principal line of fortifications was made of bales of cotton covered with earth; and to give the reader some idea of the extent of them and their invulnerability, the fact need only be stated that two thousand bales of cotton were used in their construction.

Johston's army, according to the testimony of rebel prisoners, was numerically as strong as ours. It was composed of a portion of Pemberton's old army, and re-enforcements from Bragg's army, and detachments from Mobile, and Charleston, S. C. In it were the divisions of Generals Breckinridge, Loring, Walker, and Gist, besides thousands of home-guards from the interior of Mississippi and Alabama. General Gist brought ten regiments with him from South Carolina, many of them of the "best blood," as a prisoner stated, of the Palmetto State, whose motto was, "No surrender." What a sorry failure they made of it!

After our army had taken possession of Jackson, strong detachments of troops, infantry, cavalry, and artillery, were sent out on all the railroads diverging from the city, with orders to tear up the track, destroy the bridges, culverts, dépôts, and water-tanks within a radius of fifteen miles. As I close this letter, the artillery of some of our advanced troops is heard in the distance. The rebels had nearly completed the railroad bridge, destroyed by our troops in May last, across the Pearl River, near Jackson. This also is to be destroyed.

Nearly every eligible or flat piece of land in and around Jackson has been taken as rebel burial-grounds. From the thousands of graves your correspondent saw in his inspection of the city, the inference is, that the mortality in the rebel army from May until our troops repossessed the city must have been very large. Some of the graves are graced with marble slabs; but the majority had plain head-boards, giving the age and date of the death of the deceased.

Rebel prisoners by hundreds, from Johnston's fugitive army, are coming in and giving themselves up as prisoners of war. They state their belief that the Confederacy is a failure, and the rebel leaders a clique of ambitious, intriguing knaves. They declare that the war was inaugurated by a few selfish politicians, and the people were dragged into it. They state that the Union sentiment is in the minds of many of the people of the South; but they dare not express it, and are biding their time, hoping and praying they may soon be liberated from the heavy yoke of Jefferson Davis and his followers.

Our trophies by the evacuation are not numerous. The most important item is that of the cotton used in the rebel fortifications, and some miscellaneous lots in and near the city; of this, I learn there are about three thousand bales, most of it in good order and ready for shipment northward. The rebels took all their cannon, of which they had fifty pieces, with the exception of one ten-inch ship's columbiad, which was too weighty an incumbrance to a flying army. In addition to the cotton, we obtained large quantities of artillery and musket ammunition The latter was of first quality, of English and Austrian manufacture. Among the different qualities of the small ammunition was the expansive, explosive Minie, and the ordinary buck and ball cartridges. The artillery ammunition was nearly all manufactured at the Augusta (Ga.) arsenal. We captured some twenty or thirty railroad cars and other railroad equipments of no present use to the army, as the railroad, railroad bridges, culverts, water-tanks, and dépôts, have all been destroyed over an area of fifteen miles from Jackson. The damage thus done, will amount to at least two millions of dollars, and should we evacuate the place the rebels could not rebuild the roads destroyed at any price, as the material is not in the Confederacy.

From May 1st up to the capture of Jackson, General Grant's army has been unremittingly at work. They have fought, within that time, seven hotly-contested battles, at the cost of many a gallant life, but with twofold victory to our arms. The trophies of these battles, in arms and prisoners, are counted by thousands; but the crowning event of the campaign *is the opening of the Mississippi River.* The rebel army of the West has been scattered to the winds, and those not killed or captured are fleeing with sheer fright from before our army of veterans. For the present, campaigning in Mississippi is ended.*

* Mr. Charles H. Farrell's dispatch to the *New York Herald.*

CHAPTER XLIII.

GENERAL GRANT AT VICKSBURG, BUT NOT IDLE.

GENERAL GRANT had remained behind at Vicksburg when General Sherman advanced, but he was not idle. He held constant communication with his various commands, and organized certain expeditions, the more effectually to clear the entire department of all vestige of rebel rule. The following dispatch explains how General Grant was employed:

VICKSBURG, MISS., *July* 12, 1863.

Major-General HALLECK, *General-in-Chief*:

General Sherman has Jackson invested from Pearl River on the north to the river on the south. This has cut off many hundred cars from the Confederacy. Sherman says he has forces enough, and feels no apprehension about the result.

Finding that Yazoo City was being fortified, I sent General Herron there with his Division. He captured several hundred prisoners and one steamboat. Five pieces of heavy artillery and all the public stores fell into our hands. The enemy burned three steamboats on the approach of the gunboats.

The De Kalb was blown up and sunk in fifteen feet of water by the explosion of a torpedo.

Finding that the enemy were crossing cattle for the rebel army at Natchez, and were said to have several thousand there, *I have sent steamboats and troops to collect them and destroy all boats and means for making more.*

U. S. GRANT, *Major-General.*

Of the Yazoo City expedition, Admiral Porter reports as follows:

UNITED STATES MISSISSIPPI SQUADRON,
FLAG-SHIP BLACK HAWK, OFF VICKSBURG, *July* 14, 1863.

HON. GIDEON WELLES:

SIR:—Hearing that General Johnston was fortifying Yazoo City with heavy guns, and gathering troops there for the purpose of obtaining supplies for his army from the Yazoo country; also that the remainder of the enemy's best transports were then showing a possibility of his attempt to escape, *Major-General Grant and myself determined to send a naval and military expedition up there to capture them.*

The Baron De Kalb, New National, Kenwood, and Signal, were dispatched, under command of Lieutenant John G. Walker, with a force of troops numbering five thousand, under command of Major-General Frank J. Herron. Pushing up to the city, the Baron De Kalb engaged the batteries, which were all prepared to receive her, and after finding out their strength dropped back to notify General Herron, who immediately landed his men, and the army and navy made a combined attack on the enemy's works. The rebels soon fled, leaving every thing in our possession, and set fire to four of their finest steamers that ran on the Mississippi River in times past.

The army pursued the enemy and captured their rear guard of two hundred and sixty men, and at last accounts were taking more prisoners. Six heavy guns and one vessel, formerly a gunboat, fell into our hands, and all the munitions of war.

Unfortunately, while the Baron De Kalb was moving slowly along she ran foul of a torpedo, which exploded and sunk her. There was no sign of any thing of the kind to be seen. While she was going down another exploded under her stern.

The water is rising fast in the Yazoo, and we can do nothing more than get the guns out of her and then get her into deep water, where she will be undisturbed until we are able to raise her. The officers and men lost every thing.

I have the honor to be, very respectfully, your obedient servant,

DAVID D. PORTER,
Acting Rear-Admiral Commanding Mississippi Squadron.

The Red River and Natchez expedition may be considered as part and parcel of one and the same operation, the success of which is reported by Admiral Porter and General Grant as follows:

FLAG-SHIP BLACK HAWK,
OFF VICKSBURG, *July* 18, 1863.

Hon. GIDEON WELLES, *Secretary of the Navy:*

SIR:—I have the honor to inform you that the expedition I sent into the Red River region proved very successful. Ascending the Black and Tensas Rivers, running parallel with the Mississippi, Lieutenant-Commander Selfridge made the head of navigation—Tensas Lake and Bayou Macon—thirty miles above Vicksburg, and within five or six miles of the Mississippi River. The enemy were taken completely by surprise, not expecting such a force in such a quarter. The rebels who have ascended to that region will be obliged to move further back from the river, if not go away altogether.

Lieutenant-Commander Selfridge divided his forces on finding that the transports which had been carrying stores to Walker's army had escaped up some of the narrow streams. He sent the Manitou and Rattler up the Little Red River—a small tributary of the Black—and the Forest Rose and Petrel up the Tensas. The night was dark and it was raining very hard. The Manitou and Rattler succeeded in capturing the rebel steamer Louisville, one of the largest and perhaps the best steamer in the Western waters. Up the Tensas, or one of its tributaries, the Forest Rose and Petrel captured the steamer Elmira, loaded with stores, sugar, and rum, for the rebel army. Finding that the steamers which had conveyed General Walker's army had returned up the Wachita, the expedition started up that river, and came suddenly upon two rebel steamers; but the rebels set them on fire, and they were consumed so rapidly that their names could not be ascertained. One steamer, loaded with ammunition, escaped above the fort at Harrisonburg, which is a very strong work, and unassailable with wooden gunboats. It is on an elevation over one hundred feet high, which elevation covers what water batteries of heavy guns there are.

Lieutenant-Commander Selfridge was fortunate enough, however, to hear of a large quantity of ammunition that had lately been hauled from Natchez, and deposited at or near Trinity, nearly due west of Natchez, and from whence stores, provisions, cattle, guns and ammunition are transported. He captured fifteen thousand rounds of smooth-bore ammunition, ten thousand rounds of Enfield rifle, and two hundred and twenty-four rounds of fixed ammunition for guns, a rifle thirty-pounder Parrott gun-carriage, fifty-two hogsheads of sugar, ten puncheons of rum, nine barrels of flour, and fifty barrels of salt—all belonging to the Confederate government. At the same time they heard of a large amount of ammunition that had started from Natchez for Trinity, and was lying in wagons on the roads half way across. He dispatched a boat around to inform me of it; but General Ransom, who had landed a few days before at Natchez, hearing of it also, sent a detachment of cavalry and captured the whole. Thus Walker's army is left almost without ammunition.

The officers and men have shown great energy on this expedition, and have met with no mishap. They procured a good deal of information by which future movements will be regulated. The people in the whole of that section are very hostile to the government—rank rebels.

I have the honor to be, etc.,

DAVID D. PORTER, *Rear-Admiral.*

VICKSBURG, MISS., *July* 18, 1863.

Major-General H. W. HALLECK, *General-in-Chief:*

Joe Johnston evacuated Jackson on the night of the 16th instant. He is now in full retreat east. Sherman says most of Johnston's army must perish from heat, lack of water, and general discouragement.

The army paroled here have to a great extent deserted, and are scattered over the country in every direction.

Learning that Yazoo City was being fortified, I sent General Herron there. Five guns were captured, many stores, and about three hundred prisoners.

General Ransom was sent to Natchez to stop the crossing of cattle for the Eastern army. On arrival he found that large numbers had been driven out of the city to be pastured: also that munitions of war had recently been crossed over to wait for Kirby Smith. He mounted about two hundred of his men and sent them in both directions.

They captured a number of prisoners and five thousand head of Texas cattle, two thousand head of which were sent to General Banks. The balance have been or will be brought here.

In Louisiana they captured more prisoners, and a number of teams loaded with ammunition. Over two million rounds of ammunition were brought back to Natchez with the teams captured, and two hundred and sixty-eight thousand rounds, besides artillery ammunition, were destroyed.

U. S. GRANT, *Major-General Commanding.*

These operations may be said to have closed the Mississippi Valley campaign, which was one of the most victorious, throughout, that had occurred from the commencement of the war. In this connection it is due to the gentleman concerned, to transcribe a portion of General Grant's official report.* "I cannot close this report," the General writes, "without an expression of thankfulness for my good fortune in being placed in co-operation with an officer of the navy, who accords to every move that seems for the interest and success of our arms, his hearty and energetic support. Admiral Porter and the very efficient officers under him have ever shown the greatest readiness in their co-operation, no matter what was to be done or what risk to be taken either by their men or their vessels. Without this prompt and cordial support my movements would have been much embarrassed, if not wholly defeated."

Among the incidents of General Grant's occupation of Vicksburg is the following: A major in the rebel army had formerly served in the same regiment of the United States army with Grant, but was then his prisoner. Grant treated him kindly, invited him to his private apartment, and after he left, gave a sketch of the rebel's former life to the members of his staff. He said, that when the rebel major was in his room and he was talking to him about being in the Confederate service, the latter replied, "Grant, I tell you, I ain't much of a rebel, after all, and when I am paroled, I will let the d—d service go to the mischief."

* Published in full in the Appendix.

CHAPTER XLIV.

HIS SUCCESS MADE SURE.—HIS DEPARTMENT SECURED.—CARE FOR THE SOLDIERS.

General Grant, having gained his victories, was not the man to allow the fruits thereof to become valueless, by neglecting the duty of firmly securing them. He had opened the Mississippi, from its source to the Gulf; it therefore became necessary that he should prevent it from ever again being closed by the enemy. For this purpose he as cheif officer located his head-quarters at Vicksburg, in order that he might be able to have control of an easy access to all parts of his department, which at this time extended to the extreme limits of the State of Mississippi.

In a very short space of time the department was restored to peace, if not to order, and General Grant allowed himself a little of that rest so much needed after the arduous work which he had accomplished.*

In honor of the victories gained by General Grant with the Army of the Tennessee, a magnificent sword was pre-

* In this connection it might be stated that General Grant's wife, who had been an anxious watcher of his military movements and success, now, that victory and peace were secured in his department, left her home for a time to visit her husband, at the noted place which had caused him so much labor and anxiety to gain the possession of, and the reduction of which had made his name forever famous in history. While at St. Louis, she was, in honor of her husband, serenaded by a fine band, attended by an immense throng of civilians. After the music had ceased, three rousing cheers were given by the crowd for General Grant, and three more for Mrs. Grant, when that lady appeared at the window, with Brigadier-General Strong standing by her side

sented to him by the officers under his command. The scabbard was of solid silver, appropriately and most beautifully finished. The handle of the sword represented a carved figure of a young giant, crushing the rebellion, and was most elaborately designed. The box in which it was placed was made of rosewood, bound with ivory, and lined with velvet and white satin. On the interior of the lid the name of General Grant was marked with crimson silk. The whole, in design, execution, and intrinsic value, displayed great taste on the part of those selected to carry out the presentation.

President Lincoln also honored the victor by appointing him to the vacant major-generalship in the regular army of the United States, with a commission dating from the occupation of Vicksburg, July 4th, 1863.

General Grant had been very strict with regard to absent soldiers and officers, during the time their presence was needed in the camp and field; but now that victory had been secured, he allowed them more latitude, as is evidenced from the following order:

and on repeated calls for a speech, the General, in behalf of Mrs. Grant, responded:

GENTLEMEN:—I am requested by Mrs. Grant to express her acknowledgment for the honor you have done her on this occasion. I know well that, in tendering her thanks, I express your sentiments, when I say the compliment through her to her noble husband is one *merited by a brave and great man, who has made his name forever honored and immortal, in the history of America's illustrious patriots, living or dead.* Mrs. Grant does not desire, in the testimony you have offered, that you should forget *the brave and gallant officers and soldiers, who have so largely assisted in bringing about the glorious result,* which has recently caused the big heart of our nation to leap with joy. She asks you also to stop and *drop a pensive tear over the graves of the noble dead, who have fallen in the struggle,* that you and I, and all of us, might enjoy the fruits of their patriotic devotion to a country second to none on the earth. We trust that the Mississippi forever will be under the control of our glorious country. Mrs. Grant is now on the way to join her husband, *who, since the commencement of the war, has not asked for one day's absence. He has not found time to be sick.* With these remarks she bids you good-night, and begs that you accept her thousand thanks.

HEAD-QUARTERS, DEPARTMENT OF THE TENNESSEE,
VICKSBURG, MISSISSIPPI, *July* 20, 1863.

[*General Orders, No.* 45.]

In pursuance of section 32, of an act entitled "An act for enrolling and calling out the national forces, and for other purposes," approved March 3, 1863, furloughs may be granted for a period not exceeding thirty days at one time, to five per centum of the non-commissioned officers and privates of each regiment, battery, independent company, and detachment, present with their respective commands in this department, for good conduct in their line of duty, by their immediate commanding officers, approved by intermediate and army corps commanders. Furloughs thus granted are intended for the benefit of well men, and the sick who have become so from fatigue or exposure in the line of duty.

Under no circumstances will furloughs be given to men who have shirked duty, or straggled on the march, or from camps. Such men must be made to perform extra fatigue duty by their immediate commanding officers, and in cases where this is not regarded as sufficient punishment, they will be fined in an amount not beyond that which a regimental court-martial is authorized to impose. The amount of such fine will be entered on the proper muster and pay rolls, opposite their respective names, and the cause for which it is imposed stated.

By order of Major-General U. S. GRANT.

T. S. BOWERS, *A. A.-G.*

The open rebel sympathizers, although despising the United States Government, and constantly giving practical aid to its enemies, were ever ready to send their negroes to be fed by the military authorities. General Grant was determined to put a stop to this proceeding, and issued the following order:

HEAD-QUARTERS, DEPARTMENT OF THE TENNESSEE,
VICKSBURG, MISSISSIPPI, *July* 21, 1863.

[*General Orders, No.* 46.]

1. Hereafter no issues of provisions will be made for contrabands, *except those serving in regiments or in contraband camps.*

2. Issues of provisions will not be made to citizens, except on certificates that they are destitute, and have no means of purchasing the necessary supplies for their families. These certificates must state the

number of the family, and the time for which they draw, which shall not exceed ten days at any one time.

3. In making issues to citizens, only articles of prime necessity will be given, *i. e.*, bread and meat, and these at the rate of one pound of flour, one half pound of salt meat, or one pound of fresh beef, to the ation.

By order of Major-General U. S. GRANT.

JNO. A. RAWLINS, *A. A.-G.*

The matter of trade with the rebels had always been a source of trouble to General Grant, as he found that persons so engaged were far more ready to secure to themselves the profits of illicit speculation than to care for the success of the Union armies. The following letter to the Hon. Secretary of the Treasury clearly sets forth his feelings upon this matter, and explains his objections to the plan of "Trade following the Flag":

HEAD-QUARTERS, DEPARTMMENT OF THE TENNESSEE,
VICKSBURG, MISS., *July* 21, 1863.

SIR:—Your letter of the 4th instant to me, enclosing a copy of a letter of same date to Mr. Mellen, special agent of the Treasury, is just received. My Assistant Adjutant-General, by whom I shall send this letter, is about starting for Washington; hence I shall be very short in my reply.

My experience in West Tennessee has convinced me that any trade whatever with the rebellious States is weakening to us of at least thirty-three per cent. of our force. No matter what the restrictions thrown around trade, if any whatever is allowed it will be made the means of supplying the enemy what they want. *Restrictions, if lived up to, make trade unprofitable, and hence none but dishonest men go into it. I will venture to say that no honest man has made money in West Tennessee in the last year, while many fortunes have been made there during the time.*

The people in the Mississippi Valley are now nearly subjugated. Keep trade out for a few months, and I doubt not but that the work of subjugation will be so complete, that trade can be opened freely with the States of Arkansas, Louisiana, and Mississippi; that the people of these States will be more anxious for the enforcement and protection of our laws than the people of the loyal States. They have experienced the misfortune of being without them, and are now in a most happy condition to appreciate their blessings.

No theory of my own will ever stand in the way of my executing, in good faith, any order I may receive from those in authority over me; but my position has given me an opportunity of seeing what would not be known by persons away from the scene of war, and I venture, therefore, to suggest great caution in opening trade with rebels.

I am, Sir, very respectfully,

Your obedient servant,.

U. S. GRANT, *Major-General.*

Hon. S. P. CHASE, *Secretary of the Treasury.*

It will, however, be seen by the last paragraph, that General Grant, like a true soldier, never allowed his private feelings to stand in the way of his duty, and was always ready to render a cheerful obedience to the orders of those in authority, no matter how it might interfere with his own plans or views.

By the end of July, 1863, General Grant had perfected a complete system of mounted patrols between Vicksburg and New Orleans, who, with the gunboats, afforded ample protection to vessels. Every thing soon became quiet, and there existed no signs of rebels on either shore. General Grant ordered all sick soldiers in hospital, able to bear the journey, to be sent home on thirty days' furlough, and all those permanently disabled to be immediately discharged or recommended for membership in the invalid corps.

The following is an evidence of General Grant's care for the soldiers under his command, and his determination that they should not be imposed upon by the cormorants that generally hang upon the trail of an army:

When General Grant issued his order, No. 45, granting furloughs to the soldiers, he also issued a special order forbidding steamboat men to charge more than five dollars to enlisted men, and seven dollars to officers, as fare between Vicksburg and Cairo. Immediately after Vicksburg had fallen a large number of steamboats cleared from Northern ports for that place, and were in the habit of charging soldiers going home on furlough from fifteen to thirty dollars' fare to Cairo. One steamer was compelled by General Grant to disgorge its ill-gotten gains, under the following circumstances:—This boat had about one thousand enlisted soldiers and nearly two hundred and fifty officers on board, *en route* for home on short leave of absence, after the fatigues of their protracted but glorious campaign. The captain had charged these men and officers from ten to twenty-five dollars each as fare to Cairo. Just as the boat was about to push off from the wharf at Vicksburg, an order came from General Grant, requiring the captain to pay back to his passengers all money received by him as fare in excess of five dollars to enlisted men, and seven dollars to officers, or submit to imprisonment for disobedience, and have his boat confiscated. The order certainly caused an amount of disagreeable astonishment to the captain; but the presence of a guard rendered it useless to refuse; and so, amid the shouts of the soldiers over their General's care of their interests, he complied with as good grace as possible, and paid back the money. A gentleman who was a passenger on this occasion had been present when General Grant issued the order above referred to. The General, upon being informed of the impositions practised upon furloughed men and officers by steamboat men, was very indignant.

"I will teach them, if they need the lesson," said the gallant General, "that the men who have periled their lives to open the Mississippi River for their benefit cannot be imposed upon with impunity."

Can it be wondered at, with such evidences of their General's care, the soldiers of the Army of the Tennessee should fairly worship him?

General Grant was determined to eradicate from his department, all bands of marauders, guerillas, and irregular troopers, who, under the disguise of citizens, committed depredations within the Union lines. Neither would he allow plundering by his own soldiers. He therefore issued the following important order to that effect:

HEAD-QUARTERS, DEPARTMENT OF THE TENNESSEE,
VICKSBURG, MISS., *August* 1, 1863.

[*General Orders, No.* 50.]

I. *All regularly organized bodies of the enemy having been driven from those parts of Kentucky and Tennessee west of the Tennessee River, and from all of Mississippi west of the Mississippi Central Railroad*, and it being to the interest of those districts not to invite the presence of armed bodies of men among them, it is announced that *the most rigorous penalties will hereafter be inflicted upon the following classes of prisoners*, to wit: All irregular bodies of cavalry not mustered and paid by the Confederate authorities; all persons engaged in conscripting, enforcing the conscription, or apprehending deserters, whether regular or irregular; all citizens encouraging or aiding the same; and all persons detected in firing upon unarmed transports.

It is not contemplated that this order shall affect the treatment due to prisoners of war captured within the districts named, when they are *members of legally organized companies, and when their acts are in accordance with the usages of civilized warfare.*

II. The citizens of Mississippi, within the limits above described, are called upon to *pursue their peaceful avocations*, in obedience to the laws of the United States. While doing so in good faith, *all United States forces are prohibited from molesting them in any way. It is earnestly recommended that the freedom of negroes be acknowledged*, and that, instead of compulsory labor, contracts on fair terms be entered into between the former masters and servants, or between the latter and other persons who may be willing to give them employment. Such a system as this, honestly followed, will result in substantial advantages to all parties.

All private property will be respected except when the use of it is necessary for the Government, in which case it must be taken under the direction of a corps commander, and by a proper detail under charge of a commissioned officer, with specific instructions to seize certain proper ty and no other. A staff-officer of the quartermaster or subsistence department, will, in each instance, be designated to receipt for such property as may be seized, the property to be paid for at the end of the war on proof of loyalty, or on proper adjustment of the claim, under such regulations or laws as may hereafter be established. All property seized under this order must be taken up on returns by the officers giving receipts, and disposed of in accordance with existing regulations.

III. *Persons having cotton, or other produce not required by the army, will be allowed to bring the same to any military post within the State of Mississippi*, and abandon it to the agent of the Treasury Department at said post, to be disposed of in accordance with such regulations as the Secretary of the Treasury may establish. At posts where there is no such agent, the post quartermaster will receive all such property, and, at the option of the owner, hold it till the arrival of the agent, or send it to Memphis, directed to Captain A. R. Eddy, Acting Quartermaster, who will turn it over to the properly authorized agent at that place.

IV. Within the county of Warren, laid waste by the long presence of contending armies, the following rules, to prevent suffering, will be observed:

Major-General Sherman, commanding the Fifteenth Army Corps, and Major-General McPherson, commanding the Seventeenth Army Corps, will each designate *a commissary of subsistence, who will issue articles of prime necessity to all destitute families calling for them*, under such restrictions for the protection of the Government as they may deem necessary. *Families who are able to pay for the provisions drawn will in all cases be required to do so.*

V. *Conduct disgraceful to the American name* has been frequently reported to the Major-General commanding, particularly on the part of portions of the cavalry. *Hereafter, if the guilty parties cannot be reached, the commanders of regiments and detachments will be held responsible*, and those who prove themselves unequal to the task of preserving discipline in their commands, will be promptly reported to the War Department for "muster out." *Summary punishment must be inflicted upon all officers and soldiers apprehended in acts of violence or lawlessness.*

By order of Major-General U. S. GRANT.

T. S. BOWERS, *Acting A. A.-G.*

The negroes in the Department having all become free by virtue of President Lincoln's proclamation, and the occupation of the country by the United States authorities, General Grant issued the following order for the care and disposition of such as were without protection or employment:

HEAD-QUARTERS, DEPARTMENT OF THE TENNESSEE,
VICKSBURG, MISS., *August* 10, 1863.

[*General Orders, No.* 51.]

I. At all military posts in States within this department, where slavery has been abolished by the proclamation of the President of the United States, *camps will be established for such freed people of color as are out of employment.*

II. Commanders of posts or districts will detail suitable officers from the army as Superintendents of such camps. It will be the duty of such Superintendents to see that suitable rations are drawn from the Subsistence Department for such people as are confided to their care.

III. *All such persons supported by the Government will be employed in every practicable way so as to avoid, as far as possible, their becoming a burden upon the Government.* They may be hired to planters or other citizens, on proper assurance that the negroes so hired will not be run off beyond the military jurisdiction of the United States; they may be employed on any public works, in gathering crops from abandoned plantations, and generally in any manner local commanders may deem for the best interests of the Government, in compliance with law and the policy of the Administration.

IV. It will be the duty of the provost-marshal at every military post, to see that every negro within the jurisdiction of the military authority is employed by some white person, or is sent to the camps provided for freed people.

V. *Citizens may make contracts with freed persons of color for their labor, giving wages per month in money, or employ families of them by the year on plantations, &c., feeding, clothing, and supporting the infirm as well as able-bodied, and giving a portion, not less than one-twentieth of the commercial part of their crops, in payment for such services.*

VI. *Where negroes are employed under this authority, the parties employing will register with the provost-marshal their names, occupation, and residence, and the number of negroes so employed. They will enter into such bonds as the provost-marshal, with the approval of the local commander, may require, for the kind treatment and proper care of those employed, and as security against their being carried beyond the employe's jurisdiction.*

VII. Nothing of this order is to be construed to embarrass the employment of such colored persons as may be required by the Government.

By order of Major-General U. S. GRANT.
T. S. BOWERS, *Acting A. A.-G.*

Having thus secured his department against every important contingency, and having made provision for minor matters that did not require his personal superintendence, General Grant devoted a little time for the purpose of visiting the more distant districts under his command, leaving General McPherson, who had been appointed commander of the District of Vicksburg, to carry out the necessary orders in that immediate neighborhood.

CHAPTER XLV.

VISIT TO MEMPHIS AND NEW ORLEANS.

On the 25th of August, 1863, General Grant arrived at Memphis, Tenn., where he was received with great honor by the inhabitants of that city, although it was late in the evening before he arrived.

At ten o'clock the next morning a committee of citizens waited upon the General to tender him the hospitalities of the city and to present to him a series of resolutions passed at a meeting of the residents of Memphis held on the day of his arrival. At the close of the address an invitation was proffered to General Grant to be present at a dinner to be given in his honor that evening. The General received the committee cordially, but without further words than the thanking of the gentlemen, and through them the citizens of Memphis, for the great courtesy conferred upon him. After these ceremonious proceedings, an interview took place as to the most desirable time for the entertainment. The General signifying his satisfaction, nine o'clock was appointed. The committee then withdrew, and proceeded to the business of preparation.

The festival and reception was on a grand scale, and is thus described by one who was present:

At precisely nine o'clock the band struck up one of the national airs, the doors of the reception-room flew open, and General Grant made his appearance. There was a great rush on the part of the enthusiastic and impatient to grasp the hero's hand. An hour, at least, though it seemed less, was thus consumed in hand-shaking and congratulations. After the lapse of this time the band again sent forth its melody in the shape of a march. The whole assemblage then formed in two ranks, headed by General Grant. This being done, the entire party marched into the dining-room, made the complete round of the tables, examining the preparations, and then seated themselves. As would be expected, no sooner had each individual fastened himself to his seat, than commenced a grand, simultaneous and destructive assault upon the various dishes before him. Under the withering gastronomic abilities of the assemblage the victory was complete, and wound up by the total wreck and dissipation of the scene which, but a few moments before, shone refulgent in all its beauty. There suddenly appeared a masked battery of champagne on our rear, which opened upon the guests a vigorous champagne cannonade. Soon the engagement became general, and, like all general engagements, everybody did pretty much as he pleased, so that he kept in the ranks and did not shirk, or leave the field.

Next followed the regular toasts of the evening.

The assemblage being called to order, the chairman arose and stated the fact.

The toasts were then read.

"The United States of America—They have one constitution and government. May they have one grand destiny while human institutions endure." Responded to by Hon. Chas. Kortrecht.

"The Army and Navy—Their deeds and heroism in this war will be the noble theme of poet and historian in all future time." Responded to by Adjutant-General Lorenzo Thomas.

"General Grant—the guest of the city."

This was the signal for the wildest applause, and it was some minutes before order could be restored. It was expected that General Grant would be brought to his feet by this; but the company were dissapointed upon perceiving that instead his place was taken by his staff-surgeon, Dr. Hewitt, who remarked:

"I am instructed by General Grant to say that, as he has never been given to public speaking, you will have to excuse him on this ocasion, and, as I am the only member of his staff present, I therefore feel it my duty to thank you for this manifestation of your good-will, as also the numerous other kindnesses of which he has been the recipient ever since his arrival among you. *General Grant believes that in all he has done he has no more than accomplished a duty, and one, too, for which no particular honor is due.* But the world, as you do, will accord otherwise."

The Doctor then proposed, at General Grant's request—

"The officers of the different staffs, and the non-commissioned officers and privates of the Army of the Tennessee."

"The Federal Union—it must and will be preserved." Responded to by Major-General S. A. Hurlbut.

"The Old Flag—May its extinguished stars, rekindled by the sacred flame of human liberty, continue to shine forever undiminished in number, and undimmed in splendor." Brigadier-General Veatch.

"The President of the United States—He must be sustained." Colonel J. W. Fuller.

The Star-Spangled Banner was here sung, the whole party joining in the chorus.

"The Loyal Men of Tennessee—Their devotion to the Union, the cause of republican government and constitutional liberty is like gold tried seven times by fire." Mr. J. M. Tomeny.*

---

* Dr. Morris here read the following lines composed in honor of General Grant:

DE SOTO, FULTON, GRANT.

The daring Spaniard, when his eyes beheld,
For the first time, yon noble river roll,
And sparkle in the sunbeams, as it bore
Its mighty current onward to the sea,
Fell upon bended knee and worshipped God
Aloud, for that his painful task was done,
The secret of the ages he had solved—
The Mississippi, sire of floods, stood forth,
Embanked in verdure, bordered by a soil
Richer than Egypt's Delta.
Science and commerce winged their pinions there,
And wrote his name, De Soto, on their scrolls.

Ages rolled by, the tawny savage fled—
The white man launched his boat upon the flood,
The forest fell, the fertile soil gave back
Unto the sower's hand a hundred-fold:
Then rose the genius Fulton, and he taught
To stem the unconquered flood, to push the weight
Of mightiest keels against the heaving mass,
That untold centuries had crowned with power,
He sent his messengers in smoke and flame
Up to the Mississippi's very fount;
And by the Spaniard's name he wrote his own—
Fulton, the nation's benefactor.

The remainder of the toasts were of a local character, with the exception of the closing one, which was as follows:

"General Grant—Your Grant and my Grant. Having granted us victories, grant us the restoration of the "Old Flag;" grant us supplies, so that we may grant to our friends the grant to us."

The festivities were kept up until near three o'clock in the morning, when General Grant withdrew from the room.

Yon sire of floods was the great bond that joined
These waters into one: his bosom bore
In precious freightage all that Nature yields
From farthest North down to a torrid clime;
Its channel was the highway of the West:
Science had made his heaving mass her own;
Pleasure danced revelry upon its floods;
Beauty and love dwelt by him all secure;
Fraternal hands joined hands along his banks;
His very waters made us all akin.

Then spoke an enemy—and on his banks
Armed men appeared, and cannon-shot proclaimed
The Mississippi closed—that mighty stream
Found by De Soto, and by Fulton won!
One thought to chain him! ignominious thought!
But then the grand old monarch shook his locks
And burst his fetters like a Samson freed!
The heights were crowned with ramparts sheltering those
Whose treason knew no bounds: the frowning forts
Belched lightnings, and the morning gun
A thousand miles told mournfully the tale,
The Mississippi closed.

Not long; from the Lord God of Hosts was sent
A leader who with patient vigil planned
A great deliverance: height by height was gained,
Island and hill and woody bank and cliff.
Month followed month, till on our natal day
The last great barrier fell, and never more
The sire of waters shall obstruction know!
Now with De Soto's name, and Fulton's, see
The greater name of Grant!

Our children's children, noble Grant, shall sing
That great deliverance! On the floods of spring
Thy name shall sparkle, smiling commerce tell
Thy great achievement which restores the chain,
Never again to break, which makes us one.

After the conclusion of the evening entertainment General Grant immediately left for the steamer City of Alton, which was lying at the wharf, and took his departure at once for Vicksburg.

Before leaving the city General Grant forwarded to the Committee of the People the following letter:

MEMPHIS, TENNESSEE, *August* 26, 1863.

GENTLEMEN:—I received a copy of the resolutions passed by the "loyal citizens of Memphis at a meeting held at the rooms of the Chamber of Commerce, August 25th, 1863," tendering me a public reception.

In accepting this testimonial, which I do at a great sacrifice of my personal feelings, I simply desire to pay a tribute to the first public exhibition in Memphis of loyalty to the government which I represent in the Department of the Tennessee. I should dislike to refuse, for considerations of personal convenience, to acknowledge, anywhere or in any form, the existence of sentiments which I have so long and so ardently desired to see manifested in this department. The stability of this government and the unity of this nation depend solely on the cordial support and the earnest loyalty of the people. While, therefore, I thank you sincerely for the kind expressions you have used toward myself, I am profoundly gratified at this public recognition, in the city of Memphis, of the power and authority of the government of the United States.

I thank you, too, in the name of the noble army which I have the honor to command. It is composed of men whose loyalty is proved by their deeds of heroism and their willing sacrifices of life and health. They will rejoice with me that the miserable adherents of the rebellion, whom their bayonets have driven from this fair land, are being replaced by men who acknowledge human liberty as the only true foundation of human government. May your efforts to restore your city to the cause of the Union be as successful as have been theirs to reclaim it from the despotic rule of the leaders of the rebellion. I have the honor to be, gentlemen, your very obedient servant,

U. S. GRANT, *Major-General.*

Messrs. R. HOUGH and others, Committee, Memphis.

The affair of all sides was a triumphant success. The hospitality of Memphis, the liberality of its citizens, and the unmistakable evidences of their loyalty, so enthusiastically set forth, will, beyond all doubt, be cherished by General Grant as one of the happiest recollections of his career. *

* *New York Herald's* Memphis correspondence.

General Grant did not long remain at Vicksburg, but proceeded down the river to inspect the posts at Natchez and other points of his department, after which he paid a visit to General Banks at New Orleans for the purpose of opening up trade between that city and the North. General Grant arrived at New Orleans on the 2d of September, within one week from the time he left Memphis, and the next day it was announced that the trade of the city of New Orleans with Cairo, St. Louis, and the cities and towns of the Upper Mississippi, the Missouri and Ohio rivers, was declared free from any military restriction whatever. The trade of the Mississippi at intermediate points within the Department of the Gulf was held subject only to such limitations as might prove necessary to prevent the supply of provisions and munitions of war to the enemies of the country.

On the morning of the 4th of September 1863, General Grant held a grand review of the Thirteenth Army Corps, which had been under his command at Vicksburg, but was afterwards transferred to that of General Banks. A correspondent thus described the appearance of General Grant as he moved from his hotel for the purpose of taking the most prominent part in the review:—

"General Banks, accompanied by a numerous staff, was at the St. Charles Hotel as early as eight o'clock, and at nine o'clock both generals left for Carrolton, where the review took place. The street was crowded to witness the departure of these officers, all present being desirous of seeing General Grant. *He was in undress uniform, without sword, sash, or belt; coat unbuttoned, a low-crowned black felt hat, without any mark upon it of military rank; a pair of kid gloves, and a cigar in his mouth.* It must be known, however, that he is never without the latter except when asleep."

During the review, General Grant, although a good horseman, being mounted on a strange horse, was suddenly thrown from his seat, and severely injured. At this particular time the mishap was of serious consequence with regard to the campaigns in the Southwest, as may be judged from the annual report of the General-in-Chief.

It will be seen by the following extract from that document, that it was intended that General Grant should have taken command, in September, 1863, of the Union forces moving towards Northwestern Georgia; but in consequence of his accident he was prevented from so doing.

As three separate armies—those of the Ohio, Cumberland, and Tennessee—were now to operate in the same field, it seemed necessary to have a single commander, in order to secure a more perfect co-operation than had been obtained with the separate commands of Burnside and Rosecrans. *General Grant, by his distinguished services* and superior rank to all the other generals in the West, seemed entitled to this general command. But, unfortunately, he was at this time in New Orleans, unable to take the field. Moreover, there was no telegraphic communication with him, and the dispatches of September 13th, directed to him and General Sherman, did not reach them until some days after their dates, thus delaying the movement of General Grant's forces from Vicksburg. General Hurlbut, however, had moved the troops of his own corps, then in West Tennessee, with commendable promptness. These were to be replaced by re-enforcements from Steele's Corps in Arkansas, which also formed part of General Grant's army. Hearing nothing from General Grant or General Sherman's Corps at Vicksburg, it was determined on the 23d to detach the Eleventh and Twelfth Corps from the Army of the Potomac, and send them by rail, under the command of General Hooker, to protect General Rosecrans's line of communication from Bridgeport to Nashville. It was known that these troops could not go immediately to the front. To send more men to Chattanooga, when those already there could not be fully supplied, would only increase the embarrassment, and probably cause the evacuation of that place. In other words, Hooker's command was temporarily performing the duties previously assigned to the re-enforcements ordered from Grant's army.

General Grant's injuries were of such a serious nature that it was feared he would never be able to take the field again. He was carried from Carrolton on a litter to the steamer "Franklin," which took him up the river; his breastbone was said to have been crushed, three ribs broken, and one side paralyzed; and his brain was thought to be affected from the concussion of the fall from his horse. Fortunately, for the country, by the aid of a good surgeon, he was enabled after over a month's illness to take the position destined for him, as Chief Commander in the West.

CHAPTER XLVI.

AN ENLARGED COMMAND.—MILITARY DIVISION OF THE MISSISSIPPI.

General Grant, as soon as he was able to move, began his voyage up the Mississippi River, agreeably to the orders from Washington. On his road he stopped at the principal dépôts of his troops along the Mississippi, and arranged for their departure eastward, at such proper times as would enable them to form a combination with the forces at Chattanooga.

While at Vicksburg, General Grant was determined that his men should be paid, and issued an order to that effect. It was also necessary for him to make a tariff of rates to prevent impositions being practised upon the war-ruined people of the Southwest. The exorbitant prices of passage on the Mississippi River called forth from department head-quarters the last paragraph of the following order in relation to river matters:

Head-Quarters, Department of the Tennessee,
Vicksburg, Miss., *September*, 29, 1863.

[*General Orders, No.* 59.]

I. All enlisted men on detached service, in army corps other than that in which their regiments, detachments, or companies are serving, except those detailed by orders from department head-quarters, as nurses in general hospitals and hospital steamers, and clerks in staff departments, are hereby relieved from such detached service, and will report to their respective commands for duty.

Army Corps commanders will see that this order is carried into immediate execution.

II. Company and regimental commanders will furnish to the officer in charge of men of their respective commands, absent in hospitals or at parole camps, proper descriptive lists and accounts of pay and clothing, *to enable them to draw their pay.* Such descriptive lists must contain the name, rank, description, where born, occupation, when, where, and by whom enrolled or enlisted, when, where, by whom, and for what period mustered, by what paymaster, and to what time last paid, the bounty paid and amount still due, and the amount due, to or from him, for clothing, with the proper remarks showing his military history, etc. Descriptive lists showing less than this are valueless. *Hereafter no enlisted man will be sent from his company or regiment without such descriptive list as is herein required being furnished to the proper officer in charge, and any neglect to comply with this order will subject the offender to trial by court-martial and dismissal from the service.*

*It will be the duty of all officers of the Inspector-General's Department to properly inspect and report any neglect of duty in this particular.**

III. Army Corps commanders will announce in general orders the acting assistant inspectors-general of districts, divisions, and brigades within their respective corps, and will authorize them to make inspections and recommend the disposal of unserviceable property, in accordance with army regulations and orders.

So much of paragraph third of General Orders, No. 30, current series, from these head-quarters, as requires the acting assistant inspectors-general of districts, divisions, and brigades, to report direct to the Assistant Inspector-General at department head-quarters, is revoked, and all reports required by army regulations and existing orders will be forwarded through the proper military channels.

IV. So much of General Orders, No. 49, current series, from these head-quarters, as establishes the rates of transportation and subsistence of commissioned officers travelling on steamboats within this department, is hereby revoked, and in lieu thereof is substituted the rates of military transportation and subsistence established by Colonel Lewis B. Parsons, Assistant-Quartermaster and General Superintendent of Transportation at St. Louis, Mo., August 1st, 1863, viz.:

TO OR FROM ST. LOUIS TO THE FOLLOWING PLACES:

Place	Rate	Place	Rate
Cairo to Columbus	$4	Vicksburg	$16
Memphis	10	Port Hudson	18
Helena	12	New Orleans	20

* General Grant was determined that soldiers should not lose their pay through the carelessness of their officers.

And to or from all intermediate points at like rates in proportion to distance transported.

Enlisted men will be entitled to travel as cabin passengers, when they desire it, at same rates.

By order of Major-General U. S. GRANT.

JOHN A. RAWLINS, *Brig.-Gen. and A. A.-G.*

General Grant, before he left the Department of the Tennessee, regulated the military civic jurisdiction over the conquered region around Vicksburg.

The administration of the city was excellent, and the numerous secessionists still remaining there were kept strictly on their good behavior in dread of "exile," as they considered the operation of sending them to their friends within the rebel lines. The following officers composed the administration:—District Commander, Major-General James B. McPherson; Post Commander, Major-General John A. Logan; District Provost-Marshal, Lieutenant-Colonel James Wilson; Post Provost-Marshal, Lieutenant-Colonel Waddell. As a reward for special bravery General Grant instituted the "Insignia of Honor" for the Seventeenth Corps. The design of the medals was a blending of the crescent, a star and a shield; the base being formed of the crescent, to the two extremities of which was fixed the star, while pendant from its lower point was suspended a shield. Upon the crescent the words "Vicksburg, July 4, 1863." The object in the presentation of these badges was to reward the meritorious members of the Seventeenth Corps for conspicuous valor on the field of battle or endurance in the march. This famous corps since its organization had been foremost in duty and deeds of glory throughout the entire campaign against Vicksburg, and no better method could have been adopted to continue in the future the same excellent spirit of emulation for which it has always been celebrated, both on the part of officers and men.

The following General Order was issued by the Corps commander, at the instigation of General Grant, in relation to the distribution of these badges:

HEAD-QUARTERS, SEVENTEENTH ARMY CORPS,
DEPARTMENT OF THE TENNESSEE,
VICKSBURG, MISS., *Oct.* 2, 1863.

[*General Orders, No.* 30.]

I. In order to encourage and reward the meritorious and faithful officers and men of this corps, a "Medal of Honor," with appropriate device, has been prepared, and will be presented by a "Board of Honor," of which the Major-General commanding is the advisory member, to all those who, by their gallantry in action and other soldierlike qualities, have most distinguished themselves, or who may hereafter most distinguish themselves, during the war.

II. The following officers will constitute the "Board of Honor" hereby appointed:

Major-General John A. Logan, commanding Third Division.

Brigadier-General John McArthur, commanding First Division.

Brigadier-General John E. Smith, commanding Second Division.

Brigadier-General M. M. Crocker, commanding Fourth Division.

Brigadier-General T. E. G. Ransom, commanding Second Brigade, First Division.

Brigadier-General M. M. Force, commanding Second Brigade, Third Division.

Brigadier-General W. Q. Gresham, commanding Third Brigade, Fourth Division.

Brigadier-General Alex. Chambers, commanding Third Brigade, First Division.

Colonel Gabriel Bouck, Eighteenth Wisconsin Infantry.

Lieutenant-Colonel A. M. Powell, Chief of Artillery.

III. Company commanders will forward to the commanding officer of their regiment a list of the names of the non-commissioned officers and men of their command whom they deem entitled to receive the "medal," accompanied by a full and complete statement of facts to guide the "Board" in their award. These lists will be revised by the regimental commander, who will forward them, with his remarks, to the commanding officer of the brigade.

IV. Regimental commanders will send similar lists of those officers of their command whom they believe entitled to the "medal," to the brigade commander, who, after revising the whole, will send them direct to the President of the "Board."

V. The "Board of Honor" will be convened upon the order of the President, at such times and places as he may direct, and they are empowered to make all needful rules and regulations for the attainment of the object of this order—the just and impartial award to the most deserving of the "Medal of Honor."

By order of Major-General JAS. B. MCPHERSON.

W. T. CLARK, *A. A.-G.*

After the repulse of the forces at Chickamauga in front of Chattanooga, important movements of troops commenced from General Grant's department toward that place. All of General Sherman's Fifteenth Army Corps, excepting General Tuttle's Division, was transported from Vicksburg to the line of the Memphis and Charleston Railroad. On Saturday, October 10th, General Osterhaus's Division entered Iuka. No considerable body of rebels were encountered anywhere on the march between Iuka and Corinth. The rebel cavalry were seen hovering on the Union flank and front continually, although they gave but little trouble or uneasiness. A reconnoissance was made on October 11th by two regiments of infantry, a section of artillery, and one company of cavalry, and revealed a battalion of cavalry at the crossing of Bear Creek, five miles east of Iuka.

In the mean time, it was known by the rebels that General Sherman was at Memphis, and intended to pass over the Memphis and Charleston Railroad to Chattanooga. A body of rebel cavalry and infantry therefore concentrated at Wyeth, a small village on the Tallahatchie, where were located the head-quarters of Colonel Chalmers. This force was further increased by the addition of a number of conscripts. Having thus gathered all the numbers they could in the country, Chalmers found himself at the head of about four thousand men of all kinds and five pieces of artillery. With this command he moved north, and on the morning of October 11th made his appearance upon the railroad, several miles beyond Colliersville. The regular passenger train, though in his power, the enemy allowed to pass, but as soon as that had run by, working parties were thrown upon the track, which was torn up in several places and the ties stacked upon the road and fired. These fires proved a fortunate circumstance, as, soon after, General Sherman and staff, accompanied by his body guard, a battalion of the Thirteenth Regulars, approached the place on an extra train. Discovering the fires, the troops on board prepared for an attack, though they did not disembark, and the entire party ran up to the station. As they were passing a certain point, as was expected, the enemy fired upon the train, particularly into the passenger car, wounding several persons. Having run up to the stockade, the enemy closed in upon the Union troops, and commenced a fire from all directions. In order to cover the transit of the United States troops from the train to the stockade, the regulars made a charge out of the cars and directly upon the enemy, who fled in all directions in a perfect panic. The entire force then succeeded in taking refuge within the stockade, and acted entirely on the defensive.

Before General Sherman arrived, the garrison had engaged the enemy in a desperate conflict, and at the time of his appearance they had been overwhelmed and driven within the fortifications of the place. The fight continued but a short time after the opportune arrival of the regulars, though while it did the General took an active part among the men. His presence had much to do with keeping up their spirits.

The enemy soon exhibited signs of discomfiture. Immediately upon the receipt of information that the enemy was in this neighborhood, a strong body of infantry re-enforcements was ordered from Memphis to the scene of operations. At the same time the cavalry, encamped at Germantown, were ordered to mount and move out. A force also demonstrated from the east.

On October 21st, the Union forces moving eastward from Corinth met with resistance near Cherokee Station, eighty-nine miles from Tuscumbia. General Osterhaus was in the advance, and had not moved far when he encountered two brigades of rebel cavalry, estimated at from four to six thousand. The fight lasted an hour, when the rebels were defeated.

General Sherman, finding that to advance along the railroad would only lead to continual fighting and delay, kept a small force moving by that direction, while he marched the main body north of the Tennessee River, and thus reached Chattanooga without any serious opposition, as the rebels had concentrated their forces to resist his advance by the route south of that stream.

Meanwhile General Grant moved up the Mississippi River to Cairo, and as he did so, he paid a short visit to all the military posts along that river. He telegraphed his arrival at each of these places to the head-quarters of the General-in-Chief at Washington, and the Secretary of War started to meet him on the route. When General Grant arrived at Indianapolis, he found that a telegram was there awaiting him at the dépôt, requesting him to delay his further journey until the arrival of that official. It was not long before they met, and as soon as the Secretary of War and General Grant had passed the usual compliments between gentlemen on their first personal acquaintance, the former handed the latter the following order:

WAR DEPARTMENT, ADJUTANT-GENERAL'S OFFICE,
WASHINGTON, *October* 16, 1863.

[*General Orders, No.* 337.]

By direction of the President of the United States, the Departments of the Ohio, of the Cumberland, and of the Tennessee, will constitute the Military Division of the Mississippi. Major-General U. S. Grant, United States army, is placed in command of the Military Division of the Mississippi, with his head-quarters in the field.

Major-General W. S. Rosecrans, U. S. Vols., is relieved from the command of the Department and Army of the Cumberland. Major-General G. H. Thomas is hereby assigned to that command.

By order of the Secretary of War.

E. D. TOWNSEND, *A. A.-G.*

The party then proceeded, with their special attendants, to Louisville, where their arrival created intense excitement. They found a wondering crowd gathered in the hall of the Galt House to catch a glimpse of the hero of Vicksburg. Numerous were the exclamations of wonder as General Grant made his appearance. There seemed to have been an impression that the General was above the ordinary stature of men.

"I thought he was a large man," said a native. "He would be considered a small chance of a fighter if he lived in Kentucky."

The medium sized frame of the General formed a strange contrast to the huge figures of the Kentuckians who swarmed to behold him.

During the afternoon, General Grant indulged in a ride on horseback around the town. He was still unable to walk without his cane and crutch, but managed to ride quite well. Even then, in his feeble condition, it would have required a strong effort on the part of a horse to unseat him.

The condition of the region of country over which General Grant was now to exercise superintendence, was such as to require immediate action; and notwithstanding his crippled condition, he at once assumed his new command, announcing the same in the following simple order:

HEAD-QUARTERS MILITARY DIVISION OF THE MISSISSIPPI,
LOUISVILLE, KY., *October* 18, 1863.

[*General Orders, No.* 1.]

In compliance with General Orders, No. 337, of date Washington, D. C., October 16th, 1863, the undersigned hereby assumes command of the "Military Division of the Mississippi, embracing the departments of the Ohio, of the Cumberland, and of the Tennessee."

The head-quarters of the Military Division of the Mississippi will be in the field, where all reports and returns required by army regulations and existing orders will be made. U. S. GRANT, *Major-General.*

The new command of General Grant was one of the most stupendous ever held by a General, below the grade of a General-in-Chief, in this or any other nation. It covered a larger area and controlled a greater number of troops than had previously been massed under one man. The Military Division of the Mississippi embraced the central zone of operations, and the nature of the territory belonging thereto rendered it absolutely essential that one mind should direct its movements. The necessity for proper co-operation alone made this imperative.

General Grant now had under his direction four of the largest armies in the field. His own army, with which he won the victories in and around Vicksburg, and throughout Mississippi; the "Army of the Cumberland;" the "Army of the Ohio," and General Hooker's Grand Division. Under him were a perfect galaxy of Marshals. His army commanders were Generals Sherman, Thomas, Burnside, and Hooker. (General Foster's column was afterwards added.) His corps commanders were as follows:

The Fourth Army Corps, General Granger; the Ninth Army Corps, General Potter; the Eleventh Army Corps,

General Howard; the Twelfth Army Corps, General Slocum; the Fourteenth Army Corps, General Palmer; the Fifteenth Army Corps, General J. A. Logan; the Sixteenth Army Corps, General Hurlbut; the Seventeenth Army Corps, General McPherson; and the Twenty-third Army Corps, General Manson.

His division and brigade leaders were not inferior, while the regiments were of the best fighting material in the world.

The country embraced within the limits of this new command included the States of Michigan, Illinois, Indiana, Ohio, Kentucky, Tennessee, Mississippi, Northern Alabama and Northwestern Georgia. One glance at the map will therefore show what comprised General Grant's Military Division of the Mississippi.

The opposing forces were not less grand in their constitution. General Bragg's army embraced his own veteran troops, and to that army were added Longstreet's and Hill's Corps from the Virginia rebel army. General Pemberton's army, which were said to be exchanged, were with Bragg. Joe Johnston had a co-operating force of 30,000 men, in addition to which there was a small rebel force in Mississippi, consisting of one brigade of infantry at Newton Station, on the Southern Road, and a cavalry division of from 5,000 to 6,000, operating between Jackson and the Big Black, under General S. D. Lee.

The rebels, however, began to dread the approaching campaign, as is evident from the following extract from one of their newspapers, published in Atlanta:

> The Yankee Army of the Cumberland holds the door to lower East Tennessee, and this door we must leave open. * * * If we continue to gaze listlessly from the bold knobs of Missionary Ridge upon the comfortable barracks of the Federals below, then may we tremble for the next campaign; for, as sure as there is any surety in the future, the

spring of 1864 must see us far from the borders of Georgia, or near to the verge of destruction. Nail it to your door-posts, men of the South, and refuse to be deluded into any other belief! Food and raiment are our needs. We must have them. *Kentucky and Middle Tennessee can only supply them. Better give up the seacoast, better give up the Southwest, aye, better to give up Richmond without a struggle, and win these, than lose the golden field, whose grain and wool are our sole hope.* The enemy has just one army too many in the field for us. We must crush this overplus; we must gain one signal Stonewall Jackson campaign. Destiny points to the very place. Be Rosecrans the victim. Defeat him, pulverize him, run him to the Ohio River, and then close the war with the next summer. And how? Nothing easier. The bee which has really stung our flank so long, once disposed of, our triumphant legions have a clear road before them. Fed sumptuously through the winter, well shod and clad, they have only to meet a dispirited foe, retake the valley of the Mississippi, secure the election of a peace democrat to the Presidency in the fall, and arrange the terms of treaty and independence. These results can be accomplished nowhere else than in this department. The Northwest is our real adversary.*

The readers of this chapter will see the position of affairs when General Grant assumed his new command. It must, however, not be forgotten that he had under him the troops that had been sorely defeated at Chickamauga, and were at that time shut up in Chattanooga by a besieging force of the rebels. The enemy believed that they had this force securely in a trap, and when they heard of the change in the command they began to make light of it. One of their journalists remarked that the Union authorities had removed a hero (Rosecrans), and placed two fools (Grant and Thomas) in command. The President is reported to have said, that "if one fool like Grant can do as much work, and win as profitable victories as he, he had no objection to two of them, as they would surely wipe out the rebellion."

* *Chattanooga—Atlanta Rebel*, Nov. 9th, 1863.

CHAPTER XLVII.

ACTIVE MOVEMENTS.—LOOKOUT VALLEY.

General Grant was not the man to stand idle when there was work to be done. He, therefore, soon left Louisville, after making certain necessary arrangements for co-operation of troops from Kentucky, and arrived in Nashville on the morning of October 21st. He was during the same evening introduced to the people of Nashville, by the Military Governor, but refused to make any speech to them. Having made certain dispositions of his forces in this vicinity, to secure his communications, and having ordered the re-gauging of the railroads, so that one continuous line of communication should exist between the Ohio River and Chattanooga, General Grant took his departure for the latter place, where he arrived on October 23d.

The situation of affairs at this time in the neighborhood of Chattanooga, is thus described by a correspondent:

The sad position of affairs is in nowise changed up to date. I trust that every warrior in this army is alive to it; *for I confess I do not see any very brilliant prospects for continuing alive in it all this winter, unless something desperate be done.* While the army sits here, hungry, chilly, watching the "key to Tennessee," the "good dog" Bragg lies over against us, licking his Chickamauga sores without whine or growl. He will not reply to our occasional shots from Star Fort, Fort Crittenden, or the Moccasin Point batteries across the river; has forbidden the exchange of newspapers and the compliments of the day between pickets; has returned surly answers to flag of truce messages; in fact, has cut us dead. They know we have been, and are being largely re-enforced, and fear a flank movement, similar to that which gave Rosecrans possession of Chattanooga. This is a synopsis of the situation. The details, so far as relates to our side of the house, about which I am only expected to know, are far less cheering.

By the Anderson road (north of the Tennessee), from Bridgeport to Chattanooga the distance is something like sixty miles, and since the heavy rains of the past week, the entire route is dismal beyond execration. Mules stage through twenty-five or thirty miles of almost unfathomable mud, toil up and over a mountain—Walden's Ridge—where a single misstep would insure their exit from life over a frightful precipice, grinding along, over enormous boulders and jagged rocks, through more mud, to the muddy banks of the river at Chattanooga. A thousand pounds of provisions or forage were an extraordinary load for the best of six mule teams on their trial trips over this route; but now it is positive inhumanity to ask half that work of the jaded, half-starved brutes. Yet all the supplies must come by this route, and every animal able to stagger under a burthen, must be kept on the move. Trains, once the pride and boast of proprietary quartermasters, have dwindled away; wagon after wagon worn out, or destroyed by Wheeler's raiders, till the transportation of the army is not half what it was, or one-quarter what it should be; and, unless we shall be able to navigate the river soon, want stares us in the face. Half rations for troops will suffice for a time; quarter rations, now darkly hinted, is rather "crowding the mourners," the troops say. A very patient and meek mule can exist on two or three pounds of corn per day; but wagon boxes, dry leaves, and woollen blankets, with harness for relish, are not conducive to mule health, strength, and longevity. Angular skeletons of artillery horses rattle past my quarters toward the Tennessee—Heaven be thanked there is plenty of water—while I write this, and within my range of vision, up and down the main street, are numbers of weak and trembling horse "frames," glandered and starving, staggering about in search of a convenient spot to die.

The mortality among these innocents is frightful to contemplate. Their corpses line the road, and taint the air, all along the Bridgeport route. In these days, hereabouts, it is within the scope of the most obtuse to distinguish a quartermaster or staff officer, by a casual glance at the animal he strides. "He has the fatness of twenty horses upon his ribs," as Squeers remarked of little Wackford; "and so he has; God help the others."

I am assured this state of things will not last long; that hordes of men are energetically at work improving our means of communication, and that we soon shall be benefited by the overflowing plenty of the North. The vigor and good spirits of the army all this time are developed in a most astonishing manner.

Major-General Grant, who presides over the destinies of this, amongst other armies, reached Chattanooga to-day. He was accompanied by Quartermaster-General Meigs, and Mr. Dana, of the War Department, who now returns after a short absence. They have come back, perhaps, to witness operations at the front, which their superior knowledge of the situation may lead them to expect. If I should write what I know of the whereabouts and movements of the troops, above and below us, on the Tennessee River, and elsewhere, all aiming at that grand object, the overthrow of "this accursed rebellion," I would, no doubt, be arrested for dealing in contraband news. Luckily, I know so little about Burnside, General Joe Hooker, and the rest, that it requires but little effort to keep my pencil quiet. They are in their proper places, however. General Grant probably knows where they are, and what they are doing; the enemy will find out when the thing is fully developed. One of Wheeler's couriers was captured the other day, with that chieftain's written reply to a dispatch from General Braxton Bragg, ordering the raider back into Middle Tennessee. Wheeler said it was utterly impossible for him to go back, on account of his impoverished and worn-out condition. His command would not hold together. (He said nothing about the Union troopers, who were following him up in vast force.) He also whined considerably about the difficulty in escaping across the Tennessee to the South. He was prevented, he said, by "Lee's Federal Jayhawkers." How Grant's cavalry could bother the rebels in Southern Tennessee, was something the raider couldn't understand.*

General Grant no sooner made his appearance at Chattanooga, than a change was at once set about in the situation of affairs. He had left directions for the management of the raiders, with the corps and district commanders outside of that position, and he, therefore, was at liberty to direct his personal attention to the re-opening of communications, by proper routes, with his dépôts of supplies.

---

* *New York Herald* correspondence, October 23d.

After the battles of Chickamauga, the post on Lookout Mountain was abandoned by the Union troops, and was immediately taken possession of by the rebels. From this point the rebels were enabled to shell the supply trains moving along the valley route towards Chattanooga from Bridgeport. From this cause the Union troops were compelled to take their supplies along the mountain roads, described in the foregoing correspondence.

To reopen the valley route was General Grant's primary and most important design. He, therefore, while at Nashville communicated his plans to General Hooker, and when he arrived at Chattanooga, he, with the assistance of his chief-engineer, Brigadier-General W. F. Smith, at once set about the work.

The following correspondence will show what was accomplished during this movement:

CHATTANOOGA, *October* 28, 1863.

The reoccupation of Lookout and the reopening of the "Southern line" to Bridgeport has for some time been the chief aim of strategists in this department. A movement of Major-General Hooker's troops from opposite Bridgeport, along the south bank of the Tennessee, through Shellmound and Whiteside, commenced a week ago.* A large additional force, under Major-General Palmer—spared from the army without weakening our lines—joined Hooker on the march up Lookout Valley, and the combined forces effected a junction with Brigadier-General Hazen's command last night, near the foot of Lookout. The valley route to Bridgeport is now ours, and I am led to believe that movements in progress will give us possession of the mountain itself, and perhaps force an evacuation by Bragg's whole army ere many weeks are gone.

I am, at present, unable to write particularly of the preliminary movements by the forces under General Hooker's immediate command; but I am able to describe the hazardous expedition of the co-operating forces from this end of the line with all the accuracy of an eye-witness. Fourteen hundred men were, on Monday night, October 26th, picked

---

* While General Grant was at Nashville.

from Brigadier-General W. B. Hazen's Brigade, Fourth Army Corps, and ordered to report at the pontoon bridge, Chattanooga, at midnight. The selection of General Hazen and his troops for the expedition was due to a reputation they had long since established for dash and daring, and the brilliant result proves it a well-founded one. So well had the secret been kept that not one of the fourteen hundred braves, aside from the General and staff, knew where they were going, as they stepped into the pontoon boats which had been provided for them. The expedition filled fifty-six boats, an average of twenty-five men to a Chattanooga built pontoon. Soon after the embarkation, when they had floated through the gap in the bridge arranged for their passage, the men of the expedition began to understand their situation and to discover the object of their midnight excursion. They were to run past the rebel batteries and sharpshooters on Lookout, and effect a landing at Brown's Ferry, eight miles below, by the river line. The moon was shining bright, but occasionally overcast by drifting clouds, and it seemed impossible to pass the frowning batteries of Lookout without discovery. At half-past one o'clock the advance guard boat, reached Chattanooga Creek, three miles below the starting point and the extreme outpost of our lines. Here a halt was made to concentrate the forces, and the General's watch marked half-past two before the final start was made. Oars were now discarded, and, hugging to the right bank, creeping along under its shadows, the boats reached the front of Lookout Brave men held their breath, every eye was fixed upon the mountain, and not a muscle moved as we approached the dangerous point. Rebel camp fires could be seen far up the dark mountain side, their signal torches working slowly, but incessantly, with now and then a stave from some secession air, drowsily sung by the rebel pickets. Not a shot or an alarm as yet, and the men breathed a little freer as the mountain was passed, and we emerged from its shadow into the modified darkness of the valley below.

The force was now divided, the First Division, comprising half the force, landing at Brown's Ferry, about one and a half miles below Lookout. A rebel cavalry picket was surprised here and fled, closely pursued, up the road, after exchanging a few shots. The second detachment landed at the foot of a ridge bordering the river, at a point two miles below Brown's Ferry. The ridge, slippery and almost inaccessible, towered three hundred feet above the level of the river; but the brave men of the expedition, under the wild excitement of the movement and the situation, pushed up the steep declivity almost at a run

A rebel picket post on the crest of the ridge was scattered by a volley and a yell, and the first point was gained. Two days before four rebel regiments were stationed in the valley behind this ridge, at the foot of Raccoon Mountain, and an attack was to be expected from them. The sequel proved they had been relieved on Monday, and the force now occupying the camp consisted of two strange regiments, with three pieces of artillery. This force moved along the rear of the ridge and attacked the First Division of the expedition, which had landed at Brown's Ferry. Their superior numbers forced the troops back to the landing, and the rebels planted guns in position to sweep the road to the ferry. It was now four o'clock in the morning, and movements could be distinguished in the gray light of dawn. The cannonading by the rebel battery worked no damage. Not a man was hurt. General Hazen threw out skirmishers, and a brisk fight ensued. The attacking force of rebels was finally driven back in the direction of Lookout Mountain and up its steep sides, while, under cover of a battery on the Union or north side of the Tennessee. Turchin's Brigade, under Brigadier-General Smith, Engineer Corps, crossed on pontoons to the support of Hazen. Being now firmly established, scouting parties were sent out, and the country once more passed into the possession of the United States. The rebels from a battery half way up the mountain, kept up a desultory fire till ten o'clock in the forenoon. Our position was secure, and camps were established on the ridge. A foraging party, on an excursion into the country thereabouts, discovered mines of forage, which was particularly acceptable to the then impoverished Union troops.*

The operations of General Hooker's column are thus described by a participant:

IN THE FIELD, LOOKOUT VALLEY,
October 29, 1863.

On the morning of October 26th, we left Bridgeport, Ala., by crossing a pontoon at that place, and moving forward to Shell Mount. The next day at daylight we moved forward to and through Lookout Valley, at a point adjacent to where the roads fork—the one going to, and being called the Chattanooga road, and the other Brown's Ferry.

Here the enemy made a short stand, but was soon driven from this position. The enemy was posted on a high and commanding elevation.

---

* Chattanooga correspondence of the *New York Herald.*

Our troops moved forward, in line, to the right and left of the hill, and when there was an evidence that the enemy would be surrounded, the latter retreated, in double-quick time, and fell back across Lookout Creek, where he was supported by a reserve rebel force.

In moving along the enemy appeared upon our right, on the Lookout Mountain ridge—as we moved parallel to it. The enemy opened upon our forces, moving in column, from Point Lookout, but did not succeed in checking the progress of the troops. The rebel signal officers, too, in plain sight, but far above us, pursued their business, and seemed to run along on a ridge, signalling with a view to attract our attention. This signalling continued thus for several miles, and until our forces got fully abreast of Point Lookout, &c. It must have been exceedingly annoying to the rebels to see our long line wind its way in and out of the woods and on the road unbroken and at a steady march, notwithstanding the fire from his high posted guns. Of course, at certain times there were many narrow escapes. Shells constantly burst to the right and left of the road (which lies almost at the base of the mountain), but few on it. The orderly passage of the troops under this fire reflected much credit on the commanders of all grades. The enemy attempted to destroy our trains, but signally failed even in this. This species of shelling was continued upon our line for several hours, and even until dark, but without inflicting any injury of consequence. So close at one time was one portion the Union troops, that the enemy threw percussion shells by hand off the mountain, and they exploded almost in our midst.

The morning of the 28th opened with a clear, bright, beautiful moonlight, the scenery on every side traced in dark sombre on the back ground of the sky. High, towering mountains—the Raccoon Mountain on one side and the Lookout Mountain on the other—and the valley diversified by open fields and small clumps of woods, formed a curious picture. On Lookout Mountain bright fires burned, and told us too plainly where to look for the enemy and his signal officers. Our camp fires burned brightly, and our line lay on a parallel with what was the enemy's on the day previous. Two divisions were encamped on the left or front of our line. Another division, General Geary's, was in bivouac, about one mile and a half from the other two divisions. Between the two sections of the command the enemy held a position on the Chattanooga road proper, as also on the railroad. In brief, the enemy had a force, in a gap between the base of the point of Lookout Mountain, along the river on the flats and some hills, partially situated in our rear.

Suddenly the Union troops were aroused by the heavy firing in the direction of General Geary's Division. At once preparation was made for a general engagement. The troops were soon in column, and the trains and ambulances got in readiness for the emergency. As they pressed forward on the road to join General Geary, the enemy opened a heavy fire of musketry from a high hill close to their line of advance. At once our commanding generals comprehended the state of affairs. The enemy had intended their movement to be a surprise; and one with a view to the probable surrounding and possible capture of Geary's force. From prisoners taken during the fight that ensued, we learned that General Longstreet, on beholding our column move up the Lookout Valley toward Chattanooga, quietly massed two divisions on Lookout Mountain, and moved them up to and across Lookout Creek, with a view to the carrying out of the plan of his surprise movement. About eight P. M. he moved his division across the creek. One division passed on to the Chattanooga road and occupied two hills commanding the road, on a parallel, leading to Brown's Ferry. The other division passed down the railroad, and from there on to the Chattanooga road, below the fork. The rebels had intrenched themselves on the hill, and from their works had opened fire upon the Union command; but this did not delay the advance of the re-enforcements, which pushed along under fire through an open space or field to the right of the front of the hills.

While this command was pressing forward, a second division was moved up on the road, and a courier sent to inform General Geary of the near approach of assistance.

An order was now given to take the hill, and the second division was assigned to the task. The advance was commenced and the enemy poured down a heavy fire of musketry. Slowly the men went up the hill, the ascent of which was so steep that it was as much as a man could do to get to the top in peaceful times, and with the help of day light. This hill was covered with briar bushes, fallen trees, and tangling masses of various descriptions, but our boys pressed forward in spite of all obstructions. The whole division at last gave a sudden start forward and gained the crest of the hill. The enemy's line wavered and broke, and the rebels composing it went down the other side of the hill with broken, flying, and disordered ranks. On gaining the crest our men found that they had not only driven the enemy off, but had taken some tolerably well-constructed earthworks, behind which the rebels had posted themselves. It was then ascertained, too, that the hill had been occupied by about two thousand rebels. The success and the gallantry with which the height was taken elicited general commendation to the skill and bravery of the troops and their commanding officers.

Soon after this a detachment from another division took the next hill to the right without much resistance.

The enemy continued a scattering fire for some time after the hills were taken, but finally ceased troubling us.

In the mean time, General Geary had bravely resisted the rebel attack, and after two hours' hard fighting the enemy retreated, without making Geary's line to waver or fall back a foot. Almost every horse in one section of artillery was shot dead. The enemy retired across the railroad, and from there to the other side of the creek.*

The success of this movement of General Grant's forces was very annoying to the rebels, as may be judged from the following extract from one of their journals:

The movements of the enemy at Chattanooga are still uncertain, Whether the occupation of Lookout Mountain indicates an advance, or is, like the last crossing of the Rappahannock at Fredericksburg by Sedgwick's Corps, merely a feint to cover a retreat, has not yet transpired; but when considered in connection with the reported retreat from Loudon, and its occupation by our forces, we are inclined to believe that Grant is preparing a "change of base" from East Tennessee to some point more accessible for supplies. This supposition becomes more probable when it is remembered that from Lookout Valley to Bridgeport his retreat could be more expeditiously made than from Chattanooga.

But whether for advance or retreat this occupation of Lookout Valley is of importance. If for the former, it demonstrates that the enemy have recovered from their defeat at Chickamauga, and taken the initiative, always one of importance in military movements. It may be useless to inquire why the enemy were permitted to regain strength, *morale*, and organization, and begin offensive movements, in the immediate front, under the very nose of General Bragg. The vanquished, flying enemy, whom General Bragg reported to be "pursued by our cavalry," have turned upon the pursuers and have occupied a threatening position upon the flank of the victors. The enemy were outfought at Chickamauga, thanks to the army, but the present position of affairs looks as though

* *New York Herald* correspondence.

we had been outgeneraled at Chattanooga. We hope these, our apprehensions, may turn out groundless, and that the strategy of General Bragg may prove equal to the prowess and gallantry of his army: but we must confess that the country will be as much surprised as pleased should success attend our arms at Chattanooga.

If the occupation of Lookout Valley by the enemy has been made to cover a retreat, an opportunity for energy, strategy, and perseverance, will be afforded General Bragg, which if promptly embraced and efficiently pursued, will do much to reinstate him in the confidence of the army and the country. As the risk is to be taken under General Bragg, we hope that every officer and private will exert his utmost endeavors to aid the General in overwhelming the enemy.

Whether General Grant intends to advance or is preparing to retreat from Chattanooga, he must be defeated either on the south side of the Tennessee or on his retreat to Nashville. The approaching winter warns both armies that their present positions may be their mutual destruction, and the spring of 1864 *open on the wasted and ruined remnonts of both.*

The railroad from "Bridgeport to Jaspar," if not as unreal and unsubstantial as the taking of Lookout Mountain by the enemy, may solve the difficulty of Grant remaining in Chattanooga for the winter.

Thus, from the contradictory and unreconcilable reports of movements, it is impossible to ascertain any thing definite and certain as regards the situation at Chattanooga. Our readers must exercise patience and hope for the best.*

General Grant had, however, no intention of retreating. About this time the rebel President paid a visit to Bragg's army, to ascertain the true condition of affairs, and it is reported that the following scene occurred on the summit of Lookout Moutain:

Looking down one bright day from the lofty eminence commanding a clear view into four States, and a very distant view into a fifth, Davis saw Grant's army almost beneath his feet, across the valley, working like beavers on their fortifications.

"I have them now," said he, "in just the trap I set for them."

* *Richmond Enquirer*, November 6th, 1863.

To which Lieutenant-General Pemberton, who was sitting on horseback beside him, replied, "Mr. Davis, you are Commander-in-Chief, and you are here. You think the enemy are in a trap, and can be captured by vigorous assault. I have been blamed for not having ordered a general attack on the enemy when they were drawing around me their lines of circumvallation at Vicksburg. Do you now order an attack upon those troops down there below us, and I will set you my life that not one G—d d—d man of the attacking column will ever come back across that valley, except as a prisoner."

CHAPTER XLVIII.

LONGSTREET'S ADVANCE UPON KNOXVILLE.

THE brilliant success of these operations relieved Chattanooga of the prospective danger of starvation, and General Grant found time to prepare for his movements upon the enemy in his front. Stores of all kinds began to make their way into storehouse, and daily parades and drills took place in front of the works, within view of the rebel pickets and sentries. Every thing had settled down into its quiet routine, and even the generals appeared at their ease. A private letter from a resident of Chattanooga had the following paragraph descriptive of this serenity:

General Grant, who has almost recovered his strength, occupies a delightful Chattanooga residence, and, with his briarwood pipe, *walks to and fro up the streets of the town, unattended, many times unobserved, but at all times observing.* Quartermaster-General Meigs has taken to a wall tent, from a regard for the fitness of things. His head-quarters are in the field, and soldiers in the field inhabit tents. Generals Thomas and Gordon Granger are workers, and are preparing their grand machine for the next campaign, their consultations often extending far into the night.

But in the midst of this quiet lay a slumbering volcano. General Grant had determined he would have no enemies around him to report his movements to the rebels or to interfere with his plans; therefore, previous to his making any advance upon the rebel positions, he issued the following order:

HEAD-QUARTERS, MILITARY DIVISION OF THE MISSISSIPPI,
IN THE FIELD, CHATTANOOGA, TENN., *Nov.* 5, 1863.

[*General Orders, No.* 4.]

The habit of raiding parties of rebel cavalry visiting towns, villages, and farms where there are no Federal forces, and pillaging Union families, having become prevalent, department commanders will take immediate steps to stop the evil, or make the loss by such raids fall upon secessionists and secession sympathizers in the neighborhood where such acts are committed. For every act of violence to the person of an unarmed Union citizen, a secessionist will be arrested and held as hostage for the delivery of the offender. For every dollar's worth of property taken from such citizens, or destroyed by raiders, an assessment will be made upon secessionists of the neighborhood, and collected by the nearest military forces, under the supervision of the commander thereof, and the amount thus collected paid over to the sufferers. When such assessments cannot be collected in money, property useful to the government may be taken at a fair valuation, and the amount paid in money by a disbursing officer of the government, who will take such property upon his returns. Wealthy secession citizens will be assessed in money and provisions for the support of Union refugees who have been and may be driven from their homes and into our lines by the acts of those with whom secession citizens are in sympathy. All collections and payments under this order will be through disbursing officers of the government, whose accounts must show all money and property received under it, and how disposed of.

By order of Major-General U. S. GRANT.

T. S. BOWERS, *A. A.-G.*

This order he carried out to the letter when the opportunity offered.

About the middle of November the head of General Sherman's column arrived at Chattanooga and formed a junction with the forces under General Thomas, on the right of the main army.

Shortly before the time that General Sherman joined General Grant, the rebel General Longstreet made several attempts to flank the Union position several miles to the eastward of Chattanooga, with the intention of advancing into Tennessee and capturing Knoxville. The advanced forces of the Army of Eastern Tennessee had heretofore resisted Longstreet's movement at the crossing of the Little Tennessee River; but after General Burnside had communicated with General Grant, Longstreet was allowed to advance upon Knoxville, the Union troops impeding his march as much as possible, and drawing him on with a show of resistance. The feint was well planned and finely carried out.

On the 14th of November, General Longstreet, after crossing the Little Tennessee River, was attacked by a force of General Burnside's Union troops, who drove the rebel advance guard back upon their reserves, which were stationed at about a mile north of the river bank. The Union troops then retreated, while the rebels crossed their whole force and moved toward Marysville. The Unionists then fell back upon Lenoir, as if to hold the railroad at that place. Three times the rebels assaulted that position on November 15th without success; but the next morning the Union troops evacuated it and retreated to Campbell's Station. Here they again made a stand, and a fight ensued lasting from before noon until dark. This detention of the rebels enabled the Unionists to secure their trains, which they sent within the defences of Knoxville. The Union troops once more fell back, stopped and repeated their resistance to the enemy, and after a fight again retreated in good order, until, on the 19th of November, Longstreet's rebel forces were before the city of Knoxville, which they began to invest—the Union troops being all safely within the defences.

General Grant was duly advised of the position of affairs, and with his "we have them now where we want them," he prepared to move on the enemy's works.

A plan had been made, by the commanding General, to raise the siege of Chattanooga and get possession of Lookout Mountain. This plan was submitted to his general officers by the General himself, and finally adopted. An examination of the enemy's line showed clearly that he had deliberately exposed himself to great danger. He had allowed a large portion of his army to go into East Tennessee, and he extended the remainder of his forces into lines almost as thin as a spider's thread. His exterior line upon Mission Ridge was something near seven miles in extent, while his inner lines of rifle pits and similar defences running through the valleys were not less than five miles long. There were upon the line two points of importance to him; the first, Missionary Ridge, being the key to his position, and Lookout Mountain, an elevation valuable to Bragg as a barrier to the purposes of the Union troops. It was supposed the enemy would defend the former with vigor, as the latter could be held by a small force. General Grant was of the opinion, that by attacking his flanks vigorously, in order to force him to keep his line lengthened, and thus weakened, it would afford the Union troops a favorable opportunity to test the strength of the centre. It was therefore decided that General Sherman, with three divisions of his own army, and General Davis, of Palmer's Corps, should move north of the river, to a point opposite the mouth of the Chickamauga, and at an early hour on the following morning throw a pontoon bridge across the Tennessee, and, under cover of artillery, cross and carry the heights of Missionary Ridge as far, at least, as Tunnel Hill. On the left rebel flank, General Hooker was to operate with three divisions, his primary object being to hold the rebels there, but authorized, in case of an opportunity presenting itself, to take posession of Lookout Mountain. In the centre, General Thomas was ordered to hold Granger and Palmer's Corps well in hand, to await an opportunity to strike at the centre, whenever in the opinion of General Grant the auspicious moment presented itself. General O. O. Howard's Corps was to be moved to the north side of the river, so as to aid either Sherman or the centre. But subsequently, at the suggestion of General Thomas, Howard was crossed into Chattanooga, and held as a movable column in reserve. Such was the general plan of operations, subject, of course, to such modifications as the movements of the enemy might necessitate.

This plan was to have been put in execution on Saturday, November 21st, almost immediately after General Grant had ascertained that Longstreet was before Knoxville; but General Sherman failed to get into position on Friday, his delay being caused by heavy rains and the partial destruction of the pontoon bridges by rafts floated down the river by the rebels. Indeed, he was prevented from getting up until the night of Monday, and only reported himself ready for his work on Tuesday morning. On Monday, however, a trivial circumstance brought about a development of interest, and which, without changing the plan in the least, rather advanced it and increased the chances of success.

CHAPTER XLIX.

THE BATTLES BEFORE CHATTANOOGA.—FIRST DAY.

SHORTLY before noon on the morning of Monday, November 23d, 1863, the order for the preliminary advance of General Grant's forces was promulgated at head-quarters, and the troops advanced as if on parade. The rebels passively watched the movements of the Union forces under the impression that they were engaged in a review, and they were not undeceived until it was too late to remedy the evil. The battles occupied several days and resulted in a complete victory for the Union forces.

The details of this important contest are thus given by one who witnessed the whole action:

Reports had come in during the morning of Monday that the enemy was evacuating the ridge in our front. On examination it was found that they were engaged in some kind of movement, and about noon General Thomas determined upon a reconnoissance to learn the meaning of his manœuvres, and also for developing his right, it being a matter of considerable interest, in view of Sherman's movements, to know how strongly Bragg was posted on the ridge about the tunnel. General Wood's Division was selected to make the reconnoissance, and at one o'clock he had moved his three brigades into line in an open field east of the city, and immediately under the siege guns of Fort Wood. General Howard's Corps having crossed the river from Lookout Valley, deployed into line as a reserve, while General Sheridan, of Granger's Corps, and the troops of the Fourteenth Corps, General Palmer, were drawn up in line in case of a necessity arising for them. General Palmer also showed himself threateningly down the valley of Chattanooga Creek, making his advance well beyond Dobb's house. Wood's route, as chosen, was to be to the left of the road to Blackford's house on Mission Ridge; but the force headed for two prominent hills a little to the north of this road, and the right hardly rested on the Blackford road when the day was over.

I have mentioned two prominent peaks or hills in Wood's front. These are exactly one mile from Fort Wood, and lie west of Citico Creek, a little stream running between this small ridge and Mission Ridge. The principal of these peaks is called by the citizens "Orchard Knob," and the rebels had used it as a redoubt in their outer line. The approach to it was down and across an open slope from Fort Wood and then across a heavily-wooded plain. General Wood began his movement down this slope, and across this plain at half-past one P. M. At the moment Wood began to move, General Granger ordered the siege guns in Fort Wood to open on the enemy's first position, and immediately the black monsters bellowed a hoarse challenge to the enemy who now began to appear on Missionary Ridge in quite a strong force, as also in the valley below and toward us. Wood moved forward in admirable style, his skirmishers driving in the strong picket line of the enemy with ease. Through the open field the line moved unwaveringly, and not with undue haste, as if seeking to gain the cover of the woods in their front, but in the style of veterans proud of their leader; and, knowing that *from the ramparts of Fort Wood they were watched by Generals Grant, Thomas, Granger, and Howard,* each seemed to feel that he was part of a scene which, even in this warlike age, has been seldom witnessed. There was no straggling. There were none who seemed so poor and spiritless as to straggle in the presence of men who had led at Vicksburg and Chickamauga, or of troops that had stood at Gettysburg. So, when they disappeared in the woods at the bottom of the hill, and their position became revealed only by the smoke of battle, which rose above the tree tops and drifted away toward Mission Ridge, a general buzz of admiration went up from the spectators in the fort, and extended to the more distinguished heroes of Vicksburg and Chickamauga. On entering the woods the advancing line became quite warmly engaged, and at a quarter of two o'clock a very brisk musketry fire enveloped the whole of Wood's front. The enemy was found posted behind rather rude but good rifle-pits, and in strong force. But, though they got in upon Wood a heavy and quite destructive fire, it did not for a moment halt him. On reaching the foot of Orchard Knob he ordered a charge, and with a cheer the men went at it, pushed up the Knob in admirable order, while the rest took the rifle-pits, driving the enemy out in confusion, and securing one hundred and fifty men and nine officers of an Alabama regiment. Another force gallantly assaulted and carried the ridge to the right of Orchard Knob, driving the rebels from their pits on the summit.

Although now far advanced toward the enemy's line of works on the ridge, General Wood found his flanks entirely unmolested. He discovered the position taken to be a very strong one, easily held, in short cannon range of the enemy's camps along Citico Creek, and within reach of the heavy line established by them on the summit of Mission Ridge; and finding, after some time, that the enemy remained quiet, Wood reported the fact to General Granger, who, on orders from General Thomas, instructed Wood to intrench himself, and at the same time sent word he would protect his flanks.

In order to support Wood in this situation, General Thomas ordered General Howard, with his two divisions, to move from his position as reserve behind Wood, and to go into line on Citico Creek, closing his right well upon Wood's left, and retiring the left of the corps. He got into position without much fighting, other than some pretty heavy skirmishing with a small force of rebels in a second line of rifle-pits beyond Citico Creek. Approaching these pits in front, General Howard found their occupants prepared, and disposed to make a strong resistance. In order to avoid a bloody affair, General Granger sent a brigade, of Wood's Division, hitherto in reserve, through some woods to the right of the rebel works. The enemy, finding himself thus flanked, and at the same time heavily pressed by Howard, hastily fled to the stronger position at the foot of the mountain.

Simultaneously with Howard's movement General Sheridan's Division —Granger's Corps—was moved forward to support Wood's right, and went into position in *échelon* on the left without any fighting. The enemy, finding that our men were intrenching themselves on Orchard Knob, began about five o'clock a vigorous shelling of that point. Although this was kept up from three batteries until darkness had set in, no damage was done.

During the night the position taken by Wood and the forces which came up to support him, right and left, was materially strengthened by building rough rifle-pits a few yards in front of those of the rebels which had been taken. A battery was moved forward from Fort Wood and posted on Orchard Knob, where it remained during the rest of the operations. There may have been other batteries on the front line at this time, but if so I did not see them. I may as well mention here that the heavy guns of Fort Wood took part in the three days' operations, throwing heavy shells upon Mission Ridge with great accuracy.

General Palmer moved during the night a portion of his corps to the left of his position during the day, and stood ready at dawn to continue his demonstrations down Chattanooga Valley, or to aid the left centre, under Granger, in an assault on the ridge. No dispositon appeared on Palmer's part to force a pathway down the valley, as this would have broken the rebel line to no purpose, as they could well afford to retire from the valley entirely in order to hold Mission Ridge. The aim of General Grant appears to have been to weaken the rebel centre on Mission Ridge, in order that he might at once take the ridge and break their army in two.

Night found the situation very slightly altered, save in the centre, where we had assumed a strong position and threatening attitude. But the rebels did not appear to be much troubled at this. They rather apprehended the movement of Sherman, which it was evident they had suspected. During the last hours of the afternoon it was seen from Orchard Knob that a long column of rebels was moving to the north, and disappearing about the more formidable hills at the tunnel or north end of Mission Ridge. It was evident that Bragg had an inkling of Sherman's purpose to cross on the ensuing morning at the mouth of the creek, and was massing against him; but whether to oppose his crossing or to hold the hill remained at that time a matter of doubt. The enemy in front of Wood allowed that enterprising officer to rest in peace during the night.*

---

* Mr. W. F. G. Shanks's dispatch to the *New York Herald.*

CHAPTER L.

THE SECOND DAY.—LOOKOUT MOUNTAIN.

THE second day's operations are thus described by the same correspondent:

Tuesday morning, November 24th, was gloomy, threatening rain, and until quite late our forces remained inactive. On the centre Granger's and Palmer's Corps maintained the silence of the night just past, and only a few guns from Fort Wood disturbed the rebel centre. The day was chosen for operations on the flanks, and for that purpose Hooker and Sherman began to move quite early.

It will be remembered that General Howard's Corps (the Eleventh) had crossed the river and gone into camp in Chattanooga on Sunday. On Monday he was held in reserve, and went in late in the day to support General Wood's left. On Tuesday morning his corps was selected by General Grant to open communications by the east side of the Tennessee River with General Sherman. It was about ten o'clock when one of his divisions crossed Citico Creek, near its mouth, and began pushing northward in search of General Sherman. Finding the centre destined to remain quiet, I pushed towards the left, and found General Howard. The whole of the valley between Mission Ridge and the Tennessee River, and between Citico and Chickamauga Creeks, is one vast corn-field. Through this lay the course of General Howard.

Learning that General Sherman's position was not over two miles and a half distant, General Howard sent one of his staff on the dangerous mission of trying to find General Sherman alone. The skirmishers were thrown forward until the line became dangerously extended, and none of General Sherman's troops were found. The staff officer departed on his mission of danger; but by keeping close to the river succeeded in crossing and recrossing the gap without being captured. General Howard, on receiving his report, ordered the division to push further to the left, and started out to seek General Sherman. I pursued the same

BATTLE AT CHATTANOOGA.

route and soon found General Sherman's troops, and was standing on the unfinished pontoon bridge which General Sherman was building, when General Howard came up. The last boat of the bridge was being placed in the centre of the stream as General Howard arrived, and introduced himself across the slight gulf between the two. At the moment of its occurrence this was a meeting of considerable interest to me, but coming to write about it I find I cannot get up the same amount of enthusiasm that I then felt at the reflection of these two men, representing the extreme armies of the country, meeting thus upon the same field. Sherman, on the north end of the bridge, dressed loosely, with a worn gum overcoat thrown around him, was directing the completion of the bridge; and, as soon as the boat was put in, sprang over and shook the hand of the princely Howard. It was exactly at noon.

I found on inquiry that General Sherman had at an early hour thrown a portion of one of his divisions across the river, under the protection of a battery, and subsequently the other divisions, the greater portion being crossed by the steamer Dunbar, which, captured two months ago, at Chattanooga, had been repaired, and was now serving good and loyal purposes. Immediately on arriving he had thrown up strong rifle-pits in two lines, covering the approach to the bridge and adding much strength to a naturally strong position. The troops of his corps at the hour of noon held these works and were waiting for a division of the Fourteenth Corps, to cross the river and take up position in the works. This division had been sent General Sherman in place of Osterhaus, who was acting with General Hooker, and was now being used by Sherman as a reserve.

This division crossed the river, and went into line within the works about an hour after the meeting between Howard and Sherman. At the same moment General Sherman gave his orders to prepare for an attack. By this hour, one o'clock P. M., the drizzly rain, which had been threatening us, began to fall, and the object of the assault was soon hid from view. General Sherman stood on a prominent hill to the left of the pontoon bridge, and having succeeded, with the aid of two orderlies, and in despite of the rain, in lighting a cigar, stood puffing away at one end, chewing at the other, and observing all that could be seen in the country before him. Around him were gathered at this time Generals Frank Blair, Morgan L. Smith, Ewing, John W. Corse, and Howard. The troops of the several divisions were encamped just in front of him, while on the left and rear Davis's artillery was thundering over the bridge. In a very quiet tone Sherman gave his orders to form for the assault, remarking that the enemy was reported heavy in his front. The formation as ordered, was *echelon* on the left, General Morgan L. Smith's Division being the left, John E. Smith the centre, and Ewing the right. The left was to keep well towards Chickamauga Creek, "and," added Sherman, "I want you to keep up the formation, 400 yards distance, until you get to the foot of the hill."

"And shall we keep it after that?" asked Ewing.

"You may go up the hill," answered Sherman, "if you like, and can."

General Davis having got into position, and the troops having been arranged as ordered, General Sherman gave the orders to move to the assault. They were couched in very common terms, but which ought to be preserved: "I see Davis is up. I guess you may as well go on, and take the hill." In a few moments after the three columns were moving.

Soldiers are very different beings under the two different circumstances of receiving and making an attack. In the first case they are seldom or never composed, cool, and quiet. Put men behind breastworks to receive an assault, and the delay in the attack creates anxiety, which develops into mental excitement, which finds vent in noise and a certain restlessness of person. Going to the assault they are different beings. I watched carefully the columns, as they moved out to the assault on Tuesday, each believing that the next step brought his advance against that of the enemy. The silence was painfully noticeable. A command given at one end of the corps, could be distinctly heard at the other. The men looked serious, and rather gruff, and were painfully quiet. They conversed with each other but seldom, and then in under tones. All appeared anxious to preserve their weapons from the rain. They moved in perfect order. But though one might fail to notice this, the most casual student of human nature could hardly fail to observe how serious those men were. And he would know, too, that it was not the rain which dampened their spirits. Ever and anon they would glance at the hill which they were approaching, and it was easy to see why they looked serious. Perhaps they compared the hills, in their own minds, to the Walnut Hills of Vicksburg; but I do not think there was one man there who feared to test the question of victory or defeat there and then.

But it was not destined that Tuesday should witness a conflict for these hills. General Sherman had anticipated skirmishing before reaching the foot of the mountain, it having been reported by citizens that the enemy held the position in strong force. But the foot of the hill was reached, after short delay, without any serious skirmishing, only a few shells, from Tunnel Hill, passed over our heads, and exploded among the colored pioneers, who followed in the rear, doing no damage, but causing the negroes to lose all respect for orders to "close up."

The enemy made no opposition to the occupation of the extreme end of the ridge. General Sherman was in possession of this at about four o'clock P. M. It then appeared that the hills occupied were separated from Mission Ridge by a narrow valley, through which the railroad runs.

The hills occupied by Sherman were three in number, and semicircular in shape, bending around and north of the end of Mission Ridge. The end of the ridge is generally and very properly called Tunnel Hill. It overlooks and commands the hills of which General Sherman found himself in peaceable possession; and on examination he found that the labor still remained to be done. A close inspection of the ground and the enemy's position determined Sherman to occupy the semicircular ridge with his centre and right, and throw his left still further to the left and in the region of Myer's mill. The division moved promptly to this position and took possession of the valley from the foot of the hills to Chickamauga River, securing at the time about one hundred rebels engaged in building rafts of fallen timber with which to destroy our pontoon bridges.

An examination of the enemy's position revealed him on the top and at the foot of the next hill—Tunnel Hill. On the summit he was engaged in strengthening a large bastion-shaped work (Fort Buckner), and was working with great vigor and a large force, as if the fort had not been previously completed. At the foot of the mountain and near the west end of the tunnel a force of about one brigade occupied and held the heavy railroad bank.

General Sherman ordered the erection of defences on the ridge he had occupied, and finding he did not propose to push further during the little of daylight left him, I left his corps and proceeded to join that of General Hooker, which had been engaged all day.

In order to carry out the proposed plan, and to keep the enemy's lines as much extended as possible, it was necessary that Hooker and Sherman should attack the lines simultaneously. General Hooker's task was to assault Lookout Mountain, and in the event of finding a weak force holding it, or the failure of the enemy to weaken the rest of their line in order to hold the mountain, to take possession of it. It was thought that as Tunnel Hill was of vast importance to the rebels, and Lookout of the same value to us, that they would strongly defend both. General Hooker had only one division of Slocum's Corps to make the assault with, but was re-enforced before the attack was made by a division of Sherman's Corps, and two brigades of the Fourth Corps.

The rebels occupied the west side or slope of Lookout Mountain in very strong force, and also the front or spur of the mountain. It must also be remembered that it is not a regular slope from the summit of Lookout to the foot, but that the first twenty-five or thirty feet of the descent is perpendicular rocks, or what is generally understood to be meant by "palisades." These are very high and grand, and there are but two routes by which they can be overcome. One of these is a gap twenty miles south of the river, and was held by the rebels. The other is by the road to Summertown, which is laid down upon the map. It winds up the east side of the mountain, ascending the palisades by a steep declivity and a narrow road. General Hooker's plan of operation was to get possession of this road. To do so was to gain possession of the mountain.

He began his operations early on the morning of Tuesday, and by eight o'clock his column was moving up Lookout Valley, and to the surprise of the enemy on the point of the mountain, it disappeared in the forest south of Wauchatchia. But here, filing his troops to the left, General Hooker began the difficult task of the ascent of the mountain; but meeting with no opposition he was enabled to do this in a short time. The head of the column having reached the palisades went into line of battle facing to the north, and with the right resting against the palisades, stretched down the mountain slope.

General Hooker then formed a second line of the two brigades of the Fourth Corps, which had been sent him, the remaining division forming a third line, and held in readiness to aid any part of the line which might need it. Thus arranged, the corps was ordered forward, with a heavy line of skirmishers thrown out, and, marching along the slope of the ridge, soon came upon the rear of the enemy, who, unsuspecting such a movement so absolutely opposed to all the military rules by which Bragg fights, were taken completely by surprise. Before those at the foot of the hill could comprehend the situation, the Union skirmishers had penetrated far towards the point of the mountain, and now got in a heavy fire upon the enemy, who were trying to escape up the hill, while our men assaulted them from above—a most complete reverse to the late situation. At the same time our batteries on Moccasin Point and those of the rebels on Lookout Mountain opened a heavy fire upon each other, and soon the whole mountain was hid from view in Chattanooga by the cloud of smoke which rose above and around it.

Thus taken in rear and flank, the enemy made but little organized resistance, but their skirmishers for a long time kept up a heavy fire from behind jutting rocks and from trees. They, however, were forced back by the heavy skirmish line under General Hooker, and the enemy on the point of the mountain gradually gave way, and fell back in some disorder to the line of breastworks on the east slope of the mountain, at Carlin's house. The Union troops then swung around until his line was parallel with that of the enemy, and again advanced; but, met by organized and well directed resistance, for a time recoiled and hesitated.

It was now that the fruits of the strange movement of Hooker began to develop themselves. The Union line had moved around the spur of the mountain and on the east side with such rapidity that the enemy stationed at the foot of the hill and along the river had no time to escape, and our troops began to secure them by hundreds. Every jutting rock, every thicket of undergrowth, and many a hollow tree, on examination, disclosed their secrets in the shape of prisoners. Each regiment engaged seemed to have secured enough to have filled their ranks, and the provost-marshal, who appeared to take charge of them, soon found his hands full. The number thus captured, General Hooker estimated on the spot at two thousand, but on counting them it was found the exact number secured was only one thousand three hundred and sixty. They represented themselves to be from Stevenson's Division, and it was soon discovered that they were the unexchanged prisoners taken by Grant at Vicksburg. I have talked with several of these men since, and I have no doubt in my own mind that they conscientiously believed that they had been exchanged. Certain it is that it had been so represented to these men, and officers and men with whom I have conversed freely on the subject, express great indignation at their own government and terror of ours. I attempted to convince these men that though our government would hold all officers who had been guilty or cognizant of this outrage to a strict accountability to the laws of nations on the subject, it would at the same time be too merciful to punish those who had already been victims to the deceptions of their friends. This was consolation to the men, who were terribly frightened at the prospect of punishment; but the more intelligent of the officers seemed to fear very little the power of the government to punish them.

An examination of the enemy's position revealed him behind very heavy and strong breastworks running diagonally across a large open field, of which Carlin's house is the centre. The works were very strong, and deep rifle-pits, and posted behind them, to the right of Carlin's house, were two pieces of light artillery. The enemy had not yet opened with these, but was preparing to do so as soon as our line should appear out of the woods and advancing across this open field. General Hooker, after a close examination of this position, made a new disposition of his force and began a systematic assault upon the works. Every advantage was now with the enemy, and, with re-enforcements to the extent of his losses in prisoners, he could have held the mountain against General Hooker's combined force. But the re-enforcements were not forthcoming. The weakened enemy had to contract his line to the works immediately across the field, and in doing so left his right flank exposed.

Now began the heavy struggle of the day. Sending two regiments to hold the road which crosses the spur of the mountain from the east, he advanced the rest of his forces to the front line. An advance was immediately ordered, and for an hour and a half (it was now two o'clock P. M.) a very heavy sharpshooters' fight was kept up. I cannot expect to give any clear idea of this engagement. It was no place to manœuvre columns. Each man and company fought upon his and its "own hook." From Chattanooga nothing was visible save the misty smoke which enveloped and hid the mountain. But beneath this the combatants saw each other, and here they continued to fight with desperation until four o'clock, when there came a tide in Hooker's fortune which he did not fail to take at the flood.

The skirmish line was enabled, under cover of the trees which grew along that part of the ridge, to advance much nearer the rebel line than those in the immediate front of the enemy and the open field. It was also upon the flank of the position; and the weakness of the enemy having compelled him to contract his left, a lodgment was found very near their rifle-pits. General Hooker, upon being informed of this, at four o'clock ordered a charge of the line, and through a heavy and rapid fire, kept up for five long minutes—and minutes are sometimes very long—the men dashed forward upon, over, and into the abandoned pits. The enemy had seen the long line of steel that glittered even amid the rain which was pouring upon them, and they couldn't stand that. They also saw troops upon their left flank, and, filled with that holy horror which old soldiers have for "flank movements," they couldn't stand that.

They fell back, abandoning works, artillery, and position, but still holding the important Summertown road.

But the enemy, though flanked and overpowered, did not appear disposed to leave us in quiet possession of his works and guns. He hastily reformed his lines and prepared to assault in turn. The Unionists had hardly occupied the captured position, or been able to remove the captured guns, before the enemy returned to the attack. He pressed forward with great vigor and gained ground very rapidly at first, but found in his way the same obstacle of the open field, while he did not have the advantage of superior numbers. As soon as it came to close work, his rapidly advancing lines were halted very suddenly by the terrible fire which was now poured in upon him. He continued, however, to fire rapidly, and with some execution upon our line, but would have been ultimately repulsed without other assistance, had not a very serious obstacle presented itself.

Men in line of battle very soon expend their ammunition. In a skirmishing engagement, like that they were then having, they dispose of it even more rapidly. We were nearly out of ammunition, and the commanding officer had serious fears he would have to relinquish possession of the works if his cartridge-boxes were not soon replenished. General Hooker, anticipating this, had sent for ammunition at an early hour after getting possession of the road across the spur of the mountain; but the difficulties of the uncertain pontoon bridges had prevented his getting any. He again asked for it, and this time it came, and at the opportune moment. The men were beginning to fall out of line occasionally, entirely out of ammunition; for when a man puts his hand behind him and into his cartridge-box, to find no cartridges there, a good deal of his confidence, if not courage, oozes out at the ends of his fingers, with which he thought to grasp the death-dealing messenger. The line was beginning to be thinned by men who had fired their sixty rounds, when the ammunition which General Thomas had sent sprang across Chattanooga Creek. The enemy had begun to perceive his advantage and to push forward, when this ammunition marched up the hill. The enemy had even ventured upon a shout of assured victory, when this ammunition deployed into line and double-quicked across the open field, and sprang into the vacated places. There were one hundred and twenty thousand rounds of it, strapped upon the backs of as good men as had stayed with Thomas at Chickamauga, and in ten minutes after it reached the works it had repulsed the enemy! The re-enforcements which so opportunely arrived consisted of a brigade of the Fourteenth Corps, and upon it devolved the remainder of the labor of the day. It was dark by the time the enemy were repulsed, and those who stayed in Chattanooga describe this fight as the most magnificent view of the grand panorama of war which we have just witnessed. It was just beginning to be dark enough to see the flash of the muskets, and still light enough to distinguish the general outline of the contending masses. The mountain was lit up by the fires of the men in the second line, and the flash of musketry and artillery. An unearthly noise rose from the mountain as if the old monster was groaning with the punishment the pigmy combatants inflicted upon him as well as upon each other. And during it all, the great guns on the summit continued, as in rage, to bellow defiance at the smaller guns of Moccasin Point, which, with lighter tone, and more rapidly, as if mocking the imbecility of its giant enemy, continued to fire till the day roared itself into darkness.

The enemy fell back after his repulse to a point covering the Summertown ascent to the summit of the mountain, and for the remainder of the night confined himself to the defence of that defile and to the evacuation of the mountain.

Subsequently, about midnight, the enemy, to cover his retreat, made an assault upon the Union lines, but though they did some execution they were handsomely repulsed.

General Hooker made a great reputation by this attack with the men of the Army of the Cumberland. As his lines would advance after night, the men could see his fires springing up and locating his new line. As each line became developed by these fires, those on the mountain could plainly distinguish the cheers of their comrades below. One of the expressions used by a private who was watching the fires from Orchard Knob has already grown into the dignity of a camp proverb. On seeing the line of camp fires advanced to Carlin's house and beyond the rifle-pits of the enemy, a soldier in General Wood's command sprang up from his reclining position on Orchard Knob, and exclaimed:

"Look at old Hooker! Don't he fight for 'keeps?'"

The sequel of the fight—the morning's handsome epilogue to the night's drama—is already known. Hooker found the enemy gone, and the assault of Lookout Mountain had not been in vain.*

The following is General Grant's modest dispatch with regard to the operations of the second day:

* Mr. W. F. G. Shanks's dispatch.

CHATTANOOGA, *Nov.* 24—6 P. M.

Major General H. W. HALLECK, *General-in-Chief, Washington, D. C.*:—

The fighting to-day progressed favorably.

General Sherman carried the end of Missionary Ridge, and his right is now at the tunnel, and his left at Chickamauga Creek.

The troops from Lookout Valley carried the point of the mountain, and now hold the eastern slope and point high up.

I cannot yet tell the amount of casualties, but our loss is not heavy.

General Hooker reports two thousand prisoners taken, besides which a small number have fallen into our hands from Missionary Ridge.

U. S. GRANT, *Major-General.*

In the above dispatch General Grant says nothing about himself, or in what manner he had participated in the struggle, although from the correspondent's account it is clearly seen, that notwithstanding his crippled condition he anxiously watched the movements of the troops at a position within cannon shot of the enemy.

The following is the rebel dispatch concerning the contest:

MISSION RIDGE, *Nov.* 24, 1863.

To General S. COOPER:

We have had a prolonged struggle for Lookout Mountain to-day, and sustained considerable loss in one division. Elsewhere the enemy has only manœuvred for position.

BRAXTON BRAGG, *General.*

CHAPTER LI.

THIRD DAY.—TUNNEL HILL.—MISSION RIDGE.

The battle raged as furiously on the third day as on those preceding, and is thus described:

General Hooker pursued the retreating enemy on top of the mountains, but did not succeed in coming up with him. He descended the mountain, however, at Hickajack trace, and, crossing the Chattanooga Creek Valley, made the ascent of Mission Ridge at or near the old battle field of Chickamauga. Here he was to the south of Rossville and in the rear of the rebel line in Chattanooga Valley, entirely cut off from the rest of our army, but perfectly able to take care of himself. He began to move north on top of Mission Ridge, and arrived at an opportune moment in the rear of Fort Breckinridge.

Weary with watching Hooker the night previous, it was late before I reached Orchard Knob on the morning of Wednesday. At the first glance I thought the situation here unchanged; but upon a closer examination I saw that the mask of night had been used to cover very extensive preparations for hard work. The relinquishing of Lookout Mountain had evinced the rebel intention to defend Mission Ridge with vigor, and in answer to this sensible play of the rebels, *General Grant had doubled the strength of forces selected to storm the ridge.* Wood had been chosen to storm the heights at Blackfords. General Grant had added to his force that of General Baird. Sheridan had been chosen to make the assault at Thurman's house, and a brigade was added to his force. General Palmer had taken command of these in person, while General Gordon Granger assumed command of the divisions of Wood and Baird. Under the cover of the forest in which they rested, these two formidable columns were hid from view from Mission Ridge, and there were no rebels on Mission Ridge to signalize the important information to Bragg, who kept head-quarters at Blackfords. The men were in excellent spirits. They had rested well from their Monday's labor, and their souls had been cheered by seeing Hooker's camp fires on Lookout and Sherman's on Mission Ridge. Daylight had revealed the signal flags waving on Lookout, and the artillery of Sherman opening from his position on Fort Buckner. General Wood was enjoying himself hugely, and called to me to stay and see the finest work of the day; but I had seen General Rawlings, of Grant's staff, dash away a few minutes before towards Fort Wood, and I knew that he had gone to fire the signal for the assault, and, putting spurs to the (not) noble ass which I had pressed into service in default of a good horse I had broken down the day before, I dashed off to see Sherman's fight.

I found General Howard's Corps moving to the left, taking care to expose itself as much as possible to rebel eyesight. The corps subsequently reached General Sherman, and were sent to strengthen his left in a movement up Chickamauga Creek.

On reaching the summit of the semi-circular shaped hills, which General Sherman had occupied on Tuesday afternoon, I found he had strengthened his position by strong rifle-pits, and had put four pieces of artillery on the right of his line, on the hills, and a section on the other extreme, thus getting in an enfilading fire on Fort Buckner. I asked the distance from the right position to Fort Buckner, and by the elevation given to the guns it was reported to be a fraction over 900 yards. A short time after my arrival this battery again became rather seriously engaged with a rebel battery in Fort Buckner, which was kept up for half an hour, to the evident discomfiture of the rebels. With the exception of the artillery, the line was as quiet and composed as if in camp, or as were three of our high privates, whom I saw sitting in a cluster to the left, making entries in their diaries. Three private soldiers, under fire, entering in diaries, in plain, legible chirography, the events of the day, is a spectacle only seen in the army of the Union. It is one of the sights which causes one to reflect, and which will long retain hold upon his memory.

The operations of the day, on General Sherman's part, began by an attack on his right upon the enemy posted behind the railroad bank at Glass Station. This attack was made at ten o'clock, and resulted in a repulse of the assaulting Union troops, after a short fight, so weakly made and so early dropped that I imagine it was intended to develop the enemy and his strength for the benefit of the artillery on the hill which began to pour upon the rebels a very destructive fire of shells, which exploded above them in handsome style. The Union commander recalled his troops after they had fully drawn the fire of the enemy, and awaited further developments on the left.

I find myself using the pronoun of the egotist rather oftener than is modest, perhaps; but the history of the first events of the battle must necessarily be matters of personal observation—and that must be my apology. On going to the left of the ridge I found gathered together there Generals Sherman, Blair, M. L. Smith and Lightburn, watching the re-enforcement by General Corse's command of three regiments of General Lightburn's Brigade, which had succeeded in effecting a lodgment on Tunnel Hill, and upon which the enemy was still at work on Fort Buckner. General Blair pointed out the situation to me, remarking, "When we take one hill it looks as if there was another to be taken." But, after a moment's pause and silent observation of Tunnel Hill, he added, "When we've got that we'll be done." I don't know that General Blair thought we should be repulsed; but I imagine he did when he made that last remark.

General Corse, with his command, mounted the hill in good style, and reached the crest without any difficulty or opposition, as other troops had also succeeded in doing; for you must understand that Fort Buckner was not built immediately on the edge of the hill. That is, you reached the top and the plateau before you got under the fire of the fort; but the moment you began to move over the plateau the fire of the enemy was likely to open out upon you. General Corse, taking command, formed the whole force under the crest of the hill, his own immediate command on the right, with the other three regiments on the left. It was just eleven o'clock when a tremendous volley from the enemy revealed the fact, patent only to good field-glasses, that Corse had marched over the crest, was on the plateau, and was charging on Fort Buckner. The opening chorus was well worthy to be the prologue of the day's drama, for it had all the merit of brevity and briskness. It lasted but ten minutes. The men fell back under the crest of the hill, but they left their dead and wounded in the enemy's rifle-pits. As they retreated our batteries opened upon the pursuing enemy, who appeared in heavy force. This ably-directed fire covered the retreat so well that the enemy were unable to pursue to the crest of the hill.

This column had hardly fallen back to its position when from the right appeared another Union brigade, pushing steadily and rapidly across some open fields in a persistent and stronger attack upon the railroad bank at this station. The enemy gave him a warm reception in front; but one of the Union regiments appearing upon their left flank, and our batteries opening on them from their right, they failed to stand the assault, and hastily abandoning it fled up the hill to the fort. Our men were soon in permanent occupation of the bank, and from it continued to fire on the retreating rebels until the last one found safety behind the mud walls of Fort Buckner.

While this had been going on, General Corse was re-enforced by a portion, perhaps all, of another brigade, and the position vacated by him was then filled by the Eleventh Corps of General Howard, which about this time double-quicked across the ridge and went into position on the left extreme. A second assault was now ordered, and General Lightburn, who had been anxiously watching the action, joined the portion of his brigade on the hill, and assumed command of the whole assaulting column. He ordered the movement to begin immediately, and a more desperate and bloody assault than the former was made. The combat had no salient point to be described; it was simply a steady and slow advance of the whole line to within a few dozen yards of the fort, occupying three quarters of an hour, and then a rapid retreat to the former position at the crest of the hill, leaving the dead and wounded in the hands of the enemy; and between their outer rifle pits and Fort Buckner, Generals Corse and Giles Smith, seriously wounded, were carried into the valley in the rear—the one to lose his leg, and the other probably to die. Corse and Smith gone, the troops were reformed in a new line of battle by Lightburn, and under orders the line lay down to rest and await the attack of the enemy should he venture to make one. From this time—quarter after twelve, was the time which this repulse took place—until half-past one there was a pause in Sherman's battle. This he occupied in inditing a message to Grant, and in preparing for a more determined assault. The centre of the line at Orchard Knob noted the time by rapid and vigorous firing. I employed the time by examining the hospitals in rear of the lately assaulting party, and I found at the old log hut, which was being used as an hospital, and in the side at the foot of the hill, many a brave heart that had grown suddenly silent to the praises which comrades were murmuring over them.

On leaving the valley and the hospitals I returned to the point on the right of the ridge, where the guns were posted. Here I found that a Union brigade had, disdaining the protection of the railroad bank, rushed forward and was now skirmishing with the enemy for the possession of an abrupt ledge of rocks, which, outcropping from the hill side, afforded a secure position to an attacking column, at a point not more than fifty yards from Fort Buckner, which, let it be noticed, was near the crest of the west side of the hill, up which the brigade was now moving. The brigade eventually gained possession of this by half-past one o'clock, when a second brigade moved upon its left and rear. This brigade got into position without any serious skirmishing. But while this force was moving up, the enemy had continued to pour into the advance not only a continuous, though harmless fire of musketry, but had devised and put into execution a system of warfare worthy of the ancients. *They began throwing stones.* And this, too, with such an effect, that they soon grew to be as great a terror to our boys as gunboats were formerly to the rebels. These stones—huge in size—partly thrown down the mountain, would leap over the outjutting rocks and fall upon onr men with great force, doing much damage. The men at length, unable to bear this fire, demanded to be led against the fort, and did rush forward, but met with such a heavy fire that in their temporarily disordered state they were unable to stand it, and breaking, turned and fled, only the color-bearer of one of the regiments remaining in position. Here he continued, waving his flag, until the retreating forces having met in descending, the second advancing brigade turned, rallied, and again marched in good order to the position formerly held by it, and rescued their colors from the enemy, who was making a charge for their possession. The color-bearer remained unhurt. The two brigades now laid down again when the enemy began again his fire of stones, but failed this time to break the line, though the troops were much harassed by this novel expedient to dislodge them.

Not content with the strength of the column which lay now resting on the hill, General Sherman ordered two other regiments to move up to the left and rear of those forces, in order to support it. These regiments moved forward and took up a strong position about nalfway up the hill. He had no sooner gotten into position than the other troops moved, and began to advance up the hill, with loud shouts of encouragement. The enemy sprang to their guns, and from six pieces of artillery and a long line of musketry a heavy and destructive fire was poured upon them Instantly the last two regiments sent by General Sherman, though out of breath in climbing halfway up the hill, pushed forward in support of this perhaps premature assault. The hill at this time fitfully flashed and flared with flame, and the columns, the flags, the figures of both foe and friend being plainly visible, there was presented the most magnificent vision of war which has yet been vouchsafed me. I cannot and dare not attempt to describe it. If the reader can imagine two hosts thus struggling, his imagination, however weak, cannot fail to draw a sublimer picture than my pen ; and however bright that imagination may be, it cannot fail to fall far short of the sublime reality.

Through a half hour of slow, toilsome ascent did this keep on. The enemy continued without intermission to pour canister and musket balls into the column whose success they appeared so much to fear. Our men toiled on slowly, making but one wild dash at the guns, from which they came back maddened with rage at their failure. From their line the fire leaped upward to almost meet that of the enemy they were approaching. Success seemed within our very grasp, and when—

It was a partial repulse, but that momentary episode of the battle will reflect undying honor on the army of which those repulsed troops formed a part. I know not the cause—the rebel artillery may have been concentrated upon it, but one brigade broke—broke in utter confusion, I thought, as I saw it, and the men came rushing down the hill. The others still stood, and the re-enforcements continued to move forward. But the retreating troops did not fly to the foot of the hill, for at the moment they were passing the re-enforcements an officer sprang forward among them, seized the standard of one of the regiments and stuck it in the ground. I saw him wave his sword once over his head and point up the hill. I could not hear his voice, but the men did, and as if by magic—which will be forever a mystery to me—that routed column turned, turned instantly, and in a single second was marching up the hill, as firmly and as strongly formed as that of the newly arrived troops, and apparently forming a part of them. Not a man went further than where the re-enforcements were met, and there all turned and re-charged as if it were a movement they had been practising for years.

And then this whole line pushed forward again—certainly the most wonderful display of human nature under thorough discipline I have ever beheld or imagined. Both brigades had broken once; yet now, after half an hour's fight, they again returned to the fight by the side of a third leader. It is to me, writing it, perfectly incomprehensible, and I turn to my notes to see if my memory is not at fault. But no—the wonderful achievement is there in black and white—the very hour marked and noted, and just beneath it is a still more wonderful achievement in the last charge and repulse.

It was just at a quarter after two o'clock that the forces then in line made a last grand charge at the rebel works, fifty yards in front of them. The line was perfect now, though the stream of wounded that straggled to the rear made it look ragged. The order was given, and they pushed forward. It was but a short walk before breakfast, that fifty yards, but it was no child's play to charge over it. Double shotted with canister, the rebel guns thundered upon our men; and, alas! we could see it was fearfully thinning our still advancing ranks. But still our boys pressed on—stern, rigid, boldly, grandly. I saw them with my glass draw the blue cloth cap down over their eyes, as if seeking to hide the fearful flame that devoured them. A few more yards and a few more lives, and the rebel battery, the rebel position was ours.

We did not win it here. The enemy was forced to call for help—to draw from his centre—and at this moment, when all was ours, they poured in from their left around the hill, and got in upon our boys a damnable flank and cross fire that it was perfectly impossible to oppose. This force proved to be very heavy, and came into the engagement at double-quick. Our line crumbled almost instantaneously. A few hundred faced about and fought a running fight to the rear; but the main body turned and retreated. But there was no panic, no despair. They saw they had failed and were overcome. They retreated, but not rushing wildly and furiously far to the rear. The powerful aided the weak, and the strong bore off the wounded.

The west side of the hill was soon cleared of all but our wounded and the rebels. These latter pushed around the hill, under the fire of our guns, until they suddenly, and apparently unexpectedly, came upon Lightburn, who had during all this remained perfectly quiet, but who now sent them howling to their holes.

At this moment I was standing near the bronze figure of Sherman. As our men retreated down the hill I saw him bite off the end of a cigar, light it, take a puff or two, and then, turning to one of his aides, said, "Tell Lightburn to intrench and go into position." He then sat down to write a dispatch. I knew the battle of Tunnel Hill was over.

We had been repulsed. I may say bloodily repulsed.

But the enemy had been forced to commit the fatal error.*

The following interesting account of the battle of Mission Ridge is given by an eye-witness.

The iron heart of Sherman's column began to be audible, like the fall of great trees in the depth of the forest, as it beat beyond the woods on the extreme left. Over roads indescribable, and conquering lions of difficulties that met him all the way, he had at length arrived with his command of the Army of the Tennessee. The roar of his guns was like

* Mr. W. F. G. Shanks's dispatches to the *New York Herald.*

the striking of a great clock, and grew nearer and louder as the morning wore away. Along the centre all was still. Our men lay as they *had* lain since Tuesday night, motionless behind the works. *Generals Grant, Thomas, Granger, Meigs, Hunter, Reynolds, were grouped at Orchard Knob, here;* Bragg, Breckinridge, Hardee, Stevens, Cleburn, Bates, Walker, were waiting on Mission Ridge, yonder. And the northern clock tolled on! At noon, a pair of steamers, screaming in the river across the town, telling over, in their own wild way, our mountain triumph on the right, pierced the hushed breadth of air between two lines of battle with a note or two of the music of peaceful life.

At one o'clock the signal flag at Fort Wood was a flutter. Scanning the horizon, another flag, glancing like a lady's handkerchief, showed white across a field lying high and dry upon the ridge three miles to the northeast, and answered back. The centre and Sherman's Corps had spoken. As the hour went by, all semblance to falling tree and tolling clock had vanished; it was a rattling roar; the ring of Sherman's panting artillery, and the fiery gust from the rebel guns on Tunnel Hill, the point of Mission Ridge. The enemy had massed there the corps of Hardee and Buckner, as upon a battlement, utterly inaccessible save by one steep, narrow way, commanded by their guns. A thousand men could hold it against a host. And right in front of this bold abutment of the ridge, is a broad, clear field, skirted by woods. Across this tremendous threshold up to death's door, moved Sherman's column. Twice it advanced, and twice I saw it swept back in bleeding lines before the furnace blast, until that russet field seemed some strange page ruled thick with blue and red. Bright valor was in vain; they lacked the ground to *stand* on; they wanted, like the giant of old story, a touch of earth to make them strong. It was the devil's own corner. Before them was a lane, whose upper end the rebel cannon swallowed. Moving by the right flank, nature opposed them with precipitous heights. There was nothing for it but straight across the field, swept by an enfilading fire, and up to the lane, down which drove the storm. They could unfold no broad front, and so the losses were less than seven hundred, that must otherwise have swelled to thousands. The musketry fire was delivered with terrible emphasis; two dwellings, in one of which Federal wounded men were lying, set on fire by the rebels, began to send up tall columns of smoke, streaked red with fire; the grand and the terrible were blended.

If Sherman did not attain the height and roll the enemy along the Ridge like a carpet, at least he rendered splendid services, for he had a huge ganglion of rebels as firmly on their right as if he held them in the vise of the "lame Lemnian," who forged the thunderbolts.

* * * * *

The brief November afternoon was half gone; it was yet thundering on the left; along the centre all was still. At that very hour a fierce assault was made upon the enemy's left near Rossville, four miles down towards the old field of Chickamauga. They carried the Ridge; Mission Ridge seems everywhere—they strewed its summit with rebel dead; they *held* it. And thus the tips of the Federal army's wide-spread wings flapped grandly. But it had not swooped; the gray quarry yet perched upon Mission Ridge; the rebel army was terribly battered at the edges, but there full in our front it grimly waited, biding out its time. If the horns of the rebel crescent could not be doubled crushingly together, in a shapeless mass, possibly it might be sundered at its centre, and tumbled in fragments over the other side of Mission Ridge. Sherman was halted upon the left; Hooker was holding hard in Chattanooga Valley; the Fourth Corps, that rounded out our centre, grew impatient of restraint; the day was waning; but little time remained to complete the Commanding General's grand design; Gordon Granger's hour had come; his work was full before him.

And what a work that was to make a weak man falter and a brave man think! One and a half miles to traverse, with narrow fringes of woods, rough valleys, sweeps of open field, rocky acclivities, to the base of the ridge, and no foot in all the breadth withdrawn from rebel sight; no foot that could not be played upon by rebel cannon, like a piano's keys, under Thalberg's stormy fingers. The base attained, what then? A heavy rebel work, packed with the enemy, rimming it like a battlement. That work carried, and what then? A hill, struggling up out of the valley, four hundred feet, rained on by bullets, swept by shot and shell; another line of works, and then, up like a Gothic roof, rough with rocks, a wreck with fallen trees, four hundred more; another ring of fire and iron, and then the crest, and then the enemy.

To dream of such a journey would be madness; to devise it a thing incredible; to *do* it a deed impossible. *But Grant was guilty of them all, and Granger was equal to the work.* The story of the battle of Mission Ridge is struck with immortality already; let the leader of the Fourth Corps bear it company.

That the centre yet lies along its silent line is still true; in five minutes it will be the wildest fiction. Let us take that little breath of grace for just one glance at the surroundings, since we shall have neither heart nor eyes for it again. Did ever battle have so vast a cloud of witnesses? The hive-shaped hills have swarmed. Clustered like bees, blackening the house-tops, lining the fortifications, over yonder *across* the theatre, in the seats with the Catilines, *everywhere*, are a hundred thousand beholders. Their souls are in their eyes. Not a murmur can you hear. It is the most solemn congregation that ever stood up in the presence of the God of battles. I think of Bunker Hill, as I stand here; of the thousands who witnessed the immortal struggle; and fancy there is a parallel. I think, too, that the chair of every man of them will stand vacant against the wall to-morrow, and that around the fireside they must give thanks without him, if they can.

At half-past three, a group of generals, whose names will need no "Old Mortality" to chisel them anew, stood upon Orchard Knob. The hero of Vicksburg was there, calm, clear, persistent, far-seeing. Thomas, the sterling and sturdy; Meigs, Hunter, Granger, Reynolds. Clusters of humbler mortals were there, too, but it was any thing but a turbulent crowd; the voice naturally fell into a subdued tone, and even young faces took on the gravity of later years. *Generals Grant, Thomas, and Granger conferred, an order was given, and in an instant the Knob was cleared like a ship's deck for action.* At twenty minutes of four, Granger stood upon the parapet; the bugle swung idle at the bugler's side, the warbling fife and the grumbling drum unheard:—there was to be *louder* talk—six guns at intervals of two seconds, the signal to advance. Strong and steady his voice rang out: "Number one, fire! Number two, fire! Number three, fire!" it seemed to me the tolling of the clock of destiny—and when at "Number six, fire!" the roar throbbed out with the flash, you should have seen the dead line that had been lying behind the works all day, all night, all day again, come to resurrection in the twinkling of an eye—leap like a blade from its scabbard, and sweep with a two-mile stroke towards the ridge. From divisions to brigades, from brigades to regiments, the order ran. A minute, and the skirmishers deploy; a minute, and the first great drops begin to patter along the line; a minute, and the musketry is in full play like the crackling whips of a hemlock fire; men go down here and there, before your eyes; the wind lifts the smoke and drifts it away over the top of the ridge; every thing is too distinct; it is fairly *palpable;* you can touch it with your hand. The divisions of Wood and Sheridan are wading breast deep in the valley of death.

I never can tell you what it was like. They pushed out, leaving nothing behind them. There was no reservation in that battle. On moves the line of skirmishers, like a heavy frown, and after it, at quick time, the splendid columns. At right of us and left of us and front of us, you can see the bayonets glitter in the sun. You cannot persuade yourself that Bragg was wrong, a day or two ago, when, seeing Hooker moving in, he said, "Now we shall have a Potomac review;" that this is *not* the parade he prophesied; that it is of a truth the harvest of death to which they go down. And so through the fringe of woods went the line. Now, out into the open ground they burst at the double-quick. Shall I call it a Sabbath day's journey, or a long one and a half mile? To me that watched, it seemed endless as eternity, and yet they made it in thirty minutes. The tempest that now broke upon their heads was terrible. The enemy's fire burst out of the rifle-pits from base to summit of Mission Ridge; five rebel batteries of Parrotts and Napoleons opened along the crest. Grape and canister and shot and shell sowed the ground with rugged iron and garnished it with the wounded and the dead. But steady and strong our columns moved on.

> "By heaven! It was a splendid sight to see,
> For one who had no friend, no brother there;"

but to all loyal hearts, alas! and thank God, those men were friend and brother, both in one.

And over their heads as they went, Forts Wood and Negley struck straight out like mighty pugilists right and left, raining their iron blows upon the Ridge from base to crest; Forts Palmer and King took up the quarrel, and Moccasin Point cracked its fiery whips and lashed the rebel left till the wolf cowered in its corner with a growl. Bridges's battery, from Orchard Knob below, thrust its ponderous fists in the face of the enemy, and planted blows at will. Our artillery was doing splendid service. It laid its shot and shell wherever it pleased. Had giants carried them by hand they could hardly have been more accurate. All along the mountain's side, in the rebel rifle-pits, on the crest, they fairly dotted the Ridge. General Granger leaped down, sighted a gun, and in a moment, right in front, a great volume of smoke, like "the cloud by day," lifted off the summit from among the rebel batteries, and hung motionless, kindling in the sun. The shot had struck a caisson and that was its dying breath. In five minutes away floated another. A shell went crashing through a building in the cluster that marked Bragg's head-quarters; a second killed the skeleton horses of a battery at his elbow, a third scattered a gray mass as if it had been a wasp's nest.

And all the while our lines were moving on; they had burned through the woods and swept over the rough and rolling ground like a prairie-fire. Never halting, never faltering, they charged up to the first rifle-pits with a cheer, forked out the rebels with their bayonets, and lay there panting for breath. If the thunder of guns had been terrible, it was now growing sublime; it was like the footfall of God on the ledges of cloud. Our forts and batteries still thrust out their mighty arms across the valley; the rebel guns that lined the arc of the crest full in our front, opened like the fan of Lucifer, and converged their fire down upon Baird and Wood and Sheridan. It was rifles and musketry; it was grape and canister; it was shell and schrapnel. Mission Ridge was volcanic; a thousand torrents of red poured over its brink and rushed together to its base. And our men were there, halting for breath! And still the sublime diapason rolled on. Echoes that never waked before, roared out from height to height, and called from the far ranges of Waldron's Ridge to Lookout. As for Mission Ridge, it had jarred to such music before; it was the "sounding-board" of Chickamauga; it was *behind* us then; it frowns and flashes in our faces to-day; the old army of the Cumberland was there; it breasted the storm till the storm was spent, and left the ground it held; the old army of the Cumberland is *here!* It shall roll up the Ridge like a surge to its summit, and sweep triumphant down the other side. Believe me, that memory and hope may have made the heart of many a blue-coat beat like a drum. "Beat," did I say? The feverish heart of the *battle* beats on; fifty-eight guns a minute, by the watch, is the rate of its terrible throbbing. That hill, if you climb it, will appal you. Furrowed like a summer-fallow, bullets as if an oak had shed them; trees clipped and shorn, leaf and limb, as with the knife of some heroic gardener pruning back for richer fruit. How you attain the summit, weary and breathless, I wait to hear; how *they* went up in the teeth of the storm no man can tell!

And all the while rebel prisoners have been streaming out from the rear of our lines like the tails of a cloud of kites. Captured and disarmed, they needed nobody to set them going. The fire of their own comrades was like spurs in a horse's flanks, and amid the tempest of their own brewing they ran for dear life, until they dropped like quails into the Federal rifle-pits and were safe. But our gallant legions are out in the storm; they have carried the works at the base of the Ridge; they have fallen like leaves in winter weather. Blow, dumb bugles! Sound the recall! "Take the rifle-pit," was the order; and it is as empty of rebels as the tomb of the prophets. Shall they turn their backs to the blast? Shall they sit down under the eaves of that dripping iron? Or shall they climb to the cloud of death above them, and pluck out its lightnings as they would straws from a sheaf of wheat? But the order was not given. And now the arc of fire on the crest grows fiercer and longer. The reconnoissance of Monday had failed to develop the heavy metal of the enemy. The dull fringe of the hill kindles with the flash of great guns. I count the fleeces of white smoke that dot the Ridge, as battery after battery opens upon our line, until from the ends of the growing arc they sweep down upon it in mighty X's of fire. I count till that devil's girdle numbers thirteen batteries, and my heart cries out, "Great God, when shall the end be!" There is a poem I learned in childhood, and so did you: it is Campbell's "Hohenlinden." One line I never knew the meaning of until I read it written along that hill! It has lighted up the whole poem for me with the glow of battle forever:

> "And louder than the bolts of heaven,
> Far flashed the red artillery."

At this moment General Granger's aids are dashing out with an order; they radiate over the field, to left, right, and front; "Take the Ridge if you can"—"Take the Ridge if you can"—and so it went along the line. But the advance had already set forth without it. Stout-hearted Wood, the iron-gray veteran, is rallying on his men; stormy Turchin is delivering brave words in bad English: Sheridan—"little Phil"—you may easily look down upon him without climbing a tree, and see one of the most gallant leaders of the age if you do—is riding to and fro along the first line of rifle-pits, as calmly as a chess-player. An aid rides up with the order. "Avery, that flask," said the General. Quietly filling the pewter cup, Sheridan looks up at the battery that frowns above him, by Bragg's head-quarters, shakes his cap amid that storm of every thing that kills, when you could hardly hold your hand without catching a bullet in it, and with a "how are you?" tosses off the cup. The blue battle-flag of the rebels fluttered a response to the cool salute, and the next instant the battery let fly its six guns, showering Sheridan with earth. Alluding to that compliment with any thing but a blank cartridge, the General said to me in his quiet way, "I thought it —— ungenerous!" The recording angel will drop a tear upon the word for the part he played that day. Wheeling towards the men, he cheered them to the charge, and made at the hill like a bold-riding hunter; they were out of the rifle-pits and into the tempest and struggling up the steep, before you could get breath to tell it, and so they were throughout the inspired line.

And now you have before you one of the most startling episodes of the war; I cannot render it in words; dictionaries are beggarly things. But I *may* tell you they did not storm that mountain as you would think. They dash out a little way, and then slacken; they creep up, hand over hand, loading and firing, and wavering and halting, from the first line of works to the second; they burst into a charge with a cheer, and go over it. Sheets of flame baptize them; plunging shot tear away comrades on left and right; it is no longer shoulder to shoulder; it is God for us all! Under tree-trunks, among rocks, stumbling over the dead, struggling with the living, facing the steady fire of eight thousand infantry poured down upon their heads as if it were the old historic curse from heaven, they wrestle with the Ridge. Ten, fifteen, twenty minutes go by like a reluctant century. The batteries roll like a drum; between the second and last lines of rebel works is the torrid zone of the battle; the hill sways up like a wall before them at an angle of forty-five degrees, but our brave mountaineers are clambering steadily on—up—upward still! You may think it strange, but I would not have recalled them if I could. They would have lifted you, as they did me, in full view of the heroic grandeur: they seemed to be spurning the dull earth under their feet, and going up to do Homeric battle with the greater gods.

And what do those men follow? If you look you shall see that the thirteen thousand are not a rushing herd of human creatures; that along the Gothic roof of the Ridge a row of inverted V's is slowly moving up almost in line, a mighty lettering on the hill's broad side. At the angles of those V's is something that glitters like a wing. Your heart gives a great bound when you think what it is—*the regimental flag*—and glancing along the front count fifteen of those colors that were borne at Pea Ridge, waved at Shiloh, glorified at Stone River, riddled at Chickamauga. Nobler than Cæsar's rent mantle are they all! And up move the banners, now fluttering like a wounded bird, now faltering, now sinking out of sight. Three times the flag of one regiment goes down. And you know why. Three dead color-sergeants lie just there, but the *flag* is immortal—thank God!—and up it comes again, and the V's move on. At the left of Wood, three regiments of Baird—Turchin, the Russian thunderbolt, is there—hurl themselves against a bold point strong with rebel works, for a long quarter of an hour three flags are perched and motionless on a plateau under the frown of the hill. Will they linger forever? I give a look at the sun behind me; it is not more than a hand's breadth from the edge of the mountain; its level rays bridge the valley from Chattanooga to the Ridge with beams of gold; it shines in the rebel faces; it brings out the Federal blue; it touches up the flags. Oh, for the voice that could bid that sun stand still! I turn to the battle again; those three flags have taken flight! They are upward bound.

The race of the flags is growing every moment more terrible. There at the right, a strange thing catches the eye; one of the inverted V's is turning right side up. The men struggling along the converging lines to overtake the flag have distanced it, and there the colors are, sinking down in the centre between the rising flanks. The line wavers like a great billow and up comes the banner again, as if heaved on a surge's shoulder. The iron sledges beat on. Hearts, loyal and brave, are on the anvil, all the way from base to summit of Mission Ridge, but those dreadful hammers never intermit. Swarms of bullets sweep the hill; you can count twenty-eight balls in one little tree. Things are growing desperate up aloft; the rebels tumble rocks upon the rising line; they light the fuses and roll shells down the steep; they load the guns with handfuls of cartridges in their haste; and as if there were powder in the word, they shout "Chickamauga!" down upon the mountaineers. But it would not all do, and just as the sun, weary of the scene, was sinking out of sight, with magnificent bursts all along the line, exactly as you have seen the crested seas leap up at the breakwater, the advance surged over the crest, and in a minute those flags fluttered along the fringe where fifty rebel guns were kenneled. GOD bless the flag! GOD save the Union!

What colors were first upon the mountain battlement I dare not try to say; bright honor itself may be proud to bear—nay, proud to follow the hindmost. Foot by foot they had fought up the steep, slippery with much blood; let them go to glory together. A minute and they were *all* there, fluttering along the Ridge from left to right. The rebel hordes rolled off to the north, rolled off to the east, like the clouds of a worn-out storm. Bragg, ten minutes before, was putting men back in the rifle-pits. His gallant gray was straining a nerve for him now, and the man rode on horseback into Dixie's bosom, who, arrayed in some prophet's discarded mantle, foretold on Monday that the Yankees would leave Chattanooga in five days. They left in three, and by way of Mission Ridge, straight over the mountains as their forefathers went! As Sheridan rode up to the guns, the heels of Breckinridge's horse glittered in the last rays of sunshine. That crest was hardly "well off with the old love before it was on with the new."

But the scene on the narrow plateau can never be painted. As the blue coats surged over its edge, cheer on cheer rang like bells through the valley of the Chickamauga. Men flung themselves exhausted upon the ground. They laughed and wept, shook hands, embraced; turned round and did all four over again. It was as wild as a carnival. Granger was received with a shout. "Soldiers," he said, "you ought to be court-martialed every man of you. I ordered you to take the rifle-pits and you scaled the mountain!" but it was not Mars's horrid front exactly with which he said it, for his cheeks were wet with tears as honest as the blood that reddened all the route. Wood uttered words that rang like "Napoleon's," and Sheridan, the rowels at his horse's flanks, was ready for a dash down the Ridge with a "view halloo," for a fox hunt.

But you must not think this was all there was of the scene on the crest, for fight and frolic was strangely mingled. Not a rebel had dreamed a man of us all would live to reach the summit, and when a little wave of the Federal cheer rolled up and broke over the crest, they defiantly cried "Hurrah and be damned!" the next minute a Union regiment followed the voice, the rebels delivered their fire, and tumbled down in the rifle-pits, their faces distorted with fear. No sooner had the soldiers scrambled to the Ridge and straightened themselves, than up muskets and away they blazed. One of them, fairly beside himself between laughing and crying, seemed puzzled at which end of his piece he should load, and so abandoning the gun and the problem together, he made a catapult of himself and fell to hurling stones after the enemy. And he said, as he threw—well, you know our "army swore terribly in Flanders." Bayonets glinted and muskets rattled. Gen. Sheridan's horse was killed under him; Richard was not in his role, and so he leaped upon a rebel gun for want of another. Rebel artillerists are driven from their batteries at the edge of the sword and the point of the bayonet; two rebel guns are swung around upon their old masters. But there is nobody to load them. Light and heavy artillery do not belong to the winged kingdom. Two infantry men claiming to be old artillerists, volunteer. Granger turns captain of the guns, and—right about wheel!—in a moment they are growling after the flying enemy. I say "flying," but that is figurative. The many run like Spanish merinos, but the few fight like gray wolves at bay;

they load and fire as they retreat; they are fairly scorched out of position.

A sharpshooter, fancying Granger to be worth the powder, coolly tries his hand at him. The General hears the *zip* of a ball at one ear, but doesn't mind it. In a minute away it sings at the other. He takes the hint, sweeps with his glass the direction whence the couple came, and brings up the marksman, just drawing a bead upon him again. At that instant a Federal argument persuades the cool hunter and down he goes. That long range gun of his was captured, weighed twenty-four pounds, was telescope-mounted, a sort of mongrel howitzer.

A colonel is slashing away with his sabre in a ring of rebels. Down goes his horse under him; they have him on the hip; one of them is taking deliberate aim, when up rushes a lieutenant, claps a pistol to one ear and roars in at the other, "Who the h—l are you shooting at?" The fellow drops his piece, gasps out, "I surrender," and the next instant the gallant lieutenant falls sharply wounded. He is a "roll of honor" officer, straight up from the ranks, and he honors the roll.

A little German in Wood's Division is pierced like the lid of a pepper box, but he is neither dead nor wounded. "See here," he says, rushing up to a comrade, "a pullet hit te preach of mine gun, a pullet in mine pocket-book—a pullet in mine coat tail—they shoots me tree, five time, and py dam I gives dem h—l yet!"

But I can render you no idea of the battle caldron that boiled on the plateau. An incident here and there, I have given you, and you must fill out the picture for yourself. Dead rebels lay thick around Bragg's head-quarters and along the Ridge. Scabbards, broken arms, artillery horses, wrecks of gun-carriages, and bloody garments, strewed the scene; and, tread lightly, oh! loyal-hearted, the boys in blue are lying there; no more the sounding charge, no more the brave, wild cheer, and never for them, sweet as the breath of the new-mown hay in the old home fields, "The Soldier's Return from the War." A little waif of a drummer-boy, somehow drifted up the mountain in the surge, lies there; his pale face upward, a blue spot on his breast. Muffle his drum for the poor child and his mother.

Our troops met one loyal welcome on the height. How the old Tennesseean that gave it managed to get there nobody knows, but there he was, grasping a colonel's hand, and saying, while the tears ran down his face, "God be thanked! I *knew* the Yankees would fight!" With the receding flight and swift pursuit the battle died away in murmurs, far down the valley of the Chickamauga; Sheridan was again in the saddle, and with his command spurring on after the enemy. Tall columns of smoke were rising at the left. The rebels were burning a train of stores a mile long. In the exploding rebel caissons we had "the cloud by day," and now we are having "the pillar of fire by night." The sun, the golden dish of the scales that balance day and night, had hardly gone down, when up, beyond Mission Ridge, rose the *silver* side, for that night it was full moon. The troubled day was done. *A Federal General sat in the seat of the man who, on the very Saturday before the battle, had sent a flag to the Federal lines with the words:*

"Humanity would dictate the removal of all non-combatants from Chattanooga, as I am about to shell the city!"

Sat there, and announced to the Fourth Corps the congratulations and thanks, just placed in his hands, from the commander of the department:

BRAGG'S HEAD-QUARTERS, MISSION RIDGE,
November 25, 1863.

In conveying to you this distinguished recognition of your signal gallantry in carrying, through a terrible storm of iron, a mountain crowned with batteries and enriched with rifle-pits, I am constrained to express my own admiration of your noble conduct, and am proud to tell you that the veteran Generals from other fields, who witnessed your heroic bearing, place your assault and triumph among the most brilliant achievements of the war. Thanks, soldiers! You have made, this day, a glorious page of history.

GORDON GRANGER.

There was a species of poetic justice in it all, that would have made the prince of dramatists content. The ardor of the men had been quenchless: there had been three days of fitful fever, and after it, alas! a multitude had slept well. The work on the right, left, and centre, cost us full four thousand killed and wounded. There is a tremble of the lip, but a flash of pride in the eye, as the soldier tells with how many he went in—how expressive that "went in!" Of a truth it was wading in deep waters—with how few we came out. I cannot try to swing the burden clear of any heart, by throwing into the scale upon the other side the dead weight of fifty-two pieces of captured artillery, ten thousand stand of arms, and heaps of dead rebels, or by driving upon a herd of seven thousand prisoners. Nothing of all this can lighten that burden a single ounce, but this thought may, and I dare to utter it: Those three days' work brought Tennessee to resurrection; set the flag, that fairest blossom in all this flowery world, to blooming in its native soil once more.

That splendid march from the Federal line of battle to the crest, was made in one hour and five minutes, but it was a grander march towards the end of rebeldom; a glorious campaign of sixty-five minutes towards the white borders of peace. It made that fleeting November afternoon imperishable. Than the assault upon Mission Ridge, I know of nothing more gallant in the annals of the war. Let it rank foremost with the storming of Fort Scharnitz and Alma, that covered the French arms with undying fame.

Reader and writer must walk together down the heights another day; press that rugged earth with the first backward step a loyal foot has made upon it, and as we linger, recall a few of the incidents that will render it historic and holy ground for coming time. Let the struggle be known as the Battle of Mission Ridge, and when, in calmer days, men make pilgrimage, and women smile again among the mountains of the Cumberland, they will need no guide. Rust will have eaten the guns; the graves of the heroes will have subsided like waves; weary of their troubling, the soldier and his leader will have lain down together; but there, embossed upon the globe, MISSION RIDGE will stand its fitting monument forever.*

General Grant announced the victory in the following few but telling words:

CHATTANOOGA, *November* 25, 1863.—7.15 P. M.

Major-General H. W. HALLECK, *General-in-Chief:*

Although the battle lasted from early dawn till dark this evening, *I believe I am not premature in announcing a complete victory over Bragg.*

Lookout Mountain top, all the rifle-pits in Chattanooga Valley, and Missionary Ridge entire have been carried, and are now held by us.

U. S. GRANT, *Major-General.*

The rebel dispatch is thus worded:

CHICKAMAUGA, *November* 25, 1863.

General S. COOPER, *Adjutant and Inspector General:*

After several unsuccessful assaults on our lines to-day, the enemy carried the left centre about four o clock. *The whole left soon gave way in considerable disorder.* The right maintained its ground, and repelled every attack. I am withdrawing all to this point.

BRAXTON BRAGG.

---

* Mr. B. F. Taylor's correspondence to the *Chicago Journal.*

CHAPTER LII.

RETROSPECT OF THE THREE DAYS' BATTLES.

PERHAPS no better retrospect of these battles could be written, than that which will be found in the following pithy dispatch from General Meigs, Quartermaster-General of the United States Army, who was present at Chattanooga during the whole action:

HEAD-QUARTERS, CHATTANOOGA, *Nov.* 26, 1863.

EDWIN M. STANTON, *Secretary of War:*

SIR:—On the 23d instant, at half-past eleven, A. M., General Grant ordered a demonstration against Missionary Ridge, to develop the force holding it. The troops marched out, formed in order, and advanced in line of battle as if on parade.

The rebels watched the formation and movement from their picket lines and rifle-pits, and from the summits of Missionary Ridge, five hundred feet above us, and *thought it was a review and drill, so openly and deliberately, so regular, was it all done.*

The line advanced, preceded by skirmishers, and at two o'clock P. M. reached our picket lines, and opened a rattling volley upon the rebel pickets, who replied and ran into their advanced line of rifle-pits. After them went our skirmishers and into them, along the centre of the line of 25,000 troops which General Thomas had so quickly displayed, until we opened fire. Prisoners assert that they thought the whole movement was a review and general drill, and that it was too late to send to their camps for re-enforcements, and that they were overwhelmed by force of numbers. *It was a surprise in open daylight.*

At three P. M., the important advanced position of Orchard Knob and the lines right and left were in our possession, and arrangements were ordered for holding them during the night.

The next day at daylight General Sherman had five thousand men across the Tennessee, and established on its south bank, and commenced the construction of a pontoon bridge about six miles above Chattanooga.

The rebel steamer Dunbar was repaired at the right moment, and rendered effective aid in this crossing, carrying over six thousand men.

By nightfall General Sherman had seized the extremity of Missionary Ridge nearest the river, and was intrenching himself. General Howard, with a brigade, opened communication with him from Chattanooga on the south side of the river. Skirmishing and cannonading continued all day on the left and centre. General Hooker scaled the slopes of Lookout Mountain, and from the valley of Lookout Creek drove the rebels around the point. He captured some two thousand prisoners, and established himself high up the mountain side, in full view of Chattanooga. This raised the blockade, and now steamers were ordered from Bridgeport to Chattanooga. They had run only to Kelley's Ferry, whence ten miles of hauling over mountain roads and twice across the Tennessee on pontoon bridges brought us our supplies.

All night the point of Missionary Ridge on the extreme left, and the side of Lookout Mountain on the extreme right, blazed with the camp fires of loyal troops.

The day had been one of dense mists and rains, and *much of General Hooker's battle was fought above the clouds*, which concealed him from our view, but from which his musketry was heard.

At nightfall the sky cleared and the full moon—"the traitor's doom"—shone upon the beautiful scene, until one A. M., when twinkling sparks upon the mountain side showed that picket skirmishing was going on. Then it ceased. A brigade sent from Chattanooga crossed the Chattanooga Creek and opened communication with Hooker.

General Grant's head-quarters during the afternoon of the 23d and the day of the 24th were in Wood's redoubt, except when in the course of the day he rode along the advanced line, visiting the head-quarters of the several commanders in Chattanooga Valley.

At daylight on the 25th the Stars and Stripes were descried on the peak of Lookout. The rebels had evacuated the mountain.

Hooker moved to descend the mountain, striking Missionary Ridge at the Rossville Gap, to sweep both sides and its summit.

The rebel troops were seen, as soon as it was light enough, streaming regiments and brigades along the narrow summit of Missionary Ridge, either concentrating on the right to overwhelm Sherman, or marching for the railroad to raise the siege.

They had evacuated the valley of Chattanooga. Would they abandon that of Chickamauga?

The twenty-pounders and four-and-a-quarter inch rifles of Wood's redoubt opened on Missionary Ridge. Orchard Knob sent its compliments to the Ridge, which, with rifled Parrotts, answered, and the cannonade, thus commenced, continued all day. Shot and shell screamed from Orchard Knob to Missionary Ridge, and from Missionary Ridge to Orchard Knob, and from Wood's redoubt, *over the heads of Generals Grant and Thomas and their staffs, who were with us in this favorable position, from whence the whole battle could be seen as in an amphitheatre. The head-quarters were under fire all day long.*

Cannonading and musketry were heard from General Sherman, and General Howard marched the Eleventh Corps to join him.

General Thomas sent out skirmishers, who drove in the rebel pickets and chased them into their intrenchments, and at the foot of Missionary Ridge Sherman made an assault against Bragg's right, intrenched on a high knob next to that on which Sherman himself lay fortified. The assault was gallantly made.

Sherman reached the edge of the crest, and held his ground for (it seemed to me) an hour, but was bloodily repulsed by reserves.

A general advance was ordered, and a strong line of skirmishers followed by a deployed line of battle some two miles in length. At the signal of leaden shots from head-quarters on Orchard Knob, the line moved rapidly and orderly forward. The rebel pickets discharged their muskets and ran into their rifle-pits. Our skirmishers followed on their heels.

The line of battle was not far behind, and we saw the gray rebels swarm out of the ledge line of rifle-pits and over the base of the hill in numbers which surprised us. A few turned and fired their pieces; but the greater number collected into the many roads which cross obliquely up its steep face, and went on to the top.

Some regiments pressed on and swarmed up the steep sides of the Ridge, and here and there a color was advanced beyond the lines. The attempt appeared most dangerous; but the advance was supported, and the whole line was ordered to storm the heights, upon which not less than forty pieces of artillery, and no one knew how many muskets, stood ready to slaughter the assailants. With cheers answering to cheers the men swarmed upward. They gathered to the points least difficult of ascent, and the line was broken. Color after color was planted on the summit, while musket and cannon vomited their thunder upon them.

A well-directed shot from Orchard Knob exploded a rebel caisson on the summit, and the gun was seen being speedily taken to the right, its driver lashing his horses. A party of our soldiers intercepted them, and the gun was captured, with cheers.

A fierce musketry fight broke out to the left, where, between Thomas and Sherman, a mile or two of the Ridge was still occupied by the rebels.

Bragg left the house in which he had held his head-quarters, and rode to the rear as our troops crowded the hill on either side of him.

General Grant proceeded to the summit, and then only did we know its height.

Some of the captured artillery was put into position. Artillerists were sent for to work the guns, and caissons were searched for ammunition.

The rebel log breastworks were torn to pieces and carried to the other side of the Ridge, and used in forming barricades across.

A strong line of infantry was formed in the rear of Baird's line, and engaged in a musketry contest with the rebels to the left, and a secure lodgment was soon effected.

The other assault to the right of our centre gained the summit, and the rebels threw down their arms and fled.

Hooker, coming into favorable position, swept the right of the Ridge, and captured many prisoners.

Bragg's remaining troops left early in the night, and *the battle of Chattanooga, after days of manœuvring and fighting, was won. The strength of the rebellion in the centre is broken. Burnside is relieved from danger in East Tennessee. Kentucky and Tennessee are rescued. Georgia and the Southeast are threatened in the rear*, AND ANOTHER VICTORY IS ADDED TO THE CHAPTER OF "UNCONDITIONAL SURRENDER GRANT."

To-night the estimate of captures is several thousand prisoners and thirty pieces of artillery.

Our loss for so great a victory is not severe.

Bragg is firing the railroad as he retreats towards Dalton. Sherman is in hot pursuit.

To-day I viewed the battle-field, which extends for six miles along Missionary Ridge and for several miles on Lookout Mountain.

Probably not so well directed, so well ordered a battle, has taken place during the war. But one assault was repulsed; but that assault, by calling to that point the rebel reserves, prevented them repulsing any of the others.

A few days since Bragg sent to General Grant a flag of truce, advising him that it would be prudent to remove any non-combatants who might be still in Chattanooga. No reply has been returned; but the combatants having removed from the vicinity, it is probable that non-combatants can remain without imprudence.

M. C. MEIGS, *Quartermaster-General.*

CHAPTER LIII.

THE PURSUIT.—FIGHT AT RINGGOLD.

THE main portion of the struggle was over, but other work had yet to be done. The siege of Chattanooga was raised, but still the beaten rebels must not be allowed to gather their remnants together within any long day's march of the battle-field. A pursuit of their flying columns was ordered, and to Generals Sherman, Hooker, and Palmer was assigned the task of completing the rebel discomfiture.

The following account of the pursuit is given by one who took part in the movements of General Hooker's column:

After the successes of the 25th, the army was again put in motion, with a view of following up the enemy to Ringgold, and doing him as much injury as possible in the shortest space of time. The army moved in three main columns, Hooker being on the right, Palmer in the centre, and Sherman on the left. Hooker took the Rossville road direct to Ringgold, and Palmer made a junction with Sherman at Greysville, Sherman having moved up the left bank of the Chickamauga. All three of the columns met at and near Ringgold, from which place they opened lines of communication.

Davis's Division of the Fourteenth Corps evacuated its position on a hill immediately adjacent to Missionary Ridge at two o'clock on the morning of the 26th, and marched to a point near where the Chickamauga empties its waters into the Tennessee River. Here the division crossed the Chickamauga on a pontoon bridge, and continued its march up the left bank of the stream. This division was immediately followed by all the divisions of the Eleventh Corps, and this again by Ewing's Division of Sherman's Corps. Towards daylight the extreme head of the column had some brief skirmishes, the rebel videttes or scouts falling back after delivering their first fire.

The morning was clear and bright, and the officers and men of the entire command in the best of spirits, for the successes of the previous day were truly of the most inspiriting character. Our movement now was to get on the enemy's flank in the course of his retreat, and strike a blow for the capture of his trains, pick up stragglers, give those willing to desert an opportunity to do so, and do what other damage we could.

During the morning of this day, as General Sherman was absent elsewhere, Major-General Howard assumed command of the column and directed its movements. On the march we took some prisoners, picked up several deserters, and no small number of stragglers. The deserters represented what they had seen of Bragg's retreat as being confused and precipitate.

About ten A. M. we reached the neighborhood of Chickamauga dépôt. After a short engagement—more of a skirmish than any thing else—we drove the rebels back from the dépôt.

We found the dépôt in flames, and two large piles of corn meal burning. The amount of commissary stores captured here was tolerably large. By the burning alone the rebels must have lost fifty thousand dollars' worth.

We captured, fit for use, one pontoon train of fifteen boats; two sixty-four-pounder rifled siege guns; twenty army wagons; sixty thousand rations of shelled corn; fifty thousand rations of corn meal; four hundred gallons of molasses; two caissons; six forges; thirty barrels of pork; one thousand pounds of bacon; some ordnance stores, artillery, and small arm ammunition.

The carriages on which the siege guns were mounted were found in flames, and became eventually totally destroyed. One of the guns was spiked with a wrought nail.

The place presented a curious sight. A burning railroad dépôt, piles of burning corn meal, barrels and boxes scattered around in the wildest confusion, piles of bacon lying on the railroad track, shelled corn scattered in piles around the railroad platform, two heavy guns pointed in the direction in which we advanced—their carriages in flames; a pontoon train, new, and apparently never used, massed near the station; army wagons—some good and some broken down—turned over, on end, and every way displayed, in whatever direction the eye might turn; small arms lying around, some broken and some not; broken open boxes of ammunition for small arms thrown here and there, by the fire and away from it; a caisson on one side, limber chest on the other, half open; shells scattered under it, broken wheels, tongues of wagons, and other things pertaining to army transportation, thrown to the right and left, far and near, on all sides, and in the most disordered manner, showing that the enemy left with the greatest precipitancy, and before he could complete the destruction of one-third of his commissary, quartermaster, or ordnance stores.

On an examination of the hills and fields around the station we found breastworks and redoubts. The latter were well constructed, and if properly manned could not have been taken without considerable loss of life, and without such manœuvring as pertains to regular operations for battle. We manned the works at once.

The inhabitants we found in the place (which is but a small one) were few. They were so frightened at what had occurred, that it was some time before we could get from them intelligent answers to our questions. Even after they had a chance to get a little quieted, all they could tell us was that on the night previous, about eleven o'clock, the rebels commenced the movement of their stores—loading their teams and moving them off as fast as possible; and that finally they set fire to what stores they could; when they found the Yankees pressing them, and left the place on a full run.

Before leaving the dépôt, the retreating rebel forces destroyed two small railroad bridges (one over the Chickamauga) near that place. When necessary, the bridges can easily be rebuilt.

Pushing on past Chickamauga dépôt, we drove the enemy to Pigeon Ridge, where he made a stand; this at a point near where we had to pass. The enemy opened on us with artillery. Not knowing what force might be on the ridge, the whole column was placed in position for battle. We then advanced. The sight presented was a beautiful one. The far stretching lines, one after another emerging from the woods and advancing over open fields, with colors flying, made up a scene of interesting peculiarity. After a short engagement, in which we brought artillery to bear against that of the enemy, a brigade, of Davis's Division, charged up the heights and took them without any material loss, the enemy precipitately retiring on finding us determined to advance. This occurred at about half-past twelve o'clock. The column then rested for a short time.

At this juncture General Sherman arrived on the field, and took direct command of the column.

General Sherman, while at Chickamauga dépôt, and in common with some other officers, assisted in putting out a portion of the fire around the railroad platform, thereby rendering service in saving some of the abandoned stores from destruction by the flames.

On our march being resumed, and as the column moved forward, we came upon wagons, caissons, and odd wheels that had been abandoned by the enemy from time to time in the course of his retreat.

No opposition worthy of mention attended our march forward until near dark, when, as we emerged out of some low, swampy ground, the enemy opened fire with musketry and artillery from a low hill. Quite a lively musketry fire ensued, lasting for about three-quarters of an hour, when we drove the enemy from the field, leaving his killed and wounded in our hands. We then bivouacked for the night.

Next morning we pressed on to Graysville, where we made a junction with the forces under command of Major-General Palmer. Here we learned that the enemy who fought us on the previous afternoon had retired to Graysville and gone into camp near that place, intending to move back to Ringgold on the following morning. Scarcely had he got into camp when he was surprised and attacked by Palmer's Corps, and immediately put to flight. In this surprise movement we captured three pieces of artillery, sixty-four prisoners, two caissons, and all the artillery horses. In subsequent movements General Palmer took this artillery with him to use it against the enemy. From the prisoners taken we learn that a General Stuart was in command of the forces thus surprised.

Other than this surprise movement and some slight skirmishing, Palmer's column met with nothing of particular interest during Thursday.

On Thursday Hooker's column had skirmishing most all day, and towards evening an engagement, that was briefly terminated by our forces pressing forward and the enemy falling back.

On Friday morning, November 27th, at half-past eight o'clock, Hooker's column moved up the Rossville road towards Ringgold and became engaged. As we pressed forward with rapidity and obstinacy, the enemy slowly fell back, through the town of Ringgold and towards the gap, being closely followed up.

Ringgold is a small place, of about two thousand five hundred inhabitants, and the county seat of Catoosa County, Georgia; is situated at the base of the White Oak Mountain Ridge, and directly in front of Ringgold Gap. The surrounding scenery is mountainous and decidedly romantic. Like all southern towns, it presents a dingy appearance, and shows evidence of neglect or decay. Among its buildings are some neat cottage residences and a few substantial structures of brick. The line of the railroad from Dalton to Chattanooga runs through the town. The railroad connects with the railroad lines to Cleveland and Atlanta. The inhabitants, both in their language and manners, and the manner in which they furnish their houses, show some considerable degree of taste and refinement. Many of the houses into which I went were neatly and even elegantly furnished.

As you pass up the main street you come to the road, narrow and straight ahead, leading through Ringgold Gap. On either side of it rises the mountainous heights of White Oak Ridge. This ridge extends along for a very considerable distance, forming a chain of low mountains. In fact, the whole of this region of country is but a succession of ridges, with narrow valleys between. The common or generally travelled roads converge to these gaps. These are so peculiarly protected by the adjacent ridges, that two or three hundred men, posted on the ridges, with a section of artillery to sweep the gap, can hold an army in check until such time as preparation is made either to take the position by direct assault in front or by a flank movement, through other gaps in the same ridge, and an advance in the valley beyond.

The enemy slowly retired towards the ridge and gap, and supposing them to be in small force, Osterhaus's Division pressed forward in line of battle with great gallantry. The enemy opened a scattering musketry fire from the top of the ridge, and also brought into action four pieces of artillery, that swept the gap and threw their shells into the town and our lines. Notwithstanding this, Osterhaus's men kept on their course, advancing at quick time up the slope, on both sides of the gap. They had almost gained the summit, when the enemy showed its strength by delivering a terrific fire from the mountain top, at the same time succeeding in throwing a brigade each on the right and left of our lines. Our men stood their ground well, but at last had to slowly retire in consequence of the enemy's superior strength and position. The enemy finding our men falling back, followed them up with great persistency, and attempted to drive them across the railroad line by making a charge, but did not succeed, as Osterhaus's men bravely held their own and kept their line unbroken.

In this emergency Geary's Division, of the Twefth Corps, was ordered into action. General Geary at once ordered a brigade around on our left, to advance up the slope for the purpose of turning the enemy's right. The General's orders were promptly obeyed. The brigade got within about thirty yards of the crest, the Seventh Ohio being in the extreme advance (their skirmishers had even got on the crest), when the enemy, by a quick movement, massed a superior force against it, and succeeded in delivering a cross fire, successfully enfilading their line. The enemy's fire was so rapid and heavy that it was totally impossible for so small a force to withstand it any length of time without being almost annihilated. Still they stood their ground firmly and nobly, when General Geary, seeing it was of no use for them to remain longer under such a heavy fire, they were withdrawn by his orders. In this advance, the Seventh Ohio lost all its officers, the regiment coming out of the action under command of a lieutenant.

The enemy continuing to press our lines, two sections of a battery were got into position, and opened a rapid fire on the right and left of the rebel line.

At this time, too, the Second and Third Brigades of Geary's Division were ordered up. Our line then became extended in view of making an assault.

The decisive moment came at last. The grand movement was made. Slowly our men advanced, and slowly the rebels retired towards the gap and up the mountain slope. Our artillery, too, kept up a steady fire, almost immediately silencing that of the enemy. Osterhaus's Division occupied the centre, one brigade of Geary's was on the extreme left and the other two on the extreme right. After much patient effort we outflanked the rebels on the right and left of the hills, gained these, and drove the remaining rebels from the gap, and held the latter position. In the final movements the rebels retreated in the most disorderly manner. They did not all of them get away, as we took about three hundred prisoners.

After the enemy were driven through and from the gap, we established our lines in the next valley beyond. The enemy fell back to Tunnel Gap, situated in the succeeding ridge to that of White Oak.

After Sherman made a junction with Palmer, on Friday morning, the Eleventh Army Corps, under command of Major-General Howard, was sent off to the left to take Parker's Gap, this being situated on the enemy's right, and the second gap from Ringgold Gap in the same ridge. The position was taken and occupied without opposition, the enemy's scouting parties falling back without firing. During the battle of Ringgold, the Eleventh Corps was in a position almost in the enemy's rear, and we could at any time have turned their right flank.

A portion of the Eleventh Corps pressed on to the line of the Dalton and Cleveland Railroad, reaching Red Clay Station about dark.

The object in destroying the railroad line at Red Clay was to prevent Longstreet from using it to make a junction with Bragg. Another point was, that if the cavalry failed of accomplishing its object at Cleveland, we would carry out the design at Red Clay.

General Grant had his head-quarters in the town of Ringgold on November 28th. The General was much pleased with the success of his plans, spoke freely on the subject, and was of opinion that this campaign had been successful to an almost extraordinary degree, and had been fruitful of results of the most unqualifiedly gratifying character. It was decided not to pursue the enemy further, as more important operations were afoot.*

The rebels having retreated as far as Dalton, Ga., and finding the Union troops did not pursue further than Ringgold, there turned and made a stand. General Bragg then telegraphed the following, four days after the pursuit had been given up:

DALTON, GA., *December* 2, 1863.

General COOPER, Richmond:

The enemy have fallen back across the Chattanooga, destroying every thing in their route, including the railroad track and bridges. Their loss was heavy in their attack on our rear guard, under General Clayborn.

BRAXTON BRAGG.

General Grant, by taking possession of Red Clay, Cleveland, and Chattanooga, thus breaking the rebel railroad triangle the corners of which rest on Dalton, Cleveland, and Chattanooga, compressed the principal artery of the heart of the rebel confederacy, and smote it in its most vital part.

* Army correspondence of the *New York Herald*, dated from Ringgold, Ga., November 28th, 1863.

CHAPTER LIV.

KNOXVILLE RELIEVED.

WHILE the operations described in the foregoing chapters were being carried out by Gen. Grant, the rebel General Longstreet was engaged in the investment of the city of Knoxville. Finding that General Bragg had been defeated below Chattanooga, Longstreet determined to do something to redeem his name from the obloquy that would attend it through being attached to Gen. Bragg's command. He therefore on November 29th, 1863, made an assault upon Fort Sanders and the other works around Knoxville. The assault proved a failure, and long before he could recover from the effects of the repulse, he found the Union columns were gathering around him, in such a manner that if he did not soon withdraw from his position he would be completely encircled by them.

Gen. Foster's column was advancing from the North, and Gen. Granger's and other forces under Gen. Sherman from Chattanooga. This was the movement that caused the withdrawal of the troops from the pursuit of the rebels beyond Ringgold, Ga.

Gen. Sherman's Cavalry arrived at Knoxville on Dec. 3, and on the night of Dec. 4, Gen. Longstreet raised the siege of that place, retreating eastward toward Virginia, pursued by both Foster and Sherman's Cavalry.

On Dec. 7 it was telegraphed to Washington that Knoxville had been relieved and re-enforced by Granger's Corps, and that Longstreet was retreating. On the same day President Lincoln issued the following proclamation of thanksgiving:

EXECUTIVE MANSION.
WASHINGTON, D. C., *Dec.* 7, 1863.

Reliable information being received that the insurgent force is retreating from East Tennessee, under circumstances rendering it probable that the Union forces cannot hereafter be dislodged from that important position; and esteeming this to be of high national consequence, I recommend that all loyal people do, on receipt of this information, assemble at their places of worship, and render special homage and gratitude to Almighty God for this great advancement of the national cause. A. LINCOLN.

The President also sent the following dispatch to Major-General Grant:

WASHINGTON, *Dec.* 8.

Major-General GRANT:

Understanding that your lodgment at Chattanooga and Knoxville is now secure, *I wish to tender you and all under your command my more than thanks—my profoundest gratitude for the skill, courage, and perseverance with which you and they, over so great difficulties, have effected that important object.* God bless you all! A. LINCOLN.

The above dispatch was embodied in an order by Gen. Grant, and so read to every regiment in his command.

In reference to this brief but decisive campaign, Gen. Halleck added the following supplementary remarks to his annual report:

HEAD-QUARTERS OF THE ARMY,
WASHINGTON, D. C., *December* 6, 1863.

In compliance with your instructions I submit the following summary of the operations of General Grant's army since my report of the 15th ult.:

It appears from the official reports which have been received here that our loss in the operations of the 27th, 28th, and 29th of October in reopening communications on the south side of the Tennessee River, from Chattanooga to Bridgeport, was 76 killed, 339 wounded, and 22 missing; total 437. The estimated loss of the enemy was over 1,500.

As soon as General Grant could get up his supplies he prepared to advance upon the enemy, who had become weakened by the detachment of Longstreet's command against Knoxville. General Sherman's army moved up the north side of the Tennessee River, and during the nights of the 23d and 24th of November established pontoon bridges and crossed to the south side between Citico Creek and Chickamauga. On the afternoon of the 23d General Thomas's forces attacked the enemy's rifle-pits between Chattanooga and Citico Creek. The battle was renewed on the 24th along the whole line. Sherman carried the eastern end of Missionary Ridge up to the tunnel, and Thomas repelled every attempt of the enemy to regain the position which he had lost at the centre; while Hooker's force, in Lookout Valley, crossed the mountain and drove the enemy from its northern slope.

On the 25th the whole of Mission Ridge, from Rossville to the Chickamauga, was, after a desperate struggle, most gallantly carried by our troops, and the enemy was completely routed.

Considering the strength of the rebel position and the difficulty of storming his intrenchments, *the battle of Chattanooga must be considered the most remarkable in history.* Not only did the officers and men exhibit great skill and daring in their operations on the field, but the highest praise is due to the commanding general for *his admirable dispositions for dislodging the enemy from a position apparently impregnable.** Moreover, by turning his right flank and throwing him back upon Ringgold and Dalton, Sherman's forces were interposed between Bragg and Longstreet so as to prevent any possibility of their forming a junction.

Our loss in killed, wounded, and missing is reported at about 4,000. We captured over 6,000 prisoners, besides the wounded left in our hands, forty pieces of artillery, five or six thousand small arms, and a large train. The enemy's loss in killed and wounded is not known.

While Generals Thomas and Hooker pushed Bragg's army back into

---

* General Scott is reported to have stated to a leading Washington official, with whom the old veteran fell into a very unreserved talk, that General Grant's operations displayed more military skill than any other general had exhibited on our side; and he was the more surprised and mystified at it, as he could only remember him in the Mexican war as a young lieutenant of undoubted courage, but giving no promise whatever of any thing beyond ordinary abilities.

Georgia, *General Sherman with his own and General Granger's forces was sent into East Tennessee to prevent the return of Longstreet and to relieve General Burnside, who was then besieged in Knoxville.* We have reliable information that General Sherman has successfully accomplished his object, and that Longstreet is in full retreat towards Virginia. But no details have been received with regard to Sherman's operations since he crossed the Hiwassee, nor of Burnside's defence of Knoxville. It is only known that every attack of the enemy on that place was successfully repulsed.

Very respectfully, your obedient servant,

H. W. HALLECK, *General-in-Chief.*

Hon. E. M. STANTON, *Secretary of War.*

On December 5, 1863, General Burnside, the commander at Knoxville, issued a congratulatory order to his troops in reference to the raising of the siege, which had lasted about three weeks.

An army correspondent writing from Knoxville, states as follows:

Now that the campaign has developed itself, it may not be considered contraband information to say that, in holding Knoxville, *General Burnside has played an important part in the grand campaign of General Grant.* Some incline to the belief that with the troops under his command, General Burnside could have checked Longstreet on the Tennessee River, and there kept him, transferring the scene of the contest from Knoxville to the vicinity of Loudon or Kingston. *But by doing so Longstreet would have been within supporting distance of Bragg. To draw him, therefore, still further away from Chattanooga, General Burnside slowly retreated before him until he reached Knoxville, where, of course, his plan was to keep him in efforts to take the city while General Thomas might fall upon and rout the army of Bragg, diminished as it was by the withdrawal of Longstreet's command. How egregiously he fell into the trap, and how successfully the other portion of the programme was carried out at Chattanooga, are now fully known* from the history of the past few weeks. Bragg, in the first place, has been thoroughly routed, and Longstreet, after vain efforts to capture this city by siege and assault, as an offset to the defeat of Bragg, has been compelled to raise the siege and retreat, an inglorious fugitive, towards Virginia. On Nov. 13, when Longstreet crossed his advance guard over the Tennessee, *it would have been an easy matter with General Burnside to have driven it back again, destroyed the pontoon bridges, and by planting his artillery on the hills this side of the river, prevented a recrossing; but the part assigned him by General Grant was to lure his antagonist on.* Longstreet discovered his mistake too late. Letters written by his officers and captured by our forces, show that when the fighting commenced at Chattanooga he was extremely puzzled as to what part he should take. The capture of Knoxville seemed a very difficult matter, and he entertained ideas of abandoning the siege for the purpose of returning to Bragg; but when the latter was defeated, and when he saw that Thomas was now between Bragg and himself, he endeavored to retrieve the disaster in a measure by the capture of Knoxville. Hence the desperate assault of the 29th ult. *That he was preparing for another attack when our re-enforcements reached us we have the best of evidence.* So far as capturing the city is concerned, we know that he could not have done it by actual fighting. The garrison was all sufficient in this respect. But, if unmolested in the siege, he might have starved us out, and hence the necessity of re-enforcements. It may be that the programme also embraced his rout, if not capture, before he could get away from Knoxville. *If so, he took the alarm in time*, and is now well on his way to reenforce Lee. How far he will succeed in escaping time will develop.*

The rebels now began to be seriously-worried about General Grant's movements, and the following article appeared in one of their principal journals:

"Sallust," the well-informed and trustworthy correspondent of the *Dispatch*, telegraphing from Resaca, under date of December, 1863, states, in substance, that the wagon roads are in a horrible condition, that the enemy cannot advance without the railroad, that they have no cars, and that the probabilities are that no movement in force upon Dalton and Atlanta will be made till next spring. With great general confidence in the accuracy of statement and correctness of judgment of this correspondent, we should, nevertheless, be exceedingly sorry to learn that his opinions are derived from the general now commanding the remnant of Bragg's army, and that they are shared by the President and

---

* Mr. James C. Fitzpatrick's correspondence to the *New York Herald*, December 6, 1863.

War Department at Richmond. *To count upon the tardiness of Grant's movements, in consequence of the condition of the turnpikes or the railroads, would be suicidal. Grant has proved that he can do what so few of our generals have been able to accomplish—follow up a victory—in spite of natural obstacles; and it is certain that he will not permit himself now to be stopped, either by mud or by a want of cars.* These difficulties are by no means insurmountable.

Every one remembers the sanguine predictions of the impossibility of carrying on the siege of Vicksburg. Gentlemen owning plantations on which Grant's army was encamped before Vicksburg, declared that the soldiers would perish for lack of water, or die like sheep with the rot, from drinking such as they could obtain. Moreover, we were told that the malarious diseases of the climate would decimate his army, and compel him to raise the siege. Further, it was stated by the same reliable operator, who is now at work in Atlanta, cheering us with the assurance that the Yankees lost at least twenty thousand men in the assault on Lookout Mountain, that Grant had lost quite fifty thousand of the flower of his army in the various attempts to storm the intrenchments at Vicksburg. How utterly fallacious all these predictions and assertions proved! *The siege of Vicksburg progressed steadily to its conclusion, without, so far as we have ever learned, any serious impediment whatever. In spite of water, climate, diseases, and repeated repulses, Grant compelled Pemberton to surrender in less than three months from the day the siege began.*

Shall we again be the dupes of ill-founded hopes? Shall we rely for safety upon mud and not upon men? Shall we trust to cars and not to energy? Heaven forbid! The railroad from Nashville to Chattanooga is, doubtless, now open, and trains running all the way through. On this railroad any quantity of cars and engines necessary to stock the road from Chattanooga to Atlanta, may be brought through in less than a week's time. Two weeks more will be all that Yankee activity and ingenuity will demand to complete the re-building of burned bridges. *But we doubt if Grant will await the arrival of cars and the completion of bridges.* He has plenty of transportation, and the whole North behind him to supply horses and wagons as fast as they break down.

* * * * * *

What is to be done must be done without one moment's delay, and much must be given up in order that something may be saved. *Grant's goal is Atlanta.* He will be there before Christmas, and half the cotton remaining in the Confederacy will be in his hands or destroyed, unless a truly great general and a great army are placed athwart his path within three weeks from this day.*

The Chattanooga-Knoxville campaign ended, General Grant issued the following congratulatory order to his command:

HEAD-QUARTERS MILITARY DIVISION OF THE MISSISSIPPI, IN THE FIELD,
CHATTANOOGA, TENNESSEE, *Dec.* 10, 1863.

[*General Orders, No.* 9.]

The General Commanding takes this opportunity of returning his sincere thanks and congratulations to the brave armies of the Cumberland, the Ohio, the Tennessee, and their comrades from the Potomac, for the recent splendid and decisive successes achieved over the enemy. *In a short time you have recovered from him the control of the Tennessee River from Bridgeport to Knoxville. You dislodged him from his great stronghold upon Lookout Mountain, drove him from Chattanooga Valley, wrested from his determined grasp the possession of Missionary Ridge, repelled with heavy loss to him his repeated assaults upon Knoxville, forcing him to raise the siege there, driving him at all points, utterly routed and discomfited, beyond the limits of the State.* By your noble heroism and determined courage, you have most effectually defeated the plans of the enemy for regaining possession of the States of Kentucky and Tennessee. You have secured positions from which no rebellious power can drive or dislodge you. For all this the General Commanding thanks you collectively and individually. The loyal people of the United States thank and bless you. Their hopes and prayers for your success against this unholy rebellion are with you daily. Their faith in you will not be in vain. Their hopes will not be blasted. Their prayers to Almighty God will be answered. *You will yet go to other fields of strife; and with the invincible bravery and unflinching loyalty to justice and right which have characterized you in the past, you will prove that no enemy can withstand you, and that no defences, however formidable, can check your onward march.*

By order of Maj.-Gen. U. S. GRANT.

T. S. BOWERS, *A. A.-G.*

At the time General Grant issued the above order he was far from being in good health, as may be gathered from the following extract from a correspondent's letter:

* *Richmond* (Va.) *Whig*, December, 1863.

General Grant is still suffering from his fall at New Orleans, has grown thin and stooping, and shows marks of so great a loss of health and strength as to create fear of his recovery, though he still works as indefatigably as ever. When it was announced at General Grant's headquarters that Bragg had been removed and Hardee put in command of the rebel army, the General quietly remarked: "He is my choice,"—an opinion that seems to be very generally entertained in both armies.*

In connection with the foregoing paragraph it is necessary to state that General Bragg was removed from his command for his defeat at Chattanooga, and was temporarily succeeded by General Hardee.

It was announced from Chattanooga on December 7th that General Grant had captured, from the commencement of the war up to that date, no less than four hundred and seventy-two cannon and ninety thousand prisoners, with small arms innumerable.

The following remarks are reported to have been written by Colonel Ely S. Parker—Indian Sachem and Chief of the Tonawanda tribe and Seneca Nation of Indians, and who became a member of General Grant's staff—in relation to the conduct of the commanding general during the battles around Chattanooga:

I need not describe to you the recent battle of Chattanooga. The papers have given every possible detail concerning it. I may only say that I saw it all, and was in the five days' fight. Of General Grant's staff only one was wounded, a Lieutenant Towner, Assistant Chief of Artillery, whose parents formerly lived at Batavia, N. Y., but now of Chicago. *It has been a matter of universal wonder in this army that General Grant himself was not killed, and that no more accidents occurred to his staff, for the General was always in the front* (his staff with him, of course), and perfectly heedless of the storm of hissing bullets and screaming shell flying around him. His apparent want of sensibility does not arise from heedlessness, heartlessness, or vain military affectation, but from a *sense of the responsibility resting upon him* when in battle. When

**Indianapolis Journal*, December, 1863.

at Ringgold, we rode for half a mile in the face of the enemy, *under an incessant fire of cannon and musketry*, nor did we ride fast, but upon an ordinary trot, and *not once do I believe did it enter the General's mind that he was in danger.* I was by his side and watched him closely. In riding that distance we were going to the front, and I could see that he was studying the positions of the two armies, and, of course, *planning how to defeat the enemy*, who was here making a most desperate stand, and was slaughtering our men fearfully. After defeating and driving the enemy here we returned to Chattanooga.

Another feature in General Grant's personal movements is, that *he requires no escort beyond his staff, so regardless of danger is he.* Roads are almost useless to him, for he takes short cuts through fields and woods, and will swim his horse through almost any stream that obstructs his way. Nor does it make any difference to him whether he has daylight for his movements, for *he will ride from breakfast until two o'clock in the morning, and that too without eating. The next day he will repeat the dose, until he finishes his work.* Now such things come hard upon the staff, but they have learned how to bear it.

General Grant has the reputation of being the best rider in the army; and an eye-witness to his movements during the battle of Chattanooga relates that when he spurred from one portion of the field to another, his staff very soon strung out like the tail of a kite. The General always leads.

The following amusing incident took place during the Chattanooga campaign: During the dark days of the siege, when food and forage were scarce, and the ghastly corpses and bleached skeletons of starved mules lined the thoroughfares thereabouts, General Grant and Quartermaster General Meigs arrived in Chattanooga. Taking an airing on horseback one afternoon, they passed the carcass of a huge mule lying by the roadside, whose "ill-savor went up" before and around them. The hero of Vicksburg removed his briar root from his lips, and remarked sorrowfully, "Ah, General, there lies a dead soldier of the Quartermaster's Department." "Yes, General," replied the Quartermaster General, in subdued tones, "in him you see the 'ruling passion strong in death' exemplified, for the old veteran has already assumed the offensive."

From a private letter from an officer the following incident has been gleaned:

> A great many prisoners have been brought in. The charge of the army on Mission Ridge astounded Bragg. Breckinridge's head-quarters were on the Ridge, in full view of our troops. A lady who lives there told our troops the following: "Before you all came up here, I asked General Bragg, 'What are you going to do with me, General?' He says to me, 'Lord! madame, *the Yankees will never dare to come up here.*' And," she added with a blubber, "it was not fifteen minutes till you were all around here."

CHAPTER LV.

HONORS TO GENERAL GRANT.—THANKS OF CONGRESS.—GOLD MEDAL.

THE intelligence of General Grant's victorious mountain campaign in Tennessee and Georgia was announced in Washington on the day of the first assembling of the United States Congress for 1863–'4. Mr. Washburne, the representative for Galena, in the House, immediately gave notice of the introduction of two bills, one "to revive the grade of Lieutenant-General of the army," and the other "to provide that a medal be struck for General Grant, and that a vote of thanks be given him and the officers of his army."

It did not require either any very acute mental penetration or a knowledge of the intimate relations of Congressman Washburne with General Grant, to understand the meaning and bearing of the above bill for the revival of the grade of Lieutenant-General. The object was nothing more nor less than the elevation of Major-General Grant to that position.

It was not the intention of those who desired the further promotion of General Grant to take him away from his command, and substitute him for the General-in-Chief. It was their conviction that he would be most useful in the field, and hence they wanted him to remain at the head of his great army, but to exercise, at the same time, from the field, the functions of a General-in-Chief.

Mr. Washburne's motion relative to the joint thanks of Congress and the Gold Medal did not require long deliberation. The members of both Houses were thoroughly convinced that General Grant deserved the thanks of the nation, and when that resolution was brought up, it was passed by both Congress and Senate without opposition, and received the President's signature within ten days of its introduction. It then became the first law of the session of 1863–'4.

The following is a copy of the official document:

LAWS OF THE UNITED STATES.

Passed at the First Session of the Thirty-eighth Congress.

[PUBLIC RESOLUTION NO. 1.]

JOINT RESOLUTION of thanks to Major-General Ulysses S. Grant and the officers and soldiers who have fought under his command during this rebellion; and providing that the President of the United States shall cause a medal to be struck, to be presented to Major-General Grant in the name of the people of the United States of America.

Be it resolved by the Senate and House of Representatives of the United States of America in Congress assembled, That the thanks of Congress be and they hereby are presented to Major-General Ulysses S. Grant, and through him to the officers and soldiers who have fought under his command during this rebellion, for their gallantry and good conduct in the battles in which they have been engaged; and that the President of the United States be requested to cause a gold medal to be struck, with suitable emblems, devices, and inscriptions, to be presented to Major-General Grant.

SEC. 2. *And be it further resolved,* That, when the said medal shall have been struck, the President shall cause a copy of this joint resolution to be engrossed on parchment, and shall transmit the same, together with the said medal, to Major-General Grant, to be presented to him in the name of the people of the United States of America.

SEC. 3. *And be it further resolved,* That a sufficient sum of money to carry this resolution into effect is hereby appropriated out of any money in the Treasury not otherwise appropriated.

SCHUYLER COLFAX,
Speaker of the House of Representatives.
H. HAMLIN,
Vice-President of the United States and
President of the Senate.

Approved December 17, 1863.

ABRAHAM LINCOLN.

The resolution having become a law of the land, it was necessary that a design should at once be made for the medal. The following by Leutze was announced* as the one selected by the committee having the matter in charge: "The obverse of the medal was to consist of a profile likeness of the hero, surrounded by a wreath of laurels; his name and the year of his victories inscribed upon it, and the whole surrounded by a galaxy of stars. The design for the reverse was original, appropriate, and beautiful. It was the figure of Fame seated in a graceful attitude on the American eagle, which, with outspread wings, seems preparing for flight. In her right hand she held the symbolical trump, and in her left a scroll on which were inscribed the names of the gallant chief's various battles, viz.: Corinth, Vicksburg, Mississippi River, and Chattanooga. On her head was a helmet, ornamented in Indian fashion, with feathers radiating from it. In front of the eagle, its breast resting against it, was the emblematical shield of the United States. Just underneath this group, their stems crossing each other, were single sprigs of the pine and the palm, typical of the North and South. Above the figure of fame, in a curved line, the motto, "Proclaim Liberty throughout the Land." The edge was surrounded, like the obverse, with a circle of stars of a style peculiar to the Byzantine period, and rarely seen except in illuminated MSS. of that age. These stars were more in number than the existing States—of course, including those of the South—thereby suggesting further additions in the future to the Union."

Other honors were paid him by societies, electing him honorary life member, &c. The following are selected as instances to show the manner in which he received these tokens of appreciation:

* New York *Evening Post.*

At the anniversary of the Missionary Society of the Cincinnati Conference held in 1863, that body elected General Grant an honorary member. Rev. J. F. Marlay communicated the fact to the General, and the following is his reply:

CHATTANOOGA, *Dec.* 7, 1863.

Rev. F. MARLAY, Secretary Society:

DEAR SIR:—Through you permit me to express my thanks to the society of which you are the honored secretary, for the compliment they have seen fit to pay me by electing me one of its members.

I accept the election as a token of earnest support, by members of the Methodist Missionary Society of the Cincinnati Conference, to the cause of our country in this hour of trial.

I have the honor to be, very truly, your obedient servant,

U. S. GRANT, *Major-General U. S. A.*

The following interesting correspondence explains itself:

MORRISTOWN, *Dec.* 9, 1863.

To Major-General U. S. GRANT:

DEAR SIR:—I have the pleasure of informing you that the church of which I am pastor, the Methodist Episcopal Church of this town, highly appreciating your services for your country, and rejoicing in the victories which God has wrought out through you and your noble army, and praying that you may be spared to see the end of this accursed rebellion, have contributed one hundred and fifty dollars ($150) to constitute you a LIFE DIRECTOR of the Missionary Society of the M. E. Church. Will you please direct where we shall send your Certificate? May God Almighty bless and keep you, and continue to crown your arms with ctory and triumph!

With sincere admiration and respect,

I am, dear General, yours truly,

LEWIS R. DUNN,

Pastor of the M. E. Church, Morristown, N. J.

HEAD-QUARTERS MIL. DIST. OF THE MISS.,
CHATTANOOGA, TENN., *Dec.* 16, 1863.

To the Rev. LEWIS R. DUNN,

Pastor of M. E. Church, Morristown, N. J.

SIR:—In reply to your letter of Dec. 19th, to Maj.-Gen. U. S. Grant, he directs me to express his gratitude to the Christian people of Morristown for their prayerful remembrance of him before the throne of the Most High, and to thank them, through you, for the honor conferred upon him. *Be good enough to send his Certificate of Membership to Mrs. U. S. Grant, Louisville, Kentucky.*

Very resp'y, your ob't ser't,
J. H. Wilson, Brig.-Gen.

As a further appreciation of General Grant's merits, and to manifest the true feeling of the people with regard to his patriotism and military success, it was recommended by one of the principal journals of the United States* that he should be tendered a popular nomination for the position of President, embracing the offices of chief magistrate, *and Commander-in-Chief of the forces* of the nation.

On the thirteenth day of January, 1864, the following resolution, moved by Mr. Reed, was adopted by the Legislature of the State of New York:

Resolved, That the thanks of the people of this State be tendered to General Grant and his Army for their glorious victories in the valley of the Mississippi, and the still more glorious victory at Mission Ridge and Lookout Mountain, and that a certified copy of this resolution be forwarded to General Grant.

The Legislature of the State of Ohio also presented him with a vote of thanks.

The following is the description of a handsome pair of revolvers in course of construction at the Colt's arm manufacturing establishment designed to be presented to General Grant:

The handles are of black horn, beautifully polished, and the barrels, magazines, and other steel parts are elaborately inlaid with pure gold, which is beaten into a design previously cut out of the steel. The other ornaments, guard, &c., are of a solid gold. The pair are to be enclosed in a handsome rosewood box, lined with velvet, and accompanied by all the tools, &c., belonging to them—the cartridge-boxes, &c., being manufactured of silver. When finished these pistols will equal any pair that has ever left the establishment.†

* *New York Herald.* † *Hartford* (Ct.) *Times.*

CHAPTER LVI.

LIEUTENANT-GENERAL.—CONGRESSIONAL NOMINATION.

THE bill introduced by Mr. Washburne for the revival of the grade of Lieutenant-General of the United States Army, having in the due course of business been read and referred to the military committee of the House of Congress, was slightly amended, and came up on February 1st, 1864, for final action of that portion of the law-making power.

The amended bill introduced was thus worded:

Be it enacted by the Senate and House of Representatives of the United States of America in Congress assembled, That the grade of Lieutenant-General be, and the same is hereby, revived in the Army of the United States of America; and the President is hereby authorized, whenever he shall deem it expedient, to appoint, by and with the advice and consent of the Senate, a commander of the army, to be selected, during war, from among those officers in the military service of the United States, not below the grade of Major-General, most distinguished for courage, skill, and ability; and who, being commissioned as Lieutenant-General, *shall be authorized, under the direction of the President, to command the armies of the United States.*

SEC. 2. *And be it further enacted,* That the Lieutenant-General appointed as hereinbefore provided, shall be entitled to the pay, allowances, and staff specified in the fifth section of the act approved May 28th, 1798; and also the allowances described in the sixth section of the act approved August 23d, 1842, granting additional rations to certain officers: *Provided,* That nothing in this bill contained shall be construed in any way to affect the rank, pay, or allowances of Winfield Scott, lieutenant general by brevet, now on the retired list of the army.

Mr. Farnsworth opened the debate by a recommendation that the bill should be passed that morning.

Mr. Garfield, formerly chief of staff to General Rosecrans, having opposed the motion,

Mr. Farnsworth addressed the House as follows:

Mr. Speaker, the argument of my colleague of the Committee on Military Affairs who has just taken his seat, is a twofold argument. I understand his first argument to be that the war has not progressed far enough, and that we have not given our generals in the field a sufficient term of trial to enable the President to select with proper judgment a man upon whom to confer the rank of lieutenant-general.

His second argument is, that the General toward whom this legislation is directed is *so great and so successful a general that it would be dangerous to take him from the field and put him in command of the entire Army of the United States.*

In answer to the first branch of the gentleman's argument I have only this to say: we are now very near to the close of the third year of this war, and while *it is true that many generals in the army may be up to-day and down to-morrow, and that their fortunes fluctuate, is not true of the general to whom this legislation applies. His star has been steadily rising.* He has been growing greater and greater day by day, *rising from an obscure position*, scarcely known out of the county in which he resided. By his masterly ability he now stands, without saying any thing to the disparagement of other generals, *head and shoulders over every other general in the Army of the United States.* He has been tried, tried long enough; and if his star were to go down to-morrow he has still done enough to entitle him to this prize.

After some further debate Mr. Ross submitted the following amendment, to be added to the act:

And that we respectfully recommend the appointment of Major General U. S. Grant for the position of lieutenant-general.

On this amendment a spirited debate ensued in favor of General Grant, when Mr. Washburne took the floor and said:

I had not intended to submit any remarks on this bill. I have made no preparation whatever to speak to its merits; and if I had I should be unable to do so on account of the present state of my health. No subject of less importance than this, no bill in which I felt a less degree of interest, could have brought me to the House to-day. I had not looked for the opposition to the bill which has been manifested. The bill having been printed, and its provisions being very simple and easy of comprehension, I supposed we should have come to a vote without extended debate, as every member of the House had undoubtedly made up his mind as to how he would vote on the question.

The proposition is to revive the grade of lieutenant-general, for the purpose of conferring it not only for the recognition of distinguished and exceptional services already rendered to the country, but for the practical purpose of investing full command of the army in the party receiving the appointment, in subordination, of course, to the Commander-in-Chief under the Constitution. I do not propose to enter upon the reasons which I supposed would control the House in passing this bill. Those reasons must suggest themselves to all men who love our country and the flag. They spring from the admiration which a great and magnanimous people must ever feel for deeds of heroism and for public service of untold value, and for which no reward can be esteemed too great. The question has been raised as to who will be appointed under the bill in the event of its passage. I take it there is no gentleman upon this floor who has really any doubt upon whom this appointment will be conferred. Under the language of the bill, referring to most eminent and distinguished service, I think one individual, and one individual alone, is pointed out so distinctly that no man can misunderstand.

A great deal has been said as to what might have happened if some such bill had passed two years ago; that such or such a man might have received the honor, and implying that the party upon whom the honor may be conferred under this bill may prove himself unworthy. How much, I would ask, is now to be required of a general before he can have the confidence of this House? *Has not General Grant earned that confidence, and proved himself worthy of full trust in the greatest positions? I demand to know what would have been our position as a nation in the present struggle had it not been for the achievements of General Grant?* Where can you point to a series of greater triumphs than he has achieved, a more complete succession of victories, which are unsurpassed in history, and which for the brilliancy of their achievement, and in furtherance of the great cause in which he has so nobly fought, have made his name and his fame as lasting as the history of the nation?

I have spoken of the interest I feel in this bill, but if I know myself it is a feeling that rises far above the considerations of personal friendship which I entertain for the distinguished soldier whose name has been connected with it. *I am not here to speak for General Grant. No man with his consent has ever mentioned his name in connection with any position.* I say what I know to be true when I allege that every promotion he has received since he first entered the service to put down this rebellion was moved without his knowledge or consent; and in regard to this very matter of lieutenant-general, *after the bill was introduced and his name mentioned in connection therewith, he wrote me and admonished me that he had been highly honored already by the Government, and did not ask or deserve any thing more in the shape of honors or promotion; and that a success over the enemy was what he craved above every thing else; that he only desired to hold such an influence over those under his command as to use them to the best advantage to secure that end.** Such is the language of this patriotic and single-minded soldier, ambitious only of serving his country and doing his whole duty. *Sir, whatever this House may do, the country will do justice to General Grant.* We can see that. I think I can appreciate that myself.

After the battle of Shiloh, a little less than two years ago, a wave of calumny and detraction swept over General Grant with a power that would have overwhelmed any man of less strength and courage. My neighbor and my friend, appointed upon my own recommendation, I sought in my place on this floor the earliest occasion to tell the country something of this general, denunciations of whom were ringing from one end of the country to the other. I believe I can say I scarcely had the sympathy of a single member on this floor in making that speech, which was only regarded as a somewhat extravagant defence of a friend. Willing to take the responsibility of standing by my record then, *I now appeal to history for my justification, and ask if General Grant has not far transcended every thing that I claimed for him.*

It cannot certainly, Mr. Speaker, be necessary for me to enter into any detail of the services of General Grant to the country. They are as familiar as household words to our constituents, if not to us here. Why necessary to recount that long list of triumphs and of victories from Belmont to Lookout Mountain? Look at what this man has done for his country, for humanity and civilization—*this modest and unpretending general* whom gentlemen appear to be so much afraid of. He

* Another evidence of General Grant's remarkably retiring modesty.

has fought more battles and won more victories than any man living; he has captured more prisoners and taken more guns than any general of modern times. To us in the great valley of the West he has rendered a service in opening our great channel of communication to the ocean, so that the great Father of Waters now goes "unvexed to the sea," which endears him to all our hearts. Sir, *when his blue legions crowned the crest of Vicksburg, and the hosts of rebeldom laid their arms at the feet of this great conqueror, the rebel confederacy was cut in twain and the backbone of the rebellion broken.*

I speak of the fall of Vicksburg. I might speak of what went before. It was my good fortune to be with General Grant, and with that noble army, every man of whom is a hero, at the commencement of the expedition which culminated in the taking of Vicksburg. We all know how ill at ease the public mind was last winter pending General Grant's operations on the lower Mississippi. The expedition by Grenada, the opening of the canal, the opening of the bayous had not succeeded: the country saw all the attempts to flank that stronghold likely to prove abortive, and there was great anxiety. *But with unshaken confidence in himself, General Grant pursued the even tenor of his way*, and with entire reliance upon his success in the plan finally adopted, and which could not be undertaken until the river and bayous should sufficiently recede to enable them to move. Then, sir, was seen *that bold and daring conception which I say is without parallel in all military history.* It was to send his army and his transportation by land on the Louisiana side from Milliken's Bend to a point below Vicksburg, and then run the frowning batteries of that rebel Gibraltar, with its hundreds of guns, with his transports, and thus enable him to cross the river below Vicksburg, and get on to the shores of Mississippi. *The country was startled* at the success which attended the running of those batteries by the frail Mississippi steamboats used as transports, and *the rebels stood aghast* when they saw seven or eight transports and all of Porter's gunboats below Vicksburg.

There was something in this matter of running those batteries by the transports which deserves more than a passing notice, as showing the indomitable spirit and courage of that magnificent army. Certain boats were detailed for the extraordinary and hazardous service of running the batteries, but, with one exception, *the crews of all the boats refused to go.* The provost marshal was then ordered to beat up for volunteers. No sooner was the notice given than *soldiers rushed in for the service*, and at once many times the number that was called for was filled—pilots, engineers, firemen, and deck-hands, in the greatest numbers offered themselves. From one regiment, known as the Lead Mine regiment, raised in my own section, no less than one hundred and sixteen men and sixteen commisioned officers volunteered for that dangerous yet glorious service. The consequence of all this was that *resort was had to lot as to who should have the privilege of risking life in that unparalleled adventure. One noble boy from my own city, who had drawn the prize, was offered $100 in greenbacks for his chance, which he refused to take*, but courageously held on and successfully passed not only the Vicksburg but the Grand Gulf batteries. What language can do justice to an army animated by such a spirit? What triumphs and what glories might not justly be expected from it?

The transports and gunboats below the batteries, the army reaches by land marches Perkins's plantation, twenty miles above, and Hard Times landing, nearly opposite Grand Gulf. It was supposed that Admiral Porter, who always seconded General Grant with a zeal equal to his courage and ability, could reduce the batteries at Grand Gulf, after which the troops were to be crossed over in the transports, and were to land and carry the place by assault. But after five hours and a half of the most desperate naval fighting ever seen upon this continent, the brave Porter drew off his shattered fleet, unable to effect a reduction of the principal battery. During all of this time the army had been waiting with intense impatience for the time to come when the guns of the batteries should be silenced and they could land, and great was the disappointment when it was known that the fleet had failed to reduce the works. It seemed then that all had miscarried, and that the expedition, on which so many hopes hung, would be a failure.

At that moment was seen in General Grant that greatest of all gifts of a military man—the gift of deciding instantly amid the pressure of the greatest emergencies. I was with him when Porter reported his inability to reduce the batteries, and *in an instant he made his new dispositions*, and gave his orders. They were, to debark all his troops, and march them down three miles below Grand Gulf, "and," said he, "after nightfall I will run every transport I have below their batteries, and not one shall be injured." And, sure enough, when it became dark, Porter again attacked the batteries with his fleet, and amid the din and clatter of the attack, the transports all safely passed Grand Gulf. And, sir, it was a noble sight as this grand army was about to bivouac at Disharoon landing, three miles below Grand Gulf, with their camp fires burning brightly on that soft April night, when these transports, one by one, escaping all serious injury from the terrific tempest through which they had passed, rounded to, responding to eager inquiries, "All is well," and which was followed by such a shout as our brave and patriotic soldiers only can give.

Early the next morning this whole army was again embarked on board the gunboats and transports, bound down the Mississippi, for "Cowes and a market," for some place where a landing could be made on solid ground on the Mississippi side. And that was a proud spectacle when the grim old iron-clad Benton, the flag-ship of Admiral Porter, on which was General Grant, led the way down the river, the entire fleet and the transports following. She landed at a dilapidated plantation called Bruinsburg, and *General Grant was the first man to go ashore to seek information.* He there met a loyal "American citizen of African descent," who gave him trustworthy information in regard to the country and the roads into the interior. Instantly the debarkation of the troops commenced, and the line of march taken up toward Port Gibson. Before two o'clock the next morning, May 1, 1863, the enemy was encountered, and the battle of Port Gibson, the first of the series resulting in the capture of Vicksburg, was fought during that whole day, ending finally in the complete rout of the enemy.

And that which must ever be regarded by the historian as the most extraordinary feature of this campaign, is the astounding fact that *when General Grant landed in the State of Mississippi and made his campaign in the enemy's country, he had a smaller force than the enemy.* There he was, in the enemy's country, cut off, in a measure, from his supplies, with a great river in his rear, and in one of the most defensible of countries, through which he had to pass. *To his idomitable courage and energy, to his unparalleled celerity of movement, striking the enemy in detail, and beating him on every field, is the country indebted to those wonderful successes of that campaign* which have not only challenged the gratitude and admiration of our own countrymen, but the admiration of the best military men of all nations. My colleague [Mr. Farnsworth] has well said that General Grant is no "carpet knight." If gentlemen could know him as I know him, and as his soldiers know him, they would not be so reluctant about conferring this honor. If they could have seen him as I saw him on that expedition; if they could have witnessed *his terrible earnestness, his devotion to his duty, his care, his vigilance, and his unchallenged courage,* I think their opposition to this bill would give way.

When he left his head-quarters at "Smith's plantation," below Vicksburg, to enter on that great campaign, he did not take with him the trappings and paraphernalia so common to many military men. As all depended on quickness of movement, and as it was important to be encumbered with as little baggage as possible, he set an example to all under him. He took with him neither a horse, nor an orderly, nor a servant, nor a camp chest, nor an overcoat, nor a blanket, nor even a clean shirt. His entire baggage for six days—I was with him at that time—was a *tooth brush.* He fared like the commonest soldier in his command, partaking of his rations and sleeping upon the ground, with no covering excepting the canopy of heaven. How could such a soldier fail to inspire confidence in an army, and to lead it to victory and to glory? Confer upon him the rank contemplated by this bill, and you excite the enthusiasm of all your armies, and all your soldiers will be eager to follow his victorious banners!

But, gentlemen say, wait and confer this rank when the war is over. Sir, I want it conferred now, because it is my most solemn and earnest conviction that *General Grant is the man upon whom we must depend to fight out this rebellion in the field, and bring this war to a speedy and triumphant close.* It is said that he will have to leave his army if this rank is conferred upon him and come to Washington. Let me say to gentlemen that they need have no uneasiness upon that score. *General Grant,* if this appointment shall be conferred upon him, *will never leave the field, but he will be with his army wherever his presence is most needed;* he will be with his soldiers to lead them on in this gigantic struggle to preserve our God-given Government, in which he, in common with all loyal men, has so great an interest.

After a few brief remarks from other members, Mr. Ross's amendment was carried by 117 votes against 19. The bill so amended was finally passed and sent to the Senate for their action.

The Senate having confirmed the bill, so far as it revived the grade of Lieutenant-Generals, and the President having, on March 1st, approved the same, Major-General Ulysses S. Grant was nominated by President Lincoln for that high rank. On the 2d of March, 1864, the nomination was confirmed by the Senate in Executive Session, and he became the ranking officer of the United States Army.

CHAPTER LVII.

PREPARING FOR A NEW CAMPAIGN.

General Grant had no sooner finished one campaign before he began making his plans for another still more brilliant. He forwarded to Washington his views of the way the war in the southwest should be conducted to insure the earliest and most complete suppression of the rebellion. What these views are in detail will be developed by time; but among other recommendations that of a concerted movement of all our armies under one policy, and, so far as practicable, under one direction, was the principal feature of General Grant's project.

In alluding to this plan, a correspondent at Chattanooga wrote as follows:

Assuming that it is true that General Grant has forwarded to Washington his plan—and whether he has or not can be ascertained by inquiry at the proper department—no one will question his title to do so, or the weight his recommendations should have. Standing before the country *the first General in the field, with results proving his great abilities, almost marvellous*, it is not to be supposed for an instant that his views will fail to excite the greatest interest. To suppose that they will not enter largely into the future conduct of the war is to imply a disposition to deny him the influence his great services entitle him to have, and a suspicion that the powers at Washington are inimical to the General, whom the country recognizes as not only having done most, but as best qualified to give counsel. It may, therefore, confidently be expected that the future movements of our armies and the policy that will prevail in the campaigns to follow, will be much in accordance with the suggestions of General Grant.

I do not pretend to speak from authority. If General Grant has not presented his views nothing will be heard of them at Washington. If he has, we may safely assume that no time will be lost in giving them that consideration to which the great eminence of the author entitles them.*

The Congress at Washington, however, gave evidence of their desire to forward General Grant's plans, and Senator Howe, of Wisconsin, offered the following joint resolution on the 7th of January, 1864, under the plea of releasing the prisoners within the rebel lines:

Resolved by the Senate and House of Representatives in Congress assembled:

SEC. 1. *That the President of the United States is hereby authorized and requested to call out and arm one million of volunteers to serve for the period of ninety days* unless sooner discharged, and to be employed to carry food and freedom to every captive held in rebel prisons, and to plant the flag of the United States upon every prison they occupy.

SEC. 2. *That the President be requested to assign Major-General Ulysses S. Grant to the command of the forces raised under this call, together with such of the forces now in the field as may be joined with them*, and he is hereby authorized to detail for the subordinate commands in the forces to be raised under the authority of these resolutions, such officers or privates now in the field as he may deem best qualified therefor; or he may assign to such commands any person or persons who may volunteer under the same authority; *provided, however*, that any officer or private, now in the military service of the United States, who may be detailed to any such command by authority hereby, shall receive no additional pay for such substituted service; and no volunteer, under the same authority, who shall be detailed to any such command, shall receive more pay than the pay of a private.

In the mean time General Grant devoted his attention to the minor duties connected with his immediate department.

Many of the rebel troops finding that all hope for the establishment of a Southern Confederacy had passed away,

* *New York Times*, December, 1863.

and that whenever General Grant moved victory was always his constant attendant, began to desert from their ranks, and came within the Union lines in large numbers. To prevent them from being retaken and summarily punished by the rebel authorities, the commanding General issued the following order for their disposition and protection:

HEAD-QUARTERS MILITARY DIVISION OF THE MISSISSIPPI, IN THE FIELD, CHATTANOOGA, TENN., *December* 12, 1863.

[*General Orders, No.* 10.]

To obtain uniformity in the disposition of deserters from the Confederate armies coming within this military division, the following order is published:

I. All deserters from the enemy coming within our lines will be conducted to the commander of division or detached brigade who shall be nearest the place of surrender.

II. If such commander is satisfied that the deserters desire to quit the Confederate service, *he may permit them to go to their homes, if within our lines, on taking the following oath:*

THE OATH.

"I do solemnly swear in the presence of Almighty God, that I will henceforth faithfully support, protect, and defend the Constitution of the United States and the Union of States thereunder, and that I will in like manner abide by and faithfully support all acts of Congress passed during the existing rebellion with reference to slaves, so long and so far as not yet repealed, modified, or held void by Congress or by decision of the Supreme Court, and that I will in like manner abide by and faithfully support all proclamations of the President made during the existing rebellion having reference to slaves, so long and so far as not modified or declared void by decision of the Supreme Court, so help me God.

"Sworn and subscribed to before me at——this——day of——186 ."

III. Deserters from the enemy will at once be disarmed, and their arms turned over to the nearest Ordnance Officer, who will account for them.

IV. Passes and rations may be given to deserters to carry them to their homes, and free passes over military railroads and on steamboats in Government employ.

V. Employment at fair wages will, when practicable, be given to deserters by officers of the Quartermaster and Engineer Departments.

To avoid the danger of re-capture of such deserters by the enemy, they will be exempt from the military service in the armies of the United States.

By order of Major-General U. S. GRANT.

T. S. BOWERS, *A. A.-G.*

General Grant also issued an order that "no encouragement will be given to traders or army followers, who have left their homes to avoid enrollment or the draft, and to speculate upon the soldiers' pay; and this class of persons will not be tolerated in the armies of the Military Division of the Mississippi."

He also promulgated orders for the better protection of the property of loyal citizens residing within the rebellious States, and for the proper seizure of the effects of rebels forfeited to the United States under the special act of Congress passed for that purpose.

The following are the orders alluded to:

HEAD-QUARTERS MILITARY DIVISION OF THE MISSISSIPPI, IN THE FIELD, CHATTANOOGA, TENN., *December* 13, 1863.

[*General Orders, No* 11.]

All Quartermasters within the Military Division of the Mississippi who now have, or may hereafter receive, moneys for rents accruing from abandoned property, or property known to belong to Secessionists within this Military Division, are hereby directed to pay such moneys into the hands of the nearest Treasury Agent, taking his receipt therefor, excepting such sums out of said moneys so collected as may be requisite to pay the necessary expenses of collection and the taxes due the United States upon the same.

Any property now held by any Quartermaster, and upon which rents are collected by him, shall, when satisfactorily proven to belong to loyal citizens, be restored to the possession of the owners, together with all moneys collected for rents upon the same, excepting only such sums as may be required to pay the necessary expenses of collection, and the taxes due to the United States upon the same.

Department and Corps Commanders and Commandants of Military

Posts and Stations within this Military Division, are hereby required and directed, whenever called upon by proper authority, to promptly afford all necessary assistance in enforcing the collection of the taxes due upon all property within this command.

Corps Commanders within this Military Division are directed to immediately seize, or cause to be seized, all County Records and documents showing titles and claims to property within the revolted States in their respective districts, and hold the same until they can be delivered to an authorized Tax Commissioner of the United States.

Where property is used by the Government without paying rent, the collection of taxes on it will be suspended until further orders.

By order of Major-General U. S. GRANT.

T. S. BOWERS, *A. A.-G.*

HEAD-QUARTERS MILITARY DIVISION OF THE MISSISSIPPI, IN THE FIELD,
CHATTANOOGA, TENN., *December* 16, 1863.

[*General Orders, No.* 12.]

1. All seizures of private buildings will be made by the Quartermaster's Department, on the order of the commanding officer. The buildings of disloyal persons alone, will be taken to furnish officers with quarters, and the need for public offices and storehouses must be supplied in preference.

2. When the urgent exigencies of the service require it, the buildings of loyal persons may be taken for storehouses and offices, but only after all suitable buildings belonging to disloyal persons have been seized.

3. In the seizure of buildings, the owner will be allowed to retain all movables except the means of heating.

4. All officers will remain in the immediate vicinity of their commands, and if having a less command than a division or a post, when the command is in tents they will occupy tents themselves.

5. Commanding officers are prohibited from quartering troops in houses, without the special written authority of the General commanding the Corps or Department to which they belong.

6. In furnishing quarters to officers not serving with troops, the Quartermaster's Department will be governed by existing regulations.

7. Ten days after the receipt and distribution of this order, Corps Commanders will cause an inspection of their commands to be made by their Assistant Inspectors General, and will arrest and prefer charges against every officer who may be occupying quarters not assigned to

him by the Quartermaster's Department, or in violation of paragraph 4 of this order.

By order of Major-General U. S. GRANT.

T. S. BOWERS, *A. A.-G.*

General Grant, ever mindful of the comforts of the soldiers under his command, ordered the following important notice to be sent on Dec. 22, 1863, from the office of the Chief Quartermaster at Louisville, Ky., to prevent any stoppage of the supplies to his army:

All requisitions made by Captain J. A. Potter, Assistant Quartermaster United States Army, for military supplies, will be immediately and promptly filled.

In case of delay or refusal on the part of any railroad, Captain Potter is authorized to take such means as may be necessary to enforce compliance.

By order of Major-General U. S. GRANT.

ROBERT ALLEN, *Brig.-Gen. and Chief Quartermaster.*

CHAPTER LVIII.

GEN. GRANT PERSONALLY INSPECTS HIS GRAND DEPARTMENT.

HAVING thus secured all that appeared at that time to require his personal attention, General Grant determined to visit the outposts of his department, and left Chattanooga for Nashville.

An army correspondent at the former place thus records his departure:

Gen. Grant left Chattanooga yesterday on the noble and fast-sailing government steam packet Point Rock, *en route* for Nashville and Louisville. Head-quarters of the Military Division of the Mississippi will soon be established in the last-named town. Gen. Sherman accompanied him.

Gen. Grant has not yet entirely recovered from the effect of the injuries received by the fall from his horse last summer, and the sickness has made sad work with his once robust frame. He walks slowly, sometimes with a cane, and has come to stoop a very little. But the cheery look, which brightens into a cordial smile so rapidly, does not convey any idea of suffering. *The soldiers and sub-officers at Chattanooga will miss him very much;* for they had cause to know him from his daily walk in the streets among them. "Then, *Grant is so easy to approach*," say they. If a sub-officer or private wishes to gain the private ear of the General, and the request is well founded, it is not necessary to wade through a "regular channel!" of thirty-two gorgeous and curt staff officers to see the chief. *General Grant will have no one between him and his army but his adjutant, Brigadier-General Rawlings,* who is a hearty, jovial, plain-spoken, hard-working staff officer, just such as is indispensable to an energetic chief like "Old Vicksburg." *

* Mr. Westfall's dispatch (Dec. 19, 1864) to *New York Herald.*

Another correspondent announces Gen. Grant's arrival at Nashville in the following language:

The first soldier of the times, the hero of Donelson, Vicksburg, and Missionary Ridge, is also here. General Grant arrived on Saturday last, December 20, 1863, occupying for a few days his head-quarters on High street, the same once occupied by General Rosecrans, being the mansion of the well-known rebel, George Cunningham, and one of the stateliest in Nashville. The General is a man of medium height, rather spare than otherwise, and of far less pretentious appearance than many a second lieutenant frequently seen flashing his finery before the eyes of wondering beholders. His apparel is plain, and a trifle, perhaps, *negligé*, as a man of his celebrity can very well afford that it should be —or, perhaps, just come in from the engrossing cares and toils of a brilliant field, the spruce exterior of the martinet seemed specially unworthy of attention. His face is but little striking. Dark brown hair surmounts a brow straight and square, though of no unusual apparent capacity. His blue eyes are sharp and expressive, while his nose, not quite straight enough for Grecian, is delicate as well as bold in outline. A short-cut reddish beard and mustache conceal mouth and chin, which one is sure, from the general contour, must express decision and energy.

This countenance seen in repose, with the smoke of a Havana (General Grant is no exception to the all but universal practice in the army of using the fragrant weed) curling up around it, who would be likely to identify it as belonging to the most successful of all our warriors, *par excellence*, and beyond a doubt the greatest? Simplicity, indeed, as well in dress as in address and manner, though not inseparable from real greatness, is its most frequent and appropriate attendant. General Grant has the substantial without the showy. *Simple as a child, modest and unassuming, of high honor and blameless integrity*, no man could wear more becomingly the clustering chaplets he has so gloriously earned. The President may well felicitate himself in having retained General Grant in command against the strongest pressure for his removal. The result has fully vindicated the President's discernment and sagacity, and secured a leader to our armies in whom they and the whole country repose a confidence hardly second to that which the Chief Magistrate himself enjoys. With such a leader the future will be sure to have other great successes in store, and the campaign about to open, to harbinger the rebellion's speedy downfall.*

* *New York Times* Nashville correspondence, December 23, 1863.

The commander did not stay longer at Nashville than was necessary to secure active work on the railroad communications with Chattanooga, and in a few days his departure was announced for Knoxville. He had heard that the communications with that post had been much cut up and endangered, and, therefore, after a brief stay, he left the State capital for that point of his department.

While at Knoxville he felt desirous of ascertaining the condition of the roads between that place and Louisville, by way of Cumberland Gap, and he resolved upon making a personal examination of that line of travel.

The following dispatch will show the amount of hardship he endured to gain the desired information, and his reception along the route:

LOUISVILLE, KY., *January* 11, 1864.

General U. S. Grant arrived here this afternoon from Knoxville, having just completed a six days' campaign against Jack Frost. He and his staff left Knoxville on the 5th instant, and crossed the country by way of Cumberland Gap, Barboursville, Big Hill, Richmond, and Lexington, to this city, *having to encounter the coldest weather and deepest snow known there for thirty years.* The trip was a most terrible one—the officers having to walk a great part of the way, driving their nearly frozen animals before them. The descent of the Gap and of Big Hill is represented to have been *not only difficult but dangerous*, and had an army been compelled at this time to cross those mountains the task would not have been much less terrible than Macdonald's passage of the Spleigen. General Grant had a much easier and shorter route to Nashville by way of Chattanooga; *but he chose this difficult and dangerous one solely from a desire to see for himself the capabilities of the country and route for supplying General Foster's army.* It is this personal attention to important details and his aggressive style of warfare which is the secret of General Grant's great success. This difficult journey, undertaken at this time, is indicative of the indomitable energy of the man.

At Lexington, Kentucky, General Grant met with a spontaneous reception from the citizens. The town was crowded with the country visitors, and nothing would satisfy them but a speech. The General, however, contented himself with making his appearance. The people insisted on his getting upon a chair that he might be seen to better advantage, and, half pushed by General Leslie Coombs, General Grant mounted the improvised rostrum. General Coombs then introduced him in a neat little speech, in which he said that "General Grant had told him in confidence —and he would not repeat it—that he never had made a speech, knew nothing about speech-making, and had no disposition to learn." After satisfying the curiosity of the people, but without ever having opened his mouth, General Grant dismounted from his chair and retired, amid the cheers of the assemblage.

His arrival at the Galt House was not generally known, and few who had not looked at the books suspected that the little man in faded blue overcoat, with heavy red whiskers and keen, bright eyes, the hero of the two rebel Gibraltars of Vicksburg and Chattanooga, stood before them. This people have been so used to and surfeited with brilliantly dressed and cleanly shaven staff officers, with every pretence star or double star that has flitted across this horizon, that they never dreamed of recognizing in the blue overcoated men who figured in the scene with him, the admirable and hard-working staff-officers who have aided in no little degree to General Grant's success. General Grant was accompanied by General Wilson, Colonel Duff, Colonel T. S. Bowers, and others of his staff. The party are to leave in the morning train for Nashville, where General Grant establishes his head-quarters for the present.*

On the 12th of January, 1864, a telegraphic dispatch announced that railroad communication was opened between Louisville and Chattanooga. A private letter from Chattanooga states that when the first train of cars from Bridgeport arrived at the military post, the fact caused the greatest rejoicing throughout the whole army, and that our soldiers, who had for so many months been on short rations were soon revelling in plenty.

General Grant immediately began the collection of a large amount of supplies at Chattanooga preparatory to the opening of the spring campaign.

The following extract will give some idea of the laboi required to effect this desirable result:

* Mr. W. F. G. Shanks's dispatch to the *New York Herald*.

An announcement of great importance appeared in our Chattanooga dispatch of yesterday. It was, that at the close of this week the cars would run through to Chattanooga. Only those thoroughly informed of the vast amount of labor required to get the road in order will appreciate the victory that has been won by our soldiers and mechanics. The heavy force that has been employed in building the bridge over the Tennessee River and Falling Waters was next used to put the road in perfect order from Nashville to Bridgeport. This road had heretofore been in a wretched condition. The track had been constantly giving way, and the trains have been badly damaged by accidents. The utmost energy was displayed to make this road first-class, and equip it so that not only can our army at Chattanooga be thoroughly supplied, but provisions and ammunition, pork, bread, salt, cartridges, clothing—the necessaries of life for a great army—be accumulated for next spring's campaign. The road swarmed with laborers from end to end, until this was accomplished. With a good road, the furloughed soldiers can be sent home promptly, and the trains returned ponderous with military indispensables. It was no less important to General Grant than the reorganization and re-enforcement of his army, that the railroad should be efficient. It would be vain to gather the manly strength of the nation at Chattanooga if we could not send to that point that which is needed to provide the men for the present, and give them a dépôt of supplies for the future. Therefore, we regard the construction of the road to Chattanooga as a significant victory. It means as much in the direction of overcoming the rebellion, as if we had gained another battle in East Tennessee or Northern Georgia.*

On the 13th of January General Grant was in Nashville, having made the circuit of his deparment in the most inclement season of the year.

It was by this personal superintendence of every little detail that he has heretofore been victorious, and was enabled to prepare for a vigorous campaign at the opening up the spring of 1864.

A Washington correspondent sent the following paragraph to a prominent daily paper during February, 1864:

An officer just in from General Grant's head-quarters states that *all through the country to the rear of the Union lines a Union officer, in his uni-*

* *Cincinnati Commercial*, January 14, 1864.

*form, can ride unmolested to any portions of Mississippi, Tennessee, and Alabama, halting at farm-houses along the road for such refreshments and shelter as he may desire.**

What an evidence of the superiority of management of the departments in that region is set forth in the foregoing short paragraph.

The following, concerning the manner in which the commander of the forces in the Southwest carries out his campaigns, appeared recently in a public journal:

General Grant appears to have been acting from the beginning of his first campaign upon a fixed principle—*to take away from the rebels whatever they declare themselves least able to spare.* In January, 1862, it was rumored that the rebel capital would presently be removed to Nashville. Grant determined to be beforehand with Davis, moved upon the works of Fort Donelson, and after very unhandsomely capturing the garrison, with General Buckner, took possession of Nashville.

Next Mr. Davis announced to all the world that the fate of the Confederacy depended upon the fate of Vicksburg. Hereupon Grant moved down and captured that place.

East Tennessee was next declared to be absolutely necessary to the safety of the rebel cause. The untiring Grant no sooner heard this than he sent Sherman to Knoxville to drive off Longstreet, and leisurely drove Bragg away from Chattanooga.†

---

* *New York Tribune.* † *New York Evening Post,* February, 1864.

CHAPTER LIX.

GENERAL GRANT AT ST. LOUIS.—PUBLIC DINNER.

On the 26th of January, 1864, having satisfied himself that all was right in his grand department, General Grant visited the city of St. Louis, for the purpose of seeing his child, who was there lying sick.

The knowledge of General Grant's arrival in that city was gained by some visitors inspecting the book of the hotel where he had put up. The entry was simply as follows:

"U. S. Grant, Chattanooga."

That entry, modest and simple as it was, spoke volumes; for, hidden under those seven letters that composed his name and initials, lay unseen the titles of "Major-General of the United States Army," "Conqueror of Vicksburg and Chattanooga," "Grand Commander of the Military Division of the Mississippi." It did not require to be written, for it was all embraced in "U. S. Grant."

As soon as it became known that General Grant was really in St. Louis—it had been doubted by many that so great a general could have entered their city without a brilliant escort, or his advent being heralded by a flourish of trumpets and rolling of drums—the citizens prepared to give him a reception worthy of his deeds. No occasion had occurred since the commencement of the war in which St. Louis had more cheerfully united to do honor to one worthy of the gratitude of all.

The following invitation to a public dinner was tendered to General Grant by the citizens of St. Louis:

ST. LOUIS, *January* 27, 1864.

To Major-General U. S. GRANT:

DEAR SIR:—Your fellow-citizens of St. Louis, in common with all the loyal men of the republic, have witnessed with the highest admiration your patriotic devotion, unsurpassed services, and commanding success in the various military positions occupied by you from the commencement of the existing war. They remember the alacrity with which you sprang to arms at the first call of your country, placing yourself at its disposal to aid in suppressing this most unjustifiable and gigantic rebellion. As citizens of Missouri they can never forget the promptness and skill with which you aided in defending this State at the beginning of the conflict, when the means at the command of those in authority were wholly inadequate to the great work committed to them; and as citizens of the great valley of the Mississippi, they owe you unbounded gratitude, not only for the first signal victories which, under your auspices, crowned our arms, and thrilled the nation with joy, but also for those later and unparalleled triumphs which gave again freedom to Western commerce, from the sources of its great rivers to the Gulf. Not with more certainty is the indivisibility of the Mississippi Valley proclaimed by its geographical features than by the devoted loyalty of the Northwest, which demands that from the lakes to the Gulf, along its broad rivers and over its fertile plains, only one flag shall be known, and that the glorious banner of our republic—"one and indivisible." You have borne that flag victoriously with your heroic legions until the Mississippi goes "unvexed to the sea;" and looking down from the mountain heights of Tennessee upon the States between you and the Gulf in one direction, and the Atlantic in the other, you have, with the inspiration which the past glories of that State should ever arouse, made at Chattanooga a glorious response to that grand utterance of an immortal hero, which crushed out incipient rebellion years gone by, "The federal Union: it shall be preserved."

As citizens of a republic consecrated to constitutional liberty, and duly appreciating the destinies of the future for our own and other lands which hang upon the results of the present conflict, we glory in the brilliant deeds and unparalleled triumphs of yourself, officers, and men. To you and the gallant soldiers whom you have led a nation's honor and gratitude are due.

In the name of ourselves and St. Louis, we earnestly request that you will, before leaving the city—once your home—meet your fellow citizens at a public dinner, where old personal friendships may be renewed and new ones formed, and where congratulations over the successes of the past and the hopes of the future may be freely interchanged.

We have the honor to be, with sentiments of profound regard, your obedient servants.

(Here follow the names of the subscribers.)

General Grant accepted the invitation, and forwarded the following written reply to the foregoing document:

St. Louis, Mo., *Jan.* 27, 1864.

Colonel John O'Fallan, Hon. John How, and citizens of St. Louis:

Gentlemen:—Your highly complimentary invitation "to meet old acquaintances and make new ones," at a dinner to be given by citizens of St. Louis, is just received.

I will state that I have only visited St. Louis on this occasion to see a sick child. Finding, however, that he has passed the crisis of his disease and is pronounced out of danger by his physicians, I accept the invitation. My stay in this city will be short—probably not beyond the 1st proximo. On to-morrow I shall be engaged. Any other day of my stay here, and any place selected by the citizens of St. Louis, it will be agreeable for me to meet them.

I have the honor to be, very respectfully, your obedient servant,

U. S. Grant, *Major-General U. S. A.*

During that day (Januaiy 27th) General Grant paid a visit to the city University, where he passed some two hours in reviewing the arrangements and listening to the recitations of the students of this institution.

The same evening he attended the St. Louis theatre with his family, and was the cynosure of the eyes of all around him during the whole of the performance. After the fall of the curtain upon the play of Richelieu, cheers were proposed and heartily given for the "famous military chieftain." The general rose from his box bowing his acknowledgments, and in response to calls was understood to say that he had never made a speech in his life and never expected to. Asking to be excused, he resumed his seat amidst a shower of cheers. The orchestra struck up "Hail Columbia," followed by "Yankee Doodle," and altogether the incident was a very pleasant one.

On Friday evening (January 29th, 1864) the old friends of the modest Lieutenant Grant of former times, the neighbors of farmer Grant, the cordwood dealer of Corondelet, and the admirers of General Grant, the redeemer of the Mississippi Valley, sat down in the dining-hall of the Lindell Hotel, St. Louis, to a grand dinner given in his honor. A stranger, unacquainted with the object of the gathering, entering the dining-hall during the dinner, would never have selected, from the guests there assembled, the quiet, modest, unassuming man at the upper end of the room, as the victorious hero of the Southwest.

The St. Louis journals thus describe the reception and appearance of General Grant on this occasion:

The guests assembled in the corridors and parlors of the hotel at half-past six o'clock. Much curiosity was exhibited to see General Grant; and when he made his appearance, arm-in-arm with Judge Treat, all were eager to go forward and be presented to him. He went through the protracted ceremony of shaking hands with the crowd, and passing a word or two with each, *with far less of pretensions and pompous deportment than many of those who sought his acquaintance.* He is a small man about five feet eight inches high, with a well-knit frame, brown hair and whiskers, both cropped close, and a manner as utterly destitute of style as could be conceived. His sharp nose, heavy lower jaw, and firm set lips, are the only features wherein one would suspect lurked the qualities that drove the Western armies like a resistless avalanche down the Mississippi and over the Southwest, in that career of consecutive victories that broke the power of rebellion, even while it was boasting of triumphs at the East.

The curiosity of the company centered mainly upon General Grant, to honor whom the demonstration was specially intended. As he lodged in the hotel, any thing like an ostentatious arrival or reception was, of course, out of the question. General Grant had a visibly mild, modest manner, and received the cordial *greetings tendered him with evident embarrassment.* The lady inmates of the house took possession of an adjoining parlor, through the open door of which they could see the General, and several of his most ardent admirers among the fair spectators took the opportunity of his near proximity to the door in question, to obtain an introduction.

The dinner was as choice as it could possibly be. There were three elegant tables spread lengthwise in the hall, provided abundantly from the larder of the hotel. In the centre of the one on the north side were seated the President of the Committee of Citizens, Judge Samuel Treat, with General Grant next on his right, followed by General Schofield, Colonel Leighton, Colonel Marcy, and Lieutenant-Governor Hall. Next on his left sat General Rosecrans, General Osterhaus, and Mr. F. Dent, father-in-law of the guest of the evening. Mr. Dent is a white-haired, florid, fine-looking gentleman, about sixty-five years old. He resided in St. Louis County, on the Gravois road. Immediately opposite Judge Treat, at the same table, sat Judge Lord, of the Land Court, flanked on the left by Major Dunn, C. B. Hubbell, Colonel Merrill, and G. Hoeber; and on the right by Colonel Callender, Colonel Myers, Colonel Haines, and Major C. P. E. Johnson.

At the centre of the south table were seated Honorable Wayman Crow, with General McNeil, General Fisk, General Brown, General Totten, and General Gray. The remaining guests, to the number of two hundred, occupied the other seats at the tables. The hall, superb in the ceiling and wall colorings which embellished it, was further decorated by the spirited drapings of the national flag from each of the arched windows, and presented a magnificent appearance.

After the dinner the various toasts, incident to such

occasions, were given. At the toast of "our distinguished guest, Major-General Grant," the band played with great spirit the air "Hail to the Chief."

General Grant arose amid a perfect storm of applause; but, true to his resolution never to make a speech, he simply said:

GENTLEMEN: In response, it will be impossible for me to do more than to thank you.

At the toast of "the City of St. Louis," the following preamble and resolutions, passed by the City Council an hour or two before the time fixed for the dinner, were read:

COUNCIL CHAMBER,
CITY OF ST. LOUIS, *January* 29, 1864.

Whereas, Major-General U. S. Grant has, since our last meeting, suddenly and unexpectedly arrived among us, and the opportunity not having presented itself whereby the city authorities and this body could testify their great esteem, regard, and indebtedness *due his modest, unswerving energies, swayed neither by the mighty successes which have crowned his genius and efforts in behalf of the government, nor the machinations of politicians—evidences of the true patriot and soldier;* therefore, be it

Resolved, That the thanks of the Common Council of the City of St. Louis are eminently due, and are hereby respectfully tendered to Major-General U. S. Grant, in behalf of the City of St. Louis.

Resolved, That his Honor, the Mayor, be respectfully requested to give his official approval to this preamble and resolutions, and cause the seal of the city to be affixed, and the same presented to Major-General U. S. Grant.

Shortly before the dinner party broke up, the following was read:

Major-General Grant—He is emphatically U. S. Grant, for he has given US and the U. S. an earnest of those victories which will finally rescue this nation from the rebellion and its cause—American slavery.

Loud applause greeted the reading of this sentiment.

During the same evening, the General was honored by the enthusiastic populace with a serenade. His appearance on the balcony was greeted with the most flattering cheers. In response to calls for a speech, he took off his hat, and, amid profound silence, said:

GENTLEMEN: I thank you for this honor. I cannot make a speech. It is something I have never done, and never intend to do, and I beg you will excuse me.

Loud cheers followed this brief address, at the conclusion of which the General replaced his hat, took a cigar from his pocket, lit it, and stood on the balcony in the presence of the crowd, puffing his Havana and watching the rockets as they ascended and burst in the air.

"Speech! speech!" vociferated the multitude, and several gentlemen near him urged the General to say something to satisfy the people, but he declined. Judge Lord, of the Land Court, appeared very enthusiastic, and, placing his hand on General Grant's shoulder, said: "Tell them you can fight for them, but can't talk to them—do tell them that!"

"I must get some one else to say that for me," replied the General; but the multitude continuing to cry out, "Speech! speech!" he leaned over the railing, blew a wreath of smoke from his lips, and said:

"Gentlemen: Making speeches is not my business. I never did it in my life, and never will. I thank you, however, for your attendance here," and with that the General retired.

At the request of a number of ladies the noted visitor agreed to stay in the city until the end of the month, as the citizens of St. Louis were organizing a Great Western Sanitary Commission Fair. The following letter from him was, however, read at a meeting held on Monday evening, February 1, 1864:

ST. LOUIS, MO., *Jan.* 31, 1864.

DR. W. G. ELIOT, GEORGE PARTRIDGE, *and others, Western Sanitary Commission:*

GENTLEMEN: Your letter of yesterday, requesting my presence at a general meeting of the loyal citizens of St. Louis on Monday evening, to make preparations for a "Grand Mississippi Valley Fair," for the benefit of the sick and wounded soldiers of the Western army, is before me. *I regret that my already protracted stay in the city will prevent any longer delay from my public duties.* I regret this, as it would afford me the greatest pleasure to advance, in any manner, the interests of a commission that has already done so much for the suffering soldiers of our Western armies. The gratuitous offerings of our loyal citizens at home, through the agency of Sanitary Commissions, to our brave soldiers in the field, have been to them the most encouraging and gratifying evidence that whilst they are risking life and health for the suppression of this most wicked rebellion, their friends, who cannot assist them with musket and sword, are with them in sympathy and heart. The Western Sanitary Commission have distributed many tons of stores to the armies under my command. Their voluntary offerings have made glad the hearts of many thousands of wounded and sick soldiers who otherwise would have been subjected to severe privations. Knowing the benefits already conferred on the army by the Western Sanitary Commission, I hope for them a full and enthusiastic meeting to-night, and a fair to follow which will bring together many old friends who have been kept apart for the last three years, and unite them again in one common cause—that of their country and peace.

I am, gentlemen, with great respect,

Your obedient servant,

U. S. GRANT, *Major-General U. S. A.*

Before the close of the meeting the General was elected an honorary member of the Commission.

General Grant when he took his departure from St. Louis stated that he felt much pleased to find he was so well aided by the residents of the Mississippi River cities. He then set about carrying out his plans for the Spring Campaign, the effects of which will doubtless help to shake the remainder of the rebel confederacy to pieces.

CHAPTER LX.

GENERAL GRANT'S PERSONAL APPEARANCE AND CHARACTER.

THE appearance of General Grant is far from what an idealist would picture of a great hero. He is a man of medium height, and but little above the minimum standard of officers of the army. The appearance of his countenance during repose is far from commanding; but on the field there seems to be something in the determined glance of his eye, the contracted brow, and the firm-set teeth, that would imply that his wishes "must and shall be carried out." Otherwise there is but little in his countenance that could be called striking. His brow is straight and square, but cannot be characterized as lofty, although it is far from ignoble. His head is covered by a fair quantity of light brownish hair.* His eyes are blue, sharp, and expressive,

* We find a letter from General Grant to the wife of General I. F. Quinby, which we quote:

CHATTANOOGA, TENN., *Dec.* 13, 1863.

MY DEAR MADAM:—The letter of my old friend and classmate, your husband, requesting a lock of my hair, if the article is not growing scarce from age—I presume he means to be put in an ornament (by the most delicate of hands no doubt), and sold at the bazaar for the benefit of disabled soldiers and their families—is just received.

I am glad to say that the stock is yet abundant as ever, though time or other cause is beginning to intersperse here and there a reminder that winters have passed.

The object for which this little requisite is made is so praiseworthy that I cannot refuse it, even though I do, by granting it, expose the fact to the ladies of Rochester, that I am no longer a boy. Hoping that the yet, at times, calm and mild. His nose is aquiline, its bold lines delicately chiseled. His mouth and chin are well formed, but are concealed under a heavy reddish beard and mustache, which is kept cut somewhat shorter than it deserves.

His manner is mild even in times of the greatest excitement, and the humblest drummer-boy can as easily reach the General with his complaints, as could his corps or departmental commanders.

His style of dress has often been alluded to in the course of this narrative. He assumes no gaudy plumes nor trappings, and takes but little consideration as to his personal appearance. This apparent carelessness is a conclusive evidence that his mind is employed with more important matters.

A correspondent from Chattanooga thus describes his appearance during the battle:

Those who had never seen General Grant would scarcely be likely to have singled him out from the hundred others on the ground around Chattanooga as the man whom the country recognizes as having done the most, and of whom so much is expected, to crush the rebellion by hard blows, and of the exercise of those qualities which enter into a character of true greatness. He was there to be seen enveloped in a rather hugh military coat, wearing a slouching hat, which seemed to have a predisposition to turn up before and down behind, with a gait slightly limping from his accident at New Orleans, giving his orders with as few words as possible, in a low tone, and with an accent which partook of the slight nervousness, intensity of feeling, yet perfect self-command, seen in all his movements. General Grant might be described best as a little old man—yet not really old—who, with a keen eye, did not intend that any thing should escape his observation. At

---

citizens of your city may spend a happy week commencing to-morrow, and that this fair may remunerate most abundantly,

I remain, very truly, your friend,

U. S. Grant,

Major-General U. S. A.

that battle he was not in his usual physical condition, his recent illness, added to his arduous labors, having made him lean in flesh, and given a sharpness to his features which he did not formerly have. Those features, however, go far to define the man of will and self-control that he is. At the critical moment of the day's operations, the muscles appeared to gather tighter and harder over his slightly projecting chin, which seems to have an involuntary way of working, and the lips to contract. There is in what he does or says nothing that has the slightest approach to ostentation or show, but the palpable evidence of a plain man of sense, will, and purpose, who has little idea that more eyes are turned on him than on any other man on the continent. From his first struggle at Belmont to his last at Chattanooga, the men led by him have fought more steadily, fiercely, and successfully than those of any other portion of our army. In looking back over the history of the war, the eye rests upon no more glorious pages than those whereon are written Fort Donelson, Vicksburg, and Chattanooga.*

There are several instances mentioned of the kindness of General Grant's heart, but one will suffice as an evidence of the whole. When General Grant heard of the death of Colonel O'Meara, one of the officers under his command at Chattanooga, he hastened to see the daring and brave man's remains which were at the landing in a coffin, waiting for transportation. The General ordered the coffin to be opened that he might take "a last look at the gallant Colonel of the Irish Legion." When the coffin was opened the General was touched at the sight of one whom he had honored and publicly thanked before he had been two months in the Army of the Tennessee. O'Meara's defence of the trestlework, a few miles north of Holly Springs, Miss., when Van Dorn made a raid there in December, 1862, and which saved Grant's army from starvation, was never forgotten by the General. The spectators were moved at the sad and touching farewell of the Commander of the Department of the Mississippi from

* *New York Herald.*

the corpse of a young Irish soldier, who had forfeited his life to the belief that "the highest and best duty of all, native or foreign born, was to stand by the flag which is the hope of the exile, the emblem of philanthropy, and the ensign of the American people."

General Grant in private is thus described by an officer of his staff:

If you could see the General as he sits just over beyond me, with his wife and two children, looking more like a chaplain than a general, with that quiet air so impossible to describe, you would not ask me if he drinks. He rarely ever uses intoxicating liquors; more moderate in his habits and desires than any other man I ever knew; *more pure and spotless is his private character than almost any man I ever knew;* more brave than any man I ever saw; with more power to command and ability to plan than any man I ever served under; cool to excess, when others lose nerve, always hopeful, always undisturbed, never failing to accomplish what he undertakes just as he expects to. He is the only General worthy to command Americans fighting for their national salvation.

Of his bravery there can be no doubt, as it has been shown on all occasions from West Point to Chattanooga; but if the fact requires an endorsement, it has it in the following remarks from General Sherman, at the public dinner given at Memphis on the 25th of January, 1864: "I was at West Point," said General Sherman, "with General Grant. The General is not a man of remarkable learning, but *he is one of the bravest I ever saw.* He smokes his cigar with coolness in the midst of flying shot. *He has no fear, because he is an honest man.* I like Grant. I do not say he is a hero; I do not believe in heroes; but I know he is a gentleman, and a good man."

General Grant has always manifested towards the officers that have served under him a full appreciation of their abilities. His dispatches to the General-in-Chief, concerning battles and other movements, have always given evidence of this fact; and the following special recommendations of distinguished officers (since promoted) by General Grant, are on file at the head-quarters of the General-in-Chief.

Under date of July 23, 1863, General Grant says:

I would respectfully, but urgently, recommend the promotion of Major-General W. T. Sherman, now commanding the Fifteenth Army Corps, to the position of Brigadier-General in the regular army.

To General Sherman I was greatly indebted for his promptness in forwarding to me, during the siege of Fort Donelson, re-enforcements and supplies from Paducah. At the battle of Shiloh, on the first day he held with raw troops the keypoint to the landing. *To his individual efforts I am indebted for the success of that battle.* Twice hit, and several (I think three) horses shot under him on that day, he maintained his position with raw troops. It is no disparagement to any other officer to say that I do not believe there was another division commander on the field who had the skill and experience to have done it. His services as division commander in the advance on Corinth, I will venture to say, were appreciated by the now General-in-Chief beyond those of any other division commander.

General Sherman's arrangement as commander of troops in the attack on Chickasaw Bluffs last December, was admirable; seeing the ground from the opposite side from the attack, I saw the impossibility of making it successful. *The conception of the attack on Arkansas Post was General Sherman's.* His part of the execution, no one denies, was as good as it possibly could have been. His demonstration at Haines's Bluff, in April, to hold the enemy about Vicksburg, while the army was securing a foothold east of the Mississippi; his rapid marches to join the army afterward; his management at Jackson, Mississippi, in the first attack; his almost unequalled march from Jackson to Bridgeport, and passage of Black River; his securing Walnut Hills on the 18th of May, and thus opening communications with our supplies, *all attest his great merit as a soldier.* The siege of Vicksburg and last capture of Jackson and dispersion of Johnston's army, entitle General Sherman to more credit than usually falls to the lot of one man to earn. The promotion of such men as Sherman always adds strength to our arms.

On the same day that he recommended the promotion of General Sherman he also requested the same honor for

General McPherson, and wrote to the General-in-Chief concerning him as follows:

General McPherson has been with me in every battle since the commencement of the rebellion, except Belmont. At Forts Henry, Donelson, Shiloh, and the siege of Corinth, as a staff officer and engineer, his services were conspicuous and highly meritorious. At the second battle of Corinth his skill as a soldier was displayed in successfully carrying re-enforcements to the besieged garrison, when the enemy was between him and the point to be reached.

In the advance through Central Mississippi last November and December, General McPherson commanded one wing of the army with all the ability possible to show, he having the lead in the advance and the rear returning.

In the campaign and siege terminating with the fall of Vicksburg, General McPherson has filled a conspicuous part at the battle of Port Gibson. It was under his direction that the enemy was driven, late in the afternoon, from a position they had succeeded in holding all day against an obstinate attack. His corps, *the advance always under his immediate eye*, were the pioneers in the movement from Port Gibson to Hawkinson's Ferry. From the north fork of the Bayou Pierre to Black River it was a constant skirmish, the whole skilfully managed. The enemy was so closely pressed as to be unable to destroy their bridge of boats after them. From Hawkinson's Ferry to Jackson, the Seventeenth Army Corps marched roads not travelled by other troops, fighting the entire battle of Raymond alone, and the bulk of Johnston's army was fought by this corps, entirely under the management of General McPherson.

At Thompson's Hill, the Seventeenth Corps and General McPherson were conspicuous, All that could be termed a battle there, was fought by the divisions of General McPherson's Corps, and Hovey's Division of the Thirteenth Corps. In the assault of the 22d of May, on the fortifications of Vicksburg, and during the entire siege, General McPherson and his command took unfading laurels. *He is one of our ablest engineers and most skilful Generals.*

These recommendations secured the nomination by the President of these officers to the positions named in the documents.

General Grant's modesty is even more remarkable than the other fine traits in his character. Every dispatch that he sent to head-quarters was full of it; his quiet acknowledgment of honors gave evidence of it; and his replies concerning the mention of his name for the Presidency—the highest honor in the gift of the people, and the proud ambition of every true American—breathed it in every syllable. One day being spoken to about that position, he said, "Let us first settle the war and it will be time enough then to talk upon that subject." On another occasion, when rallied about the persistent use of his name by the *New York Herald* for the Presidency, he said: "I aspire only to one political office. When this war is over I mean to run for Mayor of Galena (his place of residence). And if elected, I intend to have the sidewalk fixed up between my house and the dépôt."

General Howard is reported to have stated in public that General Grant is a strictly temperate man, and religious. His marked characteristic is a wonderful faith in his success, amounting almost to the fatality in which Napoleon so strongly believed. General Howard's statements can be relied on.*

Prominent military men of every age have had some particular method of fighting, which might be considered peculiar to themselves; but at the same time the world's great generals have all adopted some acknowledged principles of strategy. On this subject General Grant made the following remarks to the members of his staff at Nashville during March, 1864: "I don't believe in strategy as you generally mean it. I use it in getting just as close to the enemy as possible, and then 'up guards and at 'em.'"

**New York Times*, February 18, 1864.

CHAPTER LXI.

AT WASHINGTON—COMMISSIONED LIEUTENANT-GENERAL.

As soon as the President's appointment of General Grant to the revived rank of Lieutenant-General had received the confirmation of the Senate of the United States, the appointee was ordered to report at the national capital. With true soldierly promptness he obeyed the order, and leaving the head-quarters of his military division "in the field," hastened on to Washington. On the 6th of March, 1864, he visited the Departmental offices at Louisville, Kentucky, to ascertain that every thing was in proper working order before he left the Division; and having satisfied himself on this subject, he started East, taking with him his son, a lad thirteen years of age. He arrived at Cincinnati the next morning, where he paid a flying visit to his father (J. R. Grant, Esq.), then residing at Covington, opposite that city, after which he proceeded to Harrisburg, Pennsylvania. He left that place on the morning of March 8th, and arrived at Baltimore about noon, where he was met at the dépôt of the Northern Central Railroad by a considerable number of soldiers and citizens. The General was plainly clad, and seemed anxious to avoid show or parade. Many, however, on seeing him, went up to shake hands, and gave vent to their feelings by enthusiastic shouts of welcome. To this greeting he remarked that, "beyond all things he was determined to avoid political demonstrations; his business was with war, while it existed, and his duty was to crush the spirit of treason and save the nation from destruction. When these things were accomplished, as he hoped and believed they surely would be, then it would be time enough for those whose tastes were toward partisanship to indulge themselves."

General Grant left Baltimore by the next train, and arrived in Washington at about five o'clock on the evening of March 8th, 1864. He at once proceeded to Willard's Hotel, where he immediately went to his room. Having divested himself of his travelling attire, he, unattended by either staff or escort, quietly walked into the long dining-room of the hotel, and took his seat for dinner. There were several hundred persons present, and the ranking officer of the whole United States army sat down in their midst in his rusty major-general's uniform, attracting but little notice. His quietude was but short-lived; and he had but half finished his dinner when one of the visitors at the table inquired of a neighbor who the strange major-general was. Looking up, the party questioned recognized the newly arrived officer at a glance, as he had before known him in Galena, and he promptly answered:

"Why, that is Lieutenant-General Grant."

The magic name was quickly whispered about, and a battery of ladies' eyes was speedily opened upon him. The General soon betrayed evidences of embarrassment, when suddenly a member of Congress arose and announced that "the hero of Vicksburg was among them," and proposed his health. Instantly all the guests were on their feet, and the proposal was met with deafening cheers. More embarrassed than before, the General merely bowed and resumed his seat; but it was some time before he could finish his dinner in consequence of the rush of the guests to gain an introduction to him.

Late in the evening General Grant visited the White House, where the President was holding a public reception. He entered the reception room unannounced; but was soon recognized and greeted by Mr. Lincoln with great cordiality. The noted visitor then became the principal feature of the reception, and, attended by the Secretaries of War and State, he modestly received the congratulations of the crowded mansion, after which he escorted Mrs. Lincoln round the East

Room, and retired. He afterwards remarked it was "his warmest campaign during the whole war."

The City Councils of Washington also tendered him the hospitalities and freedom of the city, together with a cordial welcome. This welcome was embodied in a series of resolutions, handsomely written, and presented to him by the Mayor.

At one o'clock in the afternoon of March 9th, 1864, General Grant was formally presented by President Lincoln with his commission as Lieutenant-General. The ceremony took place in the presence of the Cabinet, the General-in-Chief, the members of General Grant's staff, that officer's son, the President's private secretary, and Representative Lovejoy. When the General entered the room the President rose and said:

General Grant: The nation's appreciation of what you have done, and its reliance upon you for what still remains to be accomplished in the existing great struggle, are now presented with this commission, constituting you Lieutenant-General in the army of the United States. With this high honor devolves upon you, also, a corresponding responsibility. As the country herein trusts you, so, under God, it will sustain you. I scarcely need to add, that with what I here speak for the nation, goes my own hearty personal concurrence.

To which General Grant replied as follows:

Mr. President: I accept the commission, with gratitude for the high honor conferred. With the aid of the noble armies that have fought on so many fields for our common country, it will be my earnest endeavor not to disappoint your expectations. I feel the full weight of the responsibilities now devolving on me, and I know that if they are met, it will be due to those armies, and, above all, to the favor of that Providence which leads both nations and men.

At the conclusion of these brief speeches, the President introduced the General to all the members of the Cabinet; after which the company were seated, and about half an hour was spent in pleasant social conversation.

General Grant, the next day, visited the Army of the Potomac, in company with General Meade, and on his return to the national capital, immediately made preparations for his departure. He left Washington with his staff on the evening of March 11th, for the West.

The day after, the following order was promulgated:

WAR DEPARTMENT, ADJUTANT-GENERAL'S OFFICE,
WASHINGTON, *March* 12, 1864.

[*General Orders, No.* 98.]

The President of the United States orders as follows:

First. Major-General Halleck is, at his own request, relieved from duty as General-in-Chief of the army, and Lieutenant-General U. S. Grant is assigned to the command of the armies of the United States. The head-quarters of the army will be in Washington, and also with Lieutenant-General Grant in the field.

Second. Major-General Halleck is assigned to duty in Washington, as Chief of Staff of the army under the direction of the Secretary of War and the Lieutenant-General Commanding. His orders will be obeyed and respected accordingly.

Third. Major-General W. T. Sherman is assigned to the command of the military division of the Mississippi, composed of the Departments of the Ohio, the Cumberland, the Tennessee, and the Arkansas.

Fourth. Major-General J. B. McPherson is assigned to the command of the Department and Army of the Tennessee.

Fifth. In relieving Major-General Halleck from duty as General-in-Chief, the President desires to express his approbation and thanks for the zealous manner in which the arduous and responsible duties of that position have been performed.

By order of the Secretary of War.

E. D. TOWNSEND, *Ass't Adjutant-General.*

It is believed that no military order has been issued in this war so universally satisfactory as the preceding, appointing Lieutenant-General Grant to the command of the armies of the United States. Not the least agreeable feature of it is the announcement of head-quarters in Washington *or with General Grant in the field.* Nobody need fear any longer lest he be persuaded to bury himself in a bureau. He is still to lead in person, and the name which is the omen of success to his soldiers, will still be their rallying cry in battle. Laureled victory attend his steps.

APPENDIX.

A.

THE BATTLE OF FREDERICKTOWN, MISSOURI.

OFFICIAL REPORT OF COLONEL PLUMMER.

HEAD-QUARTERS, CAMP FREMONT,
CAPE GIRARDEAU, MO., *October* 26, 1861.

COLONEL PLUMMER TO GENERAL GRANT.

GENERAL:—Pursuant to your order of the 16th, I left this post on the 18th inst., with about fifteen hundred men, and marched upon Fredericktown, *via* Jackson and Dallas, where I arrived at twelve o'clock on Monday, the 21st instant; finding there Colonel Carlin with about three thousand men who had arrived at nine o'clock that morning. He gave me a portion of his command, which I united with my own, and immediately started in pursuit of Thompson, who was reported to have evacuated the town the day before and retreated toward Greenville. I found him, however, occupying a position about one mile out of town, on the Greenville road, which he has held since about nine o'clock A. M., and immediately attacked him. The battle lasted about two hours and a half, and resulted in the total defeat of Thompson, and rout of all his forces, consisting of about three thousand five hundred men. Their loss was severe, ours very light. Among their killed was Lowe. On the following day I pursued Thompson twenty-two miles on the Greenville road, for the purpose of capturing his train, but finding further pursuit useless, and believing Pilot Knob secure and the object of the expedition accomplished, I returned to this post, where I arrived last evening, having been absent seven days and a half.

I brought with me forty-two prisoners, one iron twelve-pounder field-piece, a number of small arms and horses taken upon the field.

I will forward a detailed report of the battle as soon as reports from colonels of regiments and commanders of corps are received.

I am, very respectfully,
Your obedient servant,

J. B. PLUMMER,
Colonel Eleventh Missouri Volunteers Commanding.

TO ASSISTANT ADJUTANT-GENERAL, Head-Quarters District South-east Missouri, Cairo, Illinois.

GENERAL GRANT TO COLONEL PLUMMER.

HEAD-QUARTERS, DISTRICT SOUTHEAST MISSOURI,
CAIRO, *October* 27, 1861.

Colonel J. B. PLUMMER, *commanding United States Forces, Cape Girardeau, Missouri.*

COLONEL:—Your report of the expedition under your command is received. I congratulate you, and the officers and soldiers of the expedition, upon the result.

But little doubt can be entertained of the success of our arms, when not opposed by superior numbers; and in the action of Fredericktown they have given proof of courage and determination which shows that they would undergo any fatigue or hardships to meet our rebellious brethren, even at great odds.

Our loss, small as it was, is to be regretted; but the friends and relatives of those who fell can congratulate themselves in the midst of their affliction, that they fell in maintaining the cause of constitutional freedom and the integrity of a flag erected in the first instance at a sacirfice of many of the noblest lives that ever graced a nation.

In conclusion, say to your troops they have done nobly. It goes to prove that much more may be expected of them when the country and our great cause calls upon them.

Yours, etc. U. S. GRANT, *Brigadier-General Commanding.*

B.

THE BATTLE AT BELMONT, MISSOURI.

FOUGHT NOVEMBER 7, 1861.

GENERAL GRANT'S REPORT.

CAIRO, *November* 12, 1861.

On the evening of the 6th instant, I left this place with two thousand eight hundred and fifty men of all arms, to make a reconnoissance towards Columbus. The object of the expedition was to prevent the enemy from sending out re-enforcements to Price's army in Missouri, and also from cutting off columns that I had been directed to send out from this place and Cape Girardeau, in pursuit of Jeff. Thompson. Knowing that Columbus was strongly garrisoned, I asked General Smith, commanding at Paducah, Kentucky, to make demonstrations in the same direction. He did so by ordering a small force to Mayfield and another in the direction of Columbus, not to approach nearer, however, than twelve or fifteen miles. I also sent a small force on the Kentucky side with orders not to approach nearer than Ellicott's Mills, some twelve miles from Columbus. The expedition under my immediate command was stopped about nine miles below here on the Kentucky shore, and remained until morning. All this served to distract the enemy, and led him to think he was to be attacked in his strongly fortified position. At daylight we proceeded down the river to a point just out of range of the rebel guns, and debarked on the Missouri shore. From here the troops were marched by flank for about one mile toward Belmont, and then drawn up in line of battle, a battalion also having been left as a reserve near the transports. Two companies from each regiment, five skeletons in number, were then thrown out as skirmishers, to ascertain the position of the enemy. It was but a few moments before we met him, and a general engagement ensued.

The balance of my forces, with the exception of the reserve, was then thrown forward—all as skirmishers—and the enemy driven foot by foot, and from tree to tree, back to their encampment on the river bank, a distance of two miles. Here they had strengthened their position by felling the timber for several hundred yards around their camp, and making a sort of abatis. Our men charged through this, driving the enemy over the bank into their transports in quick time, leaving us in possession of every thing not exceedingly portable. Belmont is on low ground, and every foot of it is commanded by the guns on the opposite shore, and of course could not be held for a single hour after the enemy became aware of the withdrawal of their troops. Having no wagons, I could not move any of the captured property; consequently, I gave orders for its destruction. Their tents, blankets, etc., were set on fire, and we retired, taking their artillery with us, two pieces being drawn by hand; and one other, drawn by an inefficient team, we spiked and left in the woods, bringing the two only to this place. Before getting fairly under way the enemy made his appearance again, and attempted to surround us. Our troops were not in the least discouraged, but charged on the enemy again, and defeated him. Our loss was about eighty-four killed, one hundred and fifty wounded—many of them slightly—and about an equal number missing. Nearly all the missing were from the Iowa regiment, who behaved with great gallantry, and suffered more severely than any other of the troops.

I have not been able to put in the reports from sub-command, but will forward them as soon as received. All the troops behaved with much gallantry, much of which is attributed to the coolness and presence of mind of the officers, particularly the colonels. General McClernand was in the midst of danger throughout the engagement, and displayed both coolness and judgment. His horse was three times shot. My horse was also shot under me. To my staff, Captains Rawlins, Logan, and Hillyer, volunteer aids, and to Captains Hatch and Graham, I am much indebted for the assistance they gave. Colonel Webster, acting chief engineer, also accompanied me, and displayed highly soldier-like qualities. Colonel Doherty, of the Twenty-second Illinois Volunteers, was three times wounded and taken prisoner.

The Seventh Iowa Regiment had their lieutenant-colonel killed, and the colonel and major were severely wounded. The reports to be forwarded will detail more fully the particulars of our loss. Surgeon Brinton was in the field during the entire engagement, and displayed great ability and efficiency in providing for the wounded and organizing the medical corps.

The gunboats Tyler and Lexington, Captains Walker and Stemble, U. S. N., commanding, convoyed the expedition and rendered most efficient service. Immediately upon our landing they engaged the enemy's batteries, and protected our transports throughout.

For particulars see accompanying report of Captain Walker.

I am, sir, very respectfully, your obedient servant,

U. S. GRANT, *Brigadier-General Commanding.*

GENERAL POLK'S DISPATCH.

HEAD-QUARTERS, FIRST DIV. WEST. DEP'T,
COLUMBUS, KY., *November* 7, 1861.

To General Head-Quarters, through General A. S. JOHNSTON:

The enemy came down on the opposite side of the river, Belmont, to day, about seven thousand five hundred strong, landed under cover of gunboats, and attacked Colonel Tappan's camp. I sent over three regiments, under General Pillow, to his relief, then, at intervals, three others, then General Cheatham.

I then took over two others in person, to support a flank movement which I had directed. It was a hard-fought battle, lasting from half-past ten A. M. to five P. M. They took Beltzhoover's battery, four pieces of which were recaptured. The enemy were thoroughly routed. We pursued them to their boats seven miles, then drove their boats before us. The road was strewn with their dead and wounded, guns, ammunition, and equipments. Our loss considerable; theirs heavy.

L. POLK, *Maj.-Gen. Commanding.*

C.

CAPTURE OF FORT HENRY, TENN.

REPORT OF GENERAL GRANT.

HEAD-QUARTERS, DISTRICT OF CAIRO,
FORT HENRY, TENN., *February* 6.

Capt. J. C. KELTON, *A. A.-General, Department of Mo., St. Louis, Mo.:*

CAPTAIN:—Inclosed I send you my order for the attack upon Fort Henry. Owing to dispatches received from Major-General Halleck, and corroborating information here, to the effect that the enemy were rapidly re-enforcing, I thought it imperatively necessary that the Fort should be carried to-day. My forces were not up at ten o'clock last night, when my order was written, therefore I did not deem it practicable to set an earlier hour than eleven o'clock to-day, to commence the investment. The gunboats started up at the same hour to commence the attack, and engage the enemy at not over six hundred yards. In little over one hour all the batteries were silenced, and the Fort surrendered at discretion to Flag-Officer Foote, giving us all their guns, camp and garrison equipage, etc. The prisoners taken are General Tilghman and staff, Captain Taylor and company, and the sick. The garrison, I think, must have commenced their retreat last night, or at an early hour this morning.

Had I not felt it an imperative necessity to attack Fort Henry to-day, I should have made the investment complete, and delayed until to-morrow, so as to secure the garrison. I do not now believe, however, the result would have been any more satisfactory.

The gunboats have proven themselves well able to resist a severe cannonading. All the iron-clad boats received more or less shots—the flag-ship some twenty-eight—without any serious damage to any, except the Essex. This vessel received one shot in her boiler, that disabled her, killing and wounding some thirty-two men, Captain Porter among the wounded.

I remain your obedient servant,

U. S. GRANT, *Brigadier-General.*

HEAD-QUARTERS, DISTRICT OF CAIRO,
CAMP IN FIELD, NEAR FORT HENRY, *February* 5, 1862.

[*General Orders, No.* 1.]

The First Division, General McClernand commanding, will move, at eleven o'clock A. M., to-morrow, under the guidance of Lieutenant-Colonel McPherson, and take a position on the roads from Fort Henry to Donelson and Dover.

It will be the special duty of this command to prevent all re-enforcements to Fort Henry or escape from it. Also, to be held in readiness to charge and take Fort Henry by storm, promptly on the receipt of orders.

Two brigades of the Second Division, General C. F. Smith commanding, will start at the same hour from the west bank of the river, and take and occupy the heights commanding Fort Henry. This point will be held by so much artillery as can be made available, and such other troops as, in the opinion of the general commanding the Second Division, may be necessary for its protection.

The Third Brigade, Second Division, will advance up the east bank of the Tennessee River, as fast as it can be securely done, and be in readiness to charge upon the fort, or move to the support of the First Division, as may be necessary.

All the forces on the west bank of the river, not required to hold the heights commanding Fort Henry, will return to their transports, cross to the east bank, and follow the First Brigade as fast as possible.

The west bank of the Tennessee River, not having been reconnoitred, the commanding officer intrusted with taking possession of the enemy's works there, will proceed with great caution, and such information as can be gathered, and such guides as can be found in the time intervening, before eleven o'clock to-morrow.

The troops will receive two days' rations of bread and meat in their haversacks.

One company of the Second Division, armed with rifles, will be ordered to Flag-Officer Foote, as sharpshooters, on board the gunboats.

By order,

U. S. GRANT, *Brig.-Gen. Commanding.*

D.

THE CAPTURE OF FORT DONELSON.

GENRAL GRANT'S REPORT.

HEAD-QUARTERS, ARMY IN THE FIELD,
FORT DONELSON, *February* 16, 1862.

General G. W. CULLUM, *Chief of Staff, Department of Missouri:*

GENERAL:—I am pleased to announce to you the unconditional surrender, this morning, of Fort Donelson, with twelve to fifteen thousand prisoners, at least forty pieces of artillery, and a large amount of stores, horses, mules, and other public property.

I left Fort Henry on the 12th instant, with a force of about fifteen thousand men, divided into two divisions, under the command of Generals McClernand and Smith. Six regiments were sent around by water the day before, convoyed by a gunboat, or rather started one day later than one of the gunboats, with instructions not to pass it.

The troops made the march in good order, the head of the column arriving within two miles of the fort at twelve o'clock M. At this point the enemy's pickets were met and driven in.

The fortifications of the enemy were from this point gradually approached and surrounded, with occasional skirmishing on the line. The following day, owing to the non-arrival of the gunboats and re-enforcements sent by water, no attack was made; but the investment was extended on the flanks of the enemy, and drawn closer to his works, with skirmishing all day. The evening of the 13th, the gunboats and re-enforcements arrived. On the 14th, a gallant attack was made by Flag-Officer Foote upon the enemy's works with his fleet. The engagement lasted probably one hour and a half, and bid fair to result favorably to the cause of the Union, when two unlucky shots disabled two of the armored gunboats, so that they were carried back by the current. The remaining two were very much disabled also, having received a number of heavy shots about the pilot-house and other parts of the vessels. After these mishaps, I concluded to make the investment of Fort Donelson as perfect as possible, and partially fortify and await repairs to the gunboats. This plan was frustrated, however, by the enemy making a most vigorous attack upon our right wing, commanded by General J. A. McClernand, with a portion of the force under General L. Wallace. The enemy were repelled after a closely contested battle of several hours, in which our loss was heavy. The officers, and particularly field officers, suffered out of proportion. I have not the means yet of determining our loss even approximately, but it cannot fall far short of one thousand two hundred killed, wounded, and missing. Of the latter, I understand through General Buckner, about two hundred and fifty were taken prisoners. I shall retain enough of the enemy to exchange for them, as they were immediately shipped off and not left for recapture.

About the close of this action the ammunition in the cartridge-boxes gave out, which, with the loss of many of the field officers, produced great confusion in the ranks. Seeing that the enemy did not take advantage of this fact, I ordered a charge upon the left—enemy's right—with the division under General C. F. Smith, which was most brilliantly executed, and gave to our arms full assurance of victory. The battle lasted until dark, giving us possession of part of their intrenchments. An attack was ordered upon their other flank, after the charge of General Smith was commenced, by the divisions under Generals McClernand and Wallace, which, notwithstanding the hours of exposure to a heavy fire in the forepart of the day, was gallantly made, and the enemy further repulsed. At the points thus gained, night having come on, all the troops encamped for the night, feeling that a complete victory would crown their labors at an early hour in the morning. This morning, at a very early hour, General S. B. Buckner sent a message to our camp under a flag of truce, proposing an armistice, etc. A copy of the correspondence which ensued is herewith accompanied.

I cannot mention individuals who specially distinguished themselves, but leave that to division and brigade officers, whose reports will be forwarded as soon as received. To division commanders, however, Generals McClernand, Smith, and Wallace, I must do the justice to say that each of them were with their commands in the midst of danger, and were always ready to execute all orders, no matter what the exposure to themselves.

At the hour the attack was made on General McClernand's command, I was absent, having received a note from Flag-Officer Foote, requesting me to go and see him, he being unable to call.

My personal staff—Colonel J. D. Webster, Chief of Staff; Colonel J. Riggin, Jr., Volunteer Aide; Captain J. A. Rawlins, A. A.-General; Captains C. B. Lagow and W. S. Hillyer, Aides, and Lieutenant-Colonel V. B. McPherson, Chief Engineer—all are deserving of personal mention for their gallantry and services.

For full details and reports and particulars, reference is made to the reports of the Engineer, Medical Director and commanders of brigades and divisions, to follow.

I am, General, very respectfully,

Your obedient servant,

U. S. GRANT, *Brigadier-General.*

REBEL REPORTS.

JEFF. DAVIS'S MESSAGE ACCOMPANYING THE REPORTS.

EXECUTIVE DEPARTMENT, *March* 11, 1862.

To the Speaker of the House of Representatives:

I transmit herewith copies of such official reports as have been received at the War Department of the defence and fall of Fort Donelson.

They will be found incomplete and unsatisfactory. Instructions have been given to furnish further information upon the several points not made intelligible by the reports. It is not stated that re-enforcements were at any time asked for; nor is it demonstrated to have been impossible to have saved the army by evacuating the position; nor is it known by what means it was found practicable to withdraw a part of the garrison, leaving the remainder to surrender; nor upon what authority or principles of action the senior general abandoned responsibility by transferring the command to a junior officer.

In a former communication to Congress, I presented the propriety of a suspension of judgment in relation to the disaster at Fort Donelson, until official reports could be received. I regret that the information now furnished is so defective. In the mean time, hopeful that satisfactory explanation may be made, I have directed, upon the exhibition of the case as presented by *the two senior generals, that they should be relieved from command*, to await further orders whenever a reliable judgment can be rendered on the merits of the case.

JEFFERSON DAVIS.

REPORT OF JOHN B. FLOYD.—(*Extracts.*)

CAMP NEAR MURFREESBORO, *February* 27, 1862.

General A. S. JOHNSTON:

SIR:—Your order of the 12th of this month, transmitted to me by telegraph from Bowling Green to Cumberland City, reached me the same evening. It directed me to repair at once, with what force I could command, to the support of the garrison at Fort Donelson. I immediately prepared for my departure, and effected it in time to reach Fort Donelson the next morning, 13th, before daylight. Measures had been already taken by Brigadier-General Pillow, then in command, to render our resistance to the attack of the enemy as effective as possible. He had, with activity and industry, pushed forward the defensive works toward completion.

* * * * * *

Soon after my arrival, the intrenchments were fully occupied from one end to the other; and just as the sun rose, the cannonade from one of the enemy's gunboats announced the opening of the conflict, which was destined to continue for three days and nights. In a very short time the fire became general along our whole lines, and the enemy, who had already planted batteries at several points around the whole circuit of our intrenchments, opened a general and active fire from all arms upon our trenches, which continued until darkness put an end to the conflict. They charged with uncommon spirit at several points along on the line, but most particularly at a point undefended by intrenchments, down a hollow which separated the right wing, under Brigadier-General Buckner, from the right of the centre, commanded by Colonel Himan.

* * * * * *

The enemy continued their fire upon different parts of our intrenchments throughout the night, which deprived our men of every opportunity of sleep. We lay that night upon our arms in the trenches. We confidently expected, at the dawn of day, a more vigorous attack than ever; but in this we were entirely mistaken. The day advanced, and no preparation seemed to be making for a general onset. But an extremely annoying fire was kept up from the enemy's sharpshooters throughout the whole length of the intrenchments, from their long-range rifles. Whilst this mode of attack was not attended with any considerable loss, it, nevertheless, confined the men to their trenches, and prevented their taking their usual rest.

* * * * * *

There was no place within our intrenchments but could be reached by the enemy's artillery, from their boats or their batteries. It was but fair to infer that, while they kept up a sufficient fire upon our intrenchments, to keep our men from sleep and prevent repose, their object was merely to give time to pass a column above us on the river, both on the right and the left banks, and thus to cut off all our communications, and to prevent the possibility of egress. I thus saw clearly that but one course was left by which a rational hope could be entertained of saving the garrison, or a part of it. That was to dislodge the enemy from his position on our left, and thus to pass our people into the open country, lying southward toward Nashville. I called for a consultation of the officers of divisions and brigades, to take place after dark, when this plan was laid before them, approved and adopted, and at which it was determined to move from the trenches at an early hour on the next morning, and attack the enemy in his position.

* * * * * *

Our troops were completely exhausted by four days and nights of continued conflict. To renew it with any hope of successful result was obviously vain, and such I understood to be the unanimous opinion of all the officers present at the council called to consider what was best to be done. I thought, and so announced, that a desperate onset upon the right of the enemy's forces, on the ground where we had attacked them in the morning, might result in the extrication of a considerable proportion of the command from the position we were in, and this opinion I understood to be concurred in by all who were present. But it was likewise agreed, with the same unanimity, that it would result in the slaughter of nearly all who did not succeed in effecting their escape. The question then arose, whether, in point of humanity and a sound military policy, a course should be adopted from which the probabilities were, that the larger portion of the command would be cut to pieces in an unavailing fight against overwhelming numbers. I understood the general sentiment to be averse to the proposition. I felt that in this contingency, whilst it might be questioned whether I should, as commander of the army, lead it to certain destruction in an unavailing fight, yet I had a right, individually, to determine that I would not survive a surrender there. To satisfy both propositions, I agreed to hand over the command to Brigadier-General Buckner, through Brigadier-General Pillow, and to make an effort for my own extrication by any and every means that might present themselves to me.

I therefore directed Colonel Forrest, a daring and determined officer, at the head of an efficient regiment of cavalry, to be present for the purpose of accompanying me in what I supposed would be an effort to pass through the enemy's lines. I announced the fact, upon turning the command over to Brigadier-General Buckner, that I would bring away with me, by any means I could, my own particular brigade, the propriety of which was acquiesced in on all hands. This, by various modes, I succeeded in accomplishing to a great extent.

* * * * *

The command was turned over to Brigadier-General Buckner, who at once opened negotiations with the enemy, which resulted in the surrender of the place.

JOHN B. FLOYD, *Brig.-Gen. Commanding.*

GENERAL PILLOW'S REPORT.—(*Extracts.*)

COLUMBIA, TENNESSEE, *February* 18, 1862.

Captain CLARENCE DERRICK, *A. A.-General:*

On the 18th instant, General A. S. Johnston ordered me to proceed to Fort Donelson and take command at that post. On the 19th instant I arrived at that place. In detailing the operations of the forces under my command at Fort Donelson, it is proper to state the condition of that work and of the forces constituting its garrison.

* * * * *

The armament of the batteries consisted of eight thirty-two pounders, three thirty-two pound carronades, one eight-inch columbiad, and one rifled gun of thirty-two pound calibre. The selection of the site for the work was an unfortunate one. While its command of the river was favorable, the site was commanded by the hills above and below on the river, and by a continuous range of hills all around the works to its rear.

A field-work of very contracted dimensions had been constructed for the garrison to protect the battery; but this field-work was commanded by the hills already referred to, and lay open to a fire of artillery from every direction except from the hills below. To guard against the effect of fire of artillery from these heights, a line of defence-work, consisting of rifle-pits and *abatis* for infantry, detached on our right, but continuous on our left, with defences for our light artillery, were laid off by Major Gilmer—engineer of General A. S. Johnston's staff, but on duty with me at the post—around the rear of the battery, and on the heights from which artillery could reach our battery and inner field-work, enveloping the inner work and the town of Dover, where our principal supplies of quartermaster and commissary stores were on deposit.

These works, pushed with the utmost possible energy, were not quite completed, nor my troops all in position, though nearly so, when Brigadier-General Floyd, my senior officer, reached that station. The works were laid off with judgment and skill, by Major Gilmer; were well executed, and designed for the defence of the rear of the works. * *

I had placed Brigadier-General Buckner in command of the right wing and Brigadier-General Johnson in command of the left. By extraordinary efforts, we had barely got the works in a defensible condition, when the enemy made an advance in force around and against the entire line of our outer works.

The first assault was commenced by the enemy's artillery against the entire line of our left wing, which was promptly responded to by Captain Green's battery of field-artillery. After several hours of firing between the artillery of the two armies, the enemy's infantry advanced to the conflict all along the line, which was kept up and increased in volume from one end of the line to the other for several hours, when at last the enemy made a vigorous assault against the right of our left wing.

* * * * *

The result of the day's work pretty well tested the strength of our defensive lines, and established, beyond question, the gallantry of our entire command, all of which defended well their portion of the line. The loss sustained by our forces in this engagement was not large, our men being mostly under shelter of their rifle-pits; but we, nevertheless, had quite a number of killed and wounded, but owing to the continued fighting which followed, it was impossible to get any official report of the casualties of the day. * * * *

On the 14th instant, the enemy was busy throwing his forces at every arm around us, extending his line of investment around our position, and completely enveloping us. We were now surrounded by immense force, said by persons to amount to fifty-two regiments, and every road and possible avenue of departure were cut off, with the certainty that our sources of supply by the river would soon be cut off by the enemy's batteries placed upon the river above us.

At a meeting of the general officers, called by General Floyd, it was unanimously determined to give the enemy battle next day at daylight, so as to cut open a route of exit for our troops to the interior of the country, and thus to save our army. We had knowledge that the principal portion of the enemy's forces were massed in encampment in front of our extreme left, commanding the two roads leading into the interior, one of which we must take in leaving our position. We knew that he had massed in encampment another large force on the Union Ferry road, opposite the centre of our left wing. His fresh arrival of troops which encamped on the bank of the river, two and a half miles below us, from which latter encampment a stream of fresh troops was continually pouring around us on his line of investment, and thus strengthening his general encampment on the extreme right. At each of his encampments and on each road he had a position, a battery of field artillery and twenty-four pound iron guns on siege-carriages. * *

* * * * * *

The operations of the day had forced the entire command of the enemy around to our right wing, and in front of General Buckner's position in the intrenchments, and when his command reached his position he found the enemy rapidly advancing to take possession of this portion of his work. He had a stubborn conflict, lasting one a half hours, to regain it, and the enemy actually got possession of the extreme right of his position, and he held it so firmly that he could not dislodge him. The position thus gained by the enemy was a most commanding one, being immediately on the rear of our river-battery and field-work for its protection. From it he could readily turn the intrenched work occupied by General Buckner, and attack him in reverse, or advance under cover of an intervening ridge directly upon our battery and field-work. While he held this position, it was manifest we could not hold the main work or battery. Such was the condition of the armies at nightfall, after nine hours of severe conflict on the 15th instant. * * *

In this condition the general officers held a consultation to determine what we should do. General Buckner gave it as his decided opinion that he could not hold his position one half hour against an assault of the enemy, and said the enemy would attack him next morning at daylight. The proposition was then made by the undersigned to again fight our way through the enemy's line, and cut our way out. General Buckner said his command was so worn out and cut to pieces and demoralized that he could not make another fight; that it would cost the command three-quarters of its present number to cut its way through, and it was wrong to sacrifice three-quarters of a command to save a quarter; that no officer had a right to cause such a sacrifice. General Floyd and Major Gilmer I understood to concur in this opinion.

I then expressed the opinion that we could hold out another day, and in that time we could get steamboats and set the command over the river, and probably save a large portion of it. To this General Buckner replied that the enemy would certainly attack him at daylight, and that he could not hold his position half an hour.

The alternative of these propositions was a surrender of their position and command. General Floyd said that he would neither surrender the command, nor would he surrender himself a prisoner. I had taken the same position. General Buckner said he was satisfied nothing else could be done, and that, therefore, he would surrender if placed in command. General Floyd said he would turn over the command to him if he could be allowed to withdraw his command. To this General Buckner consented. Thereupon General Floyd turned the command over to me. I passsed it instantly to General Buckner, saying I would neither surrender the command nor myself a prisoner. I directed Colonel Forrest to cut his way out. Under these circumstances General Buckner accepted the command, and sent a flag of truce to the enemy for an armistice for six hours to negotiate for terms of capitulation. Before this flag and communication were delivered, I retired from the garrison. * * * * *

GID. J. PILLOW, *Brigadier-General, C. S. A.*

E.

GENERAL GRANT'S OFFICIAL REPORT.

HEAD-QUARTERS, DISTRICT OF WESTERN TENNESSEE,
PITTSBURG, *April* 9, 1862.

Captain N. H. McLEAN, *Assistant Adjutant-General, Department of Mississippi, St. Louis.*

CAPTAIN:—It becomes my duty again to report another battle, fought by two great armies, one contending for the maintenance of the best government ever devised, and the other for its destruction. It is pleasant to record the success of the army contending for the former principle.

On Sunday morning our pickets were attacked and driven in by the enemy. Immediately the five divisions stationed at this place were drawn up in line of battle to meet them.

The battle soon waxed warm on the left and centre, varying at times to all parts of the line. There was the most continuous firing of musketry and artillery ever heard on this continent kept up until nightfall.

The enemy, having forced the entire line to fall back nearly half way from their camps to the landing, at a late hour in the afternoon a desperate effort was made by the enemy to turn our left and get possession of the landing, transports, etc.

This point was guarded by the gunboats Tyler and Lexington, Captains Gwin and Shirk commanding, with four twenty-four pounder Parrott guns, and a battery of rifled guns.

As there is a deep and impassable ravine for artillery or cavalry, and very difficult for infantry, at this point, no troops were stationed here, except the necessary artillerists and a small infantry force for their support. Just at this moment the advnce of Major-General Buell's column and a part of the division of General Nelson arrived. The two generals named both being present, an advance was immediately made upon the point of attack, and the enemy was soon driven back.

In this repulse much is due to the presence of the gunboats Tyler and Lexington, and their able commanders, Captains Gwin and Shirk.

During the night, the divisions under Generals Crittenden and McCook arrived.

General Lewis Wallace, at Camp Landing, six miles below, was ordered, at an early hour in the morning, to hold his division in readiness to move in any direction it might be ordered. At eleven o'clock the order was delivered to move it up to Pittsburg; but, owing to its being led by a circuitous route, it did not arrive in time to take part in Sunday's action.

During the night all was quiet, and, feeling that great moral advantage would be gained by becoming the attacking party, an advance was ordered as soon as day dawned. The result was the gradual repulse of the enemy at all points of the line, from nine until probably five o'clock in the afternoon, when it became evident the enemy was retreating.

Before the close of the action, the advance of General T. J. Wood's division arrived in time to take part in the action.

My force was too much fatigued from two days' hard fighting, and exposure in the open air to a drenching rain during the intervening night, to pursue immediately.

Night closed in cloudy, with a heavy rain, making the roads impracticable for artillery by the next morning.

General Sherman, however, followed the enemy, finding that the main part of their army had retreated in good order.

Hospitals, with the enemy's wounded, were found all along the road as far as pursuit was made. Dead bodies of the enemy, and many graves were also found. I inclose herewith a report of General Sherman, which will explain more fully the result of the pursuit and of the part taken by each separate command.

I cannot take special notice in this report, but will do so more fully when the reports of the division commanders are handed in.

General Buell, commanding in the field, with a distinct army long under his command, and which did such efficient service commanded by himself in person, on the field, will be much better able to notice those officers' commands, who particularly distinguished themselves, than I possibly can.

I feel it a duty, however, to a gallant and able officer, Brigadier-General W. T. Sherman, to make a special mention. He not only was with his command during the entire two days of the action, but displayed great judgment and skill in the management of his men. Although severely wounded in the hand on the first day, his place was never vacant. He was again wounded, and had three horses killed under him. In making this mention of a gallant officer, no disparagement is intended to other division commanders or Major-Generals John A. McClernand and Lewis Wallace, and Brigadier-Generals S. A. Hurlbut, P. M. Prentiss and W. H. L. Wallace, all of whom maintained their places with credit to themselves and the cause.

General Prentiss was taken prisoner on the first day's action, and General W. H. L. Wallace was severely and probably mortally wounded. His Assistant Adjutant-General, Captain Wm. McMichael, is missing, and was probably taken prisoner.

My personal staff are all deserving of particular mention, they having been engaged during the entire two days, in carrying orders to every part of the field. It consists of Colonel J. D. Webster, Chief-of-Staff; Lieutenant-Colonel, J. B. McPherson, Chief of Engineers, assisted by Lieutenants W. L. B. Jenney, and Wm. Kossac; Captain J. A. Rawlins, Assistant Adjutant-General W. S. Hilger, W. R. Rawley, and C. B. Lagow, Aides-de-Camp; Colonel G. Pride, Volunteer Aide, and Captain J. P. Hawkins, Chief Commissary, who accompanied me upon the field.

The Medical Department, under direction of Surgeon Hewitt, Medical Director, showed great energy in providing for the wounded, and in getting them from the field, regardless of danger.

Colonel Webster was placed in special charge of all the artillery, and was constantly upon the field. He displayed, as always heretofore, both skill and bravery. At least, in one instance, he was the means of placing an entire regiment in position of doing most valuable service, and where it would not have been but for his exertions.

Lieutenant-Colonel McPherson, attached to my staff as Chief of Engineers, deserves more than a passing notice for his activity and courage. All the grounds beyond our camps for miles, have been reconnoitred by him, and the plans, carefully prepared under his supervision, give the most accurate information of the nature of the approaches to our lines. During the two days' battle, he was constantly in the saddle, leading the troops, as they arrived, to points where their services were required. During the engagement, he had one horse shot under him.

The country will have to mourn the loss of many brave men who fell at the battle of Pittsburg, or Shiloh, more properly.

The exact loss in killed and wounded, will be known in a day or two. At present I can only give it approximately at fifteen hundred killed, and thirty-five hundred wounded.

The loss of artillery was great, many pieces being disabled by the enemy's shots, and some losing all their horses and many men. There were probably not less than two hundred horses killed.

The loss of the enemy, in killed and left upon the field, was greater than ours. In the wounded an estimate cannot be made, as many of them must have been sent to Corinth and other points.

The enemy suffered terribly from demoralization and desertion.

A flag of truce was sent in to-day from General Beauregard. I inclose herewith a copy of the correspondence.

I am, respectfully, your obedient servant,

U. S. GRANT, *Maj.-Gen. Commanding.*

F.

THE BATTLE OF PITTSBURG LANDING AND MAJOR-GENERAL GRANT.

Remarks of Hon. E. B. WASHBURNE, *of Ill., in the House of Representatives, May* 2, 1862.

MR. SPEAKER:—I will only trouble the House for a few moments, but when justice claims to be heard, it is said that a nation should be silent. Lamartine, in his celebrated History of the Girondins, speaking of one of those incidents so characteristic of the French Revolution, says:

"The news of the victory of Hondschoote filled Paris with joy. But even the joy of the people was cruel. The Convention reproached as a treason the victory of a victorious general. Its commissioners to the army of the North, Hentz, Peyssard, and Duquesnoy, deposed Houchard, and sent him to the revolutionary tribunal." * * * "The unfortunate Houchard was condemned to death, and met his fate with the intrepidity of a soldier and the calmness of an innocent man." * * * "It was shown that even victory was not protection against the scaffold."

It may be inquired whether in this rebellion history is not repeating itself. I come before the House to do a great act of justice to a soldier in the field, and to vindicate him from the obloquy and misrepresentations so persistently and cruelly thrust before the country. I refer to a distinguished general who has recently fought the bloodiest and hardest battle ever fought on this continent, and won one of the most brilliant victories. I refer to the battle of Pittsburg Landing, and to Major-General Ulysses S. Grant. A native of Ohio, he graduated at West Point, July 1st, 1843, with the brevet rank of second-lieutenant, and was appointed second-lieutenant, September 30th, 1845. Though but 40 years old, he has been oftener under fire and been in more battles than any other man living on this continent, excepting that great chieftain now reposing on his laurels and on the affections of his countrymen, Lieutenant-General Scott. He was in every battle in Mexico that was possible for any one man to be in. He followed the victorious standard of General Taylor on the Rio Grande, and was in the battles of Palo Alto, Resaca de la Palma, and Monterey. He was with General Scott at Vera Cruz, and participated in every battle from the Gulf to the city of Mexico. He was breveted first-lieutenant September 8, 1847, for gallant and meritorious conduct at the battle of Molino del Rey, and on the 13th of the same month he was breveted captain for gallant and meritorious conduct at the battle of Chapultepec. He has received the baptismal of fire. No young officer came out of the Mexican war with more distinction than Grant, and the records of the War Department bear official testimony to his gallant and noble deeds. He resigned in 1855, and afterwards settled in Galena, in the district I have the honor to represent on this floor. I will read from reports in the War Department.

[The reports alluded to were then read aloud.]

Grant was among the first to offer his services to the country at the commencement of hostilities, saying that as he had been educated by the Government, that Government was entitled to his services in its time of peril. Early made a colonel of one of the Illinois regiments, he went into actual service in Missouri. His commands there were important, and he discharged every duty with great fidelity and advantage to the public service. With a military head and a military hand, he everywhere evoked order from chaos. Military discipline, order, and economy, travelled in his path. In time he was made a brigadier-general, and intrusted with the important command of the district of Cairo; and how diligently, how faithfully, how satisfactorily he discharged all his duties is well known to the country. While in that command, learning of a movement about being made by the rebels at Columbus to send out a large force to cut off Colonel Oglesby, who had gone into Missouri after that roaming bandit, Jeff Thompson, by a sudden and masterly stroke he fell upon Belmont, and after a brilliant and decisive action, in which he and all his troops displayed great bravery, he broke up the rebel camp with great loss, and then returned to Cairo. The expedition was broken up, Oglesby's command was saved, and every thing was accomplished that was expected.

In time came the operations up the Cumberland and Tennessee Rivers, and I state what I know. By a singular coincidence, on the 29th day of January last, without any suggestion from any source, General Grant and Commodore Foote, always acting in entire harmony, applied for permission to move up those rivers, which was granted. The gunboats and land forces moved up to Fort Henry. After that fort was taken it was determined to attack Fort Donelson. The gunboats were to go round and up the Cumberland River, while the army was to move overland from Fort Henry to Fort Donelson.

The roads were the worst ever known, and almost any other general or any other troops would have despaired of moving. But they did move. If General Grant had been told that it was impossible to move his army there, he would have made a reply like to that of the royal Pompey, when he was told that his fleet could not sail: "It is necessary to sail, not necessary to live." It was necessary for this western army to march, but it was not necessary to live. The country knows the result —Donelson fell. The enemy, twenty thousand strong, behind his intrenchments, succumbed before the unrelenting bravery and vigor of our troops, no more than twenty-eight thousand engaged. We took there, not twelve thousand, not fifteen thousand, but more than *sixteen thousand* prisoners. I have it from General Halleck that we have actually paid transportation for more than sixteen thousand prisoners. That, in most countries, would have been called a most brilliant military achievement. Napoleon surrounded Old Mack at Ulm, and captured twenty thousand or more prisoners, and that exploit has filled a great space in history.

While the capture of Donelson filled the country with joy, there was a cruel disposition to withhold from the commanding general the meed of gratitude and praise so justly his due. Captious criticisms were indulged in that he did not make the attack properly, and that if he had done differently the work might have been better accomplished. It was not enough that he fought and gloriously conquered, but he ought to have done it differently, forsooth. Success could be no test of merit with him. That was the way the old generals spoke of the young Napoleon when he was beating them in every battle, and carrying his eagles in triumph over all Europe. He did not fight according to the rules of war. But there was a more grievous suggestion touching the general's habits. It is a suggestion that has infused itself into the public mind everywhere. There never was a more cruel and atrocious slander upon a brave and noble-minded man. There is no more temperate man in the army than General Grant. He never indulges in the use of intoxicating liquors at all. He is an example of courage, honor, fortitude, activity, temperance, and modesty, for he is as modest as he is brave and incorruptible. To the bravery and fortitude of Lannes, he adds the stern republican simplicity of Guvion St. Cyr. It is almost vain to hope that full justice will ever be done to men who have been thus attacked. Truth is slow upon the heels of falsehood. It has been well said that "falsehood will travel from Maine to Georgia while truth is putting on its boots."

Let no gentleman have any fears of General Grant. He is no candidate for the Presidency. He is no politician. Inspired by the noblest patriotism, he only desires to do his whole duty to his country. When the war shall be over he will return to his home, and sink the soldier in the simple citizen. Though living in the same town with myself, he has no political claims on me, for, so far as he is a politician, he belongs to a different party. He has no personal claims upon me more than any other constituent. But I came here to speak as an Illinoisian, proud of his noble and patriotic State; proud of its great history now being made up; proud above all earthly things of her brave soldiers, who are shedding their blood upon all the battle-fields of the Republic. If the laurels of Grant shall ever be withered, it will not be done by the Illinois soldiers who have followed his victorious banner.

But to the victory at Pittsburg Landing, which has called forth such a flood of denunciation upon General Grant. When we consider the charges of bad generalship, incompetency, and surprise, do we not feel that "even the joy of the people is cruel?" As to the question of whether there was, or not, what might be called a surprise, I will not argue it; but even if there had been, General Grant is nowise responsible for it, for *he* was not surprised. He was at his head-quarters at Savannah when the fight commenced. Those head-quarters were established there, as being the most convenient point for all parts of his command. Some of the troops were at Crump's Landing, between Savannah and Pittsburg, and all the new arrivals were coming to Savannah. That was the proper place for the head-quarters of the commanding general at that time. The general visited Pittsburg Landing and all the important points every day. The attack was made Sunday morning by a vastly superior force. In five minutes after the first firing was heard, General Grant and staff were on board a steamboat on the way to the battle-field, and instead of not reaching the field till ten o'clock, or, as has been still more falsely represented, till noon, I have a letter before me from one of his aides who was with him, and who says he arrived there at eight o'clock in the morning, and immediately assumed command. There he directed the movements, and was always on that part of the field where his presence was most required, exposing his life, and evincing in his dispositions, the genius of the greatest commanders. With what desperate bravery that battle of Sunday was fought! what display of prowess and courage! what prodigies of valor! Our troops, less than forty thousand, attacked by more than eighty thousand of the picked men of the rebels, led by their most distinguished generals!

But it is gravely charged by these military critics who sit by the fireside while our soldiers are risking their lives on the field of conflict, that Grant was to blame in having his troops on the same side of the river with the enemy. I suppose they would have the river interpose between our army and the enemy, and permit that enemy to intrench himself on the other side, and then undertake to cross in his face. It was, in the judgment of the best military men, a wise disposition of his forces, placing them where he did. To have done otherwise, would have been like keeping the entire army of the Potomac on this side of the river, instead of crossing it when it could be done, and advancing on the other side.

After fighting all day with immensely superior numbers of the enemy, they only drove our forces back two and one half miles, and then it was to face the gunboats and the terrible batteries so skilfully arranged and worked by the gallant and accomplished officers, Webster and Callender, and which brought the countless host of the enemy to a stand. And when night came, this unconquerable army stood substantially triumphant on that bloody field. I am not here to speak disparagingly of the troops of any other State, but I will speak in praise of the troops of my own State. No Illinois regiment, no Illinois company, no Illinois soldier, fled from the battle-field. If any did flee, they were not from Illinois, and they would be the ones who, after their own flight, would seek to cover up their own disgrace, but only add to it, by attacks upon an Illinois general.

Now, sir, I have something to say about the generals and the soldiers who fought in the battle. I have a word to say about the brave McClernand, so lately our colleague here, who, as I learn from a man who was on the battle-field on that Sunday, and was seen riding at the head of his division, holding his flag in the face of the enemy, daring them to come on. I would say something in relation to the bravery and skill of Hurlbut, from my own district, who commanded another division there, and won great glory. I would say something in defence of another man who has been charged with having his division surprised, and having been taken prisoner at the time. I mean General Prentiss. I have a letter upon my desk which says, that instead of being surprised on Sunday morning, the writer saw him at half past two o'clock of that day fighting most gallantly at the head of his division. I rejoice to have this opportunity to make that statement in justice to a brave man and true soldier.

Sir, if I had time I would like to speak of others; I would speak of General Wallace of my State, who fell nobly fighting at the head of his division, a soldier by nature, a pure and noble man, whose memory will be ever honored in Illinois. I would speak of the gallant Colonel Ellis, falling at the head of the Fifteenth, and of Major Goddard, of the same regiment, also killed; of Davis, of the Forty-sixth, terribly wounded while gallantly bearing in his own hands the colors of his regiment. I would speak of the deeds of valor of the lead-mine Forty-fifth, covering itself with undying honor; of Captains Connor and Johnson, falling at the head of their companies; of the genial and impetuous young Irishman, Lieutenant George Moore, mortally wounded; of Captains Wayne and Nase and Brownell, all killed. Nor would I fail to mention Brigadier-General McArthur and Acting Brigadier-General Kirk, who boldly led their brigades everywhere where duty called and danger threatened, and were at last carried from the field badly wounded. And of Colonel Chetlain of the old Twelfth, rising from a sick-bed and entering into the thickest of the fight. And, too, I would like to speak of the dauntless valor of Rawlins and Rowley and Campbell, and of many others who distinguished themselves on that field.

I see before me my friend from Pennsylvania [Mr. McPherson], which reminds me of a friend of us both—young Baugher, a lieutenant in the lead-mine regiment, who, wounded six times, refused to leave the field; and when finally carried off, waved his sword in defiance to the enemy. But who shall attempt to do justice to the bravery of the soldiers and the daring and skill of the officers; who shall describe all the valor exhibited on those days; who shall presume to speak of all the glory won on that blood-stained field? I have spoken of those more particularly from my own part of the State; but it is because I know them best, and not because I claim more credit for them than I know to be due to the troops from all parts of the State. They all exhibited the same bravery, the same unbounded devotion, the same ardor in vindicating the honor and glory of the flag, and maintaining the prestige of our State.

Mr. WILSON. I desire to ask the gentleman whether he denies that the army was surprised at Pittsburg on the morning of Sunday?

Mr. WASHBURNE. I state that I have the fullest authority for making a substantial denial of that charge. I said, however, that I did not intend to argue that question; that it was not necessary for the defence of General Grant. But I say, whether there was a surprise or not, the manner in which all those gallant troops fought on that day has conferred upon them and upon the country imperishable renown.

Mr. WILSON. I desire to ask, admitting that it was a surprise, whose fault it was?

Mr. WASHBURNE. I suppose if there had been a surprise it would have been the fault of the man who commanded the division surprised. I come not here, however, to speak of the faults of anybody, but to do justice.

Mr. WILSON. I desire the gentleman to follow that a little further.

Mr. KELLOGG, of Illinois. I want to say a word before the gentleman from Iowa proceeds. My colleague (Mr. Washburne) has defended his friend well. I regret the disposition to find fault with our generals in the field, who have done so nobly, so bravely, and so well. Let us remember only their prowess and their glory, and let there not be crimination and recrimination. Let us rather glory in the success of our arms in our brilliant achievements on the well-fought field, and say all have done well. I regret that this matter of crimination of officers in the field should be brought up.

Mr. WILSON. I will state that I fully concur in the remark of the gentleman from Illinois (Mr. Kellogg) last on the floor, that this matter ought not to have been brought up here, and I for one do not intend to join in any crimination or recrimination. I have thought the whole thing out of taste. I have thought it improper and uncalled for. There was no occasion for it at all that I can discover. No charge has been made here against General Grant or any other officer engaged in that contest, although there are very grave differences of opinion in relation to certain matters connected with the fight.

Mr. WASHBURNE. I cannot yield further. Whatever may be my friend's opinion on the subject, I say to him that whenever I find a general from my own State at the head of an army attacked as General Grant has been, I will feel myself called upon, in all places and upon all occasions, to defend him, and I think this is the best occasion I shall have, and I intend to avail myself of it. I believe, notwithstanding the desperate fighting on Sunday, and the partial repulse of our troops, that, aided by the fresh troops of the brave Lew. Wallace, that army could have whipped the enemy on Monday without further re-enforcements. That army could never have been conquered. But I would not detract from the glorious fighting of Buell's troops on Monday, for they behaved with great gallantry and fought bravely, successfully, and well. Justice must be done to all. By a general order, General Halleck, now on the spot and cognizant of all the facts, has publicly thanked the generals, Grant, Buell, and Sherman, indorsing their bravery and skill.

Sir, I have detained the House too long, but I have felt called upon to say this much. I came only to claim public justice; the battle of Pittsburg Landing, though a bloody one, yet it will make a bright page in our history. The final charge of General Grant at the head of his reserves will have a place, too, in history. While watching the progress of the battle on Monday afternoon, word came to him that the enemy was faltering on the left. With the genius that belongs only to the true military man, he saw that the time for the final blow had come. In quick words he said, "Now is the time to drive them." It was worthy the world-renowned order of Wellington, "Up Guards, and at them."

Word was sent by his body-guard to the different regiments to be ready to charge when the order was given; then, riding out in front amid a storm of bullets, he led the charge in person, and Beauregard was driven howling to his intrenchments. His left was broken, and a retreat commenced which soon degenerated into a perfect rout. The loss of the enemy was three to our two in men, and in much greater proportion in the demoralization of an army which follows a defeat. That battle has laid the foundation for finally driving the rebels from the Southwest. So much for the battle of Pittsburg Landing, which has evoked such unjust and cruel criticism, but which history will record as one of the most glorious victories that has ever illustrated the annals of a great nation.

G

CAPITULATION OF VICKSBURG.

REPORT OF THE OPERATIONS OF THE ARMY OF THE TENNESSEE, FROM THE DAY MAJOR-GENERAL U. S. GRANT ASSUMED IMMEDIATE COMMAND OF THE EXPEDITION AGAINST VICKSBURG TO THE SURRENDER OF THAT PLACE.

HEAD-QUARTERS, DEPARTMENT OF THE TENNESSEE,
VICKSBURG, MISS., *July* 6, 1863.

COLONEL:—I have the honor to submit the following report of the operations of the Army of the Tennessee and co-operating forces, from the date of my assuming the immediate command of the expedition against Vicksburg, Mississippi, to the reduction of that place.

From the moment of taking command in person I became satisfied that Vicksburg could only be turned from the south side, and, in accordance with this conviction, I prosecuted the work on the canal, which had been located by Brigadier-General Williams, across the peninsula, on the Louisiana side of the river, with all vigor, hoping to make a channel which would pass transports for moving the army and carrying supplies to the new base of operations thus provided. The task was much more herculean than it at first appeared, and was made much more so by the almost continuous rains that fell during the whole of the time this work was prosecuted. The river, too, continued to rise and make a large expenditure of labor necessary to keep the water out of our camps and the canal.

Finally, on the 8th of March, the rapid rise of the river and the consequent great pressure upon the dam across the canal, near the upper end, at the main Mississippi levee, caused it to give way and let through the low lands back of our camps a torrent of water that separated the north and south shores of the peninsula as effectually as if the Mississippi flowed between them. This occurred when the enterprise promised success within a short time. There was some delay in trying to repair damages. It was found, however, that with the then stage of water some other plan would have to be adopted for getting below Vicksburg with transports.

Captain F. E. Prime, Chief Engineer, and Colonel G. G. Pride, who was acting on my staff, prospected a route through the bayous which run from near Milliken's Bend on the north and New Carthage on the south through Roundaway Bayou into the Tansas River. Their report of the practicability of this route determined me to commence work upon it. Having three dredge boats at the time, the work of opening this route was executed with great rapidity. One small steamer and a number of barges were taken through the channel thus opened, but the river commencing about the middle of April to fall rapidly, and the roads becoming passable between Milliken's Bend and New Carthage, made it impracticable and unnecessary to open water communication between these points.

Soon after commencing the first canal spoken of I caused a channel to be cut from the Mississippi River into Lake Providence; also one from the Mississippi River into Coldwater, by way of Yazoo Pass.

I had no great expectations of important results from the former of these, but having more troops than could be employed to advantage at Young's Point, and knowing that Lake Providence was connected by Bayou Baxter with Bayou Macon, a navigable stream through which transports might pass into the Mississippi below, through Tansas, Wachita, and Red Rivers, I thought it possible that a route might be opened in that direction which would enable me to co-operate with General Banks at Port Hudson.

By the Yazoo Pass route I only expected at first to get into the Yazoo by way of Coldwater and Tallahatchie with some lighter gunboats and a few troops, and destroy the enemy's transports in that stream and some gunboats which I knew he was building. The navigation, however, proved so much better than had been expected, that I thought for a time of the possibility of making this the route for obtaining the foothold on high land above Haines's Bluff, Mississippi, and small class steamers were accordingly ordered for transporting an army that way. Major-General J. B. McPherson, commanding Seventeenth Army Corps, was directed to hold his corps in readiness to move by this route; and one division from each the Thirteenth and Fifteenth Corps were collected near the entrance of the pass to be added to his command. It soon became evident that a sufficient number of boats of the right class could not be obtained for the movement of more than one division.

Whilst my forces were opening one end of the pass the enemy was diligently closing the other end, and in this way succeeded in gaining time to strongly fortify Greenwood, below the junction of the Tallahatchie and Yallobusha. The advance of the expedition, consisting of one division of McClernand's Corps from Helena, commanded by Brigadier-General L. F. Ross, and the Twelfth and Seventeenth regiments Missouri Infantry, from Sherman's Corps, as sharpshooters on the gunboats, succeeded in reaching Coldwater on the 2d day of March, after much difficulty, and the partial disabling of most of the boats. From the entrance into Coldwater to Fort Pemberton, at Greenwood, Mississippi, no great difficulty of navigation was experienced, nor any interruption of magnitude from the enemy. Fort Pemberton extends from the Tallahatchie to the Yazoo at Greenwood. Here the two rivers come within a few hundred yards of each other. The land around the fort is low, and at the time of the attack was entirely overflowed. Owing to this fact no movement could be made by the army to reduce it, but all depended upon the ability of the gunboats to silence the guns of the enemy and enable the transports to run down and land troops immediately on the fort itself. After an engagement of several hours the gunboats drew off, being unable to silence the batteries. Brigadier-General J. F. Quimby, commanding a division of McPherson's Corps, met the expedition under Ross with his division on its return near Fort Pemberton, on the 21st of March, and, being the senior, assumed command of the entire expedition, and returned to the position Ross had occupied.

On the 23d day of March I sent orders for the withdrawal of all the forces operating in that direction, for the purpose of concentrating my army at Milliken's Bend.

On the 14th day of March Admiral D. D. Porter, commanding Mississippi squadron, informed me that he had made a reconnoissance up Steele's Bayou, and partially through Black Bayou towards Deer Creek, and so far as explored these water courses were reported navigable for the smaller iron-clads. Information given mostly, I believe, by the negroes of the country, was to the effect that Deer Creek could be navigated to Rolling Fork, and that from there, through the Sunflower to the Yazoo River, there was no question about the navigation. On the following morning I accompanied Admiral Porter in the ram Price —seven iron-clads preceding us—up through Steele's Bayou to near Black Bayou.

At this time our forces were at a dead-lock at Greenwood, and I looked upon the success of this enterprise as of vast importance. It would, if successful, leave Greenwood between two forces of ours, and would necessarily cause the immediate abandonment of that stronghold.

About thirty steamers of the enemy would have been destroyed or fallen into our hands. Seeing that the great obstacle to navigation, so far as I had gone, was from overhanging trees, I left Admiral Porter near Black Bayou and pushed back to Young's Point for the purpose of sending forward a pioneer corps to remove these difficulties. Soon after my return to Young's Point, Admiral Porter sent back to me for a co-operating military force. Sherman was promptly sent with one division of his corps. The number of steamers suitable for the navigation of these bayous being limited, most of the force was sent up the Mississippi River to Eagle's Bend, a point where the river runs within one mile of Steele's Bayou, thus saving an important part of this difficult navigation. The expedition failed, probably more from want of knowledge as to what would be required to open this route than from any impracticability in the navigation of the streams and bayous through which it was proposed to pass. Want of this knowledge led the expedition on until difficulties were encountered, and then it would become necessary to send back to Young's Point for the means of removing them. This gave the enemy time to move forces to effectually checkmate further progress, and the expedition was withdrawn when within a few hundred yards of free and open navigation to the Yazoo.

All this may have been providential in driving us ultimately to a line of operations which has proven eminently successful.

For further particulars of the Steele's Bayou expedition see report of Major-General W. T. Sherman, forwarded on the 12th of April.

As soon as I decided to open water communication from a point on the Mississippi near Milliken's Bend to New Carthage. I determined to occupy the latter place, it being the first point below Vicksburg that could be reached by land at the stage of water then existing, and the occupancy of which, while it secured to us a point on the Mississippi River, would also protect the main line of communication by water. Accordingly, the Thirteenth Army Corps, Major-General J. A. McClernand commanding, was directed to take up its line of march on the 29th day of March for New Carthage, the Fifteenth and Seventeenth Corps to follow, moving no faster than supplies and ammunition could be transported to them.

The roads though level were intolerably bad, and the movement was therefore necessarily slow. Arriving at Smith's plantation, two miles from New Carthage, it was found that the levee of Bayou Vidal was broken in several places, thus leaving New Carthage an island.

All the boats that could be were collected from the different bayous in the vicinity, and others were built, but the transportation of an army in this way was found exceedingly tedious. Another route had to be found. This was done by making a further march around Vidal to Perkins's plantation, a distance of twelve miles more, making the whole distance to be marched from Milliken's Bend to reach water communication on the opposite side of the point thirty-five miles. Over this distance, with bad roads to contend against, supplies of ordnance stores and provisions had to be hauled by wagons, with which to commence the campaign on the opposite side of the river.

At the same time that I ordered the occupation of New Carthage, preparations were made for running transports by the Vicksburg batteries with Admiral Porter's gunboat fleet.

On the night of the 16th of April Admiral Porter's fleet and the transports Silver Wave, Forest Queen, and Henry Clay, ran the Vicksburg batteries. The boilers of the transports were protected as well as possible with hay and cotton. More or less commissary stores were put on each. All three of these boats were struck more or less frequently while passing the enemy's batteries, and the Henry Clay, by the explosion of a shell or by other means, was set on fire and entirely consumed. The other two boats were somewhat injured, but not seriously disabled. No one on board of either was hurt.

As these boats succeeded in getting by so well, I ordered six more to be prepared in like manner for running the batteries. These latter, viz.: Tigress, Anglo-Saxon, Cheeseman, Empire City, Horizonia, and Moderator, left Milliken's Bend on the night of the 22d of April, and five of them got by, but in a somewhat damaged condition. The Tigress received a shot in her hull below the water line, and sunk on the Louisiana shore soon after passing the last of the batteries. The crews of these steamers, with the exception of that of the Forest Queen, Captain D. Conway, and the Silver Wave, Captain McMillen, were composed of volunteers from the army. Upon the call for volunteers for this dangerous enterprise, officers and men presented themselves by hundreds, anxious to undertake the trip. The names of those whose services were accepted will be given in a separate report.

It is a striking feature, so far as my observation goes, of the present volunteer army of the United States, that there is nothing which men are called upon to do, mechanical or professional, that accomplished adepts cannot be found for the duty required in almost every regiment.

The transports injured in running the blockade were repaired by order of Admiral Porter, who was supplied with the material for such repairs as they required, and who was and is ever ready to afford all the assistance in his power for the furtherance of the success of our arms. In a very short time five of the transports were in running order, and the remainder were in condition to be used as barges in the moving of troops. Twelve barges loaded with forage and rations were sent in tow of the last six boats that run the blockade; one-half of them got through in a condition to be used.

Owing to the limited number of transports below Vicksburg it was found necessary to extend our line of land travel to Hard Times, Louisiana, which, by the circuitous route it was necessary to take, increased the distance to about seventy miles from Milliken's Bend our starting point.

The Thirteenth Army Corps being all through to the Mississippi, and the Seventeenth Army Corps well on the way, so much of the Thirteenth as could be got on board the transports and barges were put aboard and moved to the front of Grand Gulf on the 29th of April. The plan here was that the navy should silence the guns of the enemy, and the troops land under cover of the gunboats and carry the place by storm.

At eight o'clock A. M. the navy made the attack, and kept it up for more than five hours in the most gallant manner. From a tug out in the stream I witnessed the whole engagement. Many times it seemed to me the gunboats were within pistol shot of the enemy's batteries. It soon became evident that the guns of the enemy were too elevated and their fortifications too strong to be taken from the water side. The whole range of hills on that side were known to be lined with rifle pits, besides the field artillery could be moved to any position where it could be made useful in case of an attempt at landing. This determined me to run again the enemy's batteries, turn his position by effecting a landing at Rodney, or at Bruinsburg, between Grand Gulf and Rodney. Accordingly, orders were immediately given for the troops to debark at Hard Times, Louisiana, and march across to the point immediately below Grand Gulf. At dark the gunboats again engaged the batteries, and all the transports run by, receiving but two or three shots in the passage, and these without injury. I had some time previously ordered a reconnoissance to a point opposite Bruinsburg, to ascertain if possible from persons in the neighborhood the character of the road leading to the highlands back of Bruinsburg. During the night I learned from a negro man that there was a good road from Bruinsburg to Port Gibson, which determined me to land there.

The work of ferrying the troops to Bruinsburg was commenced at daylight in the morning, the gunboats as well as transports being used for the purpose.

As soon as the Thirteenth Army Corps was landed, and could draw three days' rations to put in haversacks (no wagons were allowed to cross until the troops were all over), they were started on the road to Port Gibson. I deemed it a matter of vast importance that the highlands should be reached without resistance.

The Seventeenth Corps followed as rapidly as it could be put across the river.

About two o'clock on the 1st of May the advance of the enemy was met eight miles from Bruinsburg, on the road to Port Gibson. He was forced to fall back, but as it was dark he was not pursued far until daylight. Early on the morning of the 1st I went out, accompanied by members of my staff, and found McClernand with his corps engaging the enemy about four miles from Port Gibson. At this point the roads branched in exactly opposite directions, both, however, leading to Port Gibson. The enemy had taken position on both branches, thus dividing as he fell back the pursuing forces. The nature of the ground in that part of the country is such that a very small force could retard the progress of a much larger one for many hours, The roads usually run on narrow, elevated ridges, with deep and impenetrable ravines on either side. On the right were the divisions of Hovey, Carr, and Smith, and on the left the division of Osterhaus, of McClernand's Corps. The three former succeeded in driving the enemy from position to position back towards Port Gibson steadily all day.

Osterhaus did not, however, move the enemy from the position occupied by him on our left until Logan's Division, of McPherson's Corps, arrived.

McClernand, who was with the right in person, sent repeated messages to me before the arrival of Logan to send Logan's and Quimby's Divisions, of McPherson's Corps, to him.

I had been on that as well as all other parts of the field, and could not see how they could be used there to advantage. However, as soon as the advance of McPherson's Corps (Logan's Division) arrived, I sent one brigade to McClernand on the right, and sent one brigade, Brigadier-General J E. Smith commanding, to the left to the assistance of Osterhaus.

By the judicious disposition made of this brigade, under the immediate supervision of McPherson and Logan, a position was soon obtained giving us an advantage which soon drove the enemy from that part of the field, to make no further stand south of Bayou Pierre.

The enemy was here repulsed with a heavy loss in killed, wounded, and prisoners. The repulse of the enemy on our left took place late in the afternoon. He was pursued towards Port Gibson, but night closing in, and the enemy making the appearance of another stand, the troops slept upon their arms until daylight.

In the morning it was found that the enemy had retreated across Bayou Pierre, on the Grand Gulf road, and a brigade of Logan's Division was sent to divert his attention whilst a floating bridge was being built across Bayou Pierre immediately at Port Gibson. This bridge was completed, eight miles marched by McPherson's Corps to the north fork of Bayou Pierre, that stream bridged, and the advance of this Corps commenced passing over it at five o'clock the following morning.

On the 3d the enemy was pursued to Hawkinson's Ferry, with slight skirmishing all day, during which we took quite a number of prisoners, mostly stragglers, from the enemy.

Finding that Grand Gulf had been evacuated, and that the advance of my forces was already fifteen miles out from there, and on the road, too, they would have to take to reach either Vicksburg, Jackson, or any intermediate point on the railroad between the two places, I determined not to march them back, but taking a small escort of cavalry, some fifteen or twenty men, I went to the Gulf myself, and made the necessary arrangements for changing my base of supplies from Bruinsburg to Grand Gulf.

In moving from Milliken's Bend, the Fifteenth Army Corps, Major-General W. T. Sherman commanding, was left to be the last to start. To prevent heavy re-enforcements going from Vicksburg to the assistance of the Grand Gulf forces, I directed Sherman to make a demonstration on Haines's Bluff, and to make all the show possible. From information since received from prisoners captured, this ruse succeeded admirably.

It had been my intention, up to the time of crossing the Mississippi River, to collect all my forces at Grand Gulf, and get on hand a good supply of provisions and ordnance stores before moving, and in the mean time to detach an army corps to co-operate with General Banks on Port Hudson and effect a junction of our forces.

About this time I received a letter from General Banks giving his position west of the Mississippi River, and stating that he could return to Baton Rouge by the 10th of May; that by the reduction of Port Hudson he could join me with 12,000 men.

I learned about the same time that troops were expected at Jackson from the Southern cities with General Beauregard in command. To delay until the 10th of May, and for the reduction of Port Hudson after that, the accession of 12,000 men would not leave me relatively so strong as to move promptly with what I had. Information received from day to day of the movements of the enemy also impelled me to the course pursued. Whilst lying at Hawkinson's Ferry waiting for wagons, supplies, and Sherman's Corps, which had come forward in the mean time, demonstrations were made, successfully, I believe, to induce the enemy to think that route, and the one by Hall's Ferry above, were objects of much solicitude to me. Reconnoissances were made to the west side of the Big Black to within six miles of Warrenton. On the 7th of May an advance was ordered, McPherson's Corps keeping the road nearest Black River to Rocky Springs, McClernand's Corps keeping the ridge road from Willow Springs, and Sherman following with his corps divided on the two roads. All the ferries were closely guarded until our troops were well advanced. It was my intention here to hug the Black River as closely as possible with McClernand's and Sherman's Corps, and get them to the railroad, at some place between Edwards's Station and Bolton. McPherson was to move by way of Utica to Raymond, and from there into Jackson, destroying the railroad telegraph, public stores, etc., and push west to rejoin the main force. Orders were given to McPherson accordingly. Sherman was moved forward on the Edwards's Station road, crossing Fourteen-Mile Creek, at Dillon's Plantation; McClernand was moved across the same creek, further west, sending one division of his corps by the Baldwin's Ferry road as far as the river. At the crossing of Fourteen-Mile Creek both McClernand and Sherman had considerable skirmishing with the enemy to get possession of the crossing.

McPherson met the enemy near Raymond two brigades strong, under Gregg and Walker, on the same day engaged him, and after several hours' hard fighting, drove him, with heavy loss in killed, wounded, and prisoners. Many threw down their arms and deserted.

My position at this time was with Sherman's Corps, some seven miles west of Raymond, and about the centre of the army.

On the night of the 12th of May, after orders had been given for the corps of McClernand and Sherman to march towards the railroad by parallel roads, the former in the direction of Edwards's Station and the latter to a point on the railroad between Edwards's Station and Bolton, the order was changed, and both were directed to move towards Raymond.

This was in consequence of the enemy having retreated towards Jackson after his defeat at Raymond, and of information that re-enforcements were daily arriving at Jackson, and that General Joe Johnston was hourly expected there to take command in person. I therefore determined to make sure of that place and leave no enemy in my rear.

McPherson moved on the 13th to Clinton, destroyed the railroad and telegraph, and captured some important dispatches from General Pemberton to General Gregg, who had commanded the day before in the battle of Raymond. Sherman moved to a parallel position on the Mississippi Springs and Jackson road; McClernand moved to a point near Raymond.

The next day Sherman and McPherson moved their entire forces towards Jackson. The rain fell in torrents all the night before, and continued until about noon of that day, making the roads at first slippery, and then miry. Notwithstanding, the troops marched in excellent order, without straggling and in the best of spirits, about fourteen miles, and engaged the enemy about twelve o'clock, M., near Jackson. McClernand occupied Clinton with one division, Mississippi Springs with another, Raymond with a third, and had his fourth division and Blair's division of Sherman's Corps, with a wagon train still in the rear, near New Auburn, while McArthur, with one brigade of his division of McPherson's Corps, was moving towards Raymond on the Utica road. It was not the intention to move these forces any nearer Jackson, but to have them in a position where they would be in supporting distance if the resistance at Jackson should prove more obstinate than there seemed reason to expect.

The enemy marched out the bulk of his force on the Clinton road and engaged McPherson's Corps about two and half miles from the city. A small force of artillery and infantry took a strong position in front of Sherman about the same distance out. By a determined advance of our skirmishers these latter were soon driven within their rifle-pits just outside the city. It was impossible to ascertain the strength of the enemy at this part of the line in time to justify an immediate assault. Consequently McPherson's two divisions engaged the main bulk of the rebel garrison at Jackson, without further aid than the moral support given them by the knowledge the enemy had of a force to the south side of the city, and a few infantry and artillery of the enemy posted there to impede Sherman's progress. Sherman soon discovered the weakness of the enemy by sending a reconnoitring party to his right, which also had the effect of causing the enemy to retreat from this part of his line. A few of the artillerists, however, remained in their places, firing upon Sherman's troops, until the last moment, evidently instructed to do so, with the expectation of being captured in the end. On entering the city it was found that the main body of the enemy had retreated north, after a heavy engagement of more than two hours with McPherson', Corps, in which he was badly beaten. He was pursued until near night, but without further damage to him.

During that evening I learned that General Johnston, as soon as he had satisfied himself that Jackson was to be attacked, had ordered Pemberton peremptorily to march out from the direction of Vicksburg and attack our rear. Availing myself of this information, I immediately issued orders to McClernand, and Blair, of Sherman's Corps, to face their troops towards Bolton, with a view to reaching Edwards's Station, marching on different roads converging near Bolton. These troops were admirably located for such a move. McPherson was ordered to retrace his steps early in the morning of the 15th on the Clinton road. Sherman was left in Jackson to destroy the railroads, bridges, factories, workshops, arsenals, and every thing valuable for the support of the enemy. This was accomplished in the most effectual manner.

On the afternoon of the 15th I proceeded as far west as Clinton, through which place McPherson's Corps passed to within supporting distance of Hovey's Division of McClernand's Corps, which had moved that day on the same road to within one and a half miles of Bolton. On reaching Clinton, at a quarter to five P. M., I ordered McClernand to move his command early the next morning towards Edwards's Depot, marching so as to feel the enemy, if he encountered him, but not to bring on a general engagement unless he was confident he was able to defeat him; and also to order Blair to move with him.

About five o'clock on the morning of the 16th, two men, employees on the Jackson and Vicksburg Railroad, who had passed through Pemberton's army the night before, were brought to my head-quarters. They stated Pemberton's force to consist of about eighty regiments, with ten batteries of artillery, and that the whole force was estimated by the enemy at about twenty-five thousand men. From them I also learned the positions being taken up by the enemy, and his intention of attacking our rear. I had determined to leave one division of Sherman's Corps one day longer in Jackson, but this information determined me to bring his entire command up at once, and I accordingly dispatched him at 5.30 A. M., to move with all possible speed until he came up with the main force near Bolton. My dispatch reached him at 7.10 A. M., and his advance division was in motion in one hour from that time. A dispatch was sent to Blair at the same time, to push forward his division in the direction of Edwards's Station with all possible dispatch. McClernand was directed to establish communication between Blair and Osterhaus, of his corps, and keep it up, moving the former to the support of the latter. McPherson was ordered forward at 5.45 A. M., to join McClernand, and Lieutenant-Colonel Wilson, of my staff, was sent forward to communicate the information received, and with verbal instructions to McClernand as to the disposition of his forces. At an early hour I left for the advance, and on arriving at the crossing of the Vicksburg and Jackson Railroad with the road from Raymond to Bolton, I found McPherson's advance and his Pioneer Corps engaged in rebuilding a bridge on the former road that had been destroyed by the cavalry of Osterhaus's Division that had gone into Bolton the night before. The train of Hovey's Division was at a halt, and blocked up the road from further advance on the Vicksburg road. I ordered all quartermasters and wagonmasters to draw their teams to one side and make room for the passage of troops. McPherson was brought up by this road. Passing to the front, he found Hovey's Division of the Thirteenth Army Corps at a halt, with our skirmishers and the enemy's pickets near each other. Hovey was bringing his troops into line, ready for battle, and could have brought on an engagement at any moment. The enemy had taken up a very strong position on a narrow ridge, his left wing resting on a height where the road makes a sharp turn to the left approaching Vicksburg. The top of the ridge and the precipitous hillside to the left of the road are covered by a dense forest and undergrowth. To the right of the road the timber extends a short distance down the hill, and then opens into cultivated fields on a gentle slope and into a valley extending for a considerable distance. On the road and into the wooded ravine and hillside Hovey's Division was disposed for the attack. McPherson's two divisions—all of his corps with him on the march from Milliken's Bend (until Ransom's Brigade arrived that day after the battle)—were thrown to the right of the road, properly speaking to the enemy's rear. But I would not permit an attack to be commenced by our troops until I could hear from McClernand, who was advancing with four divisions, two of them on a road intersecting the Jackson road about one mile from where the troops above described were placed, and about the centre of the enemy's line; the other two divisions on a road still north and nearly the same distance off.

I soon heard from McClernand, through members of his staff, and my own, whom I had sent to him early in the morning, and found that by the nearest practicable route of communication he was two and a half miles distant. I sent several successive messages to him to push forward with all rapidity. There had been continuous firing between Hovey's skirmishers and the rebel advance, which, by eleven o'clock, grew into a battle. For some time this division bore the brunt of the conflict; but, finding the enemy too strong for them, at the instance of Hovey I directed first one and then a second brigade from Crocker's Division to re-enforce him. All this time Logan's Division was working upon the enemy's left and rear, and weakened his front attack most wonderfully. The troops here opposing us evidently far outnumbered ours. Expecting McClernand momentarily with four divisions, including Blair's, I never felt a doubt of the result. He did not arrive, however, until the enemy had been driven from the field, after a terrible contest of hours, with a heavy loss of killed, wounded, and prisoners, and a number of pieces of artillery. It was found afterward that the Vicksburg road, after following the ridge in a southerly direction for about one mile, and to where it intersected one of the Raymond roads, turns almost to the west, down the hill and across the valley in which Logan was operating on the rear of the enemy. One brigade of Logan's Division had, unconscious of this important fact, penetrated nearly to this road, and compelled the enemy to retreat to prevent capture. As it was, much of his artillery and Loring's Division of his army was cut off besides the prisoners captured. On the call of Hovey for more re-enforcements, just before the rout of the enemy commenced, I ordered McPherson to move what troops he could by a left flank around to the enemy's front. Logan rode up at this time and told me that if Hovey could make another dash at the enemy, he could come up from where he then was, and capture the greater part of their force. I immediately rode forward, and found the troops that had been so gallantly engaged for so many hours, withdrawn from their advanced position, and were filling their cartridge-boxes. I directed them to use all dispatch, and push forward as soon as possible, explaining to them the position of Logan's Division. Proceeding still further forward, expecting every moment to see the enemy, and reaching what had been his line, I found he was retreating. Arriving at the Raymond road, I saw to my left and on the next ridge a column of troops, which proved to be Carr's Division and McClernand with it in person; and to the left of Carr, Osterhaus's Division soon afterward appeared, with his skirmishers well in advance. I sent word to Osterhaus that the enemy was in full retreat, and to push up with all haste. The situation was soon explained, after which I ordered Carr to pursue with all speed to Black River, and cross it if he could, and to Osterhaus to follow. Some of McPherson's troops had already got into the road in advance; but having marched and engaged the enemy all day, they were fatigued, and gave the road to Carr, who continued the pursuit until after dark, capturing a train of cars loaded with commissary and ordnance stores and other property.

The delay in the advance of the troops immediately with McClernand was caused, no doubt, by the enemy presenting a front of artillery and infantry where it was impossible, from the nature of the ground and the density of the forest, to discover his numbers. As it was, the battle of Champion's Hill, or Baker's Creek, was fought mainly by Hovey's Division of McClernand's Corps and Logan's and Quimby's Divisions (the latter commanded by Brigadier-General M. M. Crocker) of McPherson's Corps.

Ransom's brigade, of McPherson's Corps, came on to the field where the main battle had been fought, immediately after the enemy had begun his retreat.

Word was sent to Sherman, at Bolton, of the result of the day's engagement, with directions to turn his corps towards Bridgeport, and to Blair to join him at this latter place.

At daylight on the 17th the pursuit was renewed, with McClernand's Corps in the advance. The enemy was found strongly posted on both sides of the Black River. At this point on Black River the bluffs extend to the water's edge on the west bank. On the east side is an open, cultivated bottom, of near one mile in width, surrounded by a bayou of stagnant water, from two to three feet in depth, and from ten to twenty feet in width, from the river above the railroad to the river below. Following the inside line of this bayou, the enemy had constructed rifle-pits, with the bayou to serve as a ditch on the outside and immediately in front of them. Carr's Division occupied the right in investing this place, and Lawler's Brigade the right of his division. After a few hours' skirmishing, Lawler discovered that by moving a portion of his brigade under cover of the river bank, he could get a position from which that place could be successfully assaulted, and ordered a charge accordingly. Notwithstanding the level ground over which a portion of his troops had to pass without cover, and the great obstacle of the ditch in the front of the enemy's works, the charge was gallantly and successfully made, and in a few minutes the entire garrison, with seventeen pieces of artillery, were the trophies of this brilliant and daring movement. The enemy on the west bank of the river immediately set fire to the railroad bridge and retreated, thus cutting off all chance of escape for any portion of his forces remaining on the east bank.

Sherman by this time had reached Bridgeport, on Black River, above. The only pontoon train with the expedition was with him. By the morning of the 18th he had crossed the river, and was ready to march on Walnut Hills. McClernand and McPherson built floating bridges during the night, and had them ready for crossing their commands by eight A. M. of the 18th.

The march was commenced by Sherman at an early hour, by the Bridgeport and Vicksburg road, turning to the right when within three and a half miles of Vicksburg, to get possession of Walnut Hills and the Yazoo River. This was successfully accomplished before the night of the 18th. McPherson crossed Black River above the Jackson road, and came into the same road with Sherman, but to his rear. He arrived after nightfall with his advance to where Sherman turned to the right.

McClernand moved by the Jackson and Vicksburg road to Mount Albans, and there turned to the left to get into Baldwin's Ferry road. By this disposition the three army corps covered all the ground their strength would admit of, and by the morning of the 19th the investment of Vicksburg was made as complete as could be by the forces at my command.

During the day there was continuous skirmishing, and I was not without hope of carrying the enemy's works. Relying upon the demoralization of the enemy, in consequence of repeated defeats outside of Vicksburg, I ordered a general assault at two P. M. on this day.

The Fifteenth Army Corps, from having arrived in front of the enemy's works in time on the 18th to get a good position, were enabled to make a vigorous assault. The Thirteenth and Seventeenth Corps succeeded no further than to gain advanced positions, covered from the fire of the enemy. The 20th and 21st were spent in perfecting communications with our supplies. Most of the troops had been marching and fighting battles for twenty days, on an average of about five days' rations, drawn from the commissary department. Though they had not suffered from short rations up to this time, the want of bread to accompany the other rations was beginning to be much felt. On the 21st, my arrangements for drawing supplies of every description being complete, I determined to make another effort to carry Vicksburg by assault. There were many reasons to determine me to adopt this course. I believed an assault from the position gained by this time could be made successfully. It was known that Johnston was at Canton with the force taken by him from Jackson, re-enforced by other troops from the east, and that more were daily reaching him. With the force I had, a short time must have enabled him to attack me in the rear, and possibly succeeded in raising the siege. Possession of Vicksburg at that time would have enabled me to have turned upon Johnston and driven him from the State, and possess myself of all the railroads and practical military highways, thus effectually securing to ourselves all territory west of the Tombigbee, and this before the season was too far advanced for campaigning in this latitude. It would have saved government sending large re-enforcements, much needed elsewhere; and finally, the troops themselves were impatient to possess Vicksburg, and would not have worked in the trenches with the same zeal, believing it unnecessary, that they did after their failure to carry the enemy's works. Accordingly, on the 21st, orders were issued for a general assault on the whole line, to commence at 10 A. M. on the 22d. All the corps commanders set their time by mine, that there should be no difference between them in movement of assault. Promptly at the hour designated, the three army corps then in front of the enemy's works commenced the assault. I had taken a commanding position near McPherson's front, and from which I could see all the advancing columns from his corps, and a part of each of Sherman's and McClernand's. A portion of the commands of each succeeded in planting their flags on the outer slopes of the enemy's bastions, and maintained them there until night. Each corps had many more men than could possibly be used in the assault, over such ground as intervened between them and the enemy. More men could only avail in case of breaking through the enemy's line, or in repelling a sortie. The assault was gallant in the extreme on the part of all the troops; but the enemy's position was too strong, both naturally and artificially, to be taken in that way. At every point assaulted, and at all of them at the same time, the enemy was able to show all the force his works could cover. The assault failed, I regret to say, with much loss on our side in killed and wounded, but without weakening the confidence of the troops in their ability to ultimately succeed.

No troops succeeded in entering any of the enemy's works with the exception of Sergeant Griffith, of the Twenty-first Regiment Iowa Volunteers, and some eleven privates of the same regiment. Of these none returned except the sergeant and possibly one man. The work entered by him, from its position, could give us no practical advantage, unless others to the right and left of it were carried and held at the same time.

About 12 M. I received a dispatch from McClernand that he was hard pressed at several points, in reply to which I directed him to re-enforce the points hard pressed from such troops as he had that were not engaged. I then rode round to Sherman, and had just reached there when I received a second dispatch from McClernand stating positively and unequivocally that he was in possession of and still held two of the enemy's forts, that the American flag then waved over them, and asking me to have Sherman and McPherson make a diversion in his favor. This dispatch I showed to Sherman, who immediately ordered a renewal of the assault on his front. I also sent an answer to McClernand directing him to order up McArthur to his assistance, and started immediately to the position I had just left on McPherson's line to convey to him the information from McClernand by this last dispatch, that he might make the diversion requested. Before reaching McPherson I met a messenger with a third dispatch from McClernand, of which the following is a copy:

HEAD-QUARTERS, THIRTEENTH ARMY CORPS,
IN THE FIELD, NEAR VICKSBURG, MISS., *May* 22, 1863.

GENERAL:—We have gained the enemy's intrenchments at several points, but are brought to a stand. I have sent word to McArthur to re-enforce me if he can. Would it not be best to concentrate the whole or a part of his command on this point?

JOHN A. MCCLERNAND, *Major-General Commanding.*

Major-General U. S. GRANT.

P. S.—I have received your dispatch. My troops are all engaged, and I cannot withdraw any to re-enforce others.

McC.

The position occupied by me during most of the time of the assault gave me a better opportunity of seeing what was going on in front of the Thirteenth Army Corps than I believed it possible for the commander of it to have. I could not see his possession of forts, nor necessity for re-enforcements, as represented in his dispatches, up to the time I left it, which was between twelve M. and one P. M., and I expressed doubts of their correctness, which doubts the facts subsequently, but too late, confirmed. At the time I could not disregard his reiterated statements, for they might possibly be true; and that no possible opportunity of carrying the enemy's stronghold should be allowed to escape through fault of mine, I ordered Quimby's Division, which was all of McPherson's Corps then present but four brigades, to report to McClernand, and notified him of the order. I showed his dispatches to McPherson, as I had to Sherman, to satisfy him of the necessity of an active diversion on their part to hold as much force in their fronts as possible. The diversion was promptly and vigorously made, and resulted in the increase of our mortality list full fifty per cent, without advancing our position or giving us other advantages.

About half-past three P. M. I received McClernand's fourth dispatch, as follows:

HEAD-QUARTERS, THIRTEENTH ARMY CORPS,
May 22, 1863.

GENERAL:—I have received your dispatch in regard to General Quimby's Division and General McArthur's Division. As soon as they arrive I will press the enemy with all possible speed, and doubt not I will force my way through. I have lost no ground. My men are in two of the enemy's forts, but they are commanded by rifle-pits in the rear. Several prisoners have been taken, who intimate that the rear is strong. At this moment I am hard pressed.

JOHN A. MCCLERNAND, *Major-General Commanding.*

Major-General U. S. GRANT, Department of the Tennessee.

The assault of this day proved the quality of the soldiers of this army. Without entire success, and with a heavy loss, there was no murmuring or complaining, no falling back, nor other evidence of demoralization.

After the failure of the 22d, I determined upon a regular siege. The troops, now being fully awake to the necessity of this, worked diligently and cheerfully. The work progressed rapidly and satisfactorily until the 3d of July, when all was about ready for a final assault.

There was a great scarcity of engineer officers in the beginning, but under the skilful superintendence of Captain F. E. Prime, of the Engineer Corps, Lieutenant-Colonel Wilson, of my staff, and Captain C. B. Comstock, of the Engineer Corps, who joined this command during the siege, such practical experience was gained as would enable any division of this army hereafter to conduct a siege with considerable skill in the absence of regular engineer officers.

On the afternoon of the 3d of July a letter was received from Lieut.-General Pemberton, commanding the Confederate forces at Vicksburg, proposing an armistice and the appointment of commissioners to arrange terms for the capitulation of the place. The correspondence, copies of which are herewith transmitted, resulted in the surrender of the city and garrison of Vicksburg at 10 o'clock A. M., July 4, 1863, on the following terms: The entire garrison, officers and men, were to be paroled, not to take up arms against the United States until exchanged by the proper authorities; officers and men each to be furnished with a parole signed by himself; officers to be allowed their side arms and private baggage, and the field, staff, and cavalry officers one horse each; the rank and file to be allowed all their clothing, but no other property; rations from their own stores sufficient to last them beyond our lines; the necessary cooking utensils for preparing their food, and thirty wagons to transport such articles as could not well be carried. These terms I regard more favorable to the government than an unconditional surrender. It saved us the transportation of them North, which at that time would have been very difficult, owing to the limited amount of river transportation on hand, and the expense of subsisting them. It left our army free to operate against Johnston, who was threatening us from the direction of Jackson, and our river transportation to be used for the movement of troops to any point the exigency of the service might require.

I deem it proper to state here, in order that the correspondence may be fully understood, that after my answer to General Pemberton's letter of the morning of the 3d, we had a personal interview on the subject of the capitulation.

The particulars and incidents of the siege will be contained in the reports of division and corps commanders, which will be forwarded as soon as received.

I brought forward, during the siege, in addition to Lauman's Division and four regiments previously ordered from Memphis, Smith's and Kimball's Divisions, of the Sixteenth Army Corps, and assigned Major-General C. C. Washburne to command of same. On the 11th of June, Major-General F. J. Herron's Division from the Department of the Missouri arrived, and on the 14th two Divisions of the Ninth Army Corps, Major-General J. G. Parke commanding, arrived. This increase in my force enabled me to make the investment most complete, and at the same time left me a large reserve to watch the movements of Johnston. Herron's Division was put into position on the extreme left, south of the city, and Lauman's Division was placed between Herron and McClernand. Smith's and Kimball's Divisions and Parke's Corps were sent to Haines's Bluff. This place I had fortified to the land side, and every preparation made to resist a heavy force. Johnston crossed Big Black River with a portion of his force, and every thing indicated that he would make an attack about the 25th of June. Our position in front of Vicksburg having been made as strong against a sortie from the enemy as his works were against an assault, I placed Major-General Sherman in command of all the troops designated to look after Johnston. The force intended to operate against Johnston, in addition to that at Haines's Bluff, was one division from each of the Thirteenth, Fifteenth, and Seventeenth Army Corps, and Lauman's Division. Johnston, however, not attacking, I determined to attack him the moment Vicksburg was in our possession, and accordingly notified Sherman that I should again make an assault on Vicksburg at daylight of the 6th, and for him to have up supplies of all descriptions ready to move upon receipt of orders if the assault should prove a success. His preparations were immediately made, and when the place surrendered on the 4th, two days earlier than I had fixed for the attack, Sherman was found ready, and moved at once with a force increased by the remainder of both the Thirteenth and Fifteenth Army Corps, and is at present investing Jackson, where Johnston has made a stand.

In the march from Bruinsburg to Vicksburg, covering a period of twenty days, before supplies could be obtained from government stores, only five days' rations were issued, and three days' of these were taken in haversacks at the start, and were soon exhausted. All other subsistence was obtained from the country through which we passed. The march was commenced without wagons, except such as could be picked up through the country. The country was abundantly supplied with corn, bacon, beef, and mutton. The troops enjoyed excellent health, and no army ever appeared in better spirit or felt more confident of success.

In accordance with previous instructions, Major-General S. A. Hurlbut started Colonel (now Brigadier-General) B. H. Grierson with a cavalry force from La Grange, Tennessee, to make a raid through the central portion of the State of Mississippi, to destroy railroads and other public property, for the purpose of creating a diversion in favor of the army moving to the attack on Vicksburg. On the 17th of April this expedition started, and arrived at Baton Rouge on the 2d of May, having successfully traversed the whole State of Mississippi. This expedition was skilfully conducted, and reflects great credit on Colonel Grierson and all of his command. The notice given this raid by the Southern press confirms our estimate of its importance. It has been one of the most brilliant cavalry exploits of the war, and will be handed down in history as an example to be imitated. Colonel Grierson's report is herewith transmitted.

I cannot close this report without an expression of thankfulness for my good fortune in being placed in co-operation with an officer of the navy who accords to every move that seems for the interest and success of our arms his hearty and energetic support. Admiral Porter, and the very efficient officers under him, have ever shown their greatest readiness in their co-operation, no matter what was to be done or what risk to be taken, either by their men or their vessels. Without this prompt and cordial support, my movements would have been much embarrassed, if not wholly defeated.

Captain J. U. Shirk, commanding the Tuscumbia, was especially active and deserving of the highest commendation for his personal attention to the repairing of the damage done our transports by the Vicksburg batteries.

The result of this campaign has been the defeat of the enemy in five battles outside of Vicksburg: the occupation of Jackson, the capital of the State of Mississippi, and the capture of Vicksburg and its garrison and munitions of war: a loss to the enemy of thirty-seven thousand (37,000) prisoners, among whom were fifteen general officers; at least ten thousand killed and wounded, and among the killed Generals Tracy, Tilghman, and Green, and hundreds and perhaps thousands of stragglers who can never be collected and reorganized. Arms and munitions of war for an army of sixty thousand men have fallen into our hands, besides a large amount of other public property, consisting of railroads, locomotives, cars, steamboats, cotton, &c., and much was destroyed to prevent our capturing it.

Our loss in the series of battles may be summed up as follows:

	Killed.	*Wounded.*	*Missing.*
Port Gibson	130	718	5
Fourteen-Mile Creek (skirmish)	4	24	—
Raymond	69	341	32
Jackson	40	240	6
Champion's Hill	429	1,842	189
Big Black railroad bridge	29	242	2
Vicksburg	545	3,688	303

Of the wounded many were but slightly wounded, and continued on duty; many more required but a few days or weeks for their recovery. Not more than one-half of the wounded were permanently disabled.

My personal staffs and chiefs of departments have in all cases rendered prompt and efficient service.

In all former reports I have failed to make mention of Company A, Fourth Regiment Illinois Cavalry Volunteers, Captain S. D. Osband commanding. This company has been on duty with me as an escort company since November, 1861, and in every engagement I have been in since that time rendered valuable service, attracting general attention for their exemplary conduct, soldierly bearing, and promptness. It would not be overstating the merits of this company to say that many of them would fill with credit any position in a cavalry regiment.

For the brilliant achievements recounted in this report the Army of the Tennessee, their comrades of the Ninth Army Corps, Herron's Division of the Army of the Frontier, and the navy co-operating with them, deserve the highest honors their country can award.

I have the honor to be, Colonel, very respectfully, your obedient servant,

U. S. GRANT,
Major-General U. S. A. Commanding

Colonel J. C. KELTON, *A. A.-G.* Washington, D. C.

"Mr. Moore has happily executed a happy thought."

THE

Diary of the American Revolution;

From Whig and Tory Newspapers and Original Documents.

In one Volume. 8vo, pp. 1100, Illustrated with Twelve Superb Steel Engravings, by RITCHIE; *with Plans of Cities, Battles, &c.*

Edited by Frank Moore.

The materials of this work are taken from WHIG AND TORY NEWSPAPERS, published during the American Revolution, Private Diaries, and other contemporaneous writings. They present to the student of this day the same view the readers of the Revolutionary period enjoyed—the manners and customs of the people, and the moral and religious, as well as political features of the time.

The work contains not only the current accounts by both WHIG AND TORY WRITERS of the different skirmishes and battles by sea and land, but, at the same time, gives a clear idea of the effect of these occurrences upon the people and their homes.

It also embraces accounts of the balls, parties, marriages and deaths, criticisms upon men and books, wedding parties, sleigh-rides, the Whigs tarred and feathered by the Tories, and *vice versâ;* fox-hunts by the officers of the British army; surprises, birth-day celebrations, practical jokes by men who we have been taught to believe were of the most serious natural disposition; patriotic songs and ballads; horse-races, games, masquerades, reviews; anecdotes of the most celebrated men and women, popular merriments and usages, and the celebrations of national festivities.

The work carries the reader back into the homes, upon the very hearthstones, the highways and battle-fields of the Revolution, and lets him hear the Whigs and Tories lampoon and abuse each other, and see the armies fight in their own way.

From the New York Evening Post.

"Mr. Moore has happily executed a happy thought: he has written a history of the most important events of the last century in the very words of its contemporaries.

"Washington presents himself, not merely as the noble and successful leader of a great people struggling for their rights, but as the *rebel and the partisan,* having many and bitter enemies, who were capable of covering his name with the filth of their abuse."

From the New York Herald.

"It is refreshing to meet with a book in which the exact color of events is preserved, and the individuality of the author lost. Every page of the work teems with facts gathered from the daily life of the Revolution, and thus, without the intervention of modern speculation, we have brought before us not merely the actors in the great drama of the Revolution, but their actual thoughts, feelings, and emotions."

From the N. Y. Independent.

"There is not—we speak advisedly and deliberately—in the whole range of volumes and libraries upon American history, there is not to be found any *single* contribution toward that history of such value as that contained in these two volumes. The author has REPRODUCED, AS BY THE PHOTOGRAPHIC ART, THE VERY TIMES AND SCENES OF THE AMERICAN REVOLUTION AS THEY WERE TO THE MEN WHO MOVED IN THE MIDST OF THEM. The labor of such a work is immense; its value is incalculable: the reader will find in it much to amuse and instruct him, and a perfect mirror of the Revolutionary era."

From the London Saturday Review.

"The feeling with which most Englishmen will rise from the perusal of this work will be one of sorrowful but profound contempt for the government under which their ancestors flourished in the good old days. Nobody, except perhaps Washington, appears in very noble colors; but the only actors who make a thoroughly despicable figure are the English ministers and their favorite generals. It was not that they committed here and there an isolated mistake—the demon of blundering possessed them from the very first measure to the very last of the twenty years' struggle."

From the Philadelphia Bulletin.

"A really original work on our revolution is, of course, a surprise. The facts are all so well known that it would seem impossible to impart to them an air of novelty. But Mr. Frank Moore has presented a most fresh and vivid picture of the whole course of events, from the beginning of 1775 till the close of the war. The plan adopted has been to take the accounts of newspapers of the time. The skilful execution of this design has given us one of the most readable and impartial narratives of our struggle for independence that has ever been produced. The events seem to pass before the reader's immediate vision, and to be reported by him while the impression they produce on his mind is entirely fresh."

This work is sold by Subscription only, at Five Dollars per Copy, in Cloth.

DERBY & MILLER, Publishers,
NEW YORK.

www.ingramcontent.com/pod-product-compliance
Lightning Source LLC
LaVergne TN
LVHW021309110826
845150LV00003B/529

* 9 7 8 1 4 2 5 5 5 8 5 7 4 *